WINNING THE PEACE

.

Bók þessi er Tileinkuð Minningu
Sigríðar Einarsdóttur; Ömmu Minnar

Acknowledgements

In the course of this research numerous debts of gratitude have been incurred. Mrs Katharine Cobbett, the daughter of A. W. A. Leeper, kindly allowed me to consult her father's letters and diaries and actively assisted my research by locating and acquiring copies of his letters from other members of the family, as well as always providing a warm and generous hospitality during my visits. The Hon. Mrs. Eric Bailey, the daughter of Lord Cozens-Hardy, not only provided me with copies of her father's papers, but also shared with me her own reminiscences of working in Admiralty Intelligence during the First World War. Mr C. W. Crawley of Trinity Hall, Cambridge, was kind enough to allow me access to the diaries of Dr G. W. Prothero, as well as discussing Prothero's career with me. The late Prof. Agnes Headlam-Morley allowed me to consult her father's papers and discussed his work with me. The late Mr E. H. Carr kindly spoke with me about his own work in the Foreign Office during the war, and his experience of working with members of the Political Intelligence Department. The late Prof. Hugh Seton-Watson discussed his father's work and the role of the New Europe group. Sir Charles Pickthorn, Bt., and Mr G. R. Wakeling both wrote to me with interesting information concerning their father's careers, as did His Honour Judge Felix Waley, Q. C. on the career of his grandfather, Prof. H. N. Dickson. Mrs. Alexandra Campbell kindly provided me with copies of papers concerning the career of her grandfather, A. F. H. Wiggin. Prof. John D. Fair of Auburn University of Montgomery very kindly shared with me his knowledge of the career of Prof. H. W. V. Temperley, of whom he is writing a biography, and provided me with extracts from the Temperley Papers, which he had been able to consult.

Unpublished Crown copyright material in the Public Record Office and in the India Office Records is reproduced by permission of the Controller of Her Majesty's Stationery Office. I am also grateful to the following for their kind permission to consult and quote from collections in their possession: the Syndics of the Cambridge University Library for the Lord Hardinge of

Penshurst papers; the Master and Fellows of Trinity College, Cambridge, and Mr Milton Gendel, for the papers of Edwin Montagu; Lord Howard of Penrith for the papers of his father, the first Lord Howard of Penrith, and the Cumbria Record Office for access to them; to Mr R. R. Meinertzhagen for permission to quote from the diary of his father, Col. Richard Meinertzhagen; and to the Warden and Fellows of New College, Oxford, for the diaries of Lord Milner.

It was decided in this work to give as place-names those in general use during the period under consideration. Many of the places discussed have gone through a number of renamings, and retaining the older forms will assist in any reference back to the documents of this time.[1]

My research was aided by the Committee of Vice-Chancellors and Principals of the Universities of the United Kingdom with an Overseas Research Students Award; Jesus College, Cambridge, through a grant from the Bane Fund; the University of Cambridge Smuts Memorial Fund with a travel grant, and the Cambridge Historical Society with a research grant.

I am greatly indebted to Dr Michael Dockrill of King's College, London, for his careful reading of my manuscript and expert criticism. Valuable advice was provided by Dr David Armstrong of the University of Birmingham, Prof. Howard Malchow of Tufts University, Dr Zara Steiner of New Hall, Cambridge, and Prof. Geoffrey Warner. Thanks are also due to Dr Anthony Morris, history editor at Oxford University Press, for his patience and support, and to Mr Peter Glazebrook of Jesus College, Cambridge, for his assistance while I was a research student. Particular thanks are due to Prof. George J. Marcopoulos of Tufts University whose advice and teaching over many years have been invaluable. The greatest debt of all, however, is due to Mr Richard Langhorne of St John's College, Cambridge, who supervised the earlier incarnation of this work as a thesis, and who has provided constant encouragement, advice and support, as well as frequent and generous hospitality, as it grew into the current book. The responsibility for whatever deficiencies may exist rests with the author.

E.G.

[1] The following is a list of some of the places referred to in the text with their current or alternative forms: Danzig/Gdańsk, Stettin/Szczecin, Schleswig/Slesvig, Lwów/Lvov, Constanza/Constanţa, Tiflis/Tbilisi; Batum/Batumi, Temesvar/Timişoara, Dedéagach/Alexandroúpolis.

Contents

ABBREVIATIONS   xii

INTRODUCTION   1

PART I. PLANS, OPERATIONS, AND ADMINISTRATION

1. The Beginning of British Preparations for Peace   9
2. The Political Intelligence Department   57
3. The Struggle for Control   90

PART II. THE EVOLUTION OF DIPLOMATIC STRATEGY

4. The European Settlement   123
5. The World Outside Europe   150
6. Non-Territorial Questions   191

PART III. IMPLEMENTATION

7. The Paris Peace Conference   229
8. Conclusion   279

BIBLIOGRAPHY   287

INDEX   299

List of Maps

1. Boundaries of Germany   xiv
2. Austria–Hungary   xvi
3. Ottoman Empire   xviii

Abbreviations

ADM	Admiralty Papers
AIR	Air Council Papers
AWAL	A. W. A. Leeper Papers
BT	Board of Trade Papers
CAB	Cabinet Office Papers
CID	Committee of Imperial Defence
DBFP	Great Britain, Foreign Office, *Documents on British Foreign Policy, 1919–1939*, First Series
DIIB	Department of Information Intelligence Bureau
DMI	Directorate of Military Intelligence
DNI	Director of Naval Intelligence
FO	Foreign Office Papers
FRUS:PPC	United States, Department of State, *Papers Relating to the Foreign Relations of the United States: The Paris Peace Conference, 1919*
M.I.2(e)	Military Intelligence, Section 2(e)
MPC	David Lloyd George, *Memoirs of the Peace Conference* (2 vols., New Haven, Conn., 1938)
MT	Ministry of Shipping Papers
PID	Political Intelligence Department
POWE	Ministry of Power Papers
T	Treasury Papers
TS	Treasury Solicitor Papers
WM	David Lloyd George, *War Memoirs of David Lloyd George* (2 vols., London, 1938)
WO	War Office Papers
WTID	War Trade Intelligence Department
WTSD	War Trade Statistical Department

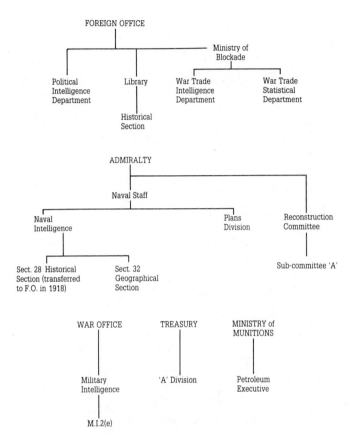

Organization of the Principal Departments involved in Peace Preparations.

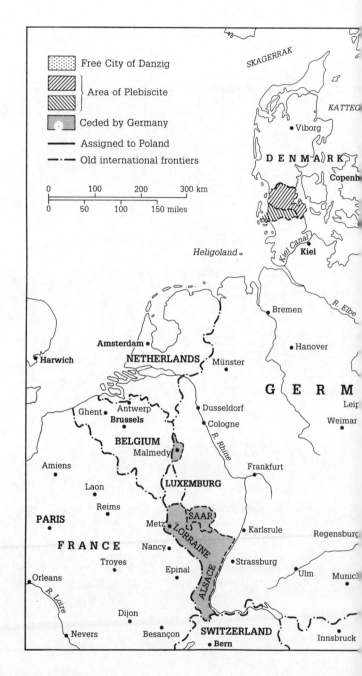

Boundaries of Germany

Austria–Hungary

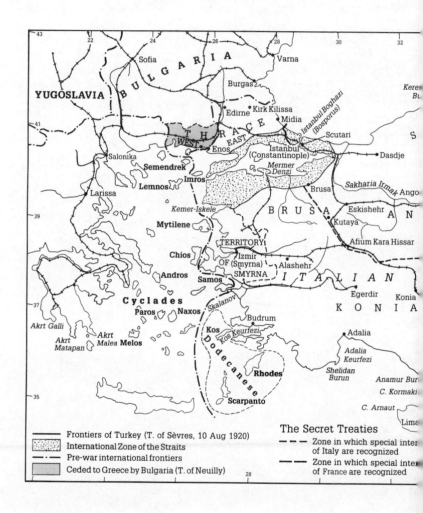

Frontiers of Turkey (T. of Sèvres, 10 Aug 1920)
International Zone of the Straits
Pre-war international frontiers
Ceded to Greece by Bulgaria (T. of Neuilly)

The Secret Treaties
Zone in which special inter...
of Italy are recognized
Zone in which special inte...
of France are recognized

Ottoman Empire

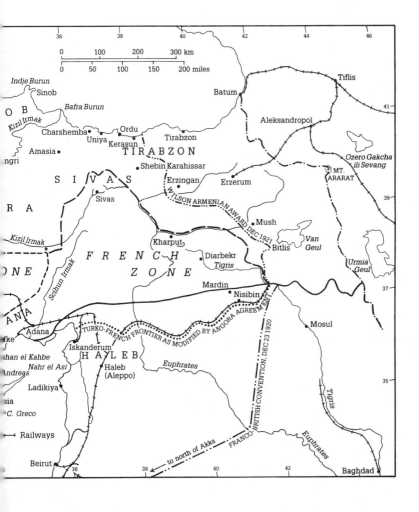

Introduction

What other worlds have we to conquer? We are like so
many Alexanders!

William Hughes, Australian premier, 1918
(cited in J. Morris, *Farewell the Trumpets: An Imperial Retreat*
(London, 1978), p.199)

Between August 1914 and November 1918 sixty-five million
men around the world went to war and thirty million people
died. The horror of this experience passed beyond all previous
conceptions of what war meant. For Britain alone the toll was
almost a million dead, from all parts of the Empire. During
these years of conflict Britain's war aims had shifted and
evolved amid the changing fortunes of war. For those who
turned their thoughts beyond the shorter-term necessity of
concluding the hostilities, there was an increasing concern as
to what sort of world should emerge from these years of destruction. It was clear that it would be a very different world
from that which had existed in 1914. Those men who became
involved in planning for the peace settlement, regardless
of their views as to how such a settlement could best be
implemented, knew that if Britain were to be spared such an
ordeal in the future, it would not be enough to win on the
battlefield — they would have to win the peace as well.

The planning phase has been a missing dimension in
attempts to understand British actions at the Paris Peace Conference. The British Empire Delegation did not suddenly arrive
at the conference without previous thought having been given
to the nature of the post-war settlement. Two years of increasingly detailed work went into preparing for this major international gathering, and any attempt to understand British
actions at Paris must integrate the preparatory phase into its
overall analysis. In 1931 the historian Robert Binkley noted that
though a third of the period between the armistice and the

signing of the Treaty of Versailles was occupied solely with preparations, 'the histories of the peace settlement have neglected it because of lack of information'.[1] A critical assessment of this period had to await the opening of the records, and the first work specifically to consider this aspect of the negotiating process was Lawrence Gelfand's masterly study of the American Inquiry.[2] British preparations are equally intriguing, for as James Headlam-Morley, himself a participant, noted in a confidential retrospective Foreign Office history of the conference, 'The critical period was not what happened in Paris during 1919, but what was done, and what was left undone, in 1918.'[3] The public archives and the private papers of those involved contain a wealth of information on this period, but as Britain's preparations were bureaucratically more diffused than those of the United States the records are scattered through many classifications, and have therefore escaped close scrutiny. A careful examination of these preparations shows that the ideas evolved, and the personnel involved, in this work did much to influence the final settlement at Paris.

It was evident by 1916 that the postwar settlement would be the most far-reaching since the Congress of Vienna assembled in 1814, and the delegates at the peace conference would be faced by a vast array of questions and problems. By 1917 some officials had become aware that the delegates at the post-war negotiating table would need more data, guidelines, and alternative solutions than had ever before been required by British negotiators. To provide these resources committees met and offices were established to prepare the material from which reasoned decisions could be made. This process culminated in the creation of a department to co-ordinate and synthesize the material being produced — the Foreign Office's Political Intelligence Department (PID). This initiative played a key part in the continuing struggle between the Foreign Office and the prime minister's office for dominance in foreign policy formulation. Lying behind these developments can be discerned some of the features which have become

[1] R. C. Binkley, 'New Light on the Paris Peace Conference', *Political Science Quarterly*, 46 (1931), 39.

[2] Lawrence Gelfand, *The Inquiry: American Preparations for Peace, 1917–1919* (New Haven, Conn., 1963).   [3] Confidential Print 13680.

characteristic of government in the twentieth century: the growth of government planning generally, the changing relations between the civil service and ministers in policy formulation, and the introduction of experts from outside the government service.[4]

In the various departments and committees assigned to preparing for the postwar settlement differing ideas emerged as to where the prime focus of British interest lay, what British interests in these areas were, and how best to implement these aims. Britain was a far-flung empire with global concerns and it is necessary to recall the dual, or even schizophrenic, nature of that empire. A great sea-borne empire with its power based on non-European possessions, it had nevertheless been engaged in a ferocious four-year struggle to determine the mastery of Europe. The identification of Britain's prime adversaries, and the priority given to critical interests, varied depending on the individual's geographical centre of concern. This critical duality was reflected in the planning stage, where European and non-European matters were considered separately, with the Ottoman empire forming something of an intermediary grey area.

The people primarily concerned with Britain's needs as an imperial state did not interest themselves deeply with the European settlement, though some supported a Carthaginian peace which would crush Germany, without paying much attention to the details of application or the possible consequences for the European balance of power. This group was interested first and foremost in the settlement outside Europe, and included such old-fashioned imperialists as Lord Curzon, as well as imperial reformers belonging to the Round Table and associated with Lord Milner, and those concerned with strategic over-extension such as Edwin Montagu.[5] An added factor here were the territorial ambitions of the dominions, each hungry for control of some part of Germany's patchwork colonial empire.

Many of the individuals involved in planning recognized the centrality of the European settlement, not just in a sweeping

[4] Dimitri Kitsikis, *Le Rôle des experts à la Conference de la Paix de 1919* (Ottawa, 1972).

[5] J. E. Kendle, *The Round Table Movement and Imperial Union* (Toronto, 1975).

strategic sense, but in a detailed tactical sense as well. Here those with the most clearly defined intellectual vision can loosely be labelled as the New Europe group, after the journal of that name published by R. W. Seton-Watson, with which many of them were associated. For them Europe was, in the words of Tomas Masaryk, 'a laboratory sitting atop a vast graveyard'.[6] They saw Europe as an entity, and concerned themselves particularly with the need to define the new borders in Eastern Europe, made necessary by the collapse of the old multi-ethnic empires. The New Europe group wished to see the frontiers of Europe redrawn on the basis of national self-determination, with future tranquillity assured by a League of Nations. This they saw as the best guarantee of future stability and equilibrium in Europe, which was after all a traditional British aim. The views of this group had a great impact on British policy, particularly after they came to dominate the PID, the hub of the peace-planning machinery.

In the negotiations at Paris the influence of the ideas developed during the planning stage can be seen, particularly as the individuals most deeply concerned with the preparations also formed the backbone of the British delegation. At Paris the diplomats had to face a complex and interlocking set of problems which dwarfed those of any previous international assemblage, and the resulting settlement has been a matter of debate ever since the ink began to dry on the treaties. Certainly many flaws can be seen in the final arrangements. In a study of the problems of a Great Power, and of the development of its diplomatic strategy at a key turning point in the international system, many factors can be considered, but the first question must be how far Britain achieved its aim at Paris. No negotiated settlement gives any one of its signatories its maximum desiderata, so one must look instead to see how far the essential core of goals was achieved. The evolution of British ideas and planning for the peace conference, and their final implementation, might seem confused in retrospect, but on careful dissection it proves to be remarkably clear-sighted strategy. The British delegation at Paris had a well defined set

---

[6] Quoted in Maurice Baumont, *La Faillite de la paix, 1918–1939* (2nd edn., Paris, 1946), p. 8.

of goals, and was more successful in achieving them than any of its allies. The differing schools of thought on the nature of the settlement avoided serious conflict because their geographical concerns were not mutually contradictory. Britain was able to carry its views in several areas in great measure because of the quality of the preparatory phase. There was no single policy document outlining British policy, but in common with the British constitution, a body of accepted wisdom emerged from the planning stage to serve as the basis of negotiation. As an exercise in diplomacy and statecraft the British actions must be seen as a seamless tale from the beginning of preparations to the conclusion of peace. Much as military staffs spend peacetime preparing for war so foreign ministries spend wartime planning for peace. In 1919 after two years of preparation it was time for the diplomats to take their place in the front lines. Paris was to be the last battle of the Great War.

PART I

Plans, Operations, and Administration

The Beginning of British Preparations for Peace

> Organized information will also be of the highest importance *in the actual making of peace*.
> Arnold Toynbee & Alfred Zimmern, Jan. 1917, CAB 21/62

As with plans for war, plans for peace take time. When the Armistice was signed in November 1918, Great Britain had been planning since 1916 for the peace conference. These preparations were naturally concentrated in the period between November 1918, when the shooting stopped, and January 1919, when the conference opened. Planning for the eventual post-war conference originated as vaguely defined discussions in a series of *ad hoc* committees and reports which started with the work of Asquith's War Committee in August 1916. This phase of peace planning stretched through the formation of the Lloyd George coalition to the Imperial War Cabinet session of 1917. In these early discussions there existed only a foggy distinction between deliberating on war aims, which involved setting out the goals for which the British Empire was fighting, and peace plans, which were the development of alternative positions on various claims, which would fit the strategic needs of British diplomacy, short and long term, for the post-war era.

AD HOC PREPARATIONS

Asquith's War Committee

On 31 August 1916 Asquith invited the members of the Cabinet's War Committee to consider the questions likely to arise in the negotiations at the end of the war.[1] Given the general lassitude of Asquith's administration it is hardly surprising that few of those so invited even bothered to reply, while those who did premised their conclusions on the optimistic expectation of a decisive military victory. It was only after the failure of the 1916 offensive that such individuals as Lord Lansdowne intervened to argue the possibility of a peace not based on a decisive victory. Among those who submitted memoranda concentrating on post-war plans were the First Lord of the Admiralty, Arthur Balfour, the Chief of the Imperial General Staff, General Robertson, the Minister of Munitions, Edwin Montagu, and for the Foreign Office Sir Ralph Paget and Sir William Tyrrell. These memoranda mark the beginning of the debate on British strategic planning for the post-war period and contain many of the basic ideas elaborated over the ensuing three years, including a concern for integrating nationality into any settlement, particularly in Eastern Europe, and the need to consider the future balance of power, especially in Western Europe. The seeds of the debate between the advocates and opponents of a punitive indemnity also begin to emerge, the precursor of a division within the British camp at Paris.

Paget and Tyrrell's memorandum was without doubt the most significant, with Lloyd George considering it 'an impressive document, well informed, bold and far seeing'.[2] They were almost alone in discussing the possibility of peace being made on the basis of an inconclusive military result to the war, and in realizing that their territorial proposals would have to be modified on the basis of geographical and military

[1] CAB 29/1/P-2, 'Negotiations at the End of the War', 31 Aug. 1916. On Asquith's War Committee memorandum see *MPC* i: 11–23; Harold I. Nelson, *Land and Power: British and Allied Policy on Germany's Frontiers, 1916–1919* (London, 1963), pp. 8–14; V. H. Rothwell, *British War Aims and Peace Diplomacy, 1914–1918* (Oxford, 1971), pp. 41–52; Sterling J. Kernek, *Distractions of Peace During War* (Philadelphia, 1975), p. 10

[2] CAB 29/1/P-5. The original with minutes by Grey and Hardinge is in FO 371/2804/180510/180510. Grey apparently did not have time to read the entire memorandum before its submission. *MPC* i: 11. Admittedly Lloyd George's observation benefits from being made with hindsight. Although this memorandum was circulated to the Cabinet, because of the inefficiencies of Asquith's government it never came up for discussion.

configurations. All they proposed at this stage was to delineate a general strategy to be followed, arguing that the territorial settlement should follow the principles of nationality, and rejecting harsh financial penalties against the defeated states which could cause resentment at a later date. Paget and Tyrrell advocated a pragmatic application of nationality advising that 'we should not push the principle of nationality so far as unduly to strengthen any State, which is likely to be a cause of danger to European peace in the future'. [3] Likewise this principle need not be too strictly applied to the disadvantage of friendly states. What they advised was a tactical application of this concept where advantage might be gained.

Paget and Tyrrell pointed out the failure of the Congress of Vienna's attempt to encircle France with a series of buffer states aimed at restraining it from further aggression: 'these creations did not fulfil that expectation, because they were artificial and did not bring contentment and prosperity to the people who formed part of them'. The lesson they drew from this was that a settlement based on nationality would be more solid and lasting, and this principle underlay all their proposed territorial changes. Alsace-Lorraine was to be returned to France, a point generally agreed throughout, but French claims to other German territory were not supported. Denmark was to receive Schleswig but not Holstein, and Poland was to be reunited as a single state. Paget and Tyrrell proposed a radical departure in British foreign policy by suggesting that an Anglo-French–Belgian permanent alliance should replace Belgian neutrality, as this was the only viable block to any future German invasion. They recognized that the era of Britain's aloofness from specific peacetime alliances was now a thing of the past.

In Eastern Europe the question of Poland's future drew the most attention. There was some concern that Russia might grab all of Poland, and they noted that 'The Western Allies might very properly take exception to the extension of Russian boundaries in Europe to within 125 miles of Berlin and about 200 miles of Vienna'. This shows another recurrent theme in British concerns, a wariness that today's allies could easily

[3] CAB 29/1/P-5.

become tomorrow's adversaries. Paget and Tyrrell recommended an independent Poland which could act as a buffer between Germany and Russia. They also noted with concern Britain's commitment to Italy under the 1915 Treaty of London, which allowed Italy much of Istria despite its Slavic population. This, they felt, 'unfortunately constitutes a very distinct violation of the principle of nationalities, and there is consequently no doubt that it involves the risk of producing the usual results, namely irredentism, and lack of stability and peace'. They were right, and the entire Adriatic crisis would eventually threaten to disrupt the peace conference.

General Robertson's views were, in contrast, quite conservative, not to say reactionary. He called for a return to the pre-war system, including the restoration of a European balance of power, the maintenance of British maritime supremacy, and the continuance of a weak power in the Lowlands. The fact that these points had not prevented a major war was ignored. Robertson's memorandum is strongly anti-Slav and anti-Latin, and although he perceived the need for a strong central European state Robertson preferred it to be German rather than Slav, believing that any Slav state would inevitably be Russophile. After the Bolshevik Revolution British policy did become Russophobe, but Robertson's views on Russia were non-ideological and simply reflected his own prejudices. He concluded that '. . . it would be to the interests of the British Empire to leave Germany reasonably strong on land but to weaken her at sea'. [4] Indeed Robertson recommended that a reduced Austria-Hungary closely associated with Germany and with a port at Fiume 'might not altogether [be] to our disadvantage on land as limiting the power of Russia and the Slav States, and on sea as preventing the Mediterranean from becoming a French and Italian lake'. Robertson did not believe that Germany would be so completely defeated that it could have a peace imposed upon it and he therefore advocated turning the defeated enemy into a new ally. According to Lloyd George, Robertson, 'After a week's reflection on his

---

[4] CAB 29/1/P-4, 'General Staff Memorandum Submitted in Accordance with the Prime Minister's Instructions', 31 Aug. 1916. Robertson was noted for his xenophobia. Lloyd George recalled that 'He had a profound and disturbing suspicion of all foreigners', WM i: 467.

own temerity ... withdrew the memorandum and cancelled it'.[5]

Arthur Balfour, First Lord of the Admiralty, a former prime minister, and soon to be Foreign Secretary, concentrated on the European settlement. He recommended the return of Alsace-Lorraine to France and the creation of a Greater Serbia and a Greater Romania, together with some sort of Czech and Polish states. This reduction in resources available to Germany and Austria-Hungary would diminish their ability to wage future wars, as Balfour estimated that under his plan twenty million people would be transferred between states. He correctly predicted that 'A revolution may upset the Hohen-zollerns, and a new Germany may arise from the ruins of militarism',[6] and he therefore recommended avoiding any Allied interference in internal German affairs in order to avoid a nationalist backlash.

Montagu was undoubtedly in favour of a Carthaginian peace. He had a strong respect for German abilities, which led to an assessment of them as dangerous adversaries. Montagu observed that 'The commonplace admission that Germany is a scientifically organised country, and pursues all of its activities methodically with a view to efficiency and wasteless working makes a sudden peace all the more likely, for although it is British and magnificent to fight when you know you have lost, it is certainly not efficient, nor scientific nor unwasteful.'[7] He was indifferent to the claims of Britain's allies and his only clear recommendation was on reparations: 'Germany has produced in me feelings which make me determined, whatever may come afterwards, to exact from her everything that can be exacted.' Montagu's view on this matter did prevail in the final settlement and did much to bedevil its efficacy.

The Mallet Committee

Just before these disorganized discussions in the Cabinet's War Committee Lord Hardinge had resumed his post as permanent under-secretary at the Foreign Office, after serving

[5] *WM* i: 467.
[6] CAB 29/1/P-7, 'The Peace Settlement in Europe', 4 Oct. 1916.
[7] CAB 29/1/P-3, 'The Problems of Peace', 29 Aug. 1916.

as viceroy of India. One of his first concerns was the lack of preparation for the peace negotiations. Writing to his old friend Valentine Chirol, he noted, 'When I got back to England I found that nothing had been done in the way of defining our desiderata when the time comes for peace negotiations. These are now being carried out. ...'[8] The result of Hardinge's concern was a Foreign Office suggestion to Asquith that it was 'very necessary that His Majesty's Government should have a clear idea of what increase of territory is desirable in the interests of the British Empire'.[9] Asquith responded by establishing an interdepartmental Sub-Committee on Territorial Changes, with Sir Louis Mallet of the Foreign Office as chairman.[10] It held five meetings between 4 September 1916 and 20 February 1917, producing four reports.[11] Its terms of reference were specifically extra-European as they were to consider 'The question of territorial changes in Africa and elsewhere outside Europe which might be expected to follow as the result of the War ....'[12] The committee's not very surprising conclusion was to recommend against allowing Germany to regain its colonial empire.

Perhaps the most revealing portions of the reports are the suggested territorial changes that might be gained at the cost of Allied states. The committee listed as British desiderata from France the cession of French Somaliland, French India, and St-Pierre and Miquelon, the abrogation of French treaty rights in Zanzibar and Muscat, and the swap of British rights in the New Hebrides condominium for the Society Islands and Rapa. The cession of Portuguese Timor was also recommended. This shows the continuing persistence of the idea that Britain's primary interests were extra-European, despite the Continental focus of the war.

Leo Amery of the Cabinet Secretariat was critical of the

[8] Hardinge to Chirol, 9 Aug. 1916. Hardinge Papers 24.
[9] CAB 16/36/TC-2.
[10] The members of the committee were Foreign Office, Mallet, Sir William Tyrrell, G. R. Clerk; Colonial Office, H. J. Read, C. Strachey, H. C. M. Lambert; India Office, Sir William Holderness, Lord Islington; War Office, Gen. Macdonough, Gen. Maurice; Admiralty, Adm. Wilson, W. F. Nicholson; Board of Trade, Sir Hubert Llewellyn-Smith, H. Fountain, P. W. L. Ashley.
[11] CAB 16/36, records of the Mallet Committee.   [12] CAB 16/36/TC-1.

committee approach to peace preparations, which were patently unrealistic. He reported to the head of the secretariat, Maurice Hankey, that after attending a meeting of the Mallet Committee he 'realised the absurdity of hoping to get anything like a coherent thought-out policy from a crowd of that character, many of whom would be useful expert witnesses, but hardly any of whom are capable of looking into the question as a whole or suggesting what matters require further investigation'.[13] Before Amery's advice was finally acted upon, one more committee was set the task of defining British desiderata.

The Curzon and Milner Committees

Lloyd George convened the first Imperial War Cabinet on 20 March 1917, and on 12 April it was decided to establish a Committee on Terms of Peace comprising two sub-committees, one under Lord Curzon on territorial desiderata and one under Lord Milner on economic and non-territorial desiderata. Both committees sat during the latter half of April with each holding five sessions, their reports being considered at meetings of the Imperial War Cabinet on 26 April and 1 May.[14]

The Curzon Committee barely touched on European matters as Lord Curzon believed 'that an exploration of these different problems in detail was hardly within the scope of the Committee, and it would be sufficient if the Committee laid

[13] CAB 21/62/f18/Q/15, minute by Amery to Hankey, 10 Feb. 1917.
[14] The Imperial War Cabinet met 20 Mar.–2 May 1917; all the dominions were represented, though Hughes of Australia was absent as a general election was in progress. The Curzon Committee consisted of Curzon, Lord Robert Cecil, Walter Long, Austen Chamberlain, J. D. Hazen, William Massey, General Smuts, Sir E. Morris, and Sir S. Sinha. The records of the committee are in CAB 21/77. A printed copy of the report and minutes is in CAB 29/1/P-16. See also W. R. Louis, *Great Britain and Germany's Lost Colonies, 1914–1919* (Oxford, 1967), pp. 81–5. The Milner Committee consisted of Milner, Arthur Henderson, Walter Long, H. A. L. Fisher, Sir Robert Borden, General Smuts, Sir Joseph Ward, Sir Edward Morris, Sir J. Meston, the Maharaja of Bikanir, and Sir Eyre Crowe. The records of the Milner Committee are in CAB 21/77.

down a few general principles'. [15] These consisted of five basic conditions for a peace settlement: the restoration of Belgian independence, the settlements in Alsace-Lorraine, Poland, and Austria-Hungary to correspond as closely as possible with the wishes of the inhabitants, that 'it should not be the purpose of British policy to destroy the national existence of any of the enemy powers ...' as the resulting ill will could lead to another war, the need to block German economic and political influence in the Near East, and a reduction of France's growing influence in Greece. [16] Obviously the term 'enemy' was taken to include wartime allies. It was realized, however, that the extent to which these policies could be carried out would depend on the degree of Allied military success.

The Dominion representatives, having thus been deftly deflected from detailed discussion of the European settlement, paid close attention to colonial concerns. The Curzon Committee started by examining the three available reports of the Mallet Committee, and its own final report closely paralleled those of Mallet's. In the Pacific, where Japan had already been promised the German islands north of the equator, Australia and New Zealand successfully argued for the southern islands, and indeed these islands passed to Australia and New Zealand as mandates at the end of the war. Walter Long added to the discussion of the Pacific that 'it would be desirable to get from the French all that we could in the Pacific'. [17] The Curzon Committee, in common with the Mallet Committee, recommended a long list of possible territorial accessions from allied and neutral states.

These claims to non-enemy territory were pressed with particular zeal by the Dominion representatives, who showed an amazing degree of imagination in the breadth of their claims. The Canadian member, J. D. Hazen, suggested that St-Pierre and Miquelon might be ceded by France in return for British support over Alsace-Lorraine, that Denmark might be induced to cede Greenland, and that the United States might exchange the Alaskan pan-handle for British Guiana. Lord Curzon,

[15] CAB 29/1/P-16, meeting of 23 Apr. 1917.
[16] Ibid., 'Report of the Committee on Terms of Peace (Territorial Desiderata)', 28 Apr. 1917.
[17] CAB 29/1/P-16, meeting of 17 Apr. 1917.

Austen Chamberlain, and Sir Satyendra Sinha all supported the idea of persuading France to cede its Indian possessions.[18]

Smuts 'considered that it was very important to secure the elimination of Portugal from the southern part of her East African territory',[19] and it was decided that the possibility of either purchasing the region south of the Zambesi River or of trading land in German East Africa (not yet even officially a British possession!) should be considered by the government. It was also recommended that the government should try to obtain French Somaliland in order to check the flow of weapons in the Horn of Africa and the Persian Gulf. In this connection it was thought that an exchange of the Gambia and French Somaliland might be practical. In the Middle East it was concluded that 'It is of great importance that both Palestine and Mesopotamia should be under British control', and that only Great Britain should exercise political influence in Arabia.[20] The revision was recommended of the 1916 Sykes–Picot Agreement, which outlined an Anglo-French division of the Middle East.

Amid its pleasant discussions the committee even found time to consider the fate of the German colonial empire. It was concluded that the colonies should not be returned and that as much as possible should be added to the British Empire, with the Dominions being given a role in their administration. There was also some discussion that German East Africa might become a field for colonial emigration from India. The Cameroons and Togoland were to be partitioned with France, with whom an agreement on these colonies' fate had already been reached. Towards the end of the committee's sittings Austen Chamberlain warned, not surprisingly, that an impression might reach the neutrals 'that we were meditating the carving up of the world to suit our own interests'.[21] Certainly

---

[18] CAB 29/1/P-16, meeting of 19 Apr. 1917. J. D. Hazen, 'The Proposed Acquisition of Greenland by Great Britain' (also in CAB 21/77). See also Robert Craig Brown, 'Sir Robert Borden and Canada's War Aims', in Barry Hunt and Adrian Preston, eds., *War Aims and Strategic Policy in the Great War, 1914–1918* (London, 1977).

[19] CAB 29/1/P-16, meeting of 19 Apr. 1917.

[20] Ibid., Report of 28 Apr. 1917.

[21] Ibid. meeting of 23 Apr. 1917.

the tendency to advocate fantastic territorial acquisitions pervaded all committee discussions on British desiderata right through to the peace conference.

The Milner Committee was somewhat more restrained in its suggestions, embodied in a rather brief report. While favouring the imposition of an indemnity, it was thought that it should be limited to compensation for lost shipping. The committee concluded that 'the surrender of the German Navy should be one of the principle objects to be aimed at in the Treaty of Peace'.[22]

The Imperial War Cabinet discussed the reports in full on 1 May. Curzon pointed out that the conclusions of the territorial committee had been unanimous and that the desire of the Dominions for a share in the captured colonies should not be overlooked. Lloyd George accepted that the committees' reports were useful in embodying aims in the event of a complete victory, but observed that they did not offer much direction for a peace conference where Germany still held a great deal of Allied territory.[23]

ORGANIZED PREPARATIONS

The Cabinet Secretariat

Two independent initiatives concerned with the necessity of adequate peace preparations developed during 1917 in the Cabinet Office and the Foreign Office, both eventually becoming entwined to form the core of the British preparatory machinery. The rather *ad hoc* nature of preparations for the post-war peace conference, illustrated by the work of Asquith's War Committee and the Mallet, Curzon, and Milner Committees, had become a matter of increasing concern to many government officials. In January 1917 Arnold Toynbee and Alfred Zimmern submitted a memorandum to the War Cabinet Secretariat proposing the establishment of a 'Peace

[22] CAB 29/1/P-15, 'Report of the Committee on Terms of Peace (Economic and Non-Territorial Desiderata)' (also in CAB 21/78).

[23] CAB 21/78/IWC13, 1 May 1917.

Terms Intelligence Section'.[24] They cited the need for information on the Allies' plans, and detailed economic and political
intelligence regarding the territories and populations affected
by either group of belligerents. Toynbee and Zimmern commented that 'Whichever party is in possession of the most detailed knowledge regarding the economic and political facts, the
plans of the enemy, and the bearing of these facts upon their
own, will have a formidable advantage over its opponents in
making peace'.[25] The discussion sparked by this memorandum
resulted in the establishment over the next year of Britain's
peace preparatory machinery, the chief components of which
were the Political Intelligence Department, the Historical
Section, and the War Trade Intelligence Department, aided by
sections of Naval and Military Intelligence.

Toynbee and Zimmern suggested that the new department
should 'collect, organise, and present all the relevant facts concerning the territories and populations affected by the plans of
either group, or of both groups of belligerents'.[26] They thought
that Naval Intelligence's Geographical Section, which already
possessed a staff trained in dealing with such matters, could be
expanded to fill this new role. The new section could also give
assistance to the propaganda departments by providing useful
information.[27] In a second memorandum on 13 February Toynbee and Zimmern clarified their proposal by outlining the exact
nature of the work to be undertaken, suggesting that the collections of information could be grouped under such headings as
nationality, trade routes and communications, economic resources, and economic policy. Under nationality a sample subject was given as the 'Croat Question', which would be looked at

---

[24] CAB 21/62/f15/E/1, 'Peace-Terms Intelligence: Suggestions for a Peace
Terms Intelligence Section to be added to the Existing Intelligence and Propa-
ganda Departments . . . .', undated, but the minute sheet suggests the end of
Jan. 1917. Toynbee was employed in the DIIB and Zimmern in the Ministry of
Reconstruction. Both were later appointed to the Political Intelligence Depart-
ment when it was established in 1918.

[25] CAB 21/62/f15/E/1.   [26] Ibid.

[27] Toynbee and Zimmern also recommended that a committee of expert
advisers be created to supervise the section's work. They recommended for
this group Sir Thomas Holding, Sir Francis Younghusband, Sir Harry
Johnstone, Wickham Steed, and Mr Fitzmaurice.

from the point of view of native, allied, enemy, and neutral interests.[28]

Toynbee and Zimmern found varying degrees of support for their idea from, among others, Sir Maurice Hankey, the head of the War Cabinet Secretariat, and two members of his staff, Thomas Jones and Leo Amery.[29] Hankey considered the proposal good, but pointed out that he thought much work of this sort had been carried out already, citing the efforts of Asquith's War Committee, the Mallet Committee, Sir Maurice de Bunsen's Committee on British desiderata in Turkey, and some special maps prepared by Naval Intelligence.[30] Hankey preferred to wait before taking any action, at least until Mallet's committee had finished its work. He did propose that after the Mallet Committee had completed its task a small committee might be established under a member of the War Cabinet, 'to look into the whole question and examine whether any further *information* is required'.[31] One member of the secretariat who disagreed with Hankey's timetable was Leo Amery, who wanted to begin outlining the work of the new section immediately.[32]

Amery perceived the critical difference between the aim of Toynbee and Zimmern, which concerned the organization of material for the peace negotiations, and the work cited by Hankey, which was essentially involved in determining the war aims towards which the military should work. It was Amery's initiative which resulted in substantive steps being taken towards organized preparatory work. He noted in his diary on 3 February that

Temperley came in with a suggestion that we should have a small historical staff to look into the past history of some of the debatable

[28] CAB 21/62/f15/E/1, 'Peace Terms Intelligence. II. Classification of Enquiries', 13 Feb. 1917.

[29] Thomas Jones, *Whitehall Diary*, vol. i: *1916–1925*, ed. Keith Middlemas (London, 1969), p. 22, entry for 11 Feb. 1917.

[30] CAB 21/62/f15/E/1, minute by Hankey, 31 Jan. 1917. The de Bunsen Committee met in 1915. Its report is in CAB 27/1.

[31] CAB 21/62/f15/E/1.

[32] Leo Amery (1873–1955); journalist for *The Times*, 1899–1909; MP (Con.), 1911–45; active service, 1914–16; assistant secretary, War Cabinet Secretariat, 1917–18; Under-Secretary for the Colonies, 1919–21; Admiralty, 1921–2, First Lord, 1922–4.

questions, more particularly in the Balkans and Poland, which will come up at the Peace Conference. This entirely fitted in with schemes I had been revolving for the last day or two for a co-ordination committee to consider peace questions in all their aspects, including what to do about our Allies' debts to us, etc. I put up to Hankey the suggestion that, while using the Royal Geographical as much as possible, I should also get under way a small staff, statistical, historical, etc. here. He entirely agreed.[33]

Amery's experiences with Mallet's committee had disillusioned him as to the work such a group could accomplish and in a minute to Hankey he noted that 'A committee, like Sir L. Mallet's for instance, has worked on very general considerations and has not been able to carry on the research that is really required if our representatives at a Peace Conference are to be able to dispose of all the arguments that may be brought up against them'.[34] Amery is here for the first time drawing a clear distinction between political debate in committee and actual research into the facts. It was dispassionate research which British policy needed as a foundation for any diplomatic planning and Amery proposed that this need be filled with a small committee under a member of the War Cabinet, assisted by a small research staff which could draw upon the services of the Naval Intelligence Geographical Section. He suggested Lord Milner, his former mentor, as a likely chief for this organization, and Amery pressed Hankey to allow himself, Mark Sykes, and Thomas Jones to start work on the details.

Hankey agreed with Amery as to the need for such information but was reluctant to create a special staff until it was unavoidable. Instead he thought, 'What should be done at this stage is to get the Departments to work on all the necessary spade work . . .'.[35] Amery thereupon 'secured Hankey's approval for getting together a research staff to work up all the information that could be conceivably required about

---

[33] John Barnes and David Nicholson, eds., *The Leo Amery Diaries*, vol. i: *1896–1929* (London, 1980), p. 141. Temperley was assigned to Military Intelligence, and his own unit, M.I.2(e), eventually became involved in peace planning.

[34] CAB 21/62/f18/Q/5, Amery to Hankey, 7 Feb. 1917.

[35] Ibid., minute by Hankey, 10 Feb. 1917.

any country in Europe or outside, that could come under discussion'.[36] To accomplish this Amery turned to Admiral Reginald Hall, the remarkable Director of Naval Intelligence, who in turn entrusted this work to Commander W. H. Cozens-Hardy.

Amery identified three areas which required research: geographical information, historical facts on all debatable territorial questions, and financial and statistical data. By 1918 departments had been created to deal with all these points. Admiral Hall expanded the duties of the Naval Intelligence Geographical Section (usually referred to by its location as Hertford House) to include the preparation of handbooks and manuals of information useful to peace conference delegates. In direct response to Amery's suggestions Hall created a Historical Section to provide background handbooks on potential problems. Hall and his deputy Cozens-Hardy were also instrumental in establishing the War Trade Intelligence Department, which together with the ancillary War Trade Statistics Department provided the needed financial facts. In addition in 1918 the Director of Military Intelligence created a new section under H. W. V. Temperley, M. I. 2(e), to deal with the military aspects of the preparations.

On 5 June 1917 Hankey circulated a note to the War Cabinet on 'Arrangements for the Eventual Peace Conference' pointing out that peace could come quite suddenly and that the mechanical arrangements at least should be thought out beforehand.[37] Hankey noted that 'Up to the present the main work accomplished in preparation for the eventual peace conference has been to block in on very broad lines the peace desiderata of the British Empire, rather as a standard to be aimed at than as practical policy'.[38] He informed the Cabinet of the work being carried out under Cozens-Hardy's direction to prepare handbooks for the benefit of the delegates.

Amery was pleased by his success in this matter, though he continued to press Hankey about establishing a small committee under a member of the War Cabinet. This time he suggested Smuts rather than Milner as chairman, commenting

---

[36] L. S. Amery, *My Political Life*, vol. ii: *War and Peace, 1914–1929* (London, 1953), p. 103.
[37] CAB 24/15/GT938.   [38] Ibid.

parenthetically, 'I think the P. M. would be a little frightened of Curzon.'[39] As events were to prove it was Smuts whom Lloyd George asked in October 1918 to co-ordinate the preparation of the peace negotiators' brief. Amery was concerned, however, that Cozens-Hardy's section was amassing information in a miscellaneous sort of way as they had no specific directions as to what was needed, and he felt that 'The thing has been left in a very unfinished state as regards many important details of the Imperial War Cabinet Committees'.[40] This matter had also begun to concern the Foreign Office, which was soon to evolve its own solution.

The Foreign Office

Amery was not the only official concerned with the state of advance planning for the peace conference. Lord Hardinge, the permanent under-secretary at the Foreign Office, was equally interested in the matter. His first term as permanent under-secretary, 1906–10, was an important period of internal reform for the Foreign Office, during which Hardinge worked closely with the Foreign Secretary, Sir Edward Grey.[41] In 1910 Hardinge was appointed Viceroy of India, where he remained until 1916. In that year he returned to Whitehall, his reputation clouded by controversy over the Mesopotamia campaign, to find the role of the Foreign Office much diminished. Hardinge was reappointed as permanent under-secretary, but Grey no longer enjoyed the same political, and physical, strength. The formation of the Lloyd George coalition in December 1916, with Arthur Balfour as foreign secretary, further diminished the importance of the Foreign Office. Lloyd George mistrusted diplomats and Balfour in his turn was willing to accept this

---

[39] CAB 21/62/f18/Q/5, Amery to Hankey, 29 June 1917.   [40] Ibid.
[41] For an account of Hardinge's work as permanent under-secretary, 1906–10, see Zara Steiner, *The Foreign Office and Foreign Policy, 1898–1914* (London, 1969), pp. 91–121, and Briton Cooper Busch, *Hardinge of Penshurst: A Study in the Old Diplomacy* (New York, 1980), pp. 91–161. Also J. Douglas Goold, 'Old Diplomacy: The Diplomatic Career of Lord Hardinge, 1910–1922' (Ph.D. thesis, University of Cambridge, 1976).

reduced status to avoid interfering with the prime minister's conduct of the war.[42]

The importance of the Foreign Office in foreign policy formulation was therefore eclipsed, in part by the war and in part by the attitude of the prime minister. Hardinge, previously an important shaper of British foreign policy, and just recently in control of the vast Indian subcontinent, now found himself confined to a largely administrative role. Increasingly he tended to busy himself with the actual operations of the Office, in particular with preparing for the moment when the Foreign Office would presumably re-emerge from its obscurity with the negotiation of a peace settlement. The successful conduct of these negotiations would also allow Hardinge to wipe away the shadow of Mesopotamia.

One of Hardinge's first concerns when he returned was the lack of any co-ordinated planning for the peace conference. His initial moves in this direction led to the formation of the Mallet Committee on Territorial Changes. However, he perceived the need for something more. He wanted to avoid that diffusion of effort which had, for instance, led to Hall in Naval Intelligence compiling detailed reports on the French role in India. What was lacking was a single department staffed by experts, similar to the American 'Inquiry', which could pull together and synthesize the available information. After much bureaucratic haggling Hardinge accomplished this aim with the creation in March 1918 of the Political Intelligence Department.

Hardinge also set about other reforms, some of them relevant to the peace negotiations. Hardinge hoped to develop the Foreign Office library into a research and reference bureau, and with this end in mind the transfer of Naval Intelligence's Historical Section to the librarian's supervision was arranged. Hardinge also established closer ties with the War Trade Intelligence Department, which was brought under the Foreign Office's Ministry of Blockade in 1917. It was clearly hoped that these new developments would become permanent after the war.

Hardinge circulated his first note about plans for the peace conference in October 1917, followed by a more detailed

[42] Roberta M. Warman, 'The Erosion of Foreign Office Influence in the Making of Foreign Policy, 1916–1918', *Historical Journal*, 15:1 (1972), 133–59. Prothero Papers (Crawley).

memorandum in November.[43] These were clearly meant to
compete with Hankey's own proposals, as both men were
staking a claim to control the machinery of the eventual peace
conference. Hardinge's purpose was to indicate a convenient
method of procedure, in the light of previous experience, and
to summarize the technical and administrative arrangements
being made. He pointed out that such plans 'must necessarily
be made in advance — so that the vast and complicated
secretarial work of the British delegation ... may proceed
with the greatest possible measure of coordination and des-
patch'.[44] Hardinge was particularly aware of the need for
speed in the opening of the peace conference and he explained
that 'The essential machinery has accordingly been devised
and laid down on such lines that, when completed, it shall be
capable of being set in motion without delay, and shall be
readily adaptable to the form in which the Congress may ultimately take shape'. The failure of the conference to move
quickly after convening in 1919 has frequently been cited as
one of its greatest technical faults. The cause of this was the
lack of adequate mechanisms for dealing with such a complicated settlement, as Lloyd George decided to reject the Hardinge plan. The conference did begin to move forward when a
system was finally evolved after several sluggish weeks, and it
is Hardinge's outline organization which, with small vari-
ations, was finally, if tardily, adopted.

Hardinge proposed that the British plenipotentiaries should
be supported by a supervising ambassador (the role he was to
play at Paris in 1919), and a secretariat consisting of six
sections, political, military, naval, financial, commercial, and
legal, and possibly aviation too. These sections would provide
précis on the questions under discussion as well as circulating
minutes on the progress of discussions. Hardinge believed
'that such a department is absolutely essential to prevent discussions proceeding on divergent lines'.[45] Reflecting current
concerns on improving the Foreign Office's registry system, a
new filing system was adopted for use at the conference, after

[43] Prothero Papers (Crawley), 'Peace Negotiations', 31 Oct. 1917, and
'Memorandum Concerning Proposed Arrangements for Dealing with the Registration of Correspondence at the Peace Congress', Nov. 1917.
[44] 'Peace Negotiations', 31 Oct. 1917.   [45] Ibid.

an examination of those in use in large commercial establish-
ments.[46]

Having established the basic infrastructure Hardinge set
about rounding up the necessary personnel and support services. The Naval Intelligence Historical Section was transferred at his instance to the Foreign Office, while the War Trade
Intelligence Department, which was another product of Hall's
imagination, was moved to the Foreign Office's Ministry of
Blockade. Finally the Political Intelligence Department was
created, largely by poaching staff from the Department of Information, in order to co-ordinate these efforts. The only
organization Hardinge did not capture was the Naval Intelligence Geographical Section, which, however, soon saw its
influence circumscribed by the Foreign Office. Hardinge
methodically acquired control of the planning machinery
established by Amery's initiative, and even the initial authors
of the plan proposed to the Cabinet Secretariat, Toynbee and
Zimmern, were recruited into the Foreign Office as part of the
Political Intelligence Department. In the evolving struggle
between the Foreign Office and the prime minister's office for
influence over foreign policy, Hardinge was making certain
that the actual bureaucratic machinery for implementation was
firmly in Foreign Office hands.

Hertford House: The Naval Intelligence Geographical Section

One of the great innovators in administration and intelligence
gathering during the Great War was Admiral Reginald Hall.[47]

[46] The delegation's registry was to consist of three branches: classification,
archives, and dispatch. A lengthy appendix outlining the divisions of correspondence was provided. Memorandum of Nov. 1917. The system used by
the Australian Imperial Forces was highly recommended. Arrangements
were also made for rapidly assembling a clerical staff and for erecting a
printing press at the conference. On the significance of the registry system see
Steiner, *Foreign Office and Foreign Policy*, pp. 154,179.

[47] The best account of Hall's career is Sir William James, *The Eyes of the Navy: A
Biographical Study of Admiral Sir Reginald Hall* (London, 1955). There is also an
unfinished draft of his autobiography with the Hall Papers, Churchill College,
Cambridge. The title of Director of the Intelligence Division was changed in Apr.
1918 to the older form of Director of Naval Intelligence. Hall apparently preferred
to recruit individuals with large, well-formed ear-lobes as an indication of good
character. Interview with the Hon. Mrs Eric Bailey, Stiffkey, 6 May 1982.

When he was appointed Director of the Intelligence Division of the Naval Staff in November 1914, he found a department engaged primarily in deciphering intercepts of German wireless signals. Under his guidance the Intelligence Division developed into a dynamic department that filled many of the gaps in the British intelligence world, even assuming some of Military Intelligence's duties. It was to Hall that Amery turned as the man most able to implement Toynbee and Zimmern's idea of a Peace Terms Intelligence Section to gather geographic, historic, economic, and statistical material. Hall accomplished this by expanding the work of the Naval Intelligence Geographical Section, establishing a Historical Section, and assisting the War Trade Intelligence Department to extend its capabilities.

The idea for a geographical section was initially proposed to Hall by Professor H. N. Dickson, a geographer at University College, Reading.[48] He had already approached the War Office with the idea of establishing a Geographical Bureau, but it was 'so crowded with work that he found it impossible to make any headway there' and he turned instead 'to the Admiralty where there was less confusion'.[49] Hall agreed with Dickson's proposal and set up the Geographical Section of the Naval Intelligence Division, code-named I. D. 32.[50] The Geographical Section was located at first at the Royal Geographical Society before moving to Hertford House, which in more peaceful times housed the Wallace Collection and whose now empty galleries provided an ideal place for map-making. After Amery's discussions with Hall, Hertford House, as Dickson's

---

[48] Henry Newton Dickson (1886–1922), educ. Edinburgh and Oxford Universities; professor of geography at University Coll., Reading, 1906–20; D.Sc. (Oxon.), 1901; CBE, 1918; assistant editor, *Encyclopaedia Britannica*, 1920–2; author of *Maps and Mapreading* (1912). Little material is available on Dickson's career, the best accounts being obituary articles in the *Geographical Journal*, 59:6 (1922) and in the *Scottish Geographical Magazine*, 38:3 (1922).

[49] Inquiry Doc 987, Report of conversation with Dickson in Maj. Douglas Johnson to Col. E. M. House, 'Confidential Report on Arrangements made by the British Government for Collecting Data for the Peace Conference', 1 May 1918.

[50] Erik Goldstein, 'Hertford House: The Naval Intelligence Geographical Section and Peace Conference Planning, 1914–1919', *The Mariner's Mirror*, 72:1 (1986), 85–8.

section was commonly called, began to focus some of its work on the needs of potential peace negotiators. A series of manuals was produced on various regions and problems, such as *The Schleswig-Holstein Question*. Dickson strove for accuracy and balance in these volumes, and when he discovered that previous British authors had relied heavily on German sources, presumably out of ignorance of Danish, he arranged translations of key Danish documents which 'put a very different complexion on the whole matter'.[51] Hertford House also planned a series of special brief reports of eight to ten pages for negotiators to use as a crib, an idea which was later taken over by the Foreign Office Library.[52]

Hertford House performed its most useful work in producing maps, usually at short notice. It was in this field that Dickson showed the greatest ingenuity, and Major Douglas Johnson, sent by the American Inquiry to study British methods of preparation, was struck by Dickson's novel use of transparencies for comparing different maps of the same region. The Section's maps were widely used, particularly by the Political Intelligence Department during the crush of work following upon the Armistice, and apparently even Lloyd George found them useful.[53]

For all its activity, though, Hertford House did not play a significant role in the final preparations for the negotiations, and alone of the department heads involved in such work, Dickson was not invited to attend the peace conference (nor for that matter was Admiral Hall). Both Hall and Dickson had acquired significant enemies in Whitehall, including the Foreign Office, which did not view favourably any poaching in its traditional preserves. When Major Johnson visited London he noted that while Dickson's operation 'is on a big scale', there were deep tensions reflecting the 'very evident slight regard in which he and his work are held by Foreign Office officials'. Johnson attributed this state of affairs to the fact that Dickson 'is a professor, and has not accomplished practical achievements sufficient to divest him of the reputation for lack

[51] Inquiry Doc. 987.
[52] The most complete run of these manuals is to be found in the Naval Historical Branch, Ministry of Defence, Empress State Building, London.
[53] FO 371/4352/f17. Inquiry Doc. 987.

of practical ideas and common sense which the profession as a whole enjoys'. Johnson summed up the situation with the observation that 'there is a marked tendency in Government circles to disown Dickson and his work'.[54] Johnson, an academic in civilian life, may well have been sensitive to such views, but it seems more likely that the Foreign Office was seeking to push Dickson into a marginal role. By eliminating Hall's organization from peace conference planning the Foreign Office would also eliminate a potentially dangerous rival.

Sir William Tyrrell, the director of the Foreign Office's Political Intelligence Department, maintained that Dickson had nothing to do with assembling data for the peace conference, while Dickson maintained that it was 'the most important part of his labours'.[55] H. W. C. Davis, vice-chairman of the War Trade Intelligence Department, told Johnson that 'Dickson's reports are not worth much, that they are too general and take in too many extraneous subjects (such as religions of people) to be of any use at the conference'.[56] Alwyn Parker, the Foreign Office Librarian, was 'particularly vigorous in his criticisms of Professor Dickson, saying that he was an impractical professor, prolix, and incapable of getting down to important facts . . . and that Dickson himself would not go [to the peace conference] if he [Parker] could help it'.[57] Hall, however, thought highly of Dickson's work, as shown by his nomination of Dickson for a CBE in 1918, but Dickson's work was clearly being belittled by the Foreign Office as part of the bureaucratic warfare in Whitehall that was being fought in tandem with the Great War in Europe.

Hertford House played a more indirect role in the final preparations than was originally intended, and the value of its contributions must be found in the material provided to the other departments which were responsible for the final arrangements. Dickson's section was hampered by the uncooperative attitude of other government departments which resented what they considered to be undue Admiralty interference in their particular spheres of concern. Other sections of the Intelligence Division suffered similar handicaps,

[54] Inquiry Doc. 987.   [55] Ibid.   [56] Ibid.   [57] Ibid.

but it is to Hall and Dickson's credit that they initiated the first systematic collection of information for use at a post-war peace conference.

The Historical Section: Origins

Under Admiral Hall the scope of the Naval Intelligence Division's work expanded to encompass political and economic affairs, war policy, and finally peace planning.[58] Dickson's organization at Hertford House was not the only section which Hall established whose brief would, in quieter times, seem tangential to the interests of the Admiralty. Leo Amery had pointed out the need to collect historical information, particularly on territorial claims, and Hall responded by establishing a Historical Section. This section was to prepare background handbooks on the various countries and issues involved in the war, on which, in many cases, no suitable work existed in English. These would be needed by the government in planning its negotiating position, in considering the claims of the various nationalities, and for reference at the peace conference. To supervise the production of these handbooks Hall recruited to his growing staff of civilian experts George Prothero, editor of the influential *Quarterly Review*.

Prothero was approached over lunch at the Athenaeum by a member of Hall's staff in May 1917, with the suggestion that he join Naval Intelligence in order 'to supervise the production of accounts, historical, geographical, economic, ethnographical etc., of all the countries likely to be discussed at the Peace Congress, for use by the Allied negotiators'.[59] Prothero was a good choice for a post requiring editorial skills and the recruitment of expert authors. Born in 1848 and educated at Eton, King's College, Cambridge, and Bonn University, he became the first professor of modern history at Edinburgh in 1894. He left in 1899 to succeed his younger brother, Rowland, at the

---

[58] James, *The Eyes of the Navy*, p. 32.

[59] Prothero Diary, 23 May 1917. The reference here to the Allied negotiators is in line with the asssumption that the Allies would first hold a preliminary meeting to co-ordinate their views before a peace conference with the Central Powers.

helm of the *Quarterly Review*.[60] Active in several organizations, Prothero served as president of the Royal Historical Society, 1901–5, and was instrumental in the founding of the British Academy. His wide range of friends throughout the academic community proved invaluable during the war when expert writers had to be found to prepare the Historical Section's handbooks. On the outbreak of war he had formed a Committee for National Patriotic Organisation aimed at educating the public through lectures and articles on the reasons for the war, and in 1916 Prothero published *German Foreign Policy before the War*, together with three bibliographical lists of books about the conflict.[61] Prothero's new section was labelled I. D. 27, though it was usually referred to as the Historical Section.

Prothero was not sanguine about the ultimate usefulness of his work, confiding to his diary, 'I doubt whether it will really be of much use — Probably even if the books are ready, our negotiators would never look at them.'[62] Despite his initial reservations about the work at hand, he greatly enjoyed the companionship of the people in his office. The staff included Lord Stanmore, Harold Russell, Gerald Fitzmaurice, Algernon Cecil, and Lieutenant Arthur Wiggin.[63] The last acted as Prothero's secretary and, though the youngest in the office, soon became a close friend of the ageing Cambridge don. Prothero and his staff immediately set about plotting out the general plan of their work.[64] At least 182 handbooks were envisaged. Such a

[60] Rowland Prothero (1851–1937), 1st Baron Ernle, 1919; educ. Marlborough and Balliol Coll., Oxford; editor of the *Quarterly Review*, 1894–9; MP (Con.) for Oxford University, 1914–19; President of the Board of Agriculture, 1916–19.

[61] The best account of Prothero is C. W. Crawley, 'Sir George Prothero and His Circle of Friends', *Transactions of the Royal Historical Society*, 5th series, vol. 20 (1970), 101–27. The co-founder of the Committee for National Patriotic Organisation was Henry Cust.

[62] Prothero Diary, 28 May 1917.

[63] A. F. H. Wiggin (1892–1935), educ. Oriel Coll., Oxford; ? .d lieutenant, Rifle Brigade, 1914; Captain, 1919; gassed in France, 1915; er .ered Diplomatic Service, 1919; first secretary, 1925. He committed suicide aboard the American liner *President McKinley* while in Tokyo harbour, apparently out of despondency over an incurable illness. A biographical sketch appeared in the *Isis* (31 Jan. 1914), pp. 11–12. His colleagues at both the Admiralty and the Foreign Office thought highly of his abilities. Wiggin Papers.

[64] Prothero Diary, 28 May–2 June 1917.

task would require the assistance of outside experts as well as the co-operation of other government offices. Within a fortnight of accepting the post Prothero was already contacting other ministries in order to secure their help.

The man appointed by Admiral Hall to supervise both I. D. 27 and I. D. 32 was Commander William Cozens-Hardy.[65] A barrister and member of the naval reserve he was posted to Naval Intelligence on the outbreak of war. He was responsible for recruiting the original staff for the Historical Section and drawing up the scheme for the series of handbooks.[66] Hall later commented about Cozens-Hardy that 'His single-mindedness of purpose was misunderstood by most people, who could not understand a man of his nature'.[67] A controversial figure, his increasingly strained relations with Prothero and the I. D. 27 staff, together with his reputation with other government departments, undoubtedly hindered the work of the Historical Section and contributed to its eventual transfer to the Foreign Office.

The India Office proved particularly recalcitrant in giving any assistance to the Historical Section. Vincent Smith, a retired India civil servant, was asked by Prothero to prepare a handbook subsequently published as *The French Possessions in India*, intended as part of the comprehensive coverage of colonial matters for any possible negotiations realigning colonial holdings.[68] The India Office, though, remained deeply suspicious of any other department concerning itself in Indian affairs, regardless of the reason. Prothero thought he had cleared the ground when he called at the India Office in June to explain the aim of his section, but when Smith requested permission to use the India Office library he was refused. John Shuckburgh, head of the India Office's Political Department, made it clear to Arthur Hirtzel, the assistant under-secretary, that he did not want 'the

---

[65] William Cozens-Hardy (1868–1924), 2nd Baron Cozens-Hardy; educ. New Coll., Oxford; barrister, Lincoln's Inn, 1893; KC, 1912; Bencher, 1916; Commander RNVR, 1914–18; MP, 1918–20.

[66] Henry Penson, 'Lord Cozens-Hardy' (obituary), *The Times*, 29 May 1924.

[67] Hall to Lady Cozens-Hardy, 1924. Cozens-Hardy Papers.

[68] V. A. Smith (1848–1920); joined India Civil Service in 1869; Judge 1st class, 1897; retired 1900. Author of the *Oxford History of India* (1919).

task of dry-nursing' Mr Smith.[69] Hirtzel responded in the same vein, commenting, 'this is another of Cozens-Hardy's stunts and is to be discouraged'.[70] When Smith again attempted to gain access to the India Office Library, this time providing extensive documentation as to the nature of his work, Hirtzel decided to contact the Foreign Office.

Hirtzel wrote to Lancelot Oliphant, then an assistant clerk at the Foreign Office, saying that he believed the matter of preparing papers for the peace conference was 'rather a FO than an Admiralty business'.[71] Oliphant was astonished to learn that the Admiralty was preparing a handbook on the French possessions in India and agreed with Hirtzel that the matter could hardly concern the Admiralty.[72] The India Office thereupon decided to demand of the unfortunate Mr Smith an official request for assistance from the Lords Commissioners of the Admiralty to the India Office. Two months later, in November, one of Hall's aides provided such an official request for assistance and Shuckburgh reluctantly gave way, noting, however, 'we find it a little hard to understand how information on the internal affairs of French India can be essential to the well being of the navy or the efficient conduct of naval policy'.[73] The incident illustrates the difficulties continually faced by the Historical Section while under the Admiralty.

There was a remarkable naïvety about the Historical Section's approach to its work. In August 1917 Prothero contacted the Dutch-based Central Organization for a Durable Peace, requesting copies of their publications. The letter was sent on Naval Intelligence Division stationery. The Foreign Office was outraged when a member of the Organization

[69] India Office, L/P&S/11/134/f1191, Prothero to Chamberlain, 6 June 1917. L/P&S/11/134/f1191/P.3358/1917, Minute by J. E. Shuckburgh to A. Hirtzel, 14 Aug. 1917. Sir Arthur Hirtzel (1870–1937); educ. Trinity Coll., Oxford; fellow of Brasenose Coll., Oxford, 1895–1902; entered India Office, 1894; secretary, Political Dept., 1909–17; assistant under-secretary, 1917–21; deputy under-secretary, 1921–4; permanent under-secretary, 1924–30.

[70] India Office, L/P&S/11/134/1191/P.3358/1917, Minute by Hirtzel, 17 Aug. 1917.

[71] Ibid., Hirtzel to Oliphant, 20 Aug. 1917.

[72] India Office, L/P&S/11/134/f1191, Oliphant to India Office, 22 Aug. 1917.

[73] India Office, L/P&S/11/134/f1191/P.3358/1917, Shuckburgh to Rayment, 21 Nov. 1917.

turned up at the British Embassy at the Hague asking if the publications requested could be sent by diplomatic bag in order to save postage. The embassy was stunned since the publications of the Central Organization were banned in Britain by the Censor, on Foreign Office orders! The Foreign Office let Hall know of their strong disapproval of such official contacts and Hall promised to stop any further such activities by I. D. 27. The incident did little to help relations with the Foreign Office.[74]

Relations with other government offices, though, were not always as disturbed as those with the India and Foreign Offices. The Colonial Office took a real interest in the Historical Section's work relating to the colonial world, although at first it too could not understand 'why the Admiralty occupied themselves with this matter'.[75] Unlike the India Office, the Colonial Office wanted to keep a watchful eye on the development of the handbooks, and Prothero soon established a good relationship with them.[76] But his relations with his own superior were not so happy.

During the autumn of 1917 tensions continued to grow among the I. D. 27 staff over the actions of Commander Cozens-Hardy, who had become a hindrance to them. In September a meeting was held to arrange a division of labour between Hertford House and the War Trade Intelligence Department during which 'All agreed that the elimination of C. H. [Cozens-Hardy] would be advantageous'.[77] Hall was asked to deal with the matter and Cozens-Hardy was moved to other work. In November, however, there was an incident in the rooms of the Historical Section, leading Prothero to note in his diary, 'Scene with Cozens-Hardy at the Admiralty: he was behaving as if still in command, had to stop him, the room was delighted'.[78] This was not the full extent of Cozens-Hardy's mischief. Politically well-connected, he was on good terms with such leading figures as Lloyd George and Lord Reading, and the prime minister occasionally used him as a private

[74] FO 371/3085/f185158/205115–211585.
[75] CO 323/750/37914, Colonial Office minute, 1 Aug. 1917.
[76] Ibid.; CO 323/758/37946; CO 323/775/13901; FO 370/84/f30550/54765, under-secretary Colonial Office to under-secretary Foreign Office, 25 Mar. 1918.
[77] Prothero Diary, 4 Sept. 1917.   [78] Ibid. 2 Nov. 1917.

envoy.[79] Prothero was disturbed to learn that Cozens-Hardy was giving out information, including the handbooks, to influential people. He noted simply, 'It must be stopped.'[80] Matters soon came to a head.

At the end of January 1918 there was another scene at the Admiralty, when Cozens-Hardy tried to turn Prothero out of his desk. Prothero naturally refused and Cozens-Hardy left in a temper. Lieutenant Wiggin, who was a particular victim of Cozens-Hardy's arrogance, was '... almost hysterical with delight' at the outcome.[81] Two days later, on 26 January, Cozens-Hardy ordered Wiggin to send him copies of all the work they had been doing. Russell, Cecil, and Stanmore thereupon presented an ultimatum to Hall, threatening a mass resignation unless Cozens-Hardy was brought to heel. Prothero went to Hall about the crisis and succeeded in obtaining the Admiral's support. He noted that when he returned to the rooms of I. D. 27, 'Russell shook me by the hand and said we must change the name of the room from Zeppelin Terrace to "Chambre du 26 Janvier"'.[82] Within weeks, however, the Historical Section was neither located in the Admiralty buildings, nor even under Admiralty control.

The effects of this skirmishing were disruptive to Hall's operations. This, together with the difficulties I. D. 27 had encountered in gathering information as an Admiralty section, must have convinced Hall that a shake-up was in order. Within a fortnight of the last incident with Cozens-Hardy a transfer of the Historical Section to the Foreign Office was under discussion and within a month the transfer was agreed to, with the Historical Section moving itself into 3 Great College Street as a part of the Foreign Office.

The Foreign Office Historical Section

The transfer of I. D. 27 to the Foreign Office fitted in neatly with Hardinge's evolving plans for the peace conference, as well as

[79] Ibid. In Aug. 1918 Cozens-Hardy wrote to Reading suggesting that he might be of use on Reading's mission to the USA, 'as my work at the Admiralty is really finished'. Reading Papers, F118/12/26–27. Reading knew Cozens-Hardy's father, who was Master of the Rolls.

[80] Prothero Diary, 2 Nov. 1917.   [81] Ibid. 24 Jan. 1918.

[82] Ibid. 26 Jan. 1918.

for longer term Office reform. In December 1917 Hardinge initiated a reform of the Foreign Office Library with the appointment of Alwyn Parker as librarian. Parker, the first professional diplomat to fill the post, was deeply involved with Hardinge in planning for the peace settlement, and his brief was to develop the library into a research organization. Since May 1917 he had been the liaison between I.D. 27 and the Foreign Office, developing in the process a good working relationship with Prothero.[83] Hardinge decided that the I.D. 27 group would complement the library reform and the new section became part of the library establishment.[84]

The idea of reforming the library was not a new one. In 1910 Eyre Crowe, in drawing up a plan for restructuring the non-political departments of the Office, recommended that the librarian's functions should include writing 'papers recording and elucidating the events of recent or contemporary history in foreign countries'. Crowe, however, did not intend that a historian be brought in to do this work, commenting that

Historians are notoriously bad at understanding and advising on current political questions, and, as a matter of fact, the habit of following the trend of contemporary affairs, and the art of writing intelligently on the subject, are outside the Foreign Offices, practically confined in most countries to men who follow the profession of journalism.

Crowe's reform proposal of 1910, though, was the predecessor of the reforms implemented in 1918, the creation of a Historical Section not being least among them.

Parker and Prothero worked out the details of the transfer during February. Prothero suggested formally christening the new organization the Foreign Office Historical Section in view of the difficulties its former ambiguous label had caused it in dealings with other agencies.[85] On 19 March the Foreign Office sent a circular notice to the other ministries announcing the establishment of the Historical Section and requesting the assistance of these departments in its work.[86] The change of title and location had the desired effect, even at the usually

[83] FO 371/3476/56911 and Prothero Diary.
[84] FO 370/84/f30550/30550, Parker to Hardinge, 14 Feb. 1918; FO 366/787/A III(a).
[85] Ibid.   [86] FO 370/84/f30550/50425.

sceptical India Office. Shuckburgh was even led to comment that 'The section certainly inspires more confidence under its present, than under its late patronage'. He remained dubious about temporary wartime offices in general, observing that 'there seems to me indications that the tendency — common to most temporary Depts. of the kind — to try to make the permanent Depts. do their work for them, has not wholly disappeared'.[87] Of course the new-found amity with the India Office may have been due to the Historical Section now being under Lord Hardinge, a former viceroy.

The Treasury, following its usual practice with regard to wartime creations, only sanctioned the funding of the Historical Section as a temporary measure. However, the Historical Section was planned as more than a wartime innovation. In April 1918 Parker recommended to Hardinge that the Historical Section 'should be permanently retained after the war, and that provision should be made for a paid Director (whoever he may ultimately be) and assistant. It is scarcely possible to exaggerate the importance of such an arrangement.'[88] Hardinge fully agreed with Parker's conclusion.

The Committee on Staffs which reviewed the Foreign Office structure in July 1918 also favoured the concept of a historical section. The committee commented that it found the remodelling of the Library with the addition of a Historical Section and the establishment of a Political Intelligence Department as being 'of the greatest importance for the future of the Foreign Office'.[89] It was certainly part of Hardinge's intention to retain these new sections as part of a general reorganization of the Foreign and Diplomatic Services.

The Historical Section under Prothero was a pleasant office to work in, leading Algernon Cecil to recall that under Prothero's 'wise and gentle influence the office in Great College Street became reminiscent of that delightful undergraduate existence which many of us left far behind; and we looked up to him almost like the undergraduates to men who have made their

---

[87] India Office, L/P&S/11/134/P.1191/1918.

[88] FO 366/787/71125. Prothero, who at first served without salary, was given a salary of £500 per annum in Aug. 1917. Prothero Diary.

[89] FO 366/787/135088, Report No. 8 of the Committee on Staffs, 11 July 1918.

mark'.[90] But Parker and Henry Penson, the head of the War Trade Intelligence Department, were concerned about the sluggish rate of production of the Peace Books. During the first week of October 1918, as the end of the war loomed, Parker, Penson, Prothero, and Cecil met to discuss a reorganization of the section.[91] Prothero blamed himself for the need of this, commenting that he 'ought to have seen the necessity of it long ago'.[92] The new arrangement was worked out by 7 October and Prothero noted sadly in his diary that it 'leaves me little direct control or responsibility'.[93] A week later Prothero celebrated his seventieth birthday.

The number of staff was increased to fifteen in order to help with the workload.[94] Among the new personnel was Captain Geoffrey Gathorne-Hardy, a barrister who had lost his left foot on the Western Front, and who, in common with Wiggin and Cozens-Hardy, was a former president of the Oxford Union. The War Office also seconded Bernard Henderson, a historian from Oxford, and E. L. Woodward.[95] Woodward, who assisted with the editorial work, recalled in his autobiography that

I was given the work of editing some of the Near and Middle Eastern books.... I found the editorial work interesting. We had asked the most learned authorities to write for us. I did not always find it easy to persuade them that they were not composing scholarly monographs at their leisure, but were compiling handbooks against time for an *ad hoc* purpose.[96]

Much of the editorial burden was assumed by the War Trade Intelligence Department which provided the services of Lillian Penson and W. W. Gregg, the latter being responsible for the geographical sections of the handbooks.[97] The rooms in Great College Street soon became insufficient and part of the staff was moved to an army hut in the then waterless lake of St. James's Park (which was emptied to prevent it being used as a landmark

[90] Algernon Cecil, 'Sir George Prothero, KBE, Litt.D.', the *Quarterly Review*, 473 (Oct 1922), 215–16.

[91] Stephen Gaselee, 'Prefatory Note', in Sir George W. Prothero, *A Select Analytical List of Books Concerning the Great War* (London, 1923).

[92] Prothero Diary, 3 Oct. 1918.   [93] Ibid. 7 Oct. 1918.

[94] Gaselee, 'Prefatory Note', p. iv.

[95] FO 370/84/f30550/174551, 172378, 172993.

[96] E. L. Woodward, *Short Journey* (London, 1942), p. 101.

[97] FO 371/4352/f17/PC17, Algernon Cecil to Roxburgh, 12 Oct. 1918.

for German aerial attack, presumably on Buckingham Palace). With this extra assistance the Peace Books now began to appear more rapidly, and by November most of the international law books were ready.[98]

The slowness with which the Peace Books were produced was not entirely Prothero's fault. No extensive work was possible until the spring of 1918 when the Section was transferred to the Foreign Office, though undoubtedly Prothero's many commitments and age must have played some part. Although he blamed himself for the difficulties, there was probably a desire to put off finishing the books until the last possible moment in order to ensure completeness. Whatever the causes and problems, Prothero's position in the Office was not affected. On 9 November Hardinge invited Prothero to attend the peace conference as Historical Advisor to the British Delegation.[99] Prothero and his now expanded staff maintained a heavy schedule after October and by the opening of the conference about fifty of the handbooks were available, with the rest soon to follow.

The Historical Section Peace Books

Between 1917 and 1919 the Historical Section produced 174 handbooks, commonly referred to as the Peace Books, or P. Books. The detailed General Plan developed by Commander Cozens-Hardy during the Section's Admiralty phase divided the Peace Books into four main sections: geography, economic conditions, political history, and present conditions, with appendices on principal treaties bearing on the subject and a bibliography. To write these handbooks Prothero recruited an impressive galaxy of authorities — some already in government service, others in private life. Over eighty experts were employed in the writing, some doing only a portion of one book while others prepared several. Prothero made full use of his friends from both the academic world and government circles. Although it 'was arranged that the books should be anonymous as a general rule', a few of Prothero's most prominent and influential authors were acknowledged, including Sir Ernest Satow, Francis Oppenheim, and Lord Phillimore.[100]

---

[98] CO 323/777/58342   [99] Prothero Diary, 9 Nov. 1918.
[100] FO 370/84/f30550/50425 and 157205.

The writers of the Peace Books were recruited in a variety of ways. C. K. Webster, the diplomatic historian, then serving in the Directorate of Military Intelligence, was seconded from May to August 1918 in order to write *The Congress of Vienna*.[101] Hardinge thought this book sufficiently important to order its immediate printing in the middle of November 1918, as useful reading for men about to meet at the first major conference for reordering the international system since Vienna.[102] E. L. Woodward, who was assigned to the Historical Section and who later became professor of international relations at Oxford, wrote *The Congress of Berlin*. He later recalled, 'I wrote what I could in a short time, and with insufficient material. My book was given a good mark by Balfour. This pleased me, since Balfour had attended the Congress as Salisbury's secretary.'[103] W. H. Dawson, an activist in social and educational work whose main interest was to interpret German life and institutions for the British people, was responsible for *German Colonisation* and the *Kiel Canal and Heligoland*.[104]

Prothero also called on the talented staff of the new Political Intelligence Department. Allen Leeper and Arnold Toynbee both wrote reports for the Historical Section, the former on Bessarabia, the later contributing to the works on the Ottoman Empire.[105] From the Foreign Office Prothero also called on retired diplomats with unusual expertise. J. H. Gubbins, who had served for thirty years in Japan and was fluent in the language, wrote the handbook on that country. C. W. Campbell, who had served almost as long in China where he had first acted as an interpreter, wrote *China*. Sir Ernest Satow provided an excellent general work entitled *International Congresses*.[106]

---

[101] Webster Papers 3/8.   [102] FO 370/84/f30550/192644.

[103] Woodward, *Short Journey*, p. 101.

[104] Dawson Papers, WHD 331–2, 335, 349, 350, 360, 362–4, 372, 387.

[105] A. W. A. Leeper Diary, 20 June 1918. AWAL. Hardinge to Toynbee, 3 June 1919, Toynbee Papers.

[106] John Hartington Gubbins (1852–1929); entered Japanese Consular Service, 1871; Japanese Secretary, 1889, Secretary of Legation, Tokyo, 1903. Author of several works on Japan. Charles William Campbell (1861–1927); Chinese Secretary, Peking, 1906–11.

Leading legal scholars, from both the Bench and the universities, were called upon. Lord Phillimore, who had chaired the committee appointed to examine early plans for a League of Nations, wrote *Schemes for Promoting a General Peace*. The German born and educated L. F. Oppenheim, Whewell Professor of International Law at Cambridge, provided the handbook entitled *Straits in International Law*. Sir Francis Piggot, formerly chief justice of the Hong Kong Supreme Court, wrote *The Freedom of the Seas: Historically Treated*.[107]

The authors of the handbooks were provided with *Instructions for Historical Writers*, prepared by Prothero, which sternly reminded them that 'They should remember that their readers will be likely to have no time to waste on matter not immediately important for the work in hand. . . . Compression and clearness should therefore be carefully studied; and the books must be severely practical.'[108] The writers were cautioned concerning the need for impartiality, though this was not meant to keep them from expressing their views. They were told explicitly that 'It is hoped that writers will not hesitate to draw such conclusions regarding the past as may seem to them fairly deducible from the facts referred to in their narratives, and also to make suggestions or recommendations concerning the future directly connected with the subject in hand.'[109] These recommendations were to be placed in a special section at the end of each book. The handbooks would thereby make available to the government the widest possible range of expert opinion.

Prothero's main task was to act as editor-in-chief of the handbooks, a role he was familiar with from the *Quarterly Review*.[110] The basic information for each of the handbook's three sections was provided by different offices. The War Trade

---

[107] Lassa Francis Oppenheim (1858–1919); educ. Universities of Göttingen, Heidelburg, Berlin, and Leipzig; professor, University of Basle, 1891; lecturer, LSE, 1895; naturalized British subject, 1900; Whewell Prof. of International Law, Cambridge, 1908. Sir Francis Piggot (1852–1925); educ. Trinity Coll., Cambridge; barrister, Lincoln's Inn, 1874; Legal Adviser to Prime Minister of Japan, 1887–91; Chief Justice, Hong Kong Supreme Court, 1905–12.

[108] FO 370/84/f30550/50425. [109] Ibid.

[110] The writers were told their page limit in terms of the *Quarterly Review*, and the P. Books were printed in the same size.

Intelligence Department was responsible for the first two sections of the handbooks. The material for the geography section was based on information abstracted from Hertford House's geographical handbooks and manuals, so Dickson's labours were not altogether lost. Information was also provided by Military Intelligence's Geographical Section. The WTID furnished the information for the economic section from data supplied by the War Trade Statistical Department. Prothero himself directly supervised the historical and political portions of the work, but the actual narrative was done by outside experts. Prothero and his staff edited the three sections into one readable report, before sending it off to the printers. After the reorganization of the Historical Section in October the WTID took over responsibility for the printing and press editing of the handbooks.[111] The galley proofs were then sent off to the interested government departments for comment, and the revised copy was printed.[112]

Table 1 gives some indication of the breadth of the subjects covered. The initial list of titles underwent some changes as the project proceeded, such as the dropping of envisaged titles on the 'Possibilities for Extension' of each of the European allies, during the autumn of 1918.[113] A handbook dealing with Alaska was also cancelled, perhaps because it was either extraneous or potentially too volatile. The Americans certainly would not have approved, especially as in 1916 there had been suggestions in the Imperial War Cabinet that the United States might be induced to trade Alaska for British Honduras![114] On the whole, though, the handbooks actually produced did reflect Allied concerns which arose at the negotiating table.

The Peace Books were of great interest to the American Inquiry, as indeed were British preparations in general. The Inquiry was heavily staffed by academics and Prothero, who had travelled and lectured in the United States, probably knew

---

[111] FO 370/84/f9308/9308.   [112] Inquiry Doc. 987, pp. 20–2.
[113] Webster Papers 3/9 contains the List of Subjects for 20 Sept. 1918 and a revised copy dated 25 Nov. 1918.
[114] CAB 29/1/P-16.

TABLE 1 *Distribution of Subjects in the Peace Book Series[a]*

Region	No. of Peace Books	Region	No. of Peace Books
Europe		America	
Austria-Hungary	15	North	2
Balkan Peninsula	8	Central	1
Belgium, Holland,		South	9
& Luxemburg	5	TOTAL	12
Denmark	1		
France	2	Oceania	6
Germany	6		
Italy	4	Asia	
Ottoman Empire		British Possessions	2
in Europe	1	China	6
Poland	5	Dutch Possessions	6
Portugal	2	French Possessions	2
Russia	7	Japan	1
Spain	3	Persia	2
Spitsbergen	1	Portuguese Possessions	3
TOTAL	60	Russian Possessions	2
		Siam	1
Africa		Turkey in Asia	14
Independent States	2	TOTAL	39
Belgian Possessions	1		
British Possessions	9	International Law	
French Possessions	10	Open Waters	1
German Possessions	4	Territorial Waters	5
Italian Possessions	3	TOTAL	6
Portuguese Possessions	6		
Spanish Possessions	4	General Questions	9
General Topics	3		
TOTAL	42	GRAND TOTAL	174

[a] FO 373 contains the P. Books.

several of its members.[115] Sir William Wiseman, the chief British agent in the United States, had established a good relationship with Colonel House, Wilson's chief confidant and nominal head of the Inquiry. In February 1918 Wiseman sent

[115] Inquiry Doc. 987, p. 5.

on to London a progress report on the Inquiry, causing Balfour
to suggest 'that there should be a full interchange of material'.[116] Substantive preparations were only just getting under
way at the Foreign Office with the establishment of the Political
Intelligence Department and the Historical Section, and Lord
Robert Cecil, bearing this in mind, also thought that 'When we
know what we are doing, we could see what exchange of information would be helpful'.[117] In March, therefore, a copy of
the Historical Section's General Plan, *Instructions to Historical
Writers*, and a list of subjects was forwarded to Colonel
House.[118]

This list of books was incomplete, as it was decided that
'certain books and groups of books it was thought undesirable
to communicate to Col. House were omitted. Such were the
books on Greenland, St. Pierre and Miquelon, the Falkland
Islands, Central and South America, various islands (Galapagos &c.) in the Eastern Pacific; also those on questions of International Law, Zionism &c.'[119] Obviously these were all topics
on which the two allies might have conflicting views, and virtually all were books which dealt with areas within the sphere
of America's Monroe Doctrine.

In April Major Johnson paid his visit to the Historical Section
and was given a sample copy of one of the Peace Books, in
galley proof, on Spitsbergen, which certainly must rank as the
most innocuous book on the entire list.[120] In May it was decided
to provide Wiseman with three copies of each book, most with
the general observations section omitted, and Wiseman was to
pass them on to House as he saw fit.[121] The Directors of Naval
Intelligence and Military Intelligence agreed to this, although
on the latter's recommendation the handbooks on Mesopotamia and Arabia were omitted, perhaps revealing not so
much concern about possible conflicts with the United States
in this region as British sensitivities.[122]

At the peace conference the United States requested and
received a full set of the handbooks.[123] R. A. C. Sperling was

[116] FO 370/98/f12608/187593.   [117] Ibid.
[118] Inquiry Doc. 989. The letter in the Inquiry file is dated 25 Apr. 1918.
[119] FO 370/98/f12608/187593.   [120] Ibid. and Inquiry Doc. 987, p. 5.
[121] FO 370/98/f12608/187593.
[122] Ibid.   [123] Ibid.

disturbed by this, as he feared that the Americans might leak them. Indeed the Americans inadvertently allowed the Italians to learn of the books' existence, who in turn immediately requested copies of those relevant to their interests, a request which was denied.[124] Nor does there seem to have been any exchange of information with the French. The United States delegates at the conference were therefore the only party to receive copies of the Peace Books, which they apparently found highly useful for reference.

It was not only the Americans who appreciated the quality of the Historical Section's product. Harold Nicolson found the handbooks to be of the utmost utility, observing that 'Should any historian doubt the quality of our preparation, I should urge him to obtain the whole collection. . . . He will agree that no more authoritative, comprehensive or lucid basis of information could possibly have been compiled.'[125] Not all of the Foreign Office were so enthusiastic about the Peace Books. Lancelot Oliphant apparently found them useless. Lord Edward Gleichen, acting head of the section during Prothero's absence in Paris, disagreed violently with Oliphant about this. Writing to Headlam-Morley, of the Political Intelligence Department, he said, 'F.O. people like Oliphant say they're [the P. Books] all rot — but then I consider Oliphant as belonging to that type of matter himself.'[126] Unquestionably the Peace Books were used.

Certainly some of the delegates at the conference made effective use of them. Lord Sumner used the handbook on indemnities with effect to counter American opposition.[127] Inevitably, though, those who were the busiest at Paris had the least time to make use of the books. Eyre Crowe commented that 'I have only a superficial acquaintance with one or two of the "Handbooks"'.[128] The Peace Books therefore appear to have been used most widely by the junior officials at Paris, such as Harold Nicolson and Robert Vansittart, rather than by the most senior

[124] Ibid. and FO 370/97/f12608/94886.
[125] Harold Nicolson, *Peacemaking 1919* (London, 1933), p. 27.
[126] Gleichen to Headlam-Morley, 7 Feb. 1919. Headlam-Morley Papers.
[127] Prothero Diary, 14 Feb. 1919.
[128] FO 608/160/511/4/1, Minute by Crowe, 17 Feb. 1919.

officials.[129] This is not surprising, in as much as it would be the junior officials who would be ordered to write reports on the matters under discussion and who would therefore have the greatest need for a ready reference source.

It was precisely their value as a source of reference which led Prothero to recommend publishing a sanitized version of the handbooks for public consumption. As early as May 1919 a question had been asked in the House of Commons about the possibility of the publication of the handbooks, 'in view of the great value to British traders of the information therein contained'.[130] On 20 November Prothero circulated a memorandum suggesting that publication would reflect credit on the Foreign Office and ease the public mind, 'if it could be shown tangible proofs and examples that the Foreign Office has long been considering the problems likely to arise in the settlement of peace'.[131] He went on to point out that 'The effect on our Allies, especially perhaps on the United States, should not be left out of sight'.[132] The project was agreed to and the last job of the Historical Section was to prepare the public version of the Peace Books, which appeared in 1920.[133] After the peace conference, when the Foreign Office was ordered to cut its expenses, most of the departments instituted during the war were eliminated, and the Historical Section was dissolved in November 1920.[134] The Historical Section's activity had in fact begun to decline after the conference opened. As Prothero noted in his diary, the 'historical work [was] really done already, with very few exceptions, in the P. books'.[135] While the Historical Section did not directly influence the outcome of the Paris Peace Conference, it did provide a firm underpinning

---

[129] Lord Vansittart, *The Mist Procession* (London, 1956), p. 201. Various officials though were anxious to receive them, such as Gen. Clayton who specially requested the handbooks on the Near and Middle East. FO 608/101/376/3/1/13803–15203.

[130] Hansard 115, 8 May 1919, Mr Betterton to Harmsworth.

[131] FO 370/84/f30550/192644.   [132] Ibid.

[133] Apparently the P. Books were not a great success in terms of public sales, most copies being sold at the universities. Webster Papers 1/5/67; also Prothero Diary, 8–9 Feb., 24 Oct., 30 Nov. 1919.

[134] FO 370/121/L1393/6/405.   [135] Prothero Diary, 3 Apr. 1919.

of fact for the British negotiating position at Paris, in turn allowing the British delegation to speak with greater accuracy, and therefore with greater force.

The War Trade Intelligence Department

The War Trade Intelligence Department was created as a result of Admiral Hall's attempts to gather useful information on the Central Powers' commercial activities. Hall came to an agreement with his counterpart at Military Intelligence in December 1914 for Naval Intelligence to set up an unofficial private censorship of the overseas post. No trace of espionage was uncovered by this operation, but it did reveal startling information about German purchases which were passing through neutral intermediaries. When Hall's unauthorized activities became known there was a flurry of consternation among some officials, but Hall's results were sufficiently impressive for the Cabinet to order the Committee of Imperial Defence (CID) to report on the need for an organization to deal with trade questions.[136]

On 14 January 1915 the CID recommended the creation of a War Trade Department which would include an intelligence division to act as a clearing house for commercial information. Hall credited Commander Cozens-Hardy with the successful execution of the new intelligence section:

It was during a Blockade that it was realized that it could only be made effectual by having the most accurate intelligence. The first step was to censor all letters and telegrams and have the information properly indexed. This was done for three weeks (by breaking the law) the outcome of which was the War Trade Intelligence Department, for which he was entirely responsible.[137]

It was Cozens-Hardy who recruited Henry Penson to head the Trade Clearing House, as the new section was named. Penson, an Oxford history don, was already involved in war work and he was described cryptically in one report as having 'been

[136] James, The Eyes of the Navy, pp. 37–42. Hall to Lady Cozens-Hardy, 1924, Cozens-Hardy Papers. Correspondence with G. R. Wakeling, son of G. H. Wakeling who was secretary of the WTID, during 1982.
[137] Hall to Lady Cozens-Hardy, 1924. Cozens-Hardy Papers.

associated in work of a varied description at 59, Palace St., S. W.'.[138] This presumably was the unsanctioned censorship group Hall had initially established. On 1 February 1915 the new intelligence section started operation as part of the War Trade Department established under Lord Emmott. The work of the Trade Clearing House grew rapidly, starting in February 1915 with 30 members at the Palace Street offices, and expanding by January 1917 to a staff of 262 (94 men and 168 women). Eventually it came to be housed in the temporary buildings erected in the drained lake at St James's Park.[139]

In February 1916 Lord Robert Cecil was appointed Minister of Blockade, within the Foreign Office, and in March the Trade Clearing House passed under his control, changing its name to the War Trade Intelligence Department (WTID). It remained under the War Trade Department for matters of staff, discipline, and salary until January 1917 when Cecil assumed full administrative control, and in April 1918 the WTID was placed under the Department of Overseas Trade for administrative purposes. Henry Penson remained as chairman at a salary of £1000 a year.[140] Penson's deputy, H. W. C. Davis, was a major force within the the department from its inception, and one member of the advisory committee later recalled that

Sir Henry Penson rarely interfered with the work of the different sections, many of which had been organised, and were maintained by Davis. He showed a curious aptitude for this, to him, entirely new form of mental activity; always a glutton for work, he displayed rare powers of handling the material that came along. . . .[141]

[138] CAB 15/6/24, part 1, pp. 22–31. 'War Trade Department'.

[139] Ibid. TS 14 contains records of the WTID's Contraband Committee, Enemy Exports Committee, General Black List, and copies of the Transit Letter Bulletin.

[140] CAB 15/6/24, part 1; BT 61/12/7; 'Origin and Development of the War Trade Intelligence Department', FO 366/787/A III (b). The WTID was initially paid for out of the War Trade Dept. vote, then the Foreign Office vote, and finally the DOT vote, BT 61/12/7; T 1/12264/50316, 'The Trade Clearing House. Section of the War Trade Department', Dec. 1915, contains a list of salaries. Powicke's salary of £350 was considered very extravagant by the Treasury.

[141] Alfred Sutro quoted in J. R. H. Weaver, *Henry William Careless Davis, 1874–1928: A Memoir* (London, 1933), p. 38. See also F. M. Powicke, 'Henry William Careless Davis', *English Historical Journal*, 43 (1928), 578–84.

Davis was highly thought of by his colleagues, many of whom he had recruited. He later became Regius Professor of Modern History at Oxford.

Sir Maurice Powicke, who served in the WTID, later wrote that it 'was an exceedingly interesting community of lawyers, historians, economists, dramatists, novelists, stockbrokers, and many other kinds of people whom Sir Henry Penson and his advisers gathered together'. [142] The WTID was well stocked with historians; besides Penson, Davis, and Powicke (who would later succeed Davis in the Regius chair at Oxford), there were such figures as J. R. H. Weaver, who before the war was professor of history at Trinity College, Dublin, and Lillian Penson, one of the few women to be employed by the department in more than a purely clerical capacity, and no relation to the chairman. She was assigned to assist the Historical Section with the editing of the peace handbooks and after the war she assisted H. W. V. Temperley and G. P. Gooch in editing *British Documents on the Origins of the War*. She subsequently went on to become vice-chancellor of the University of London, the first woman to hold such a position in the kingdom.

It was as a result of Toynbee and Zimmern's proposals in January 1917 for a peace intelligence section that the WTID became involved in the preparation of material for the negotiations. Leo Amery had defined the need for geographical, historical, and economic information. The first part was assigned to Dickson's Geographical Section, and the second to the newly created Historical Section. It was therefore natural for Hall and Cozens-Hardy to turn to the WTID for economic information.

The War Trade Intelligence Department's first involvement with the peace work was in connection with the Historical Section, then still part of Hall's Naval Intelligence Division. Cozens-Hardy had undoubtedly intended from the start that the WTID would provide the information for the economic sections of the proposed handbooks, while Dickson's staff would provide the geographical section. [143] In August 1917 Prothero, Dickson, Henry Penson, and Davis met to discuss the division of work between the Admiralty and the WTID[144] Davis

---

[142] Ibid. 581.   [143] Prothero Diary, 23 May 1917.
[144] Ibid. 9 Aug. 1917.

was not satisfied by the tentative conclusion, and it was not until September that an arrangement was worked out.[145] The WTID also had some difficulty sorting out its relations with the Board of Trade. Prothero, who attended these discussions, remarked in his diary on the Board's high and mighty attitude toward statistics.[146]

In October 1918 when it became apparent that the work of the Historical Section would have to be reorganized if the peace handbooks were to be ready in time for the now inevitable peace conference, it was Penson who came to the rescue. He arranged for the WTID to carry out the final editing of the work, with which the department had been involved since 1917.[147] The WTID also worked closely with the Political Intelligence Department, particularly in providing the economic information and statistics for the peace memoranda.[148]

As the war drew to a close so too did the original purpose of the WTID. Hardinge therefore made use of its excellent staff to help him with the arrangements for the peace conference, selecting Henry Penson to head the Intelligence Clearing House at Paris.[149] Penson was also responsible for overseeing accommodation at Paris, and the WTID handled the courier service with London.[150] After the conference there was some discussion of continuing the WTID as the commercial intelligence section of the Department of Overseas Trade, but no action was taken. Admiral James, the deputy director of Naval Intelligence, considered the WTID 'one of our most powerful war winning weapons. If Hall had done nothing else but found this department he would have earned the lasting gratitude of his countrymen.'[151]

Mention must be made of the small War Trade Statistical Department which assisted in providing material for the

[145] Prothero Diary, 4 Sept. 1917.   [146] Ibid. 22 May 1918.
[147] Ibid. 8 Nov. 1918.
[148] FO 371/4352/f8/PC8. Roxburgh was the PID's liaison officer with the WTID, where he worked with Sir John Keltie, who was responsible for handling requests from the PID.
[149] ADM 1/8542/284.   [150] BT 61/12/7.
[151] James, The Eyes of the Navy, p. 42. Prothero noted that 'Penson told me he had to wait from March till end Sept. to know whether they intended the WTID to come to an end or not — they decided — ultimately — to dissolve it, which is a great pity.' Prothero Diary, 24 Oct. 1919.

WTID, for the peace handbooks and the peace memoranda. It was established in 1915 as a result of the same concerns which led to the creation of the War Trade Department and the Trade Clearing House. It commenced operations on 26 April 1915 and was soon given rooms at 22 Queen Anne's Gate. R. E. Harwood was borrowed from the National Health Insurance Commission to act as principal, with W. T. Matthews as assistant principal. Its function was '(1) — to obtain correct statistics of exports from the United Kingdom to the neutral countries contiguous to the enemy. (2) — compile correct statistics of the imports into each of these neutral countries from sources other than the United Kingdom.'[152] Together with the WTID it was transferred to the Ministry of Blockade in 1917. At the time of its transfer it employed 26 men and 45 women and assisted in the collection of material for the peace conference by providing data on economic questions.[153]

The Military

In 1918 the Directorate of Military Intelligence established a new section code-named M.I.2(e) to prepare 'special papers on historical, political, and ethnographical matters'.[154] In command of M.I.2(e) was H. W. V. Temperley, a graduate of King's College, Cambridge, and a fellow of Peterhouse when war broke out. Temperley had travelled in Serbia and Slovakia before the war, and saw service at the Dardanelles before being invalided home and assigned to Military Intelligence. In 1918 he was promoted to the rank of major and on 15 October sent to Serbia in order to evaluate the distribution of territories envisaged by the 1915 Treaty of London. He remained there until April 1919 when he joined the British delegation at Paris, where he played an important part in the settlement of the

---

[152] CAB 15/6/24, part 1.

[153] Ibid. FO 370/80/f83428/83428. The WTSD was paid for out of the Foreign Office vote, FO 366/782/A III.

[154] J. R. Wade, ed., *The War Office List* (London, 1918), p. 94. The 1919 edition notes that M.I.2(e) liaises with the PID. Webster was the liason officer with the Foreign Office on matters concerning the peace conference, Webster Papers 3/9/8.

Fiume crisis.[155] After the war he edited the six-volume *History of the Peace Conference of Paris*, for which he commissioned contributions by many former members of M. I.2(e). In 1938, the year of his death, he was elected master of Peterhouse.

The other members of the section were J. A. Arland, J. R. M. Butler, C. R. M. F. Crutwell, R. G. D. Laffan, K. W. M. Pickthorn, B. H. Sumner, and C. K. Webster.[156] These men had all seen active service and several were assigned to Military Intelligence after being invalided home. Half of the section's members had served in South-Eastern Europe, which helps to explain the number of reports prepared on this region. For many of these men their work in M. I.2(e) was a critical step in their careers. One historian has commented of Webster's transfer to Military Intelligence that 'This feat of wizardry was performed by his friend and former teacher Harold Temperley. . . . It was the turning point in his career.'[157] Sumner was the most prolific writer, producing almost half of the reports.

[155] I am indebted to Prof. John D. Fair for sharing with me his knowledge of the career of H. W. V. Temperley.

[156] J. R. M. Butler (1889–1975); educ. Harrow and Trinity Coll., Cambridge; Pres. Cambridge Union, 1910; Scottish Horse, 1914–18; OBE, 1919; MVO, 1920; MP (Ind.), 1922–3; Regius Prof. of Modern History, Cambridge, 1947–54. C. R. M. F. Crutwell (1887–1941); educ. Rugby and Queen's Coll., Oxford (triple 1st); fellow of All Souls Coll., 1911; lecturer in history, Hertford Coll., Oxford, 1912; 2nd lieut., Aug. 1914; served in Belgium and France; invalided home; Principal of Hertford Coll., 1930–9. R. G. D. Laffan (1887–1972), educ. Eton and Balliol Coll., Oxford; Pres. Oxford Union, 1909; fellow of Queens' Coll., Camb., 1912; Temp. Chaplain to the Forces, 1914–18; attached to Serbian Army, 1916–18. K. W. M. Pickthorn (1892–1975). Educ. Trinity Coll., Cambridge; fellow of Corpus Christi Coll., Cambridge, 1914; served London Regt. and RFC in France and Macedonia; wounded 1917; MP (Con.), 1935–66; Baronet, 1959. Butler, Laffan, and Pickthorn shared an office, with Pickthorn responsible for German problems. (Communication from Sir Charles Pickthorn, 2nd Bt., 21 Apr. 1982.) B. H. Sumner (1893–1951); educ. Winchester and Balliol Coll., Oxford; active service, 1914–18; Warden of All Souls Coll., Oxford, 1945–51. Sumner, who had learned Russian while at school, was responsible for Russian affairs. C. K. Webster (1886–1961); educ. King's Coll., Cambridge; Prof. of Modern History, Liverpool, 1914–22; Subaltern RASC, 1914–17; Secretary Military Sect., British Delegation, Paris, 1919; Stevenson Prof. of International History, LSE, 1932–55.

[157] S. T. Bindoff, 'Charles Kingsley Webster', *Proceedings of the British Academy*, 48 (1961), 427–47.

M. I.2(e) staff produced 35 reports, which were subsequently circulated as General Staff papers. Most of these were sent to the PID, with which close relations were maintained. These connections are not surprising when the number of Cambridge and Oxford historians employed in these departments is considered. The focus of M. I.2(e)'s work can be seen in the following list, which keeps the section's own topical classification.[158]

Alsace-Lorraine	2	Yugoslavia	4
South-Eastern Europe	4	Romania	2
Belgium and Luxemburg	4	Schleswig	1
Caucasia	4	Syria	1
Czechoslovakia	3	Armenia	1
Finland	2	Russia	2
Italian Claims	3	Zionism	1

Most of the section's staff were sent to Paris for the conference, to assist with these questions.

The Army and Navy both played a role in the organized preparation of material through the special sections created within their intelligence services. In addition the Army, Navy, and Air staffs also provided memoranda covering topics of particular strategic concern. The General Staff was the last to produce such a report, in February 1919, which was based on the earlier M. I.2(e) memoranda.[159] The Admiralty, despite its early involvement through Admiral Hall, did not begin to make any preparations on specifically naval questions until the autumn of 1918. On 10 November 1918 the Plans Division drew up a memorandum containing seven recommendations for a peace settlement which were considered by the Admiralty Board on 14 November.[160] This report was concerned with such purely naval matters as the surrender of German submarines, the razing of Heligoland, and the appropriation of the German cable system.

Oswyn Murray, the secretary of the Admiralty Board, suggested a scheme for setting up six committees 'for dealing rapidly with the questions included in the summary circulated

[158] Much of the material on M.I.2(e) is based on C. K. Webster's papers, especially Webster Papers 3/7 and 3/9. There is also some information in the J. R. M. Butler Papers (uncatalogued).

[159] Webster Papers 3/7/34.

[160] ADM 167/55, Board Meeting, 14 Nov. 1918, item 12.

to the Board'.[161] These committees concerned the North Sea and Baltic, Mediterranean and Near East, the Empire, international law, financial and economic questions, and peace terms. Each committee consisted of five or six members, with Admiral Hall having representatives on all of them. On 5 December the Admiralty Board agreed to Murray's plan.[162] The Board approved the results of the committee's labour on 9 January.[163] The final report classified naval interests into four sections: naval conditions for peace, general policy questions in which the Navy was vitally concerned, questions of lesser naval interest, and minor naval questions.[164]

The Air Board paid little attention to peace questions, though it did stay in close contact with the PID. The Board had earlier submitted a report to the Mallet Committee on the need for seaplane, airplane, and airship bases. Otherwise the Air Board seems to have paid little attention to post-war settlement questions. On 22 January 1919 it finally submitted a memorandum to the delegation on some of its aims.[165]

Finance and International Law

In February 1917 the Treasury created a new department, known as the 'A' Division, which was to be exclusively concerned with the problems of external finance. The head of this new section was John Maynard Keynes, and it comprised mostly temporary civil servants. Among those employed in 'A' Division were Geoffrey Fry, Andrew Mcfadyean, Frank Nixon, Rupert Trouton, and Dudley Ward.[166] When in October 1918

[161] ADM 167/55, Oswyn Murray, 'Naval Terms of Peace', 5 Dec. 1918.

[162] ADM 167/53, Board meeting, 5 Dec. 1918, minute 520.

[163] ADM 167/56, Board meeting, 9 Jan. 1919, minute 575.

[164] ADM 167/57, 'Notes on Matters Affecting Naval Interests connected with the Peace Settlement', Jan. 1919 (3rd revise). Many of the most important documents were put together in 1935 on Murray's instance, now in ADM 116/1861. Relevant material is also in ADM 116/1852, ADM 167/55.

[165] CAB 21/77, Harvey to Amery, 'Necessity of Providing Sea Plane and Airship Bases and Aerodromes for Safeguarding Flying Rights', 18 Apr. 1917. See Nelson, Land and Power, p. 109. A memorandum was also submitted on 22 Jan. 1919, in CAB 29/2/P-100.

[166] R. F. Harrod, The Life of John Maynard Keynes, (London, 1963), pp. 219–20, and Andrew McFadyean, Recollected in Tranquillity (London, 1964), pp. 65–6.

the War Cabinet asked the Treasury to prepare a memorandum on reparations this work was assigned to 'A' Division. 'Information was assembled from every quarter. The team laboured under Keynes' guidance . . . their knowledge of the details of world trade, which came to them from their day-to-day experience, must have been unrivalled at that time.'[167] Their memorandum on reparations and indemnities was complemented by one of a similar nature from the Board of Trade.[168]

Preparations on international law topics, particularly the League of Nations and the freedom of the seas, were more complex than those on economic problems. Initial planning was carried out in a number of committees appointed by the Cabinet, such as the Phillimore Committee on the League of Nations and the Cave Committee on International Law. Eventually the PID attempted to bring some organization to this work by creating a League of Nations Section, but this attempt was hampered by the failure to appoint a head of section during the first weeks after the Armistice. The legal adviser to the Foreign Office, Cecil Hurst, who served on several of these committees, also provided drafts of potential treaty clauses. None of the groups working on economic and legal problems had been specifically established to prepare for the peace conference, but they were all drafted into temporary service during the period from November to December to assist in the preparation of material for the peace brief.

Conclusion

During the *ad hoc* discussion stage in British planning for the peace conference little of any substance was accomplished, other than a growing recognition that organized preparations were essential. Several officials independently came to the conclusion that if Britain was to succeed at the negotiating table, the level of planning would have to be raised above the fantasy world of committee discussion. It was Admiral Hall, in

[167] Harrod, *Life of John Maynard Keynes*, p. 229.
[168] A number of specialized committees were established to consider financial problems. These included the Sub-Committee on the Policy of the 'Clean-Slate' (CAB 29/1/P-21) and the Enemy Debts Committee (CAB 29/1/P-23).

response to Amery's suggestions, who took the first critical steps towards resolving this problem, and by 1917 preparations for the eventual peace conference were well under-way. Admiral Hall took a bold initiative when he decided to establish the Geographical and Historical Sections. Their work in preparing for the peace conference was not confined to the parochial interests of the Admiralty, but covered instead the widest possible range of potential British interests. That the Naval Intelligence Department, in the last instance, played no direct role in the peace work was not due to any lack of ability on the part of the staff recruited, but was a reflection of the bureaucratic difficulties and overlapping jurisdictions which inevitably beset the work of a government at war.

The Foreign Office recognized the importance of the work being performed by Naval Intelligence's Historical Section when it agreed to legitimize its activities by transferring it into the Office, thereby allowing the Section's staff to proceed more efficiently with the work at hand. The task facing the Historical Section's staff was not an easy one, as it had to predict the issues which could possibly arise at an international congress. As a result the number of topics covered by the Peace Books exceeded the number of subjects actually discussed at Paris, but it is to the Historical Section's credit that all of the issues that did arise were covered.

In 1918 the Foreign Office set up the Political Intelligence Department under Sir William Tyrrell and J. W. Headlam-Morley to co-ordinate the material now being produced. A War Trade Intelligence Department and a War Trade Statistics Department were placed under the Ministry of Blockade, while Military Intelligence established a section under H. W. V. Temperley to look into the military aspects of peace planning. In addition the Phillimore Committee was drafting a British plan for a League of Nations, and non-governmental bodies, such as the Royal Geographical Society, were brought in to assist with specialized work. By the end of the war Britain had succeeded in developing a sophisticated, if complex, machinery for providing the essential preparations for the peace negotiations.

2

The Political Intelligence Department

I do not know whether the so-called 'Ministry of All the Talents' had fully deserved its name, but in the PID, a century later, there was a concentration of talent that was immensely stimulating.

A. J. Toynbee, *Acquaintances*, p. 161

Origins of the Political Intelligence Department

In 1918 the Foreign Office embarked upon an early experiment in the central co-ordination of political intelligence when it created the Political Intelligence Department (PID). Since the turn of the century there had been a growing awareness of the need for foreign intelligence, a development which finally resulted in the creation of an espionage agency in 1909, the ancestor of the Secret Intelligence Service. This service, however, concentrated primarily on military-related intelligence.[1] During the First World War it became evident to Lord Hardinge that while there were numerous sources of political intelligence, no systematic method had been established for collecting and collating this information, verifying it against collateral sources, and synthesizing the result in succinct reports which would be of value to policy makers. Military intelligence was clearly the preserve of the Admiralty and the War Office, and Hardinge wished to establish that political intelligence fell within the purview of the Foreign Office. The creation of the PID was in effect the last phase of the reforms initiated by Lord Hardinge during his previous tenure as permanent under-secretary, 1906–10. The establishment of the

---

[1] On the origins of the SIS see Christopher Andrew, *Secret Service* (London, 1985).

PID formed part of the same reorganization which brought the Historical Section to the Foreign Office, and was intended to complement the existing departments by providing a small group of experts to co-ordinate and analyse the mass of information flowing into the Foreign Office. It was this innovative new department, and its expert personnel, which emerged during 1918 as the cornerstone of British preparations for the peace conference.

Hardinge was clearly motivated by the obvious eclipse of the Foreign Office in policy formulation since the formation of the Lloyd George coalition. He was especially resentful of the amateurs the prime minister chose to consult in preference to members of the Foreign Office. In particular Hardinge disliked Lloyd George's personal secretariat, the 'Garden Suburb'. Writing in March 1917 to Valentine Chirol he noted that 'It makes me boil when I see a young man like Philip Kerr, of whom I can say nothing but good, employed in a sort of secretariat by the Prime Minister at a salary of £1000 a year when in the War Department of this office we have a young man like Harold Nicolson who is quite first rate and a thorough expert in all his subjects, receiving a pittance of £150 a year ....'[2] Hardinge's solution was to counter with a Foreign Office equivalent of the Garden Suburb, to be composed not of amateurs but of the best available experts. What resulted became known as the Political Intelligence Department.

The proposed new department encountered some opposition within the Foreign Office, where radical innovations were not always welcome. Lord Robert Cecil, parliamentary under-secretary and Minister of Blockade (and Balfour's cousin), wrote angrily to the Foreign Secretary in January 1918 that he was 'very much grieved with Hardinge for ... having installed a new Department of Political Intelligence with Tyrrell at its Head. This seems objectionable to me on several grounds ....'[3] Hardinge was nevertheless given permission to proceed

[2] Hardinge to Chirol, 26 Mar. 1917. Hardinge Papers 2. Valentine Chirol (1852–1929), Foreign Editor of *The Times*, 1896–1912; Special Mission to the Balkans for the FO, 1915; present at the Paris Peace Conference, 1919.

[3] Cecil to Balfour, 8 Jan. 1918, Balfour MS 49738. Cecil was more concerned with the transfer of the News Dept. to the Department of Information.

with the creation of the new department. The next difficulty he faced was how to obtain expert personnel in wartime.

To resolve this problem Hardinge, with bureaucratic ruthlessness, proceeded to poach an entire department of experts from a rival ministry. His target was the Department of Information's Intelligence Bureau (DIIB). The DIIB was established in April 1917 with a view to reporting on conditions in foreign countries 'and providing the Propaganda sections of the other portion of the Department of Information with suggestions for effective propaganda in other countries'.[4] The staff consisted of twelve experts, mostly with academic backgrounds, working under Count (later Lord) Edward Gleichen, with James Headlam-Morley as assistant director.[5] They were divided into six regional sections:

1 Germany: J. W. Headlam-Morley, E. R. Bevan,
   G. Saunders;
2 East and Central Europe: R. W. Seton-Watson,
   L. B. Namier;
3 Russia: R. W. A. Leeper, J. Y. Simpson;
4 Balkans: A. W. A. Leeper;
5 Middle East: A. J. Toynbee;
6 France, Spain, and Italy: J. Bailey, J. C. Powell.[6]

Hardinge saw the DIIB as consisting of just the sort of experts he wanted to staff his new department, individuals 'who had already had long and valuable experience in watching the course of events and opinion in foreign countries, and who already knew one another and had learned to co-operate with one another'.[7]

---

[4] FO 395/148/85465/117714.

[5] Count Edward Gleichen (1863–1937), son of Admiral Prince Victor of Hohenlohe-Langenburg; he served as an army officer in the Boer War, and commanded the 37th Division, Apr. 1915–Oct. 1916; Director DIIB, 1917–18; Acting Director Historical Section, 1919.

[6] Hugh Seton-Watson and Christopher Seton-Watson, *The Making of a New Europe* (London, 1981), p. 207. FO 366/787/44472, Headlam-Morley to Foreign Office, 25 Feb. 1918. In addition an Armenian, a Mr Safrastian, was employed to write on affairs in Armenia and the Caucasus region. He eventually fell on hard times and during 1942 Toynbee was approached about helping him. Capt. W. E. D. Allen to Toynbee, Toynbee Papers (Individuals-A).

[7] FO 371/4382/PID 619.

Hardinge offered the DIIB members employment in the Foreign Office, with the widest possible access to intelligence, and the possibility of involvement in the foreign policy process. An added inducement was a minimum annual salary of £400.[8] Such a move was in line with recent proposals for the reorganization of the British propaganda services. At the request of the prime minister a report on the British propaganda effort had been prepared by Robert Donald, editor of the *Daily Chronicle*, who recommended that as the DIIB had already 'developed into a source of political intelligence from other countries . . . [it] could be useful as an adjunct of the Foreign Office but not as a branch of propaganda'.[9] This view was agreed to by both Gleichen and John Buchan, the head of the Department of Information.

As a result of the Donald report, and of Hardinge's own initiatives, the War Cabinet approved a memorandum from Balfour on 18 February requesting the Department of Information to transfer the functions of the DIIB to the Foreign Office.[10] On 21 February the Foreign Office wrote to Headlam-Morley of the DIIB asking him to determine if the twelve-member staff was willing to transfer to the newly created, and as yet unmanned, Political Intelligence Department.[11] However, problems suddenly arose in the same month with the elevation of the Department of Information into a Ministry under Lord Beaverbrook. On 20 February the new Minister asked the War Cabinet to rescind its decision, proposing instead a central political intelligence department under his own control.[12] The War Cabinet assigned General Smuts the joy of settling this dispute, perhaps because he was its only member with combat experience. Beaverbrook and Hardinge were now engaged in a traditional form of bureaucratic warfare, with each attempting to conserve and enhance his own administrative preserve.

As a first step to achieving his end Beaverbrook refused to sanction the transfer of any of his staff to the Foreign Office.

[8] FO 366/787/44472.   [9] CAB 27/18/PAC 3.
[10] CAB 23/5/WC349, CAB 24/41/GT3547.
[11] FO 366/787/44472.
[12] See Philip Taylor, 'The Foreign Office and British Propaganda during the First World War', *Historical Journal*, 23(1980), 893–4, and A. J. P. Taylor, *Beaverbrook* (London, 1972), pp. 146–50.

What defeated Beaverbrook's ploy was the temptation posed to the DIIB's experts of working within the Foreign Office, perhaps combined with a disinclination to serve under the new Minister of Information. When on 5 March Smuts recommended as a compromise that the DIIB remain under Beaverbrook, but that the Foreign Office be allowed to proceed with the establishment of its own political intelligence department, the entire staff of the DIIB resigned. 'The reason for this action was their firm conviction that it would be impossible for any satisfactory work in foreign Political Intelligence to be carried on except in the Foreign Office itself, and they did not feel justified in taking work which would only have meant the duplication of service and the weakening of the Foreign Office in its conduct of foreign affairs.'[13] Emotions were running high, as one member of the DIIB remarked in his diary at the time: 'heard that Beaverbrook had been presented with our office by the War Cabinet. All determined to resign.'[14] Certainly Beaverbrook was not considered a desirable chief by many, leading George Prothero, who was well aware of the problems of difficult superiors, to note that the DIIB staff had 'resigned rather than serve under Beaverbrook, and no wonder'.[15] In a last attempt to avoid defeat Beaverbrook asked Smuts to enforce the interdepartmental 'no poaching' understanding and to rule that 'these gentlemen should not be engaged in the Intelligence Department of the F.O. after their resignation from this department'.[16] Smuts declined observing that 'they were not civil servants but independent experts voluntarily serving their country in war time, and as the F.O. represented (no doubt with perfect truth) that their expert services could not be spared . . . if they did not work under the Ministry of Information, they should be allowed to work under the F.O.'.[17] Beaverbrook as usual never forgave and continued the struggle for several months, even threatening to resign as late as May 1918 over this issue. It was Balfour, exercising his political skills, who finally succeeded in calming Beaverbrook's anger.[18] Hardinge thus emerged victorious

[13] FO 371/4382/PID619, Memorandum by Headlam-Morley, 28 Oct. 1919.
[14] A. W. A. Leeper Diary, 7 Mar. 1918.   [15] Prothero Diary, 8 Mar. 1918.
[16] CAB 24/45/GT3939.   [17] Ibid.
[18] FO 800/207, Beaverbrook to Balfour, 21 May 1918.

from his duel with Beaverbrook and could now proceed with organizing the PID.

Early Days of the Political Intelligence Department

On 11 March 1918 Hardinge circulated a minute in the Office in which he announced, 'The new department which has been created under Sir W. Tyrrell for the purpose of collecting, sifting, and co-ordinating all political intelligence received from our own, Admiralty and War Office sources will enter upon its functions at once. It will be called the Political Intelligence Department.'[19] He went on to point out the importance of all departments keeping the PID well informed and asked them to, 'err, if anything, on the generous side in marking papers for P.I.D. or otherwise furnishing it with information which may prove of use to it'.[20] By March, then, all the arrangements for establishing the new intelligence department were complete.

Ten former DIIB members finally moved to their new quarters at the Foreign Office on 27 March.[21] They were joined over the next two months by five more experts recruited from other government departments, and one from the diplomatic service. Only Seton-Watson refused to move from the DIIB to the Foreign Office, believing that the PID's director, Tyrrell, was too wedded to the old diplomacy. Instead he went to the Department of Propaganda in Enemy Countries (Crewe House), serving under Beaverbrook's journalistic rival, Lord Northcliffe. Seton-Watson's move was undoubtedly over-precipitous, for as events proved the supporters of the New Europe dominated the PID Tyrrell made no attempt to stifle his new staff, and they were in frequent and unfettered communication with Seton-Watson. His refusal not only deprived the PID of a leading expert on Eastern Europe, but also deprived himself of an unusual opportunity to influence policy.

The PID continued most of the functions of the old DIIB, providing a weekly telegram for the Dominion governments,

---

[19] FO 371/3476/52636.   [20] Ibid.
[21] FO 366/787/91660, Minute by Koppel, 27 May 1918. FO 366/787/45225 implies that the PID may have already moved by 12 March, but A. W. A. Leeper in his diary gives 26 Mar. as the date of the move.

another weekly telegram about internal conditions in Germany for the heads of neutral states, and a monthly report on foreign affairs for the Inter-Parliamentary Associations.[22] Its most important activity was the preparation of special reports on the political situation in a wide variety of states. These ranged from a memorandum on 'The Social Democratic Parties and Leaders in Germany' to 'Japanese Pan-Asiaticism and Siberia' as well as such issues as 'The Separatist Movement in Iceland' and 'Norwegian Bolshevism'. The following list gives some indication of the output of these memoranda by the PID staff from March 1918 until the end of the Paris Peace Conference.[23]

Argentina	1	Muslim	4
Austria	11	Norway	4
Belgium	4	Poland	2
Bulgaria	3	Romania	3
China	2	Russia	26
Denmark	7	Spain	9
Finland	3	Sweden	11
France	9	Switzerland	4
Germany	38	Turkey	4
Greece	1	United States	7
Italy	12	General	3
Japan	3	Miscellaneous	2
League of Nations	2	TOTAL	175

All these reports were circulated to the War Cabinet and the principal officers of state.[24] The detailed knowledge of the current political situation in these countries acquired by the members of the department, and indicated in the breadth and scope of these reports, was later reflected in the quality of their peace preparatory material. Harold Nicolson observed that from their location on the top floor, 'It was not long before their influence permeated to the executive departments on the floors below.'[25]

[22] FO 371/4382/PID619.
[23] Virtually no memoranda in this series were produced during the period Nov. 1918–Jan. 1919, when the attention of the department shifted to the production of reports for the British delegation to the peace conference.
[24] FO 371/4382/PID619
[25] Harold Nicolson, 'Allen Leeper', *The Nineteenth Century and After*, 118 (Oct. 1935), 478.

The Treasury viewed the Foreign Office's new department as being quite temporary. Indeed the Treasury was assured by the Foreign Office that there was no question of the PID being made a permanent department.[26] Such a decision would have to await the end of the war, and PID personnel were warned, at Treasury insistence, of the conditions for work in a temporary department.[27] Hardinge, however, undoubtedly had other ideas, and was well aware that just as he had skirmished with Beaverbrook to create the department, he would eventually have to engage in battle with the Treasury over the permanency of his wartime reforms. On 27 March 1918 in a private letter to Sir Esme Howard, the minister at Stockholm, Hardinge informed him of 'the new Dept. of Political Intelligence that I have just started in the FO & from which I expect great things. It is only in its infancy at present, & is under Tyrrell, but I intend to develop it rapidly not only for our benefit but for that also of our Missions abroad.'[28] During the first week of May Hardinge had a note circulated to the overseas missions, announcing the establishment of the new department, 'with the purpose of making it a permanent integral part of our organisation'.[29] He went on to explain that the work of the PID was to keep up to date on events in other countries and on current problems in foreign policy and that 'every effort will be made in the future to base these memoranda on the reports of our Missions abroad, as well as on a reading of the Foreign press and other sources of information'. Hardinge was careful to assure the diplomats that these memoranda were not intended to override their own reports, and that for this system to work effectively the co-operation of the overseas missions was required. Hardinge ended his note by pointing out that 'the establishment of the

[26] FO 366/787/91660, 'Establishment of the Political Intelligence Department in the FO', 23 May 1918.

[27] Ibid., Heath (Secretary at the Treasury) to Hardinge, 22 May 1918. A. W. A. Leeper clearly thought when first asked to transfer that the PID would be a permanent department. He wrote to his father in Australia on 4 Mar. 1918 that he planned to resign from the British Museum, 'as we are now going to the Foreign Office as a permanent Intelligence Department'. AWAL.

[28] Hardinge to Howard, Howard of Penrith Papers DHW 4/Personal/15.

[29] FO 371/4382/PID619, Minute, 5 May 1918.

new Department is meant to stimulate, not to discourage, reports from Missions, and that criticisms will be welcomed'.[30] Hardinge hoped to minimize at the outset any bureaucratic resistance to his innovations.

The Experts: Personnel of the PID

What made the PID such an unusual government office was its personnel. Arnold Toynbee, who served in the PID, recalled that 'I was fortunate, in the First World War, in finding my way into the Political Intelligence Department of the Foreign Office. I do not know whether the so-called "Ministry of All the Talents" had fully deserved its name, but in the PID a century later, there was a concentration of talent that was immensely stimulating.'[31] These experts filled an important gap in the Foreign Office's range of expertise, and one Member of Parliament noted, 'I think it is a remarkable circumstance that when the Foreign Secretary came to the task of strengthening his own Intelligence Department, he found his most useful assistance not in the ranks of the official professional Diplomatic Service, but almost altogether in outsider circles.'[32] The introduction of outsiders, however, inevitably created difficulty with older Foreign Office hands. E. H. Carr, who was a clerk in the Foreign Office at the time, later wrote, 'The Political Intelligence Department had never been wholeheartedly accepted by the traditional Foreign Office departments; it housed too many eccentric intellectuals.'[33] Potential friction was minimized by Hardinge's appointment of Sir William Tyrrell to head the department. Hardinge was well aware that a new and unconventional department, such as the PID, would inevitably arouse resentment from the more traditional departments of the Foreign Office. Tyrrell's role was to act as a father figure for the group and protect them from the more irascible elements in the Office.[34] Harold Nicolson later recalled that 'Sir William Tyrrell, with his genius for lubricating incongruous

[30] Ibid.   [31] Arnold J. Toynbee. *Acquaintances* (London, 1967), p. 161.

[32] Hansard 109, 31 July 1918, A. F. Whyte.

[33] E. H. Carr, *From Napoleon to Stalin and Other Essays* (London, 1980), p. 166.

[34] Interview with E. H. Carr, Cambridge, 20 May 1981.

machinery, was able to secure that no friction arose,' and it was Tyrrell whom Nicolson credits with the PID's acceptance by the traditional Office staff.[35]

It was not only from the career Foreign Office clerks that Tyrrell had to protect his staff, but from Britain's allies as well. The transfer of one of the DIIB experts, Lewis Namier, caused a minor controversy. Namier, who was born in Austrian Poland, had angered Roman Dmoski, president of the Polish National Committee, by articles he had written in Seton-Watson's the *New Europe*.[36] Namier in his articles had clearly explained where Polish demands were in conflict with the stated ideals of the Allies, and when Dmoski learned of Namier's appointment to the PID he came to London to denounce him as a German and Austrian agent, through the press as well as to Military Intelligence.

Tyrrell was determined to protect Namier, who at the time wrote an account of an April 1918 meeting between the Polish leader and Tyrrell in which he reported, 'I have it from an absolutely authoritative source that when Dmoski entered the room, Tyrrell stopped him near the door, saying he refused to discuss anything unless Dmoski first withdrew all his accusations.'[37] Dmoski nevertheless persisted in his attacks and after another article appeared attacking him on 12 July Namier went to Tyrrell with a copy. As he later recounted, 'Tyrrell was furious, and took the article straight away to Hardinge.'[38] Dmoski was finally brought to heel when the Foreign Office threatened to cut its subsidy to his committee.[39]

William Tyrrell was a twenty-nine year veteran of the Foreign Office. He was a Roman Catholic, born in India in 1886 of Anglo-Indian ancestry, where his father had been a high court judge. Tyrrell's sister had married Prince Radolin (later the German ambassador in Paris at the outbreak of the First World War) who arranged for Tyrrell to attend school in

---

[35] Nicolson, 'Allen Leeper', p. 479.

[36] Roman Dmoski (1864–1939); Polish statesman, Leader of National Democratic Party; member of 2nd and 3rd Russian Dumas; President Polish National Committee, 1917–18; Polish Delegate to the Paris Peace Conference, 1919.

[37] Julia Namier, *Lewis Namier: A Biography* (London, 1971), p. 129.

[38] Ibid. 128.   [39] Ibid., 126–9.

Germany prior to going up to Oxford. After completing his education at Balliol he entered the Foreign Office, becoming Grey's private secretary in 1907. In this position he played an influential role in the formulation of pre-war foreign policy. During Hardinge's first term as permanent under-secretary Tyrrell had been one of his protégés and supporters in the implementation of internal reforms.[40] In early 1915, however, he suffered a nervous breakdown after the death in action of his younger son.[41] Less taxing work was found for him at the Home Office, but by 1918 he had recovered sufficiently for Hardinge to bring him back to the Office as Director of the PID.

A colleague in the Foreign Office, Owen O'Malley, described Tyrrell as 'a little man as quick as a lizard with scintillating eyes and wit and a great aversion to any work not transacted orally'.[42] Lewis Namier later wrote of him,

complex, versatile, talkative, but exceedingly secretive, he was ami-able, and even yielding on the surface, but a stubborn fighter under-neath. He avoided, if he could, personal collisions, and professed a preference for 'long-range artillery': yet he disliked writing — active and restless, he shunned the drudgery of office drafts, and cultivated the laziness which Talleyrand enjoined on diplomats, was selective even in his reading of office files.[43]

Namier recalled one instance of Tyrrell's indolence over office written work: 'An administrative question concerning our de-partment was once submitted to Tyrrell in a long minute on the jacket of its file. Tyrrell, uninterested in the subject, initialled the minute unread. It was returned to him with the remark, "This matter requires your decision." Reply: "I agree, W. T." The decision was then obtained orally, and the jacket of the file was changed.'[44] But Hardinge approved of Tyrrell's overall perfor-mance, recommending him for promotion to assistant under-

---

[40] Steiner, *The Foreign Office and Foreign Policy, 1898–1914* (London, 1969), pp. 102, 118–20.

[41] Hardinge Papers 93, Chirol to Hardinge, 3 May, 24 May, 23 June 1915, and Hardinge to Chirol, 31 May 1915.

[42] Owen O'Malley, *The Phantom Caravan* (London, 1954), p. 45.

[43] L. B. Namier, *Avenues of History* (London, 1952), p. 86.

[44] Ibid., 87.

secretary in October 1918.[45] This also had the effect of enhancing the status of the PID, as all the permanent Foreign Office departments were headed by assistant under-secretaries.

Given Tyrrell's somewhat relaxed methods of administration much of the work fell to the assistant director, Headlam-Morley. James Headlam-Morley (1863–1929) was educated at Eton and King's College, Cambridge, where he received a double first in the classical tripos, going on to become a fellow of King's. While studying in Germany he married Else Sontag. 'From this marriage he derived a lifelong knowledge of German language and literature. His wife never learnt to speak fluent English, and remained an impenitent German nationalist — without, however, in this respect influencing her husband in the slightest degree.'[46] From 1894 to 1900 he was professor of Greek and Ancient History at Queen's College, London. In 1902 he became a staff inspector of secondary schools for the Board of Education, and at the beginning of the war he was attached to Wellington House (the propaganda department), becoming in 1917 assistant director of the DIIB. In 1918, upon inheriting the Morley estate, he assumed the additional surname of Morley. Before the outbreak of war Headlam-Morley had already achieved recognition as a historian. His fellowship dissertation *Election by Lot in Athens* won the Prince Consort's Prize in 1890. Ten years later he published *Bismarck and the German Empire* and in early 1914 he collaborated on *A Short History of Germany and her Colonies*. His best known work is *The History of the Twelve Days*, an examination of the events leading up to the war.

Headlam-Morley was well liked by his colleagues. E. H. Carr, who served with him in the Foreign Office, described him as 'the strongly marked product of a classical education and of the British civil service in its heyday before the First World War. He was considerate, enlightened, rational, and commonsensical, averse from every fanaticism, from any emotional indulgence.'[47] As Tyrrell left most of the day to day management of the department to him, it was Headlam-Morley

---

[45] FO 366/762/173991. Hardinge wrote to Balfour concerning Tyrrell's promotion on 10 Oct. 1918. Hardinge Papers 39. On the same day Hardinge sent Balfour his plans for the peace conference.

[46] Carr, *From Napoleon to Stalin*, p. 165.   [47] Ibid. 166.

who organized the writing of reports. He was also one of the few Foreign Office officials who got on with Philip Kerr, thus providing an extra channel to the prime minister for the views of the PID.[48] At Paris he served on committees dealing with Belgium and Denmark, Danzig, the Saar, Alsace-Lorraine, Germany's eastern frontier, and minorities.

The experts who were under the supervision of Tyrrell and Headlam-Morley were an unlikely lot to find in Whitehall. They did have the traditional educational background, public or grammar school followed by Cambridge or Oxford. Of the sixteen clerks employed in the PID (if one includes Headlam-Morley) nine had been to Oxford, with Tyrrell's old college, Balliol, accounting for five, while four had been to Cambridge, with one each from Edinburgh and London. Many of these men, however, had also been educated abroad. Two had taken first degrees in Australia, at least two had attended German universities, and one had attended the Universities of Lwów and Lausanne. What marked them out was their catholicity of background, highly unusual in the Foreign Office at this time. Three of the PID clerks had been born and raised abroad and had not come to Britain until they were in their twenties. Two had Jewish backgrounds, one had a German parent, three had German wives, and one was married to an American. It is not surprising that the permanent clerks at the Office found their new brethren unusual. An examination of the backgrounds and experience of the men Hardinge recruited into his new department reveals just what an unusual group inhabited the PID.

John Cann Bailey (1864–1931) was educated at Haileybury and New College, Oxford. In 1892 he was called to the Bar at the Inner Temple, but never practised. He was twice deputy-editor of the *Quarterly Review*, of which George Prothero was editor. Before 1918 Bailey had already established a reputation

---

[48] A good memoir of Headlam-Morley is in James Headlam-Morley, *A Memoir of the Paris Peace Conference, 1919*, ed. by Agnes Headlam-Morley, Russell Bryant, and Anna Cienciala (London, 1972). See also Toynbee, *Acquaintances*, pp. 161–8, and Carr, *From Napoleon to Stalin*, pp. 165–9. Another avenue to Kerr was provided by Simpson, who corresponded with him about Russian affairs during the negotiations. Lothian Papers GD 40/17/838–864.

for himself as a writer on English literature and poetry, and he served as chairman of the English Association from 1912 to 1915. At the DIIB he dealt with France, Spain, and Italy, though during the peace work he concentrated on France.

Edwyn Bevan (1870–1943), the son of a banker, had a brilliant academic career at New College, Oxford, where he received a double first in classical moderations and Literae Humaniores. Afterwards he travelled to India where he became interested in Indian problems, and then spent a year at the British School of Archaeology at Athens, together with some time in Egypt. A man of inherited wealth, he devoted the pre-war years to the study of the Hellenistic age, writing at this time *The House of Seleucus* (1902), *Jerusalem Under the High Priests* (1904), and *Stoics and Sceptics* (1913), as well as *Indian Nationalism* (1913). In 1914 he joined the Artists Rifles but was discharged so that he could join the DIIB. During this period he produced a stream of war-related books, *The Method in the Madness*, *The Land of the Two Rivers (Mesopotamia)*, *German War Aims*, and *German Social Democracy during the War*, as well as articles for, among others, the *New Statesman* and the *Westminster Gazette*.

Two brothers from Australia, Allen and Rex Leeper, were employed in the PID. After the war they both received regular appointments in the Foreign Office, the first of many Australians to enter the British Diplomatic Service during the inter-war years. Both were born in Melbourne where their father was warden of Trinity College in the University of Melbourne. They were educated at their father's college before being sent to Oxford, Allen to Balliol and Rex to New College.

Allen Leeper (1887–1935) was one of the young men deeply influenced by the New Europe group. Having taken a first in Latin and Greek at Melbourne, Allen went on to take another first in Greats at Oxford in 1911. From Balliol he went to the Egyptian and Assyrian Department of the British Museum. At the outbreak of war in 1914 he attempted to enlist, but was rejected as medically unfit. He finally found war work in the Propaganda Department (Wellington House), moving from there to the DIIB, and in 1918 to the Political Intelligence Department. An excellent linguist, 'He could read fifteen languages with ease and could converse with varying degrees of proficiency in seven or eight.'[49] Among the languages he knew were Greek, Latin, Hebrew, French, German, Italian, Spanish, Dutch, Flemish, Swedish, Danish, Norwegian, Russian, Czech, Serbo-Croat, Bulgarian, Romaic, and Romanian.

Leeper worked closely with Harold Nicolson in the South Eastern Europe section of the PID before and during the peace conference. Nicolson wrote of him,

Having been born in Australia he was able to approach our problems from an Antipodean rather than an insular point of view; having been educated at Balliol he had learnt that knowledge is of small value unless interpreted in terms of understanding, that intelligence is but a gaudy thing unless translated into terms of creative action: having never suffered from the routine of a large Government office his eyes shone undimmed by the dust of civil service files: being a citizen of the New World, he could approach the Old with the romantic zest of a scholar on his first trip to the Parthenon: being unimpeded by the trammels of an English public school education it never occurred to him that a passionate interest in the work before us might be regarded as bad form. He was a man of high ideals, the purest Wilsonism, some philological ambition, intermittent health, unfailing energy, and unashamed curiosity.[50]

Among Leeper's colleagues in the DIIB was R. W. Seton-Watson, the proprietor of the *New Europe*. Allen Leeper and Seton-Watson became good friends, with Seton-Watson frequently dropping by at Leeper's flat in the evening to discuss the East European situation. This was to be 'one of the closest friendships in Seton's life'.[51] Allen and Rex began to write for the *New Europe*, Allen under the pseudonym 'Belisarius', with Rex signing his articles on Russian affairs as 'Rurik'. Allen Leeper was active in the Anglo-Rumanian Society along with Seton-Watson and acted as its honorary secretary. At Paris Leeper played an important role in the drawing of Eastern Europe's new frontiers. Rex Leeper (1888–1968) followed his brother from Oxford to Wellington House, the DIIB, and finally the PID. Along with his regular duties he also acted as the unofficial link between the Foreign Office and the Bolshevik representative in London, Maksim Litvinov.[52]

[49] Nicolson, 'Allen Leeper', p. 477.   [50] Ibid.

[51] Seton-Watson and Seton-Watson, *The Making of a New Europe*, p. 201 n.

[52] He was given this task by Lord Robert Cecil on 10 Jan. 1918. A. W. A. Leeper Diary, 10 Jan. 1918.

Lewis Namier (1888–1960) was one of the most colourful members of the department. Raised in Eastern Galicia of a Polonized Jewish family, he had studied at the Universities of Lwów and Lausanne, and at the London School of Economics, before finding his way to Balliol College, Oxford, where in 1908 he took a first in modern history. At Balliol he came to know Arnold Toynbee, who recalled of Namier that 'if you once let him fix you with his eye, you might find yourself a prisoner without writ of Habeas Corpus'.[53] E. H. Carr described him as an 'angular personality, relentless and sometimes overbearing in argument. Gifted by nature with acute powers of perception, he nevertheless became, when mounted upon his hobbyhorse of the moment, impervious to the reactions of the listener.'[54] He was fluent in Polish, German, and English, and his detailed knowledge of Eastern Europe was invaluable to the PID.

In 1913 he travelled to the United States, returning in 1914 to enlist in the Royal Fusiliers. He was discharged in 1915 to join Wellington House, from which he went on to the DIIB, where his main work was compiling and editing summaries of the Austrian press.[55] While working for the DIIB Namier began studying Russian with a teacher, Clara Edeleff-Poniatowska, recommended by the Leeper brothers, who were also studying the language. In 1917 they married, with Allen Leeper and Edwyn Bevan as the witnesses, but the partnership proved most unhappy.[56] In the PID he wrote on Polish affairs and on matters relating to Austria-Hungary, thereby filling in part the gap left by the failure to obtain the services of Seton-Watson. His publications included *Germany and Eastern Europe* (1917), and articles in the *Quarterly Review*, the *New Europe*, *The Times*, the *Nation*, the *Daily Chronicle*, and the *Westminster Gazette*. Namier was originally a strong Polonophile, but he subsequently became disenchanted with the new Polish state and became an ardent Zionist.[57]

[53] Toynbee, *Acquaintances*, p. 63.   [54] Carr, *From Napoleon to Stalin*, p. 191.
[55] Seton-Watson and Seton-Watson, *The Making of a New Europe*, p. 167 n.
[56] J. Namier, *Lewis Namier*, p. 132.
[57] An excellent biography of Namier was done by his second wife, Julia Namier. See also chapters on Namier in Toynbee, *Acquaintances*, pp. 62–85 and Carr, *From Napoleon to Stalin*, pp. 184–91. See also Tarras Hunczak, 'Sir Lewis Namier and the Struggle for Eastern Galicia, 1918–1920', *Harvard Ukrainian Studies*, 1:2 (1977), 198–210.

One of Namier's strongest critics in the Foreign Office was J. D. Gregory, head of the Russia department, who believed Namier to have been foisted on the Office by Philip Kerr and Lord Eustace Percy. Gregory wrote at the time that 'Mr. Namier and I have been unspeakable enemies, but I must frankly say now that I think I have been wrong in taking up a position antagonistic to him'.[58] Gregory admitted that part of the difficulty had been his inability to work harmoniously with Namier, and certainly Namier was a person who often provoked strong reactions on the part of his colleagues. Gregory observed, however, that Namier, 'knows more about Poland than anyone else in this country'.[59] Nevertheless he was unhappy with what he felt to be Namier's anti-Polish bias. In response to this Hardinge wrote a stout defence of Namier, and Curzon commented that 'It would be a great shame in any way to disown him'.[60]

Lord Eustace Percy (1887–1958) was the seventh son of the seventh duke of Northumberland. Educated at Eton and Christ Church, Oxford, he had a brilliant academic record, receiving the Stanhope Historical Prize in 1907. After a period of study on the Continent he was appointed third secretary in the diplomatic service and posted to Washington, where he served 1910–14 and 1917–18. Upon his return to London in April 1918 he was attached to the PID to deal with questions concerning the League of Nations.[61]

George Saunders (1859–1922) was a successful and noted journalist prior to the First World War. He was educated at Balliol College, Oxford, where he won prizes in moral philosophy and English literature, and he also attended the Universities of Glasgow, Bonn, and Göttingen. At Glasgow he studied law, receiving a LLD, but his attempts to establish a legal practice proved unsuccessful. In 1885 he moved to Germany where he eventually became the *Morning Post*'s Berlin correspondent, 1888–97, subsequently moving to *The Times*, 1897–1908. In 1893 he married the daughter of a Berlin banker. From 1908 to 1914 he was *The Times* correspondent in Paris. Saunders's highly articulate reports on the German army and

[58] FO 800/149, Minute by Gregory, 6 Dec. 1918.   [59] Ibid.   [60] Ibid.
[61] For an account of Percy's career see his autobiography, Eustace Percy, *Some Memories* (London, 1958).

German military manœuvres were widely read and commented upon in Great Britain and his writings display a clear antipathy towards German militarism. When he was recruited for the Propaganda Department he was considered important enough to be offered a salary of £800, double that of any other member.[62]

James Simpson (1873–1934) was one of the PID's two Russian experts, along with Rex Leeper. He was professor of natural science at the University of Edinburgh, where he had earned his D.Sc. in 1899, and was married to an American. Simpson had travelled extensively in European and Asiatic Russia before and during the war, and E. H. Carr later recalled him as a valuable member of the department, really knowing the northern countries — the Baltic Provinces and Finland. He had heard of peoples of whom nobody else in the department had a knowledge.[63] Before the war Simpson published three works, *Sidelights on Siberia* (1898), *Life of Henry Drummond* (1901), and *The Spiritual Interpretation of Nature* (1912). He joined the DIIB during the war and produced two further books on Russia, *The Self-Discovery of Russia* (1916) and the no doubt stimulating *The State-Sale Monopoly and Prohibition of Vodka in Russia* (1918). He also contributed to *The Times* and the *Daily Chronicle*.

Arnold Toynbee (1889–1975) was educated at Winchester and Balliol College, Oxford. At Oxford he came to know Alfred Zimmern, who was a lecturer, and Lewis Namier, who was then a student. Toynbee went on to become a fellow at Balliol, where he began his notable academic career. At the outbreak of the war he joined Wellington House and then the DIIB, before going to the PID. His published output during the war was immense, thirteen books as well as articles in *The Times*, the *Round Table*, the *New Europe*, and the *Daily Chronicle*. Among his war-related books were such propagandistic pot-boilers as *Microbe Culture in Bucarest*, *The Death of Edith Cavell*, *The Murderous Tyranny of the Turks*, and *The Destruction of Poland*. Of the members of the PID Toynbee undoubtedly produced the most

---

[62] For an interesting comment on Saunders's role in Germany see 'Hazard Zet Forward', an unfinished autobiographical fragment by R. W. Seton-Watson in Seton-Watson and Seton-Watson, *The Making of a New Europe*.

[63] Based on an interview with E. H. Carr at Cambridge, 20 May 1981.

memoranda, consistently of the highest quality. Toynbee later recalled of the writing of these reports,

Six weeks before the Armistice of 11 November 1918 I had received the following instructions: 'Tell the Registry to send up to you all the papers dealing with the commitments that His Majesty's Government have made during the war regarding the Near and Middle East; report what these commitments are: and write an opinion on whether they are compatible with each other.' Mountains of files appeared on my desk, and I have never again had to work so desperately hard against time; for, though we could not predict the date of the coming armistice, we did know that hostilities were now nearing their end.[64]

Despite such pressures Toynbee succeeded in producing a remarkable collection of reports.

Alfred Zimmern (1879–1957) came from a well-to-do German Jewish family which had emigrated to England after the 1848 revolution. Educated at Winchester and New College, Oxford, where he took a double first in honour moderations and Literae Humaniores, he became a fellow of his old college and lecturer in ancient history, 1904–9. It was during this period that he produced his greatest work, *The Greek Commonwealth* (1911). In 1912 he joined the Board of Education as an inspector. In 1915 he moved to the Committee (later Ministry) of Reconstruction, where he remained until his former Education Board colleague, Headlam-Morley, brought him over to the PID. During the war Zimmern produced two books, *The War and Democracy* (1914) and *Nationality and Government* (1918). In addition he wrote articles in several journals including the *Round Table*, the *Manchester Guardian*, *The Times*, and the *New Statesman*. Zimmern had a sharp analytical mind, and as Toynbee later recalled of his former Oxford lecturer, 'Alfred could, and did, draw subtle distinctions, for he was sensitive and perceptive to an unusual degree. He was endowed with some special psychic organ that served him like a seismometer or like a butterfly's antennae. This organ of his could register the slightest tremors in the structure of society and could foresee things that were to come when they were still far off in the future.'[65]

[64] Toynbee, *Acquaintances*, p. 203.
[65] For an account of Zimmern's life see ibid. 49–61.

The remaining five clerks who served in the PID during this period had backgrounds similar to those of their colleagues. E. H. W. Fullerton-Carnegie (1870–1955) was the department's Scandinavian expert. He was a close friend of Headlam-Morley, and like him was married to a German (though from Uruguay). His older brother, John, had been a captain in the Prussian Army and was married to the daughter of Field Marshal Baron Goltz. A. W. G. Randall (1892–1977) was the sole London graduate among the staff. He was described by a contemporary as 'a man of singular literary attainments and ability'.[66] A convert to Roman Catholicism, he prepared the peace memorandum on the status of the Vatican enclave, as well as the memorandum on Switzerland. Percy Koppel (1876–1932) had been educated at Magdalen College, Oxford. A barrister, he was employed before the war by the National Health Insurance Commission. Like many of his colleagues he started at Wellington House, moving then to the DIIB, and finally to the PID. R. F. Roxburgh (1889–1981) was educated at Trinity College, Cambridge, where he won the Whewell International Law Scholarship, before being called to the Bar in 1914. J. C. Powell (1860–1943) a graduate of King's College Cambridge, was a schoolmaster when the war began. He served in the DIIB before moving to the PID.

Two members of the diplomatic service were lent to the PID in November to aid in the peace work. Harold Nicolson (1886–1967) had been educated at Balliol before entering the diplomatic service. His father, Arthur Nicolson (Lord Carnock) had been permanent under-secretary, 1910–16. Nicolson's memoranda on South East Europe are among the most lucid produced by the PID. The other diplomat on loan to the PID was Robert Vansittart (1881–1957). He had served in Tehran and Cairo and had a knowledge of both Persian and Arabic. During the war he was joint head of the Contraband Department and subsequently head of the Prisoners of War Department. Both Nicolson and Vansittart went over to Paris in January 1919 as part of the British delegation.

The question of salaries for the new personnel led to a long correspondence between the Foreign Office and the Treasury. When the DIIB personnel were invited to join the PID they

[66] J. D. Gregory, *On the Edge of Diplomacy* (London, 1928), p. 106.

were guaranteed the same rate of pay as they were already receiving. In February Headlam-Morley had written to the Foreign Office proposing rises for certain members of the DIIB. Lewis Namier's salary of £260 per annum was described by Headlam-Morley as 'almost a starvation wage'. Powell refused to come over unless his salary of £260 was raised to £400. Headlam-Morley also had to lobby for Saunders to retain his £800 salary, which had been offered to him when he was first appointed. Headlam-Morley simply argued that 'His services are quite indispensable'.[67] In the end Hardinge cajoled the Treasury into raising the minimum to £400 per annum. Table 2 shows the changes in salary involved.[68]

TABLE 2. *Salaries of Members of the PID*[a]

Name	Before joining PID	After joining PID	Previous Department
Bailey	200	200	DIIB
Bevan	300	400	DIIB
Fullerton-Carnegie	—	500	
Koppel	—	500	Dept. of Info. News Dept.
A. Leeper[b]	339	400	DIIB
R. Leeper	327	400	DIIB
Namier	260	400	DIIB
Powell	260	400	DIIB
Randall[c]	260	350	DIIB
Roxburgh	260	350	Dept. of Information
Saunders	800	800	DIIB
Simpson	260	400	DIIB
Toynbee	400	400	DIIB
Zimmern[d]	250	400	Reconstruction Ministry

[a] FO 366/787/4472.

[b] The British Museum was to continue to pay Leeper his salary of £230 as an assistant and the Foreign Office was to pay the difference.

c T/12/39/2580(18), Health (Treas.) to Min. of Information, 19 Apr. 1918. This note seems to have been sent to the Min. of Information and redirected to the Foreign Office. The same applied in the case of Roxburgh.

[d] FO 366/787/91660, Minute by Headlam-Morley, 2 July 1918, and minute from Tilley, 5 June 1918. Also Tilley to Zimmern, 12 Aug. 1918, informing him of his appointment as a temporary clerk at £400 p.a. with effect from 1 May 1918. Zimmern Papers 15.

[67] FO 366/787/44472, Headlam-Morley to Foreign Office, 25 Feb. 1918.

[68] Headlam-Morley himself served without a salary. Interview with Prof. Agnes Headlam-Morley, Wimbledon, 26 Feb. 1982.

Salaries also had to be negotiated for the four members who subsequently joined the PID. In April the Treasury sanctio ied a salary of £500 for Koppel, as well as for Fullerton-Carnegie.[69] The Treasury again balked at paying what they considered an inflated salary, this time the £400 salary of Alfred Zimmern, but were told bluntly that this was the agreed base salary and that he could not be paid less because of his age and standing. It was agreed, however, that Roxburgh should continue at a salary of £350, as he was younger and less experienced than the other members of the department. Tilley, the chief clerk of the Foreign Office, in a minute to Tyrrell about Roxburgh's salary, noted that he was unfit for military service and that the Treasury would want justification for the jump in Zimmern's salary.[70] Zimmern thereby got his rise, while Roxburgh was used to appease the Treasury. It can be seen from these instances that Hardinge was willing to push for salaries attractive enough to bring the best experts available into the fledgeling department.

Hardinge's wartime reforms of the Office's internal structure entailed improvements in the existing support facilities. As early as January 1918 Hardinge was planning improvements in the Library along with the newly appointed librarian, Alwyn Parker.[71] The Library was essential to the work of both the PID and the Historical Section. Hardinge obtained a starting salary of £900 per annum for Parker, £100 above the normal rate. The reason given to the Treasury for this was the heavy load which would be borne by the Library in peace preparatory work. Parker was also the first librarian to be appointed from the diplomatic service.[72]

A Standing Library Committee on the Purchase of Books

[69] T 12/39/11825(18), Bradbury (Treas.) to Hardinge, 13 Apr. 1918.

[70] FO 366/787/91660, Tilley to Tyrrell, 6 June 1918. Tilley's comment on Roxburgh being unfit for military service was quite pointed, as Tyrrell had lost his second (and only remaining) son to the war only a month previously.

[71] FO 366/787/f17/1364. Alwyn Parker (1877–1951) joined the Diplomatic Service in 1900, served at FO, 1906–20; Asst. Clerk, 1906; Head of Contraband Dept., 1914–17; Librarian, 1918–20; Private Secretary to Hardinge at Paris, 1919.

[72] FO 366/787/f17/1364, Hardinge to Treasury, Jan. 1918. Possibly written on Hardinge's behalf by Crowe, and a personal note from Hardinge to Heath (Treas.), 26 Apr. 1918.

was established to assist in the upgrading of the Office Library's holdings. It met on a monthly basis and comprised Tilley as chairman, with Prothero, Tyrrell, Headlam-Morley, Henry Penson, Parker, and Cecil Hurst, the legal adviser. It was obviously not coincidental that it was these individuals who headed the departments most deeply involved in work for the peace conference.[73] The PID also maintained its own specialized library.[74] In addition it aided in the creation of a Foreign Office Economic Library, which Penson saw as fulfilling the twofold purpose of acting as a guide to economic theory, commerce, industry, banking, and business as well as supplying the needs of the PID.[75]

Working for Peace: The PID Peace Memoranda

As the end of the war loomed Hardinge launched his offensive to move the Foreign Office back into the centre of diplomatic activity. In a carefully detailed memorandum submitted to Balfour on 10 October 1918 Hardinge proposed a format for the coming peace conference. His plan was based on the common assumption that an inter-allied co-ordinating conference would precede the final peace congress. Hardinge suggested that the work of the conference be assigned to five Grand Committees, of which one, the Political and Territorial Adjustment Committee, would be divided into six regional sub committees. The plan was for each inter-allied Grand Committee to have a matching internal delegation committee to advise the British delegate. This territorial division closely parallels the rearrangement effected on 15 November in the organization of the PID, which was now divided into nine subsections, each under the supervision of one of the British delegates-designate to the peace conference.[76] These heads of section held their first meeting on 19 November.[77]

The Western European Section was assigned to Sir Eyre

[73] Confidential Print 10968, 'Foreign Office Library', 26 Apr. 1918.
[74] FO 371/4366/PID298 & 312 (also in Confidential Print 11004). 'Arrangements for Purchase of Books for PID'. See also FO 371/4366/PID343 and FO 371/4382/PID619.
[75] FO 371/4366/PID398, 'Suggestions for a Foreign Office Economic Library'.
[76] FO 371/4352/f18/PC20, 'Preparation for the Peace Conference'.
[77] Howard of Penrith Diary, 19 Nov. 1918.

Crowe (1864–1925), a twenty-eight year veteran of the Foreign Office, fluent in French and German. Crowe possessed strong personal links with Germany: his mother was German, he was educated at the gymnasia in Düsseldorf and Berlin, and while visiting his German relatives had met and married a cousin. These connections had made Crowe a target for the wave of anti-German hysteria which swept Britain during the war, ironically, as his warnings on German aims before the war had been among the most prescient and insistent. During Hardinge's first tenure as permanent under-secretary Crowe had worked closely with him on reforming the Office. Despite this Hardinge had mixed feelings towards his brilliant protégé, writing in 1913, 'Much as I admire Crowe's ability, I shall be sorry if he becomes head of the Foreign Office. It will lower the prestige of the office as he is so palpably German. . . . Further, I mistrust the soundness of his judgements.'[78] Nevertheless it was Crowe who succeeded Hardinge in 1920 and who had to pilot the Foreign Office into the post-war era. Crowe emerges as a key figure in this period, despite by his own admission having, 'always been made to feel that I had come in as an outsider'.[79] He rose to the top of the Foreign Office's greasy pole by sheer ability, and as the negotiations at Paris show, it was Crowe who was the colossus, or rather the Atlas, of the British delegation. It was his involvement with the PID and the peace conference which lifted him from the doldrums to which wartime passions had relegated him.

The Western Europe Section was subdivided as follows: France (Bailey), Belgium and Luxemburg (Powell),[80] Germany (Headlam-Morley and Saunders), Switzerland (Randall), and Spain and Portugal (Bailey and Koppel). No substantive reports were produced dealing with Spain and Portugal. An expert was supposed to be assigned to deal with Dutch affairs, but this was not done, though E. H. Carr did provide a report on the only Dutch question to arise, the Scheldt.[81]

[78] Hardinge to A. Nicolson, 18 June 1913. Hardinge Papers 93.

[79] FO 800/243, Typescript report of conversation with Lord Curzon, 15 Oct. 1919.

[80] Powell fell ill during this period and Akers-Douglas prepared the Belgium memorandum.

[81] FO 371/4355/f77/PC77.

The Northern Europe Section came under the direction of Sir Esme Howard (1863–1939), an old ally of Hardinge's who brought him back at short notice from the Stockholm embassy to participate in the conference's work.[82] Howard, a Harrovian, was a sprig of the aristocratic clan headed by the Duke of Norfolk. In 1893, upon his marriage, he was received into the Roman Catholic church, which brought him into conformity with much of his extended family. Howard, who had spent the war years in Stockholm, where he was deeply involved in Russian affairs as well, noted in his diary upon his appointment to head the section that 'While I know something about Russia, I am quite ignorant of the Ukraine and Caucasus'. [83] His section consisted of four sub-divisions, Scandinavia (Fullerton-Carnegie), Baltic Provinces and Finland (Simpson), Russia (R. Leeper), and Poland (Namier). Howard implemented a system whereby he drafted the final memoranda based on the reports submitted to him by his staff, and as a result he had a far greater impact on the contents than many of his fellow section chiefs.

The South-Eastern Europe Section was placed under Sir Ralph Paget (1864–1940), who had just returned from two years as minister at Copenhagen. He had entered the diplomatic service in 1888 and had served in Vienna, Cairo, Zanzibar, Washington, Tokyo, Munich, Constantinople, Guatemala, and Bangkok. From 1910 to 1913 he was minister in Belgrade, returning to London as an assistant under-secretary, 1913–16. His section was subdivided into three, Italy (Powell), Former Territories of the Austro-Hungarian Monarchy (Namier), and the Balkans (A. Leeper and Nicolson).

The Middle East Section was headed by Sir Louis Mallet (1864–1936), who had first become involved in peace planning as chairman of one of the original committees of inquiry into territorial changes. He had entered the diplomatic service in 1888, the same year as Paget, had served in Brazil, Rome, and Cairo, and was Grey's private secretary, 1905–7, becoming an assistant under-secretary in 1907 and being placed in charge of the Eastern Department, a post he held until his appointment

---

[82] Howard received his summons on 8 Nov. and arrived at the Foreign Office on 13 Nov. Howard of Penrith Diary. On his career see B. J. C. McKercher, *Esme Howard: A Diplomatic Biography* (Cambridge, 1989).

[83] Howard of Penrith Diary, 13 Nov. 1918.

as the last British ambassador to the Ottoman Empire, 1913–14. Mallet was one of Hardinge's favourite protégés, who hoped that Mallet would be his successor in preference to Crowe.[84] Toynbee, who was initially the only expert assigned to the Middle East Section, requested an assistant due to the breadth and complexity of the problems involved. His assignment included Turkey, the Arabian peninsula, and in part Tripoli, Egypt, Abyssinia, the Caucasus, Persia, and Central Asia.[85] He noted that 'Personally, I am weakest in Egypt, Egypt–Tripoli frontier, and Persia. I could undertake Abyssinia, Caucasus, Central Asia.'[86] Tyrrell in response to this request arranged for Robert Vansittart, who had once served in Egypt, to assist Toynbee.

Headlam-Morley and Tyrrell agreed that the Caucasus should be handled by the Northern Europe section, though Headlam-Morley was careful to note that 'it would have to be understood that this does not imply Russian dominion should be established over what was formerly part of the Russian Empire'. [87] The India Office was to be contacted over issues involving Central Asia and Persia. It was decided that Morocco was to be treated as a European question as the problems concerning it were not really African or Muslim. Toynbee warned of the need for close co-operation between the Middle East and South-East Europe sections on 'questions affecting Italy since it is important that Italian claims in Tripoli, Albania, Dodekanese, Anatolia and Abyssinia, should be considered as a whole, in order to decide in which direction concessions to these claims can be made with least disadvantage'. [88] The sections involved seem to have co-operated easily on all the issues of common interest.

The African Section was placed under the supervision of Gerald Spicer (1874–1944), who had entered the diplomatic service in 1898, but who had served in the Foreign Office establishment since 1906. In 1912 he was promoted to senior clerk. Lord Eustace Percy and Edwyn Bevan were assigned to

[84] Steiner, *The Foreign Office and Foreign Policy*, pp. 74–5.
[85] FO 371/4352/f18/PC18, Toynbee to Headlam-Morley, 15 Nov. 1918.
[86] Ibid.
[87] FO 371/4352/f18/PC18, Headlam-Morley to Tyrrell, 15 Nov. 1918.
[88] FO 371/4352/f18/PC18.

him, the latter presumably because of the importance of France and the Iberian states in any colonial settlement.

The Far East Section and the Colonial Questions Section were directed by Ronald Macleay (1870–1943). Educated at Charterhouse and Balliol College, Oxford, before joining the diplomatic service he had served in various foreign capitals, becoming counsellor at the embassy at Peking in 1914. No staff were allotted to him. The League of Nations Section and the Economic and Labour Problems Section did not initially have a head appointed to them, though in December Lord Robert Cecil took over the League of Nations Section. Both were staffed by Lord Eustace Percy and Alfred Zimmern.

Introductory memoranda were planned on each country likely to be considered at the conference, to be followed by memoranda on more specific topics. These introductory reports were divided into seven subsections: (1) territorial, dealing with any boundary delimitations; (2) 'External relations including such points as the possibility of establishing a Federation or some laxer union of states'; (3) internal questions which might have an international impact, such as the Jews of Poland or the Germans of Bohemia; (4) special commercial questions (more general commercial matters would be dealt with by the Board of Trade); (5) international channels of communication, and the possible establishment of free ports, with Danzig being used as a possible example; (6) colonial questions regarding the economic and political relationship with the imperial metropole, with colonies otherwise being dealt with in separate memoranda by the appropriate geographical section; (7) military matters were to be dealt with by the War Office and the Admiralty, but where there was a definite Foreign Office view, it was to be put forward. The writers were clearly warned that 'These memoranda should be as brief as possible, separate points should be clearly indicated and suggestions as to the best possible solution included'.[89] There was no need to overload the reader with historical details, as the Historical Section would be providing detailed background handbooks. Legal points were to be referred to Cecil Hurst, the legal adviser of the Foreign Office. Sections

[89] FO 371/4352/f18/PC20.

working on overlapping topics were cautioned that close co-operation would be expected. Roxburgh and subsequently Koppel were made responsible for the registration, circulation, and eventually the printing of the draft reports. Each draft was sent to Headlam-Morley and through him to Tyrrell for their observations, and then after any revision it was sent to the head of the writer's section for final approval before printing. Roxburgh also acted as liaison with other departments.[90]

On 15 November Headlam-Morley requested Tyrrell to clarify PID procedure, partly as a result of Lloyd George's appointment of General Smuts to prepare the British delegation's official position. Headlam-Morley assumed that 'the work of this Department in collecting material for the Peace Conference does not include matters connected with the indemnities and reparation. Presumably the full case in respect to this is being prepared by the other Departments.'[91] He recommended, however, that all papers dealing with these matters be sent to the PID so that they could be embodied in a general statement. He recommended that any critical differences of opinion be referred to Smuts. Headlam-Morley clearly perceived the role of his department as that of a central clearing house, which would provide the final reports for the peace delegation.

The output of reports prior to the opening of the Paris Peace Conference in January 1919 was substantial. By the beginning of January each member of the British negotiating team was to have before him a brief memorandum on every important country or topic. The following list gives some indication of the topical distribution of reports.

Western Europe	
France	3
Belgium and Luxemburg	4
Germany	3
Switzerland	6
Northern Europe	
Scandinavia	3
Baltic Provinces and Finland	2

90 FO 371/4352/f18/PC20.
91 FO 371/4352/f15/PC15, Headlam-Morley to Tyrrell, 15 Nov. 1918.

Russia	5
Poland	3
South Eastern Europe	
Italy	1
Former Austro-Hungarian Territories	4
Balkans	4
Other	
Middle East	18
Colonies	1
Africa	3
Far East	2
League of Nations	3
Economic and Labour	3
General	3
TOTAL	71

These reports were usually under twenty pages in length and were circulated to General Smuts and the War Cabinet. Crowe was awake to the danger of producing too much paper for circulation to the politicians, an ailment which afflicted the Inquiry, and he noted on one report, 'Circulation had better be limited to our own office. If we flood the outside authorities with too many papers which it is not essential they should read, we run the risk that they will read none at all.'[92] These reports were the closest Britain came to drafting instructions for its diplomats, and they at least provided the basis for a unified approach in the negotiations. As Crowe indicated, it was the diplomats and not the politicians who had the most immediate need of the peace brief, though copies were usually sent to the principal officers of state and the Dominion representatives.[93]

As 1919 dawned the PID completed its work, and several members went over to Paris to assist with the peace conference which was assembling during early January. Tilley, the chief clerk at the Foreign Office, became acting head of the PID in London and the writing of regular reports on current events was resumed by the London-based staff.[94] In Paris Tyrrell was made assistant to Hardinge, who became the superintending

---

[92] FO 371/4368/f480/PID549, Minute by Crowe, 18 Nov. 1918.
[93] FO 371/4356/f177/PC177 discusses the need for guidance.
[94] FO 371.4374/PID15.

ambassador of the British delegation. This was the zenith of the PID's influence on British policy, for as the conference wound down so too did the PID.

The End of the PID

Although the creation of the PID was viewed with suspicion by some of the more traditional elements of the Foreign Office, it slowly earned their respect, and by mid-1919 most of the senior officials were convinced of the need for such a department. Koppel informed Headlam-Morley that 'I gather that not only Hardinge, but Tyrrell, Montgomery, & practically everyone in the office is persuaded as to the utility of the PID & that they all intend to use their influence in order to make it permanent.'[95] The PID was central to all that Hardinge had been attempting to achieve in his reforms of the Foreign Office. Lord Eustace Percy in support of this vision argued that

It is vital that the Foreign Office should be made, and recognised as, a central repository of information and knowledge, detailed, comprehensive and exact. Only when this is recognised, only when this recognition is embodied in a branch of the Foreign Office definitely charged with the task of collection, comparison, digestion, record and, we may perhaps add, dissemination, will members of the Foreign Office be stimulated to real activity or will think it worth while to make themselves closely acquainted with every phase and factor in the life of foreign nations.[96]

The PID was clearly the key to breathing new life into the centenarian Foreign Office, rejuvenating it to participate in the brave new world, not only of the new diplomacy, but of the new Europe.

The department had succeeded in establishing its place by the unflagging industry of its excellent staff during the last year of war and the months of the peace conference. The uncertainties which surrounded its future were, however, destroying its effectiveness. According to the Treasury it was still no more than a temporary wartime creation. Eric Forbes-Adam in writing to Toynbee on the future of the PID observed that 'The FO

[95] Koppel to Headlam-Morley, 24 Mar. 1919. Headlam-Morley Papers.
[96] Eustace Percy, 'Foreign Office Reform', New Europe, 11:137 (29 May 1919).

can't do without some kind of liaison intelligence officers. . . .
There are many of us who will insist on it.'[97] Lord Eustace Percy
attempted to bring public pressure to bear on this problem in
an article in the *New Europe* on 8 May 1919 in which he observed
that the PID was 'the most important step recently taken by the
Foreign Office towards the creation of a new foreign policy, but
it is common knowledge amongst all who are interested in
foreign policy that the Intelligence Department is, at the
present moment, in considerable danger of falling to pieces'.[98]
Percy's article had some effect as on 21 May, in a debate on the
Foreign Office in the House of Commons, Lt.-Col. Murray
observed that 'I hope the Political Intelligence Department of
the Foreign Office will not be allowed to disintegrate. I have
some experience of the great value to the country of the Political Intelligence Department during the war. It was created
during the war and did great work . . . .'[99] Clearly as its product
became known the PID's stock had begun to rise.

The ultimate failure to maintain the PID as a unit of the
Foreign Office was due to external factors. From about March
1919 onwards the Treasury, in a frantic effort to reduce the
budget to peacetime levels, began to move for the closure of
temporary wartime creations. Headlam-Morley later observed
that 'Apparently the Treasury wanted the PID to be broken
up and dispersed among the other departments of the Foreign
Office'.[100] The final blow came in July 1920 when Hardinge, at
last wearied of the bureaucratic battles of Whitehall, accepted
the offer of the Paris embassy. With Hardinge's passing his two
major wartime innovations at the Foreign Office, the Political
Intelligence Department and the Historical Section, bereft of
their benefactor, could not long hope to survive in the face of
the stringent economies being imposed, as well as the continuing opposition of some of the older members of the Office.
Although Headlam-Morley presented a plea for the continuance of the department, its dismantling was ordered.[101] As

[97] Forbes-Adam to Toynbee, 24 May 1919. Toynbee Papers.
[98] Percy, 'Foreign Office Reform', *New Europe*, 11:134 (8 May 1919).
[99] Hansard 116, 21 May 1919, p. 515.
[100] Headlam-Morley to A. W. A. Leeper, 12 Mar. 1919. Headlam-Morley
Papers.
[101] FO 371/4382/PID619.

the end became evident most of the wartime staff of experts left. The last months of the PID were no more than a shadow existence. Some of the PID's experts received appointments as members of the Foreign and Diplomatic Service, such as the Leepers, Koppel, Randall, and Roxburgh. Saunders was considered too senior to receive such an appointment, and with regret the Foreign Office had to let him go.[102]

Hardinge's innovative department did have a notable impact on the future of the Foreign Office. Not only did some of the PID experts become career diplomats, but Hardinge was succeeded as permanent under-secretary first by Crowe, then by Tyrrell, and eventually by Vansittart. In the PID, and its various links, Hardinge provided a fertile training ground for the most talented diplomatists who would guide the Foreign Office and foreign policy through the following decades. The failure to retain the most outstanding of its experts during a period of bureaucratic indecision as to the future of the department was fatal to the PID's survival. It also deprived Britain in the inter-war years of the services of a group whose sole purpose was to collate and analyse information from the world's trouble spots. Whereas regular diplomats would rotate through appointments, the political intelligence experts would remain in their posts, providing the benefits of continuity in an otherwise migratory service. A retrospective acknowledgement of the importance of this department was provided when the PID was re-established in 1939, one of the first actions taken upon the declaration of war. The value of the original PID staff is shown by the recruitment of the surviving alumni of Hardinge's PID into this Second World War successor.[103]

Hardinge clearly foresaw the PID as fulfilling more than a fleeting role. It would be one of the innovations which would help the Foreign Office to reassert its traditional role in foreign policy formulation. The first major opportunity to do this would be at the post-war peace conference, and Hardinge began plotting his strategy for it nineteen months before the

[102] Saunders Papers, Box 3, GS/2/70. Simpson would also have liked to stay on, Simpson to Howard, 13 Sept. 1920. Howard of Penrith Papers DHW/Personal/4.

[103] Clifton Child, 'Introduction', in Great Britain, Foreign Office, *Weekly Political Intelligence Summaries*, vol. i (Millwood, NY, 1983), pp. v–xxii.

war ended.[104] The PID was left to develop its own methods and to prove its ability during the spring and summer prior to the Armistice. Hardinge's plans were disrupted when General Smuts was appointed to prepare the government's negotiating position, but the PID with its unusually talented staff of experts played the role Hardinge had envisaged, by filtering the Foreign Office's view through General Smuts, and indirectly through the prime minister's staff, to the negotiating table.

[104] Confidential Print 11022.

3

The Struggle for Control

> The critical period was not what happened in Paris during
> 1919, but what was done, and what was left undone, in
> 1918.
>
> J. W. Headlam-Morley, Confidential Print 13680

Administrative Arrangements: Hardinge and Hankey

On 6 October 1918 President Wilson received a note from the
German chancellor, Prince Max von Baden, requesting an
armistice. Four days later Hardinge began his offensive to
move the Foreign Office back into the centre of diplomatic activity. In a carefully articulated memorandum submitted to Balfour he reviewed the administrative arrangements made by
the Foreign Office over the last eighteen months.[1] Hardinge's
report revealed the thoroughness of the Foreign Office's preparations, with such innovations as the overhauled library to
deal with demands for information, the writing of 180 handbooks by the Historical Section, and the compilation of a War
Aims Index on the probable claims of the Allied, enemy, and
neutral states. What it avoids is direct mention of the work of
the PID. This was perhaps still potentially too explosive, given
the prime minister's jealous accumulation of control over
foreign policy. Hardinge was attempting initially to get the
Foreign Office's foot in the door by offering only seemingly
innocuous technical services.

---

[1] Confidential Print 11022, 'Peace Negotiations', 10 Oct. 1918. Also in Lloyd
George Papers F/3/3/35. This memorandum is very similar to Hardinge's Oct.
1917 memorandum (see Chap. 1, n. 44).

Hardinge, assisted by Alwyn Parker, had developed a complex plan of organization for the peace conference which proposed that the conference create a number of Grand Committees to examine the issues. Hardinge suggested five probable committee titles: Political and Territorial Adjustments, Financial Adjustments, Economic and Commercial Adjustments, Prevention of Future Wars, and Revision of International Law Conventions. For each inter-allied Grand Committee there was to be a corresponding British committee to advise the Grand Committee delegate, and the PID was soon reorganized with this arrangement in mind.

Hardinge was aware of the complexity of his proposed arrangements but felt that 'however cumbrous and slow the machinery may appear, there is no part of it that can be dispensed with'. [2] Hardinge hoped that the conference would avoid concentrating the chairmanships of committees in the hands of the principal powers, to avoid spreading suspicion and distrust. He wanted the best qualified person to fill these important positions, commenting that 'A competent French Chairman is infinitely preferable to an incompetent English one'. [3] Hardinge's wish on this was not always fulfilled at Paris.

Hardinge believed that it was vital to have negotiating machinery which would be 'capable of being set in motion without any delay, and shall be readily adaptable to the form in which the Congress may ultimately take shape'. [4] In his covering note to Balfour, Hardinge pointed out that these arrangements had been made as 'it was undesirable that we should find ourselves unprepared'. [5] The Foreign Office plans had been made under cover of some bureaucratic haze as Hardinge suggested that 'the moment has now arrived when we should get these preparations regularised'. [6] He proposed

---

[2] Confidential Print 11022.   [3] Ibid.

[4] Ibid. Hardinge had already trained a staff of précis writers, clerical help, and stenographers who could record discussions in French. A staff of printers and printing presses were also in readiness for use at the conference. On administrative problems at the conference see Sally Marks, 'Behind the Scenes at the Paris Peace Conference of 1919', the *Journal of British Studies*, 9:2 (May 1970), 154–80.

[5] Hardinge to Balfour, 10 Oct. 1918. Hardinge Papers 39.   [6] Ibid.

that if this were achieved other government departments should be contacted in order to create a nucleus organization for each of the proposed sections.

Hardinge concluded his note to Balfour with the observation that it was the duty of the Foreign Office to prepare this machinery. He added somewhat tersely, 'I presume that the Prime Minister would have to be consulted.'[7] Hardinge was still unaware of what role Lloyd George intended to play. From Hardinge's memorandum it appears that he did not expect the prime minister to attend the conference in person, and that Balfour would be the chief delegate. Lloyd George's decision to attend probably came as a great shock to Hardinge, just as Wilson's decision to represent himself surprised the State Department. Lloyd George in general proved himself to be a disruptive influence when it came to Hardinge's carefully laid plans.

Balfour's private secretary, Eric Drummond, wrote on three occasions to the prime minister's secretary, J. T. Davies, vainly requesting that Hardinge's memorandum on 'Peace Negotiations' be circulated to the War Cabinet.[8] There was no reply. Although Hardinge's report appeared in the confidential print series, and must have been seen by some ministers, there seems to have been no mention of it at any of the cabinet's meetings. But Harold Nicolson has left us with a memorable account of Lloyd George's reaction to Hardinge's plan. Alwyn Parker had prepared three elaborate charts to illustrate the Foreign Office's proposed arrangements. As Nicolson recalled,

Mr. Alwyn Parker, Librarian of the Foreign Office, devoted his marked talents for administration to the elaboration of a whole Peace Conference in being. He even prepared a coloured chart of the future systematization of the British Section of the Conference. Upon this reeling orrery, Prime Ministers and Dominion Delegates whirled each in his proper orbit, coloured green, or red, or blue. Mr. Parker himself could be discerned revolving modestly as a moon, attendant upon Jupiter, Lord Hardinge of Penshurst, the 'Organising Ambassador.' Mr. Parker's planisphere did not, it is true, play that part in the

---

[7] Hardinge to Balfour, 10 Oct. 1918.

[8] Drummond to Davies, 12, 16, and 19 Oct. 1918. Lloyd George Papers F3/3/35,37,38.

eventual peace conference which its designer had hoped. Mr. Lloyd George, on seeing it, laughed aloud.[9]

Lloyd George had other ideas on how arrangements for the conference should be made, and he decided to entrust the administrative planning to Maurice Hankey and the preparation of the peace brief to General Smuts. In retrospect, however, it can be seen that Hardinge's ideas played a greater role than Lloyd George had intended.

Lloyd George decided that Hankey should handle the organizational side of the peace conference. Hankey realized the wisdom of not ignoring the Foreign Office and at a meeting on 22 November he and Hardinge agreed on a division of responsibilities. Hankey noted in his diary that it was decided that he, 'would look after meetings of British delegates outside the conference, while he [Hardinge] should be in charge of all conference arrangements. — this of course depends on the P.M. who doesn't much like Hardinge'.[10] This arrangement was maintained until the delegation arrived in Paris, when Lloyd George decided to increase Hankey's role. Hardinge on the basis of this understanding with Hankey proceeded with the administrative work of setting up the machinery for British participation at the peace conference. In November he began contacting the various offices of state and asking them to appoint liaison officers to keep in touch with Parker and Tyrrell, who would be overseeing this work.[11] It is worth noting that Hardinge appointed for this task the men who headed the two departments which had been at the centre of Foreign Office innovations.

Each of the offices contacted by Hardinge received a copy of Parker's planisphere and the other outlines relating to organization. Hardinge explained in his covering note that although these arrangements were only 'mechanical and secretarial arrangements, the subject is one of vast magnitude and complexity'.[12] Most of the departments responded constructively,

[9] H. Nicolson, *Peacemaking 1919* (London, 1933), p. 26.

[10] Hankey Papers 1/5. Also in Stephen Roskill, *Hankey: Man of Secrets* (London, 1970–4), II. 22; M. P. A. Hankey, *The Supreme Command at the Paris Peace Conference, 1919: A Commentary* (London, 1963), p. 11.

[11] ADM 1/8542/284. Hardinge to Murray, 8 Nov. 1918.   [12] Ibid.

but the response from Edwin Montagu at the India Office can only be described as petulant. Montagu was greatly disturbed by Hardinge's note and wrote in reply to Lord Robert Cecil that

I feel that it is really my duty to complain to you about the method of procedure. Lord Hardinge's Minute mentions that he has been engaged for eighteen months on elaborate preparations for the administrative arrangements for the British delegates at the Peace Conference.... When Lord Hardinge, an ex-viceroy, has for eighteen months been considering matters connected with the Middle East, I may legitimately express some surprise that neither he nor anybody in the Foreign Office thought it proper or right that the India Office should be in any way consulted.[13]

Balfour's private secretary, Eric Drummond, drafted a diplomatic reply to what he described as 'this somewhat querulous letter'.[14] Montagu was apparently soothed by the response, which noted that 'As far as I am aware questions of policy have not been considered by Lord Hardinge except those for which the Foreign Office is responsible'.[15] Certainly the India Office's attitude contrasted sharply with its earlier desire to avoid any involvement with the Historical Section's work.

The Peace Brief: General Smuts and Lord Hardinge

Though the War Cabinet ignored Hardinge's memorandum on arrangements, it did not avoid the issue altogether. On 17 October, 'the War Cabinet gave some preliminary consideration to the preparations required for an eventual Peace Conference'.[16] It was decided to have a negotiating brief drawn up. Lloyd George thought that a lawyer might be a suitable person for such a task and asked Lord Reading to recommend someone. Four days later, however, the prime minister asked General Smuts to be responsible for preparing the brief.[17]

Smuts had indeed been a brilliant lawyer in his youth, and

[13] FO 800/207, Montagu to Cecil, 13 Nov. 1918.
[14] Ibid., marginal note by Drummond.
[15] FO 800/207, Balfour (drafted by Drummond) to Montagu, 14 Nov. 1918.
[16] CAB 23/8, 488(1), 17 Oct. 1918.
[17] Smuts to Lloyd George, 21 Nov. 1918. Lloyd George Papers F/45/9/23. Also in Smuts Papers 101/37, and CAB 24/70/GT6349.

he certainly commanded Lloyd George's respect. It was an imaginative and remarkable choice when it is recalled that only fourteen years before, after the collapse of the Boer cause, Smuts had sat as the enemy's representative on the opposite of the negotiating table from the British Empire. In a letter to his wife Smuts simply commented that 'I am very busy putting our whole case in order for the conference. I have been charged with this work by the Cabinet.'[18] Smuts's task was now to oversee the negotiating preparations for the peace conference with the British Empire's most recently vanquished foes.

Smuts was desperately busy in the period leading up to the peace conference. From his headquarters at the Savoy Hotel he worked with tremendous energy on his task as chairman of the Demobilisation Committee, as a member of the War Cabinet until 14 December, and with setting out South Africa's own claims, and the question of Dominion representation at the conference.[19] On the peace brief he 'worked himself nearly to death, but did not read most of the papers submitted to him'.[20] To assist him Smuts appointed Sir Erle Richards, counsel to the India Office.[21] Richards, although supposedly working on the general brief, concerned himself almost totally with questions relating to Germany's former colonies.[22] His reports were not highly thought of, and the Foreign Office sidetracked them. Toynbee noted, 'I understand that it is not proposed to submit Sir Erle Richards' series of memoranda to the Conference.'[23] Inevitably Smuts was forced to rely on the existing machinery.

---

[18] W. K. Hancock and Jean van der Poel, *Selections from the Smuts Papers*, vol. IV (Cambridge, 1966), Doc. 856, Jan Smuts to S. M. Smuts, 14 Nov. 1918.

[19] On this period in Smuts's career see W. K. Hancock, *Smuts: The Sanguine Years, 1870–1919* (Cambridge, 1962), pp. 492–504.

[20] Agnes Headlam-Morley, 'Introduction', in James Headlam-Morley, *A Memoir of the Paris Peace Conference, 1919*, ed. Agnes Headlam-Morley, Russell Bryant, and Anna Cienciala (London, 1972), p. xxiii.

[21] Smuts to Lloyd George, 21 Nov. 1918. Lloyd George Paper F/45/9/23. Sir (Henry) Erle Richards (1861–1922); educ. Eton and New Coll., Oxford; barrister, 1887; KC, 1905; Counsel to the India Office, 1911–21; KCSI, 1909; Chichele Prof. of International Law, Oxford, 1911–22.

[22] CAB 29/1/P-34. Smuts Papers 101/58.

[23] FO 608/105/384/1/1/604, Minute by Toynbee, 25 Jan. 1919. These reports were so innocuous as to be considered suitable for showing to the Americans. As instructions to negotiators they were useless.

To prepare much of the actual substance of the brief Smuts therefore turned to the Political Intelligence Department.

Leo Amery wrote to Smuts on 1 November about Smuts's new assignment and suggested that he should contact Pro- thero, Tyrrell, and Dickson.[24] Hardinge also wrote to Smuts on 1 November explaining the arrangements he had already made, noting that this had been done with Hankey's support and approval, and offering to meet Smuts to discuss the plans.[25] Hardinge's offer of assistance was obviously accepted, for on 15 November the PID was reorganized with the specific aim of assisting Smuts with the peace brief. The PID took on the task of co-ordinating with other departments in order to avoid Smuts receiving uncorrelated reports.[26]

The relationship between Smuts and the Foreign Office was a curious one. The professional diplomats had mixed feelings about the South African general's ability to handle the in- tricacies of what was mainly a European settlement.[27] During the peace conference, though, they would develop a high regard for his statesmanship. The procedure adopted by the Foreign Office was that the peace memoranda, 'after receiving the approval of the Permanent Under-Secretary of State, were submitted to General Smuts'.[28] As the PID was co-ordinating much of the material coming from other departments, this allowed Hardinge and the Office staff to control and revise the information going to Smuts. Crowe edited out of Headlam- Morley's introductory note to Smuts a passage he found over- strident on the role of public opinion in the western democra- cies.[29] Tyrrell had a cavalier view of Smuts's role. Commenting on the South-Eastern Europe memorandum, on which he wanted minor changes, Tyrrell nevertheless felt that 'for the immediate purpose of "feeding" General Smuts I think they

[24] Hancock and van der Poel, *Selections from the Smuts Papers*, vol. iii, Doc. 848. Amery rather loosely described Dickson as being someone who 'has also been getting together a lot of geographical stuff'.
[25] Hardinge to Smuts, 1 Nov. 1918. Smuts Papers 101/22.
[26] FO 371/4352/f15/PC15.
[27] Agnes Headlam-Morley, 'Introduction', in *A Member of the Paris Peace Conference*, p. xxiii.
[28] FO 371/4382/PID 619.   [29] FO 371/4353/f23/PC23.

will do'.[30] Smuts, however, clearly had no desire to usurp the Foreign Office's role on political and territorial questions, believing instead that they 'must remain responsible for the details of this work'.[31] Smuts did not alter any of the reports he received, and they were issued to the delegates as originally submitted. This may have been due to lack of time on Smuts's part or perhaps to lack of information from alternative sources.

In his letter to Lloyd George on 21 November Smuts defined two sets of documents which were to comprise the peace brief. The first was to be general summaries for use by the delegates at the conference, while the second was to be a detailed series of technical memoranda for use by the experts serving on the technical committees, to which Smuts assumed much of the conference's work would be assigned.[32] In this view Smuts is clearly reflecting Hardinge's ideas on how the conference would be organized. Smuts also followed Hardinge's line on the need for expert advisers and he suggested to Lloyd George that the delegates would need not only the peace brief, 'but a number of experts whom they may be able to consult on all the numerous subjects which will come up for consideration'.[33] It is not surprising that when the conference actually began the British delegation's expert advisers were drawn almost totally from the staffs of the departments which had been the most deeply engaged on preparations.

Smuts relied on the PID for most of the brief, but he also obtained the assistance of other departments. The Board of Trade dealt with trade, tariff, and shipping questions. The various military staffs provided reports on strategic questions. The Treasury assigned John Maynard Keynes to assist with indemnity and reparations problems.[34] With all these departments actively involved it is not surprising that the brief soon

---

[30] FO 371/4355/f68/PC68, Minute by Tyrrell, 8 Dec. 1918. Another example is provided by Tyrrell's deleting Smuts's name from the circulation list of the report by Simpson on 'The Future Settlement of Trans Caucasia', 1 Nov. 1918. FO 371/4368/f480/PID511 and FO 371/4352/f5/PC5.

[31] Smuts to Lloyd George, 21 Nov. 1918. Lloyd George Papers F/45/9/23.

[32] Ibid.

[33] Ibid.

[34] Hancock and van der Poel, *Selections from the Smuts Papers*, vol. iv, Doc. 862.

assumed a great size. When Smuts reported to the Cabinet on 21 November 1918 he pointed out that the brief was assuming large proportions, and enquired whether the Cabinet wished to read it.[35] Given the immediate crush of work and the anticipated general election, Smuts's query undoubtedly dissuaded them from much interference. It is nevertheless surprising that such an important document was not automatically submitted to the Cabinet for consideration. The result was that the existing preparatory work co-ordinated by Hardinge reached the Paris conference more or less intact.

In the end Smuts submitted no single, well-packaged peace brief comparable to the American Inquiry's 'Black Book'. Instead the basis of the negotiating materials was the PID's 'P' series of memoranda, supplemented by the specialized reports from other departments. Lloyd George had been anxious to circumvent the Whitehall bureaucratic establishment, especially the Foreign Office, and to do so he had placed in charge of the preparations a person who was not only not a regular government official but who was not even British. Smuts, however, soon perceived the enormous size of the task and was willing to trust to the machinery which had already been created. To an extent Lloyd George's aim was carried out in that the departments were manned by outsiders, brought in temporarily for the war. Nevertheless Whitehall, and the Foreign Office in particular, played the principal role in the preparations for the Paris Peace Conference.

The Allies

Great Britain was not alone among the Allied powers in preparing well in advance for the peace conference. Both the Americans and the French had created elaborate organizations for the gathering of information and the planning of negotiating positions. The United States entrusted this work to a special commission known as the Inquiry, which in terms of numbers employed and material produced was the largest such effort. The French established several independent committees which suffered severely from lack of overall co-ordination, and

[35] CAB 23/8/505(6).

as a result France's preparations never developed as fully as those of its English-speaking counterparts. French planning for the conference was entirely Eurocentric, with no work being done until after the Armistice on non-European questions. Allied success in co-ordinating military planning was not mirrored by co-operation over peace preparations, and such efforts as were made were those of the Americans, who established contact with both the French and British organizations.

The American preparatory organization was established in September 1917, only half a year after the United States entered the war.[36] The first suggestions for a planning organization for the eventual peace conference were put forward in the spring of 1917 when plans were proposed independently by the diplomat Henry White, by Felix Frankfurter who was then a special assistant to the Secretary of War, and by members of the State Department. Under such prodding the Secretary of State, Robert Lansing, began to make plans, only to be foiled, as he so often was, by the independent designs of President Wilson. On 2 September 1917 Wilson wrote to his confidant, Colonel House, proposing that he should head a body independent of the State Department not only to prepare America's case for the conference, but also to ascertain the probable claims of the Allies. House's organization effectively ignored the State Department until the imminence of peace forced it to turn to the department for help in providing essential data.

One difficulty facing the Inquiry was that few Americans had studied the world outside Europe and the Americas, and few had a knowledge even of the languages of Eastern Europe, much less of the non-European world. The result was that House in recruiting his staff often had to rely on ancient and medieval historians. The personnel of the Inquiry were undoubtedly competent, though not necessarily expert, in the fields to which they were assigned. Among those who later

---

[36] The best work on the Inquiry is Lawrence Gelfand, *The Inquiry: American Preparations for Peace, 1917–1919* (New Haven, Conn., 1963). Material on the Inquiry, unless otherwise stated, is based on this work. See also Arthur Walworth, *America's Moment: 1918* (New York, 1977), which makes use of much of the primary and secondary literature which appeared after Gelfand's work.

became eminent figures in their fields were Samuel Elliot Morrison, Walter Lippman, James Shotwell, Robert Lord, Archibald Cary Coolidge, and Manley Hudson. To head this group House chose his brother-in-law, Sidney Mezes, a philosopher of religion and university president. Though presumably chosen for his administrative talents, his difficulties in overseeing the Inquiry later led to his effective replacement by the geographer, Isaiah Bowman.

This peace planning organization was at first located in the New York Public Library, its existence kept secret even from most of the library's staff. To avoid attracting undue attention the members dubbed themselves 'the Inquiry'. In November 1917 the Inquiry moved to the building of the American Geographical Society in New York. Much as the British Naval Intelligence Geographical Section found a headquarters in the buildings of the Royal Geographical Society, so the Inquiry found the proximity to works of reference and cartographic materials particularly useful. Not all the Inquiry's staff were located in New York. It was a widely dispersed body with the Eastern European Division at Harvard, the Austrian Division at Yale, and the Ottoman Empire Division at Princeton. Monthly meetings were held in New York to bring the divisional directors together.

At its maximum size the Inquiry employed 126 experts. Despite Europe being the focus of the war, it was not the centre of the Inquiry's activities. Thirty-one of these experts were involved in the entire range of European questions, while twelve alone were employed on Latin America. In common with the PID there was no special section assigned to German problems. The disproportionate interest in Latin America was due to the influence of Bowman, who used the opportunity to further his own studies of the region, despite the doubtful utility of these reports for the peace conference.

The Inquiry compiled approximately two thousand reports, mostly between one and thirty pages in length, though some were as long as five hundred pages. Some officials questioned the massiveness of the Inquiry's preparations, and would have preferred an organization along the lines of the PID which would make use of existing studies, summarize important information, and act as a clearing house. As it was, House, though taking an interest in the Inquiry's work, exercised little supervision once it was established. Probably the Inquiry's greatest contribution to policy was assisting in the preparation of Wilson's speech of the Fourteen Points, which was based in part on an Inquiry report on suggested peace terms.[37]

Many of the Inquiry's personnel went on to become members of the American Commission to Negotiate Peace at Paris, along with technical advisers from the military and the Department of State. Wilson had his first meeting with the experts aboard the *George Washington* on his way to the peace conference in December 1918, when he told them, 'Tell me what's right and I'll fight for it; give me a guaranteed position.'[38] The Inquiry responded on 21 January 1919 with an 'Outline of Tentative Recommendations', commonly called the Black Book.

The first contact between the Inquiry and its British equivalents was brought about by Sir William Wiseman, the head of British intelligence in the United States. Wiseman had cultivated a close friendship with Colonel House, to the point of taking an apartment in the same building in New York. The result was an unofficial line of communication between London and Washington by way of Wiseman and House. The colonel took a great liking to the young English baronet and kept him informed of developments, including the work of the Inquiry. Wiseman was particularly interested in the work on German colonies and on the League of Nations, and was given access to the confidential reports of the Inquiry.[39]

Wiseman reported on the progress of the Inquiry to the Foreign Office in February 1918, and Balfour responded with the suggestion that there should be a full exchange of information.[40] At the end of March an edited list of the projected Historical Section handbooks was sent to Colonel House, and in

[37] Gelfand, *The Inquiry*, pp. 79–113, 134–53.

[38] James T. Shotwell, *At the Paris Peace Conference* (New York, 1937), p. 78.

[39] On Wiseman and House see Inga Floto, *Colonel House in Paris: A Study of American Policy at the Paris Peace Conference, 1919* (Princeton, NJ, 1980); W. B. Fowler, *British–American Relations, 1917–1918: The Role of Sir William Wiseman* (Princeton,NJ, 1969); Gelfand, *The Inquiry*, pp. 116–26; Walworth, *America's Moment*, pp. 32–4.

[40] FO 370/98/f12608/187593.

June Wiseman passed on more material.[41] In April Major Douglas Johnson arrived in London on a study tour of Allied peace preparations, and was well received by the staffs involved. This was undoubtedly the most important direct contact between the American and British preparatory organizations. Johnson was given copies of the various Historical Section outlines and instructions, as well as a proof sample of one of the books.[42]

In May Wiseman was back in London and met with Parker and Prothero to decide which handbooks should be sent to Colonel House. They agreed to provide Wiseman with three copies of each, which could be passed to House at his discretion, though Military Intelligence objected to the books on Arabia and Mesopotamia being included. Because of the slowness with which the handbooks were produced, most were not ready until January 1919 and the American delegation received copies only in February 1919.[43] Although the handbooks were unable to aid the Inquiry's researches, there was some direct contact between the personnel involved. In May 1918 Dana Munro, head of the Inquiry's Western Asia division, wrote to George Prothero suggesting a meeting to discuss their work.[44]

A fairly regular flow of information was established, although there seems at no point to have been the full exchange of views proposed by Balfour, as well as members of the Inquiry. From April 1918 onwards the PID began to receive the American intelligence reports forwarded to the British government, while many of the PID's weekly intelligence reports can be found among the papers of the Inquiry.[45] In November 1918, after the Armistice, Robert Cecil proposed

[41] FO 370/98/f12608/187593. Also Gelfand, *The Inquiry*, p. 125.

[42] Johnson submitted three reports on his London visit: 'Confidential Report on Arrangement Made by the British Government for Collecting Data for the Peace Conference', 1 May 1918, Inquiry Doc. 987; 'A Statement of Geographical War Work in Great Britain', June 1918, Inquiry Doc. 984; 'Lists of Confidential Reports Prepared or in Preparation by the Authorities of Great Britain for Use at the Peace Conference', June 1918, Inquiry Doc. 989.

[43] FO 370/98/f12608/187593.

[44] Munro to Prothero, 17 Mar. 1918. Prothero Papers (RHS), 3/I/1.

[45] FO 371/3457–3460/f1771. On Anglo-American co-operation at the peace conference see Seth P. Tillman, *Anglo-American Relations at the Paris Peace Conference of 1919* (Princeton, NJ, 1961).

that Toynbee's important memorandum on the British case in respect to Arabia and Turkey should be sent to Colonel House and President Wilson.[46] Mallet agreed that sections of the report showing British commitments could usefully be shown to the Americans, but added that the reports should be edited to eliminate anything which might prejudice the British case.[47] As the members of the Inquiry made their way to Europe in readiness for the conference personal contacts increased. In December two members of the Inquiry, Archibald Cary Coolidge and Captain Alfred Dennis, lunched with Headlam-Morley and Allen Leeper at Brown's Hotel, where in Leeper's words they had an 'interesting talk'.[48]

One of Major Johnson's recommendations upon his return from his study trip in the spring of 1918 was to suggest closer co-ordination between the preparatory organizations of the United States, Great Britain, and France. Within the alliance, however, 'there was a noticeable attitude of suspicion and even distrust between London and Paris regarding the preparations for the eventual peace'.[49] Johnson was amazed that the French and British were entirely ignorant of each other's work. The British had explained to him that a French agent had visited them and been given the information he requested, but that subsequently they had received no reciprocity from Paris. This had aroused British suspicions of French duplicity. Johnson upon visiting Paris heard another version from the Comité d'études, which claimed never to have heard of the purported agent.[50] Johnson unsuccessfully recommended that the Allied preparatory work should be co-ordinated by a special inter-allied group, so as to avoid confusion when it came time to sit down at the negotiating table with the Central Powers. As the Allies never did confront the Central Powers directly across a negotiating table, at least this one area of confusion was avoided.

French preparations were on a far less elaborate scale than

[46] FO 371/4368/f480/PID541, Minute by Cecil.
[47] Ibid., Minute by Mallet, 18 Nov. 1918.
[48] A. W. A. Leeper Diary, 9 Dec. 1918. AWAL.
[49] Gelfand, The Inquiry, p. 128.
[50] This story is recounted in Gelfand, p. 127.

those of the American Inquiry. What formal French preparations there were resulted from the work done by the Comité
d'études under Ernest Lavisse, together with a last minute
effort by André Tardieu to co-ordinate the reports and plans
produced by the various ministries. It has been observed that
with the end of the war the French government 'received two
months' grace in which to prepare its programme of peace
aims. It failed to do so.'[51] Attempts had been made since early
1917, however, to pull together the documentary information
which France would need to support her claims, in particular
for financial compensation and territorial acquisitions from the
German Empire.

The first steps towards creating a preparatory machinery
were taken in early 1917 by the Briand government, under
prodding from President Poincaré.[52] Three great commissions
were charged with this work: a Bureau d'études economiques
under Senator Jean Morel, a committee on the mines and industries of the north-east frontier area, and a Comité d'études
under Ernest Lavisse.[53] Morel's Bureau had been established in
July 1915 to examine economic questions which would have to
be settled after the war, and under Briand's plan Morel's group
was also to look at the financial consequences of neutralizing
the Rhineland. Subsequently, however, 'the Bureau's influence diminished, but it was briefly close to the heart of policy
making when economic war aims became a major government
concern in the spring of 1916'.[54] Tardieu in summarizing France's case apparently found the Bureau's notes
useful.[55] The Bureau consisted of Morel, with Henri Lorin

[51] Christopher M. Andrew and A. S. Kanya-Forstner, *France Overseas: The
Great War and the Climax of French Imperial Expansion* (London, 1981).

[52] Inquiry Doc. 270. Johnson, 'Report on Origin, Personnel, and Organization of the French Comité d'études, appointed to assemble data for the peace
conference'.

[53] Georges Suarez, *Briand: sa vie — son œuvre*, vol. iv: *La Pilote dans la tourmente, 1916–1918* (Paris, 1940), p. 130. Jean Morel (1854–1927); Deputy,
1898–1912; Senator, 1912–27; Minister of the Colonies, 1910–11 and Jan.–Dec.
1913.

[54] D. Stevenson, *French War Aims Against Germany, 1914–1919* (Oxford,
1982), p. 24.

[55] André Tardieu, *The Truth About the Treaty* (Indianapolis, 1921), p. 86.

as secretary, together with a small number of politicians and officials.[56]

The Comité d'études was organized in February 1917 by Charles Benoist, a deputy in parliament, who later served as vice-president of the Comité. Benoist was apparently not given detailed instructions as to organization, other than to study first the question of the left bank of the Rhine. He therefore selected for the Comité experts who had recently published on this issue. 'As a result, the organization naturally was not, in its personnel, the best possible one for studying the complex European questions.'[57] Benoist was a professor at the École libre des sciences politiques, though the ubiquitous Major Johnson reported that he was 'not regarded as one of the Comité intellectually'.[58] Benoist's role was to act as liaison between the Comité and the government. The president of the Comité d'études was Ernest Lavisse, director of the École normale supérieure and a well-known historian. Paul Vidal de la Blache, one of France's leading geographers, served as vice-president until his death in 1918, when he was succeeded by Benoist.

Much of the actual planning of the work and the administration was carried out by the secretary, Emmanuel de Martonne, professor of geography in the University of Paris. An active member of the Commission de Geographie of the Service Geographique de l'Armée, he prepared most of the maps and edited the reports of the Comité. The Comité d'études consisted entirely of geographers and historians and at one time or another involved about twenty-two experts. The one non-academic member was General Bourgeois, director of the Service Geographique de l'Armée, who provided the facilities for the study of problems and production of maps and reports.

The Comité adopted the seminar method for its meetings, which were held weekly from the end of February 1917 until the peace conference at the Salle des Cartes of the Geographical Institute at the Sorbonne.[59] Members submitted reports for criticism and would then revise their work before it was printed. The aim was for the reports to be 'scientifically accurate, but

[56] Inquiry Doc. 988. 'Detailed Information on French Official Preparations for Studying Condition of Peace'.

[57] Inquiry Doc. 270.   [58] Ibid.   [59] Gelfand, The Inquiry, p. 125.

expressed in terms of easy comprehension by those not specialists in the matters discussed'.[60] Half the material produced
concerned Alsace-Lorraine and France's north-east frontier, while the remainder dealt with European questions and the
Ottoman Empire. Colonial matters were not discussed. The
Comité had not finished its work when the conference began,
but when it was completed the reports filled two volumes.[61]
These reports were never widely read, and only President Poincaré seems to have studied them with any frequency.[62] In
fragmentary form, however, its work was of use to France's
last-minute effort to organize material for the conference.

Major Johnson visited the Comité d'études on behalf of the
Inquiry and was shown the index to the volume concerning
Alsace-Lorraine. General Weygand later obtained Cambon's
permission to allow Lavisse to provide copies of these documents to the Americans.[63] Inasmuch as the Comité was meant
to provide a factual backbone to the French case and not to
provide negotiating policy, giving the Americans the volume
on Alsace-Lorraine could only add to the propaganda in
support of French claims.

Despite the early date at which consideration of peace preparations had begun, the bulk of French planning was accomplished after the signing of the Armistice. On 12 November
1918 Clemenceau summoned his subordinates to the War
Office to outline French strategy for the peace conference.[64]
Foch was made responsible for preparing the case on German
disarmament, Lucien Klotz the economic and financial questions, and Paul Cambon the Rhineland. On 15 November the
foreign minister, Stephen Pichon, invited the ministries to
submit position papers on the treaty, together with drafts of
the clauses they wished included, a practice similar to the draft
treaties prepared by Cecil Hurst for the Foreign Office. The

[60] Inquiry Doc. 270.
[61] Comité d'études, *Travaux du Comité d'études* (Paris, 1918–19), vol. i:
L'Alsace-Lorraine et la frontière du nord-est, vol. ii: *Questions Européens*.
[62] Stevenson, *French War Aims Against Germany*, p. 154.
[63] Inquiry Doc. 988.
[64] Frederick J. Cox, 'The French Peace Plans, 1918–1919: The Germ of the
Conflict Between Ferdinand Foch and Georges Clemenceau', in Cox *et al.*,
Studies in Modern European History in Honor of Franklin Charles Palm (New York,
1956), p. 84.

response, like that to Asquith's request of August 1916, was belated and incomplete.[65] In early December Clemenceau turned to his protégé, André Tardieu, and charged him with co-ordinating the material and preparing a plan of organization for the peace conference. 'It was Tardieu chain-smoking into the small hours, who more than any other man prepared and then defended the Government's negotiating aims.'[66] His work concentrated on two areas, Germany's frontiers, especially with France, and economic questions. A number of less important topics were handled by others. General Bourgeois dealt with the League of Nations, while the Foreign and Colonial ministries prepared for colonial questions. Tardieu made full use of the available reports of the Comité d'études in his memoranda on territorial questions, and the economic preparations of Lucien Klotz and Étienne Clementel on financial problems. The territorial questions were considered in a series of meetings in January, which were attended by General Le Rond from Foch's staff, members of the Foreign Ministry, and the Comité d'études.

The American Inquiry had achieved some degree of co-operation with their French counterparts through visits to Paris and personal contacts.[67] The secretary of the Comité, de Martonne, visited New York and met with officials of the Inquiry and subsequently wrote a 'Rapport sur le Comité d'Enquête'.[68] The British archives on the other hand show no trace of contact or knowledge of these French organizations. The first Anglo-French contacts on preparations came on 26 November when Paul Cambon gave Lord Hardinge a copy of his 'Examination of the Conditions of Peace'.[69] This was part of Clemenceau's

[65] Stevenson, *French War Aims Against Germany*, p. 152.

[66] Ibid. 152. André Tardieu (1876–1945); Deputy, 1914–24, 1926–36; High Commissioner to the USA, Apr.–Sept. 1917; subsequently three times premier, 1929–30, 1930, 1932.

[67] An example is Maj. Douglas Johnson who met several old friends on his visit to Paris, including Henri Lorin from Morel's Economic Bureau. He was also familiar with Lavisse, Benoist, and Vidal de la Blache. Inquiry Doc. 988.

[68] Walworth, *America's Moment*, p. 78 n.

[69] FO 371/3446/f157260/198800. Cambon told Hardinge that he had prepared this document along with Fleurian. See also Stevenson, *French War Aims Against Germany*, p. 145, who states that the financial section of Cambon's memorandum was based on a Finance Ministry memorandum of 18 Nov. 1918.

effort to reach an agreement with the British on the important issues of the peace before the less amicable President Wilson arrived in Europe.

French preparations took a very different course from those of Great Britain and the United States. An important factor behind this difference was that unlike its British and American allies, France had immediate irredentist and security goals on the continent of Europe. The entire French effort was geared towards one object, which had two facets — reclaiming the territories lost in 1871 and the destruction of German power. French preparations therefore necessarily concerned the topics of German frontiers and the possible extent of reparations. The result was that France entered the conference with a well documented case for the return of its lost provinces and high reparations, a plan which for the most part was achieved. On the negative side France 'entered the Peace Conference without a coherent imperial plan'.[70] The inevitable result, given American lack of interest in colonial possessions, was that the already vast overseas British Empire grew even vaster.

No other countries seem to have created machinery specifically for dealing with peace preparations.[71] All the belligerents and nationalist groups had some form of propaganda agency which produced materials supporting their claims, and so came to Paris laden with statistics and reports. 'Most of this was purely *ex parte* pleading, but it at least secured that every side of the case would be buttressed by all the arguments that the ingenuity and industry of its supporters could produce, while many of the briefs were prepared by historians, geographers, and economists of international reputation.'[72] Only in the United States, the British Empire, and to a lesser degree France was an attempt made to pull together data based on 'scientific' research, not only to support their own national policies but to assist in untangling the claims and counter-claims of the supplicant states at the conference.

The factors which led to an attempt to organize material for

[70] Andrew and Kanya-Forstner, *France Overseas*, p. 165.

[71] The Italians apparently did have a 16-member commission working on international law, FO 372/1186/f539/192594.

[72] H. W. V. Temperley, ed., *A history of the Peace Conference of Paris* (6 vols., London, 1920–4), i. 241.

the peace negotiations, and the development of mechanisms for conducting such work, varied greatly between the three major Allied and Associated Powers, but certain common factors do emerge. Interest in such planning began in all three states in the spring of 1917, which suggests that the idea of a peace settlement was perceived as an increasingly likely event. Lloyd George, Wilson, and Clemenceau all revealed a marked distrust of their own foreign ministries. All of them ignored as much as possible the attempts of their professional diplomats to play a role in the shaping of peace aims. Wilson formally took the matter entirely out of the hands of his State Department and put it into the charge of a private individual who held no government position. Clemenceau ignored all the diplomats and turned instead to a parliamentary protégé, while Lloyd George turned to Smuts, the only person in the cabinet who was not from Great Britain. Beneath this deliberate policy of the governmental leaders lies the common fact that all three governments found it necessary to create bureaux of experts to advise on the details of the settlement. Diplomacy had now reached the age of specialization, and the professional diplomat clearly required the support of experts in the conduct of negotiations. All three states borrowed their experts from the academic world and these men provided the material upon which the political figures appointed to prepare the peace briefs based their reports. The process followed in Great Britain was not unusual, but rather followed a pattern clearly discernible among all the Great Powers.

The signing of the armistice on 11 November 1918 ended the military phase of the Great War. There was one campaign yet to be waged, the diplomatic battle which would be fought at the negotiating table. It was for this last contest of the Great War that the Allies now mobilized their departments charged with preparing for the peace talks. In America the Inquiry was getting ready to move its personnel and files to Paris, and would join President Wilson on board the *George Washington* for the voyage to Europe. In Paris the French were not only arranging their own plans for a Carthaginian peace, but were also busy with the logistics of hosting what has proved to be the greatest peace conference of the century. In London the preparations started nineteen months previously and the offices created to pursue the research at last came to the fore. The most important of these, the PID, was smoothly assisting Smuts with the peace brief. After four years of war the final and most vital objective was now to win the peace.

The Experts Go to Paris

The Paris Peace Conference, intended as the greatest meeting for reordering the international system since the Congress of Vienna in 1814–15, opened with much fanfare on 18 January 1919. As with so many events at the conference the timing was determined by historical imperatives, in this instance the anniversary of the proclamation of the German Empire in 1871. The Great Powers dominated the conference from the very outset not only by their political power but also by the sheer size of their delegations. President Wilson was supported by a staff of over 300 while the majesty of the British Empire required no fewer than 200 delegates. Paris, which had not fallen before the German menace during the war, was now occupied by an army of peace conference delegates. Lord Milner when he arrived at the British headquarters at the Hotel Majestic described the scene which met his eyes as a 'circus', and indeed almost all these individuals were ornamental.[73] There was a notable discrepancy between the notional size as opposed to the effective complement of the British Empire Delegation, and Allen Leeper was already complaining in early January that 'we are grievously understaffed'.[74] Despite the vast size of the British delegation most of the work of drafting the five peace treaties was left to a mere handful of overworked men, and the few British delegates who emerge from the records of the conference as significant figures are for the most part those who were deeply involved in the preparatory work. Hardinge had envisaged an orderly conference. Instead what met was a gathering of Allied leaders who lurched from topic to topic, uncertain at first even as to whether this was a preliminary conference or the final peace congress. In this situation what

[73] Milner Diary, 5 Feb 1919. Milner MSS dep 90. Nicolson, *Peacemaking 1919*, p. 45.
[74] A. W. A. Leeper to R. W. A. Leeper, 9 Jan. 1919. AWAL.

effect could the labour expended in all that early planning hope to have?

The flurry which attended the opening of the long awaited peace conference only marked the beginning of a long period of sluggish activity. At first the conference met in plenary session, followed by the emergence of a Council of Ten, consisting of the leaders and foreign ministers of the five Great Powers. The dominant figures were Lloyd George representing the British Empire, Georges Clemenceau for France, Woodrow Wilson for the United States, and Vittorio Orlando for Italy. This council then proceeded in a rather aimless way to hear the claims of the smaller allied states, a process later likened to hearing auditions. It was almost as if the central figures were avoiding tackling the key issues in the knowledge that unpleasant divergences of view were bound to occur. The opening weeks of the conference were no more than the Indian summer of the wartime alliance; the Paris conference, unable to decide whether it was a preliminary conference or the final event, did not establish a coherent agenda. The idea of the Great Powers hearing the smaller states emerged from the notion that this would assist in informing the Allied leaders of their junior partners' concerns prior to their negotiations with the Central Powers. As the gathering in Paris slowly transformed itself into the final peace congress which would dictate a settlement, so its requirements changed. The leaders of the Great Powers now needed to judge the claims of their smaller allies, as well as to arrange the final details of a much redesigned world. Inevitably this work was turned over to expert committees, bodies on which Britain was well prepared to argue its case because of the wealth of pre-conference planning. Much as Churchill was later praised, despite his role in other crises, for the fact that the fleet was ready, so Hardinge and those involved in establishing the preparatory machinery deserve credit for the fact that Britain was ready for the sort of international conference which occurred at Paris in 1919.

The staff of the British delegation to the peace conference began to arrive in Paris just after New Year's Day 1919.[75] Many

[75] On the Foreign Office role see M. L. Dockrill and Zara Steiner, 'The Foreign Office at the Paris Peace Conference in 1919', *International History Review*, 2 (1980), 55–86.

of those involved in the preparatory phase were included. Tyrrell and Parker attended as Lord Hardinge's private secretaries. Of the ten members of the political section, seven were connected with the PID: Crowe, Mallet, Howard, Macleay, Vansittart, Akers Douglas, and Nicolson.[76] The Intelligence Clearing House, which acted as the delegation's co-ordinating body, was headed by Henry Penson from the WTID, with Headlam-Morley, Toynbee, and Allen Leeper being initially assigned to its political sub division. George Prothero was present as historical adviser, Cecil Hurst acted as director of the legal and drafting section, while Cecil and Percy served in the League of Nations section. The Financial section included Keynes, Falk, and Ward from the Treasury's 'A' Division. A number of the other experts were also brought over to Paris for short periods to assist on problems as they arose.

Conditions during those first days in Paris were chaotic, and as Lloyd George had laughingly rejected Hardinge and Parker's organizational plan, without substituting one of his own, nobody was quite certain what their particular duties were. Headlam-Morley later noted, 'As to my duties and functions I received then and throughout the whole of the time I have been in Paris no single word of instruction.' The result he recalled was that 'I had, therefore, to determine my own duties for myself'.[77] No doubt in the spirit of the new diplomacy Headlam-Morley applied the doctrine of self-determination to his problem, and that of his PID colleagues, and the solution which emerged was certainly better than what was originally intended.

Several of the members of the PID were dispatched to Paris with the expectation that they would form part of the Intelligence Clearing House being organized under Sir Henry Penson. The difficulty was that the purpose of the Intelligence Clearing House was poorly defined, though the basic idea was that it would act as a general enquiries bureau which would also issue a daily bulletin of meetings and maintain a registry of the available documents. The hope was that such a bureau would facilitate the flow of information.[78]

---

[76] Only Paget did not in the end attend the conference.

[77] Headlam-Morley, *Memoir*, p. 89, Apr. 1919.

[78] ADM 1/8542/284, 'British Diplomatic Department Intelligence Clearing House', 12 Nov. 1918.

Headlam-Morley and his fellow political intelligence analysts, however, had no desire to be engaged in what was general clerical work. Allen Leeper observed that while the Clearing House's work would be valuable to the general running of the conference, 'It is not PID work at all'.[79] Nicolson later observed that 'The members of the PID had for years been concentrating their great abilities, not so much upon the conduct of war, as upon the theories of peace'.[80] Headlam-Morley believed that they should be deployed upon matters of which they had special knowledge.[81] Indeed it was individuals with particular expertise who were badly required, and it was not long before Nicolson and Leeper were involved in Balkan affairs, Toynbee in Near Eastern matters, and Headlam-Morley in Polish and Western European questions, while other PID experts were brought over to Paris as the need arose. By the middle of January these experts had definitely managed to re-establish their separate identity, leading Allen Leeper to comment that 'Our real function is however political advisory work & that I hope is now recognised'.[82] The difficulty now was to find somebody to advise.

The first fortnight of the conference saw the delegation painfully reinventing the system projected by Hardinge and Parker. Headlam-Morley noted that 'While all subordinate officials are producing their material and are ready to take up and to bring to a practical solution the matters with which they are charged, there remains as before a complete absence of leadership, statesmanship, decision and apparently, of any sense of responsibility above'.[83] The need for a well-organized secretariat was obvious, and at last, two days after the conference opened, Lloyd George appointed Hankey to this critical role.[84] As a consolation Hardinge was awarded the title

[79] A. W. A. Leeper to R. W. A. Leeper, 19 Jan. 1919. AWAL.

[80] Nicolson, 'Allen Leeper', p. 479.

[81] Headlam-Morley to Tyrrell, 13 Jan. 1919, in Headlam-Morley, *Memoir*, pp. 1–2.

[82] A. W. A. Leeper to R. W. A. Leeper, 19 Jan. 1919. AWAL.

[83] Headlam-Morley, *Memoir*, p. 4, diary entry for 19 Jan. 1919.

[84] FO 608/162/515/1/5/530, 1355, Hankey, 'Peace Conference', 22 Jan. and 29 Jan. 1919.

of 'supervising ambassador'. The Foreign Office had continued to fight to the end in support of Hardinge, even making a last ditch appeal through Philip Kerr, but given Lloyd George's personal inclinations such a move was probably inevitable.[85] The struggle between Hankey and Hardinge for control of the negotiating apparatus thus ended in victory for Hankey, who after all had the inestimable advantage of having the prime minister's confidence. Foreign affairs were now clearly a prime ministerial prerogative. No action could have so clearly symbolized the erosion of Foreign Office influence than the appointment of the prime minister's man, Hankey, over the Foreign Office's man, Hardinge. With this issue resolved the British Empire delegation could now get on with the business of dealing with the peace settlement.

The PID experts during this first fortnight of the conference were struggling not only to establish a separate identity from the Intelligence Clearing House, but also to make their presence felt. Both Nicolson and Leeper felt deep frustration at having the experts ignored. With some justification they believed this could only lead to diplomatic disaster. Nicolson in writing to his father observed that the Great Powers were deciding 'important questions *in camera* and on what seems a wholly empirical and irresponsible basis. They seldom take the trouble to notice facts and arguments prepared for them by their staffs. Sooner or later this disregard for technical opinion will lead to a smash.'[86] Leeper in writing to his brother expressed a similar view: 'Few of us are satisfied as to the way the conference is going. So far the expert adviser has been almost ignored & the plenipotentiaries left to their own devices — with what results!'[87] Seton-Watson must have been aware of his friends' frustration for within a fortnight of these comments he was writing in the *New Europe* that the political leaders 'have filled the Paris hotels with armies of experts and a vast apparatus of documentary material, but when it comes to action they almost invariably disregard the advice of these

[85] Drummond to Kerr, 16 Jan. 1919. Lothian Papers, GD/40/17/55/14.
[86] Nicolson to Lord Carnock, 26 Jan. 1919, in Nicolson, *Peacemaking 1919*, pp. 249–50.
[87] A. W. A. Leeper to R. W. A. Leeper, 25 Jan. 1919. AWAL.

experts, and sometimes do not even ask for it'.[88] No doubt Seton-Watson was trying to wake the politicians up to the need to make use of these people. What the experts were doing was odd job work as the conference haphazardly discussed various issues. Their time was spent jumping from topic to topic, one day Czechoslovakia, the next Fiume, the day after Greece, and then back again. All they were doing was commenting on the actual claims being put forward by the supplicant states, though this was useful. Having spent the preparatory phase in part guessing what these claims would be, they could now test their knowledge against the facts.

This early period of drift had another side-effect in allowing the experts of the different delegations to come to know one another. The result was the creation of a good working relationship between the British and American delegations, while useful contacts were also established with the delegations of the smaller states. Leeper's friendship from Balliol days with Rhys Carpenter of the American delegation facilitated their introduction. Charles Seymour of the American delegation noted that Carpenter 'is a very useful man, for he is an Oxford man, and Nicolson and Leeper are among his best friends. I find that my being a Cambridge man has been a great help.'[89] These personal contacts were particularly important with delegates from the new Eastern European states who were not well known by the professional diplomats. Allen Leeper made full use of these contacts, writing exultantly to his brother that

I'm in constant touch with them & hear news & exchange views long before you get [them] in London. Here I can influence them, in London *not at all*: there I should have only a few skimpy wires & out-of-date newspapers to go on & to write reports on such evidence! when everything is actually arranged here in an hour's personal conversation.[90]

The experts also were coming to know their political leaders, frequently being summoned to attend Lloyd George or Balfour

[88] *New Europe*, 6 Feb. 1919, quoted in H. Seton-Watson and C. Seton-Watson, *The Making of a New Europe: R. W. Seton-Watson and the Last Years of Austria-Hungary* (London, 1981), p. 343.

[89] Charles Seymour, *Letters from the Paris Peace Conference* (New Haven, Conn., 1965), pp. 102–3, letter of 12 Jan. 1919. Seymour had studied at King's College, Cambridge, taking a BA in 1904.

[90] A. W. A. Leeper to R. W. A. Leeper, 11 Jan. 1919. AWAL.

in the early talks, not as advisers but to refresh their masters' memories on details. This early period of contact allowed the comparatively junior experts to establish good relations with senior political figures. Inevitably the experts' knowledge and ability must have become evident, and it can be no accident that when the time came to set up specialist territorial committees it was these individuals who were appointed as Britain's representatives.

As the conference ground on the political leaders themselves became increasingly frustrated with the procedures they had condoned, at the very least by their collective act of omission in not establishing a more effective system. They had spent the initial weeks listening to the recitation of the desires of their smaller allies, a process originally embarked upon in part to assuage the irritation of these states at being excluded from the main negotiations. This policy of hearing all the material themselves was clearly doing the leaders of the Great Powers no good. In a peace settlement as complicated as this the leaders needed to set the general strategy and leave the details to their staff, reserving their direct involvement in details for problems which proved irreconcilable at the lower levels. Charles Seymour of the American delegation concluded that it was 'wasteful that the premiers and foreign ministers should listen to all the detail of the claims, which they cannot understand, and far better that the claims should be heard first by the specialists and then reported to the big men'.[91] Wilson and Lloyd George were rapidly coming to the same conclusion and by the end of January were clamouring to be released from their diplomatic purgatory, suggesting that committees of experts be appointed to examine the claims of the smaller powers. This would have the simultaneous effect of leaving the leaders free for the discussion of more urgent matters, while allowing these questions to be considered by those with some experience of the specific problems. It was the creation of the territorial committees which provided an institutionalized role for the experts and allowed them to play a significant role in shaping the final settlement.

The first such committee was appointed on 1 February on

[91] Seymour, *Letters from the Paris Peace Conference*, p. 148.

Romanian (later expanded to Romanian and Yugoslav) Affairs, to be joined rapidly by four other such committees dealing with Greek and Albanian Affairs, Czechoslovakia, Poland, and Belgium and Denmark.[92] Slowly the experts began to tighten their grip on the machinery, and it was the creation of the territorial committees which gave them their opportunity. This turn in events led Headlam-Morley to comment wryly to Edwyn Bevan in March that 'Self-determination is quite *démodé*. Leeper and Nicolson determine for them what they ought to wish, but they do it very well.'[93] Leeper observed at the time, 'all the commissions will be linked up through Crowe, Harold & me'.[94] The work of the various committees was to pass through a Co-ordinating Committee, where the British representative was Crowe, which put him in a position to control and influence the flow from the technical committees to the Supreme Council. Thus one month into the conference the leaders were finally adopting the system of committees that Hardinge and Parker had so clearly foreseen months before. The delay in rediscovering this structure proved costly to the peace settlement, and the extended negotiations over the future of Europe only increased the prevailing air of uncertainty and in turn spawned increased instability.

While there were many experts and would-be advisers at Paris, the group with the clearest strategic conception of the post-war order were the experts of the New Europe group, together with Sir Eyre Crowe. The individuals who can be loosely gathered under the label of the New Europe group were men who shared the ideals embodied by the journal of that name published by R. W. Seton-Watson. They held ideas very similar to those expounded by Woodrow Wilson, but were not simply followers of the American president. They were in a sense the European product of the same development of ideas about the future organization of the international system. A significant difference was that these men were Europeans, and for the most part possessed of a detailed

[92] F. S. Marston, *The Peace Conference of 1919: Organization and Procedure* (London, 1944), Chap. 9.

[93] Headlam-Morley, *Memoir*, p. 44, letter to Bevan, 5 Mar. 1919.

[94] A. W. A. Leeper to R. W. A. Leeper, 5 Feb. 1919. AWAL.

knowledge of the ethnic intricacies involved in any large-scale reshaping of the European state system. Whereas President Wilson confined himself to some vague generalities as to the framework for change in Europe, the New Europe group had very specific ideas. Their common aim is summed up in the October 1916 inaugural editorial of the *New Europe*: 'Its highest ambition will be to provide a rallying ground for all those who see in European reconstruction, on a basis of nationality, the rights of minorities, and the hard facts of geography and economics, the sole guarantee against an early repetition of the horrors of the present war.'[95] It was this ideal which inspired many of the young men employed in the negotiating apparatus. As Nicolson later remarked, 'I thought only in terms of the New Europe.'[96] The core of supporters of this view within the foreign policy machinery were located in the PID, with several of its members contributing to the *New Europe*, including the Leepers, Headlam-Morley, Toynbee, Namier, and Percy. Allen Leeper and Nicolson in particular continually consulted Seton-Watson during the peace conference.[97] As a result of these strong links the PID in particular became the nucleus within the diplomatic machinery for a vision of Europe suited to the conditions of the post-war world. The link they forged during the negotiations with Eyre Crowe provided the hard practical edge to their general ideals, and helped to convert political philosophy into diplomatic strategy.

Crowe came into contact with the PID during the preparatory phase, and this connection evolved at Paris. Crowe was not directly involved with the *New Europe*, but there was a similarity of ideas between Crowe, one of the outstanding diplomatists in British history, and the New Europe group. While Crowe dismissed the more idealistic aims of the group as impracticable and unworkable, he was deeply concerned about the altered nature of the international system in the aftermath of the Great War and how the British Empire would

[95] *The New Europe*, i: 1 (19 Oct. 1916), 1.

[96] Nicolson, *Peacemaking 1919*, p. 209.

[97] Ibid. 126. Seton-Watson expressed his own high opinion of these experts in R. W. Seton-Watson, *Treaty Revision and the Hungarian Frontiers* (London, 1934), p. 22.

secure itself in this new world. Crowe recognized the significance of the emergence of the new states based on roughly
national lines for the future European balance of power, and he
knew that Britain would have to find a way to utilize this
situation. Crowe unquestionably emerges as the driving force
within the British delegation. By mid-March Hardinge was
thoroughly disillusioned and as he began to recede as a major
figure in Foreign Office activities, so Eyre Crowe began to
emerge as the dominant individual within the diplomatic
section of the delegation. It was Crowe who oversaw the remarkable resurgence in Foreign Office influence, and his
demonstrated ability at Paris did much to lift him from the diplomatic doldrums to which wartime hysteria had consigned him.
One of his colleagues commented of Crowe's performance as
head of the British delegation at the very end of the conference,
'It is no exaggeration to say that he dominates that Assembly
and that there is hardly any limit to his power of making his
colleagues accept his proposals.'[98] At Paris he worked closely
with the available PID experts, and they in turn acquired an
admiration for him bordering on hero worship. Nicolson, who
dedicated his history of the peace conference to Crowe, wrote,
'He was so human. He was so super-human.'[99] Allen Leeper
told his brother that 'One of the discoveries of the whole thing
to me was the great charm of Crowe: he *is* a splendid person &
so frightfully nice to his juniors even when he is most obstinate
(which is not seldom). But he has extraordinary skill in
negotiation & apart from that he is such an entirely honest &
kind hearted man that one likes him through & through.'[100]
The idealists of the New Europe engaged in the reality of diplomacy at Paris learnt pragmatism from Crowe, while Crowe
seems to have absorbed some of their idealism into his *realpolitik*. The combination did much to determine the face of
modern Europe.

[98] Norman to Campbell, 18 Dec. 1919. FO 794/2.
[99] Nicolson, *Peacemaking 1919*, p. 211.
[100] A. W. A. Leeper to R. W. A. Leeper, 9 Mar. 1919. AWAL.

PART II

The Evolution of Diplomatic Strategy

4

The European Settlement

> We started full of confidence to draft memoranda giving
> our views as to how best to deal with the innumerable and
> complex problems involved.
>
> Lord Howard of Penrith, *Theatre of Life*, ii. 275

It was in Europe that the war had primarily been fought and in Europe therefore that the peace had to be successfully won. The fall of the dynasties and the rise of several new national states had already radically altered the face of the Continent. The breadth of the topics which would have to be discussed ensured that this would be no ordinary peace conference. Time would be at a premium once the conference began, and as Headlam-Morley commented in discussing Eastern Europe, 'It is . . . important that His Majesty's Government should have at their disposal full information with regard to these matters, and with this object the following [PID] memoranda have been drawn up.'[1] Such information would give the negotiators an edge in the talks which in turn would assist Britain to obtain the most advantageous settlement.

The main burden of the preparatory work fell on the Political Intelligence Department. For this assignment the PID had been reorganized into nine sections, three of which were assigned to European questions. Headlam-Morley in a note on the PID's memoranda intended for General Smuts observed

that nothing less than a bold handling of the settlement from the broadest constructive point of view can be expected to satisfy public opinion in the Western democracies. If H.M.G. do not themselves take the lead in raising questions of ultimate international policy far

---

[1] FO 371/4353/f23/PC55.

beyond the points immediately affecting British interests, that lead will be taken by the United States or by international labour.[2]

This paragraph was struck out by Sir Eyre Crowe as unsuitable for a Foreign Office paper, but it reflects the motivation of the PID.[3]

On 19 November Headlam-Morley submitted a memorandum on the European settlement which attempted to deal with questions and principles common to the European negotiations.[4] He drew a clear distinction between the European and non-European peace settlements, as Great Britain had no territorial claims to press in Europe. What it desired was 'peace and order and open facilities for trade'. These were of course traditional British aims on the Continent, and anything which might involve Britain in another great Continental war was to be avoided. Headlam-Morley divided Britain's general concerns in the negotiations into four main topics: the balance of power, the security of the opposing coastline, the territorial redistribution, and an international guarantee for free commercial intercourse. On a strategic level the security of the coastline opposite Britain was of primary importance. Due care had to be taken to ensure that neither France nor Germany would in future be able to extend their control over this region. Otherwise Headlam-Morley noted that territorial questions of interest to Britain were almost totally confined to Eastern Europe.

Headlam-Morley was very much in accord with the aims of the *New Europe*, views which are often wrongly lumped together with Wilsonism. While there was unquestionably real support for such proposals as a League of Nations, followers of New Europe ideas were concerned about the implications of the collapse of the old order on the future structure of European power. There were principles inherent in the old system which could assist the new, and one of these was the balance of

[2] FO 371/4353/f23/PC23, Headlam-Morley and Percy, 'The United Settlement', Nov. 1918. Meant as an introduction to the Foreign Office memoranda. Also in CAB 29/2/P.-53.

[3] Ibid., Minute by Crowe, 23 Nov. 1918.

[4] FO 371/4353/f23/PC55, Headlam-Morley, 'The Settlement: Europe', 15 Nov. 1918. Originally put forward as a draft instruction for the Foreign Office. Also in CAB 29/2/P.-52.

power. Headlam-Morley observed that 'It is to be regretted that public opinion appears to countenance the view that the doctrine of the Balance of Power can be neglected. It is, and will remain, a fundamental point just as much after the establishment of a League of Nations as it has been before.'[5] His interpretation of the balance of power followed traditional British thinking on the matter, which was to prevent a single power dominating the Continent. Headlam-Morley had already written forcefully in the *New Europe* on what he believed was the German alternative, commenting that German

statesmen and historians alike are never tired of telling us that that for which their people are fighting is a Europe which shall be free from the English doctrines of the balance of power, a Europe that is in which one state shall become so powerful as, under whatever form it may be, to dominate the whole. For this they require a formula; all men require formulas, none so much as the Germans, and their formula is *Mittel-Europe*.[6]

Headlam-Morley concluded that the result of German policy would be that 'the balance of power in Europe will be gone; there will be substituted for it the balance of power in the world'.[7] In other words Germany would dominate Europe.

With the collapse of German aspirations Headlam-Morley and others were concerned to insure Europe against future threats of preponderance by a single state. He noted that in the past British policy had achieved this by maintaining the full independence of the different states. The adaptation required by the radically altered situation was simple, as Headlam-Morley observed, 'now our object is to establish national States'.[8] Such states would, it was hoped, be more durable than the old states produced by historical accident and without any true cohesion. This marriage of the balance of power to the concept of national self-determination was in Britain's best interests, as Headlam-Morley concluded: 'In this matter our interests entirely coincide with the principle of nationality and the doctrine of self-determination, though there must be very great difficulties in applying it.' Headlam-Morley was indeed aware that in the new Europe there would continue to be

[5] Ibid.
[6] 'Mittel-Europe Again', *New Europe*, 6:74 (14 Mar. 1918), 257–63.
[7] Ibid.   [8] FO 371/44353/f23/PC55.

security threats, accurately predicting that 'So far as it is possible to foretell the future, if Europe were more or less divided
into national States, there are two, and two only, which, as a
result of their great population and internal strength, might
become a danger to the independence of others. These are
Germany and Russia.'[9] A properly maintained balance of
power could, however, prevent such disequilibrium. Nicolson
later recalled that 'Benes taught me that the Balance of Power
was not necessarily a shameful, but possibly a scientific, thing.
He showed me that only upon the firm basis of such a balance
could the fluids of European amity pass and repass without
interruption.'[10] The experts saw the balance of power as a
delicate mechanism for ensuring equilibrium and peace on the
Continent, which was not only a historic British aim, but a vital
necessity for the future.

Western Europe

Germany was Britain's prime adversary throughout the war,
and its frontiers and international influence concerned all three
of the PID's European sections.[11] Headlam-Morley prepared a
memorandum which pulled together most of the issues central
to the German settlement, the broad outlines of which were simple enough.[12] The range of Allied demands against Germany
was restricted by Germany's agreement to the Armistice on
the understanding that any subsequent peace treaty would
be in accord with Wilson's Fourteen Points. Headlam-Morley
did point out that 'it is entirely an obligation of honour and not
one which we can by force be compelled to regard'.[13] Certainly
in the final treaty this pledge was honoured more as an exception than as the rule. Headlam-Morley cited two territorial
demands clearly agreed upon by the Allies, the return of
Alsace-Lorraine to France and the cession of the Polish districts

[9] FO 371/44353/f23/PC55.   [10] H. Nicolson, *Peacemaking 1919* (London,
1933), p. 210.
[11] Although Crowe was responsible for Western Europe he was concerned
that no one was co-ordinating the overall case in regard to Germany. Crowe
mentioned this to Hardinge on 27 Nov. 1918, and shortly after he was given
this responsibility in addition to his other duties. FO 371/4354/f56/PC56.
[12] Ibid., 'Memorandum on the Settlement with Germany', Nov. 1918.
[13] Ibid.

of Prussia to the new Polish state. Headlam-Morley also enumerated four areas to be discussed on the basis of national
self-determination; Memelland, the cession of Malmédy to
Belgium, the transfer of North Schleswig to Denmark, and the
incorporation of German Austria into Germany. Each of these
was in itself the subject of a separate memorandum.

Headlam-Morley recommended that Britain should not take
a position on the question of Memelland, but should support
Lithuania if it put forward a claim. Sir Esme Howard, chief of
the Northern Europe section, advocated the outright cession of
the region to Lithuania.[14] Crowe, who was co-ordinating the
German brief, interceded in this discussion with the more
classical opinion that he 'would strongly advise our not pulling
the chestnuts out of the fire for the Poles or Lithuania. Let them
worry the other powers first and let us reserve our opinion
when we see how the situation develops',[15] a view with which
Lord Hardinge concurred.[16]

On the question of Germany's western frontiers there was
general support for Belgian claims to Malmédy, though its
claims against the Netherlands were more troublesome.[17]
Belgium coveted the Scheldt, along with a large slice of Dutch
Flanders. Crowe saw no need to explore this topic in depth
since it was unlikely that the Dutch would cede any territory,
especially that inhabited by Dutchmen, and he pointed out
that the Netherlands was a neutral and not a belligerent state
and could not be ordered about by the Allies, as the matter of
extraditing the Kaiser subsequently proved.[18] The Scheldt
question illustrates some of the difficulties facing the PID in its
co-ordination of material for the conference. Headlam-Morley

[14] Ibid., Esme Howard, 'Note on Mr. Headlam-Morley's memorandum re:
Settlement of Germany', 29 Nov. 1918.

[15] Ibid., Minute by Crowe, 30 Nov. 1918.

[16] Ibid., Minute by Hardinge, undated.

[17] There was also general agreement that Belgium should have the neutral
district of Moresnet, which had been overlooked at the Congress of Vienna.
See Sally Marks, *Innocent Abroad: Belgium at the Paris Peace Conference of 1919*
(Chapel Hill, NC, 1981), pp. 144–7.

[18] FO 371/4353/f27/PC95, Minute by Crowe, 21 Nov. 1918. Hardinge had
commented on the problem, 'I fail to see on what reasonable grounds we
could press Holland to make territorial concessions to Belgium.' FO
371/4353/f27/PC69.

had underlined the importance of the coast opposite Britain in his memorandum on the European settlement. The PID's resources were under great strain at this time, and the department suffered from the lack of anyone working on Dutch affairs. Eventually the services of E. H. Carr were obtained from the regular Office establishment to prepare a report on 'The Scheldt Question'.[19] In the discussion on Carr's report Hardinge suggested that the Admiralty's view should be ascertained, but Tyrrell acidly pointed out in a minute to Crowe, 'I am not hopeful of getting an authoritative answer from the Admiralty having tried for 3 years, but your persuasive powers may be greater. What about trying through D.N.I.?'[20] Eventually Crowe by working through Admiral Hall was able to prise loose the Admiralty's opinion, and it finally concluded that British policy should be to support a return to the *status quo ante bellum*, with the Scheldt being closed to ships of war.[21]

On the question of Germany's northern frontiers, the fate of North Schleswig showed the potential for departmental overlap. The PID issued a memorandum of 'The Slesvig Question' on 4 December, and the next day Military Intelligence released a report on the same topic. Although both departments tried to co-operate, and did exchange reports, Fullerton-Carnegie could not refrain from commenting that 'There is a sad duplication of labour in these memos'.[22] The reports do, however, show that there was a consensus of opinion on North Schleswig, with both offices supporting approximately the same solution. This involved the return of the Danish-populated regions, with plebiscites to be held in questionable areas. The proposed frontier ran through thinly populated marsh, heath, and woodland, which formed a natural frontier. The restrained nature of Danish claims, limited only to the ethnically Danish

[19] FO 371/4355/f77/PC77, E. H. Carr, 'The Scheldt Qustion' (P.20), 4 Dec. 1918. Also in CAB 29/2/P-61.

[20] Ibid., Minute by Tyrrell, 9 Dec. 1918.

[21] The final Admiralty views were expressed in the Board's 'Notes on Matters Affecting Naval Interests Connected with the Peace Settlement', Jan. 1919 (3rd revise). ADM 167/57.

[22] FO 371/4355/f76/PC123, Minute by Carnegie, 5 Dec. 1918.

portions of the duchy lost in 1864, made such interdepart-mental agreement easier.[23]

The question of an Austro-German union in contrast was a particularly vexing one. To oppose such a move after the Allied statements on national self-determination would discredit the supposed ideal of the New Diplomacy. The Allies, however, had no wish to create a potentially stronger new Germany. Namier, one of those strongly opposed to the Habsburg regime, nevertheless observed that

We cannot exterminate the Austrian Germans; we cannot make them cease to feel Germans. They are bound to be somewhere. Nothing would be gained by compelling them to lead an existence separate from that of Germany. Such enforced separation would merely stimulate German nationalism, but could not prevent co-operation between the two branches nor their final reunion.[24]

This was an opinion with which Hardinge was in full agree-ment, commenting in a minute on another memorandum on the same subject that 'If German Austria wishes to join Ger-many no clause in the Treaty of Peace will prevent its ultimate consummation'.[25] This summed up the general consensus, that at best the Allies could hinder an anschluss, but they could not halt it. Headlam-Morley in his summary of Britain's negotiating position advised that an Austrian request for in-corporation should be agreed to in the peace treaty.[26] Common to all the reports on this question was an assumption that such a union would dilute what were seen as dangerous Prussian influences on German society. The idea of preventing an an-schluss was dismissed, 'both on the grounds of principle and of expediency'.[27] The general opinion at this stage reflects support for the old idea of a *Kleindeutsche Lösung*.

[23] FO 371/4355/f76/PC76, Carnegie, 'The Slesvig Question', 4 Dec. 1918. FO 371/4355/f76/PC123, Pickthorn, 'Recent Evidence on the Slesvig Question', 5 Dec. 1918.

[24] FO 371/4355/f90/PC90, Namier, 'German Austria', Dec. 1918.

[25] FO 371/4354/f65/PC65, Minute by Hardinge, undated.

[26] FO 371/4353/f23/PC55, Namier also supported Austrian claims to Burgenland, the heavily German province of Hungary bordering Austria. FO 371/4355/f90/PC90.

[27] FO 371/4355/f68/PC68, 'South-Eastern Europe and the Balkans', 13 Dec. 1918. Namier's earlier memorandum on 'German Austria' was amalgamated in this, with minor modifications as to detail.

Eastern Europe

It was the Eastern European settlement which lay at the heart of any successful peace plan for Europe, for as Headlam-Morley pointedly noted,

In Eastern Europe ... the territorial problem is that which will assume the first importance, and the future peace of the world will depend on the method in which this will be settled. . . . the Germans in Bohemia and the Magyars must be treated on exactly the same principle as the Czechs and the Romanians.[28]

Headlam-Morley was an advocate of a peace based on Wilsonian–New Europe principles. As Britain had no interests directly antagonistic to these successor states, Headlam-Morley believed that London could enhance its stature by assuming the role of 'honest broker'. In this mediating role he believed it could expect the 'cordial co-operation of the United States'.[29] Headlam-Morley admitted that the motives behind such a policy were not wholly altruistic, for 'It is needless to say that the position is one which will give an unprecedented opportunity for the legitimate extension of British influence'.[30] A fund of goodwill built up now would pay dividends for Britain in the future.

The brief over most of Eastern Europe was co-ordinated by Sir Ralph Paget, aided by Allen Leeper, Nicolson, Namier, and Powell. The PID was hampered by the lack of an expert working specifically on Austro-Hungarian affairs, a gap left by the failure to secure the transfer of Seton-Watson to the department. Headlam-Morley, looking back on the PID's activities at this time, recalled that the absence of such a person 'was a grave want which was severely felt when the critical situation arose at the end of the war and in consequence important work was left undone'.[31] Nevertheless the PID did produce a number of crucially important reports on the region and it was here that the experts gathered together in the Foreign Office probably had their greatest impact on the territorial settlement.

The PID has generally been considered by historians to have been a hotbed of anti-Habsburg opinion, and the association of many of its most important members with the *New Europe* adds

---

[28] FO 371/4353/f23/PC55.   [29] Ibid.   [30] Ibid.
[31] FO 371/4382/PID619.

weight to this view. In the opinion of one historian, 'The arch-foes of the [Habsburg] Monarchy remained without a foothold in the Foreign Office until the setting up of the Political Intelligence Department in 1918',[32] while another historian believes that the PID's proposed policies were effective because 'They were the only ones who had firm ideas and a detailed knowledge to offer for its execution'.[33] Certainly opinion was split within government circles between those who favoured the nationalist movements and those who preferred merely to reform the Empire. The very completeness of the Dual Monarchy's collapse at the war's end and the proclamation of the new national states healed this rift among the policy makers. There was a general consensus in London that a power vacuum should not be allowed to occur and it was hoped that the most useful of the common links between the successor states would not be broken and that some form of customs or economic union might be effected.[34]

The situation in Central Europe became exceedingly fluid and increasingly complex when the Habsburg Empire foundered in October 1918, and the internal collapse of the Dual Monarchy fundamentally altered the nature of post-war planning for the region. While President Wilson had only spoken in his Fourteen Points of 'the freest opportunity of autonomous development' for the peoples of Austria-Hungary, the Allies were now faced with the often competing claims of six successor states. It was to Seton-Watson that Headlam-Morley turned for a report on the new situation.[35] In his report on

[32] V. H. Rothwell, *British War Aims and Peace Diplomacy, 1914–1918* (Oxford, 1971), p. 224.

[33] Wilfried Fest, *Peace or Partition: The Hapsburg Monarchy and British Policy* (London, 1978), p. 224.

[34] On the attitudes towards Austria-Hungary see K. J. Calder, *Britain and the Origins of the New Europe, 1914–1918* (Cambridge, 1976); Rothwell, *British War Aims*, pp. 221–8; Fest; and H. Seton-Watson and C. Seton-Watson, *The Making of a New Europe: R. W. Seton-Watson and the Last Years of Austria-Hungary* (London, 1981).

[35] FO 371/4354/f52/PC52. Seton-Watson, 'Austria-Hungary: The Legal Factors Replacing the Dual Monarchy', Nov. 1918. It was later amalgamated with the comprehensive memorandum on 'South-Eastern Europe and the Balkans' (FO 371/4355/f68/PC68). It was printed as a cabinet paper on 13 Dec. 1918, CAB 29/2/P-51. Also reprinted in *R. W. Seton-Watson and the Yugoslavs* (2 vols., London and Zagreb, 1976), Doc. 249.

Austria-Hungary, submitted at the end of November, Seton-Watson opens with the dramatic statement, 'Austria-Hungary has ceased to exist'.[36] In Seton-Watson's view,

The only logical principle upon which the Governments of the Entente can act in their relations with the former Dual Monarchy is a recognition of the duly accredited National Assemblies of each of the above nations (German-Austrians, Magyars, Czechoslovaks, Jugoslavs, Poles, Roumanians, and Ukrainians — it being assumed in all this that the Italian Irredentist populations are automatically united with Italy) and of their National Councils as possessing mandates from them.[37]

Of these states Seton-Watson did not believe that Austria, Hungary, and Czechoslovakia could be denied a place at the peace conference, while the others would be represented by the countries with which they wished to be united.[38]

In a separate memorandum on 'The Future Frontiers of Hungary' Seton-Watson supported the idea of national unity for the Czechoslovaks, Romanians, and Yugoslavs, together with special guarantees for the rights of minorities.[39] He recognized that there were certain 'grey areas' on the borders of the new states, and recommended that the frontiers in these regions should be delineated by boundary commissions, while in the mean time placing them under international control. He hoped that this would have the effect of 'allaying inter-racial friction'.[40] Seton-Watson's proposals, could not completely avoid the problem of creating pockets of minorities. His proposed Hungarian-Romanian frontier left 600,000 to 700,000

[36] FO 371/4354/f52/PC52.   [37] Ibid.

[38] This memorandum was reprinted in *MPC* II. 588–91. He considered the reports lucid and reliable on the irreparable disintegration of the Empire. Seton-Watson's biographers have commented on Lloyd George's opinion, 'In the climate of 1938, when the peace settlement of 1919 was widely held responsible for the imminence of a second war, Lloyd George was anxious to underplay his responsibility for that settlement by demonstrating — what was true — that the disappearance of Austria-Hungary was a *fait accompli* long before the peacemakers assembled in Paris.' Seton-Watson and Seton-Watson, *The Making of a New Europe*, p. 332.

[39] FO 371/4354/f52/PC52, Seton-Watson, 'Frontier Delineation between Hungary and her Neighbours', Nov. 1918. Also in CAB 29/2/P-66, Annex I, and in *R. W. Seton-Watson and the Yugoslavs*, Doc. 249. It was later amalgamated in 'South-Eastern Europe and the Balkans', FO 371/4355/f52/PC52.

[40] Ibid.

Magyars in Romania. Recognizing this, he called for 'a definite charter, assuring to all certain definite linguistic rights in church, school, and law courts'.[41] The protection of minority rights was a matter which was presented in several of the PID's memoranda, particularly in relation to Eastern Europe.[42]

The PID memorandum on 'South-Eastern Europe and the Balkans' was one of the most comprehensive reports produced by the department.[43] Prepared by Allen Leeper and Harold Nicolson, and amalgamating reports by R. W. Seton-Watson and Lewis Namier, it was a country by country assessment of possible terms of peace. The principle of national self-determination was generally adhered to by the authors, if for no other reason than that they considered that it offered the greatest possible opportunity for long-term peace.

Leeper and Nicolson opened their comprehensive report with a statement of the principles which it was believed should guide the settlement, and which simultaneously show their New Europe views. The aim of the peace should be 'To obtain a just permanent settlement based on the principles of nationality, self-determination, security, and free economic opportunity'.[44] They believed that a viable settlement must 'leave no avoidable cause for future friction' and that it should 'liberate the main economic routes and outlets in such a way as will draw the trade of Central Europe to the Mediterranean, while at the same time laying the foundation for a future Customs Union'.[45] Leeper and Nicolson supported the principles laid down by President Wilson in the eleventh of his Fourteen Points, which stated 'That the relations of the several Balkan States to one another should be determined by friendly counsel along historically established lines of allegiance and nationality, and international guarantees of the political and economic independence and territorial integrity of the several Balkan states should be entered into'. It was thought that 'These principles undoubtedly offer the best prospect of a

[41] Ibid.
[42] On Seton-Watson's memorandum see Seton-Watson and Seton-Watson, *The Making of a New Europe*, pp. 324, 332.
[43] FO 371/4355/f68/PC68, Leeper and Nicolson, 'South-Eastern Europe and the Balkans', 13 Dec. 1918.
[44] Ibid.   [45] Ibid.

permanent peace in South-Eastern Europe, and as such are the most desirable and advantageous from the point of view of British interests'.[46] They warned, however, that 'In the matter of territorial divisions too pedantic a formula should not be followed based on racial and linguistic affinity, but so far as possible the desires of the inhabitants themselves should be ascertained'.[47] Leeper and Nicolson's territorial proposals were for the most part extremely well drawn, and in retrospect were among the best to be suggested.

Bulgaria was to be treated leniently in comparison with the other defeated states although, 'Strictly speaking, Bulgaria is not entitled to any consideration from the Allies'.[48] To penalize Bulgaria would, however, 'leave in the Balkans a centre of discontent which would most certainly result in a disturbance of the peace at some future date'.[49] It was suggested that should Yugoslavia and Romania both obtain their ethnic irredenta, the Southern Dobrudja lost by Bulgaria in the Second Balkan War should be returned. Bulgaria, though, would lose its Aegean coastline, with its admittedly miserable little port of Dedéagach. It was thought that continued Bulgarian access to the Aegean could be maintained by granting Bulgaria transit rights to Dedéagach, which would become a free port. The authors acknowledged that this solution could not eradicate all Bulgarian resentment, and suggested that similar port facilities could be made available at Salonica and Kavalla. This view was shared by H. W. V. Temperley of M.I.2(e), who in a note on the subject of Bulgarian access to the Aegean recommended that Bulgarian economic aspirations could best be met by making Kavalla a free port and internationalizing the Straits. He readily accepted that such a solution would not match Bulgaria's political ambitions.[50]

A harsher view on Bulgarian claims was taken by R. G. D. Laffan, one of Temperley's colleagues. He noted that 'Bulgaria has shown herself a treacherous ally in 1913 and 1918, and a brutal conqueror. Should her claims, therefore, conflict with equally well substantiated claims of our Allies,

---

[46] FO 371/4355/f68/PC 68.   [47] Ibid.   [48] Ibid.   [49] Ibid.

[50] FO 371/4356/f135/PC135, Temperley, 'Notes on the Claims of Bulgaria to an Outlet on the Aegean Sea', 1 Oct. 1918.

the former may be dismissed.'[51] Laffan recognized that the Allies were committed to a peace on the basis of nationality, and recommended that where Bulgarian claims were justified and did not conflict with vital Allied interests, they should be agreed to.

Albania, which had only become independent in 1913, presented a problem of a different nature. Its constitution had been arranged by the Great Powers in 1913 in a settlement which was now obsolete.[52] Three options were proposed by the PID. The first would involve a Serbo-Greek partition of the country, leaving a rump Muslim Albania. This, however, would not only violate the theory of national self-determination, but would certainly be unacceptable to the Italians. The second solution would leave Albania with virtually the same frontiers as in 1913, though Serbia and Montenegro would be allowed to advance up to the Drin, while Greece annexed the region between the Voiussa and Valona. This solution suffered from the same defects as the first.

The third solution, and the one clearly favoured by the philhellenic PID, involved no frontier changes in the north, but with Greece obtaining a large slice of northern Epirus, while Italian aspirations would be met with a mandate over the remainder. Recommendations were also made for the future internal organization of Albania, where a cantonal system was thought most likely to reconcile tribal and religious differences, and an Italian prince, possibly the Duke of Abruzzi, could be given the throne.[53] In return the Italians would be required to agree to the neutralization of the Albanian coast and the Corfu channel. This in turn would benefit Britain by preventing the Italians from turning the Adriatic into an Italian lake, while allowing them the dubious glory of ruling Albania. Temperley

[51] FO 371/4356/f193/PC193, Laffan, 'Notes on Bulgarian Territorial Aspirations', 27 Dec. 1918. Also in Webster Papers 3/7/6.

[52] Albanian independence was recognized by the Council of Ambassadors meeting in London on 29 July 1913. A boundary commission was sent out, but never fully reported on the north and north-eastern frontiers.

[53] Wilhelm zu Wied (1876–1945) had been the first *mbret* (prince), but ruled in Albania only from Mar. to Sept. 1913. He served in the German army during the First World War. Luigi, Duke of Abruzzi (1873–1933) was grandson of Victor Emmanuel I of Italy, and 3rd son of Amadeo, Duke of Aosta and King of Spain (1870–3).

in a separate General Staff report reached virtually the same conclusions as the PID experts, with some minor differences about where to draw the Albanian–Greek frontier.[54] Their conclusions were similar enough for Nicolson to comment 'It is satisfactory, however, to see that the D.M.I. & the F.O. are agreed as regards essentials.'[55]

The question which Leeper and Nicolson found 'the most important of racial and territorial questions in South-Eastern Europe is that connected with the Jugoslav peoples'.[56] In common with Seton-Watson and the views expressed in the *New Europe* they strongly advocated a united Yugoslavia, either as a monarchy under the Karageorgevitch dynasty, or as a republic. It was hoped that Serbia and Romania could agree as to the frontier in the Banat, but as events developed Leeper was to spend a great deal of his time at the peace conference working out the details of this frontier. As regards the question of the Adriatic frontier which was subsequently to bedevil the conference, Leeper and Nicolson said little, assuming that Britain was bound by the 1915 Treaty of London.[57]

The problem of Montenegro was particularly sticky. Union with the new Yugoslav state was clearly thought desirable, but the king of Montenegro was unlikely to agree to losing his throne. Leeper and Nicolson suggested that given King Nicholas's questionable actions during the war he merited little from the Allies, and they proposed that an international commission should be sent to Montenegro to determine the wishes of the inhabitants, thereby minimizing problems with the king. The inclusion of Montenegro within the new Yugoslav state was clearly important, not only in terms of ethnicity, but for creating a viable country.

As regards Romania, Leeper and Nicolson suggested that 'The frontiers of the new state [are] to be drawn as far as

[54] FO 371/4356/f137/PC137, Temperley, 'The Proposed Settlement for Albania', 17 Sept. 1918. Also in Webster Papers 3/7/3.
[55] FO 371/4355/f68/PC68.   [56] Ibid.
[57] An excellent analysis of the problems caused by this issue is Sterling J. Kernek, 'Woodrow Wilson and National Self-Determination Along Italy's Frontier: A Study of the Manipulation of Principles in the Pursuit of Political Interests', *Proceedings of the American Philosophical Society*, 126:4 (1982), 243–300.

possible on ethnical lines, and not on those of the 1916 Treaty'.[58] Bessarabia was to have the right of self-determination, and as previously mentioned the Southern Dobrudja was to be returned to Bulgaria. The Romanian claim to all Bukovina was not accepted, instead it was thought that the province should be divided between Romania and the Ukraine along the Seret. Leeper was the leading expert on Romania, having also written the Historical Section handbook on Bessarabia. Arland and Sumner of Military Intelligence proposed that in the final settlement with Russia, Romanian claims to Bessarabia should be acknowledged up to the route of the Czernowitz–Kiev railway, and that British support for Romanian claims in Bessarabia should be used to get Romania to modify its claims in the Banat.[59]

Both Leeper and Nicolson were ardent philhellenes and both wished to see Greece receive a substantial amount of its irredenta. They envisaged Greece as the dominant Aegean power, suggesting that it should receive an Anatolian enclave around Smyrna, that the Dodecanese should be ceded by Italy, although they anticipated Italian reluctance, and that Greece should receive Bulgaria's Aegean littoral. In addition they indicated tentative support for Greek claims to northern Epirus, pending further investigation, and even discussed the idea of Britain ceding Cyprus to Greece. Toynbee was already concerned at this stage about the implications of a Greek Smyrna enclave, and recommended that Greece should receive Eastern Thrace instead. The result would be a contiguous and therefore more stable Greek state.[60] Toynbee at this stage was still numbered among the philhellenes, but his concerns over the longer term implications of a dispersed Greek state on regional stability are already in evidence. The vision of a Greater Greece was a powerful one, though, with deep romantic and

[58] Ibid.

[59] FO 371/4356/f166/PC166, Arland and Sumner, 'Notes on the Frontier of Bessarabia', 20 Dec. 1918. On Romanian frontier questions see Sherman D. Spector, *Rumania at the Paris Peace Conference: A Study in the Diplomacy of Ioan I. C. Bratianu* (New York, 1962). Also R. G. D. Laffan, 'Romania and the Redemption of the Romanians', in H. W. V. Temperley, ed., *A History of the Paris Peace Conference* (6 vols., London, 1920–4), iv. 213–36.

[60] FO 371/4356/f162/PC162, Toynbee, 'Memorandum on Alternative Territorial Settlements in Thrace and the Straits', 31 Dec. 1919.

political roots in Britain, and at the peace conference a phil-hellenic grouping emerged within the British delegation which pushed through a settlement much in Greece's favour.

Considering the strong links between the New Europe group and the Czech leadership it is not surprising that recognition of Czechoslovakia was strongly supported by members of the PID.[61] Namier, who contributed the section on Czechoslovakia to the memorandum on South-Eastern Europe and the Balkans, wrote, 'The Czechs have been throughout the war our most devoted and efficient Allies in Eastern and Central Europe, and in the very process of their recent revolution have proved themselves a nation capable of carrying on an orderly government in the most difficult circumstances.'[62] Through strongly supporting the principle of national self-determination the report recommends against a plebiscite in the Germanic portions of Bohemia and Moravia, fearing that the Czechs might lose some strategic districts.

Namier tried to create a mental image of the geographical situation by pointing out that 'The Bohemian mountain bastion is one of the most striking features of the map of Europe; its unity is almost as clearly marked as that of an island.'[63] With wonderful understatement he then goes on to note, 'On the other hand, it is obvious that the inclusion in the new Czecho-Slovak State of a large German minority inhabiting districts contiguous on German territory is extremely inconvenient, if not downright dangerous, to the Czechs . . . .'[64] It was suggested therefore that the Allies should try to reconcile the two peoples as far as possible to the new situation.

Namier in his minute on Leeper and Nicolson's report raised a suggestion originally put forward by Lord Eustace Percy for the protection of minorities in South-Eastern Europe. He proposed a multinational commission of inquiry to develop safeguards for the minorities in the Balkans.[65] Lord Robert Cecil was interested in the idea and called for a memorandum on cultural autonomy as well as a detailed report on the actual minorities involved in the Balkan settlement. Cecil added with some asperity that 'As usual I do not

---

[61] See Seton-Watson and Seton-Watson, *The Making of a New Europe.*
[62] FO 371/4355/f68/PC68.
[63] Ibid.   [64] Ibid.   [65] Ibid., Minute by Paget, 31 Dec. 1918.

want comments or arguments, still less rhetoric but FACTS.'[66] This suggests that he did not fully approve of the more strident passages in some of the PID's work.

A report on 'Minority Rights' had already been submitted by E. H. Carr in mid-November in which he suggested that inducements should be offered to minorities to migrate to their own national states, though compulsion was out of the question.[67] Howard approved of the report and had it circulated. Headlam-Morley did point out two particular difficulties, noting the need to recognize the Jews as a nationality, and mentioning that the exact method of protection seemed a bit vague.[68] His comments foreshadow the insertion of minority protection clauses into the treaties with the new states of Europe.[69]

The question of Italian claims was bound up with the 1915 Treaty of London under which Britain had agreed to recognize Italian claims to the Trentino, the Southern Tyrol up to the Brenner Pass, Trieste, and the Istrian peninsula to the outskirts of Fiume. It was Hardinge's view that 'We stand pledged to our word, & it is not for us to suggest any modifications of our engagements, except of course in the case of a decision by the contracting Powers to take them into consideration'.[70] Paget agreed with Hardinge's view, though he did note, 'But there is no doubt that the pledges given to Italy constitute a flagrant violation of a settlement according to nationalities and my idea therefore was that we should in the first instance call the attention of the Italians to this in a friendly and confidential manner.'[71] The experts assigned to Paget were also sceptical about allowing excessive Italian claims to irredenta. The memorandum on Italian claims was written by Leeper and Nicolson, and while they recognized that the government was bound by its treaty commitments, they suggested that the Italians should

---

[66] Ibid., Minute by Cecil, undated.

[67] FO 371/4353/f33/PC33, Carr, 'Minority Nationalities', 20 Nov. 1918.

[68] Ibid., Minute by Headlam-Morley, 20 Nov. 1918.

[69] See Alan Sharp, 'Britain and the Protection of Minorities at the Paris Peace Conference', in A. C. Hepburn, ed., *Minorities in History* (London, 1978), pp. 170–88.

[70] FO 371/4356/f177/PC177, Hardinge to Tyrrell, 10 Dec. 1918.

[71] Ibid., Minute by Paget, 11 Dec. 1918.

be informed that it would be advantageous not to adhere too rigidly to the treaty.[72]

On the question of Italian claims to extend its northern frontiers to the Brenner Pass, Headlam-Morley commented, 'No question which will come up for decision at the Peace Conference presents such difficulties as the future of the Upper Valley of the Adige, for in regard to this, just as in regard to the Italian Yugo-Slav frontier, the British government is pledged to two inconsistent policies.'[73] He noted that if Germany and Austria united, Italy would need a strong frontier. As a possible compromise he put forward the idea of an independent Tyrol, which would be something of a second Switzerland.

Charles Oman, professor of modern history at Oxford, who contributed a memorandum on Italy's northern frontiers, stoutly opposed Italian claims on the basis that 'giving Italy up to the Brenner on purely strategical grounds is inconsistent with all honest observance of our pledges. "Strategical grounds" are only less immoral than "compensations" from our point of view.'[74] Oman was advocating the new diplomacy in preference to the mechanisms of the old. Strategic considerations were still a reality, however. Gaining the Brenner was unquestionably important to Italy, but the question could have been put bluntly as to whether it was useful for Britain to see this vital pass come under the Italian tricolour. Certainly as the negotiations evolved it would have been useful if this point had not already been conceded by secret treaty but could have been deployed to counter the more extreme Italian demands.

Northern Europe and Russia

At Paris Russia's future role in world affairs was to perplex the negotiators. Russia was neither one of the defeated Central Powers, nor was it any longer one of the victorious Allies. The

[72] FO 371/4356/f131/PC131, Allen Leeper and Nicolson, 'The Question of Italian Claims', 18 Dec. 1918. Leeper noted in his diary on 10 Dec., 'Conference with Paget, Spicer, Harold N., & Arnold T. at 11:30 when my paper on Italian claims was discussed and passed.'

[73] FO 371/4353/f26/PC134, Headlam-Morley, 'Note on the Northern Frontier of Italy', 30 Dec. 1918.

[74] FO 371/4355/f98/PC98, note by C. Oman, 13 Dec. 1918.

collapse of the Russian Empire, the rise of the Bolshevik government, and the establishment of several national governments had altered the situation in Eastern Europe as greatly as had the collapse of the Hohenzollern and Habsburg empires. Finland, Poland, Estonia, Latvia, Lithuania, the Ukraine, Armenia, and Azerbaijan had all proclaimed their independence, with Romania annexing Bessarabia. This situation caused Esme Howard to observe in his diary, 'There is little positive to be said when one is dealing with something which is today hardly a geographical expression.'[75] The Allies would nevertheless have to consider the situation on the fringes of the old Romanov empire if any lasting settlement was to be achieved for Europe.

Sir Esme Howard, recently returned from the Stockholm embassy, was placed in charge of preparing the brief on Northern Europe. His experiences in Sweden during the war had made him familiar with Scandinavian, Baltic, and Russian affairs. In addition to his PID experts, Rex Leeper, J. Y. Simpson, and Edward Fullerton-Carnegie, the Foreign Office had assigned E. H. Carr and Michael Palairet to assist him.[76] Their central concern was of course Russia. Howard later recalled that 'Nothing could exceed my satisfaction at taking part in the Conference and nothing could have pleased me better than this particular job, though dealing with Russia, which was then in the throes of civil war between Russian 'Whites' and Bolsheviks was not an exhilarating prospect.'[77] The whole matter was complicated by the fact that as yet no state had recognized the government in power in Moscow.

[75] Howard of Penrith Diary, 30 Nov. 1918.
[76] Lord Howard of Penrith, *Theatre of Life*, vol. ii: *Life Seen from the Stalls* (London, 1936), p. 275. Howard thought very highly of Carr and Palairet in particular. (Charles) Michael Palairet (1882–1956); educ. Eton; entered Diplomatic Service, 1905; served Rome, Vienna, Paris, Athens, 1906–18; received into Roman Catholic Church, 1916; British Delegation, Paris, 1919; Minister to Romania, 1929–35, Sweden, 1935–7, Austria, 1937–8, Greece, 1939–42; Ambassador to Greece, 1942–3; assistant under-secretary, Foreign Office, 1943–5; KCMG, 1938. Edward Hallett Carr (1892–1982); educ. Trinity Coll., Cambridge; Foreign Office, 1916–36; Wilson Prof. of International Politics, Aberystwyth, 1936–47; Ministry of Information, 1939–40; Assistant Editor, *The Times*, 1940–6; tutor, Balliol Coll., 1953–5.
[77] Howard, *Theatre of Life*, p. 275.

The question of what to do about the Bolshevik government was of particular importance. Rex Leeper in a preliminary memorandum on 14 November 1918 had commented that 'Whatever may be the exact frontiers of Russia it is obvious that Russia in its present state of anarchy not only makes the League of Nations inadequate, but it is a grave menace to civilisation.'[78] He recommended, therefore, that the Allies either intervene militarily to establish a new democratic government, or alternatively that Russia should be ringed with armed forces and the Bolsheviks starved into submission. Rex Leeper's career was marked at both ends by dealings with Communist movements, starting with his role as adviser on what to do with Bolshevik Russia and ending three decades later as British ambassador to Greece during the civil war, and his views on how to cope with Communist insurgency show a notable consistency throughout.[79]

The PID in both its preliminary and final memoranda recommended a mild policy in any Russian settlement. Territorially this involved recognizing *de jure* what already existed *de facto*.[80] There was concern that a Russia which felt hard done by could potentially become a dangerous revisionist state, and Professor Simpson warned that Russia and Germany might be drawn together out of bitterness for the loss of territory and military defeat, a prediction proven at Rapallo in 1922.[81] Headlam-Morley accurately forecast that while Poland and Finland would remain independent, the Ukraine would revert to Russian control.[82] Clearly the PID was not short of experts who could gauge both the short-term and long-term international situation.

Howard's final memorandum, 'Russia', drew on the earlier versions submitted by Rex Leeper and Professor Simpson, supplemented by lengthy annotations from Headlam-Morley

[78] FO 371/4352/f13/PC13, R. W. A. Leeper, 'Russia', 14 Nov. 1918.

[79] Leeper's Greek experience is recounted in Sir Reginald Leeper, *When Greek Meets Greek* (London, 1950).

[80] FO 371/4352/f13/PC24, R. W. A. Leeper, 'Russia and the Peace Conference', 18 Nov. 1918. This replaced his report of 14 Nov.

[81] FO 371/4352/f13/PC57, Simpson, 'The Future of Russia and British Policy', 25 Nov. 1918. Simpson's proposals were similar to Leeper's, though he expressed his views with greater temperance.

[82] FO 371/4352/f13/PC13, Minute by Headlam-Morley, 15 Nov. 1918.

and Toynbee.[83] Dealing only with European Russia, Howard warned that the situation was still too nebulous for a policy to be decided upon and thought it best to wait upon events. Howard did recommend that it might be possible to deal with the Bolsheviks on a semi-official basis and to provide them with food, if they met certain conditions. These conditions were clearly fantastic and involved surrendering the Russian fleet for internment, the cessation of foreign propaganda activities, and the ousting of Lenin, Trotsky, and Zinoviev. Nevertheless it is significant that the idea of at least dealing with the Bolshevik government was raised in an important government briefing paper.

Russia's western frontier was of particular concern. It was undecided whether the Baltic provinces should be recognized as independent states, or whether they should be considered as part of a Russian federation. Rex Leeper and Alfred Zimmern strongly recommended the latter solution, but Howard disagreed, as he clearly favoured recognizing the independence of the Baltic provinces.[84] A linked concern was the future of the Åland Islands. Ethnically Swedish but geographically Finnish, the islands had been a key Russian military base. The new Finnish state was as yet unrecognized and under a cloud of suspicion from suspected Germanophile leanings. Within the PID Fullerton-Carnegie advocated Swedish sovereignty over the islands after a plebiscite, with a guarantee to Finland about the demilitarization of the islands.[85] Howard, the war-time ambassador to Stockholm, supported this view: 'Looking at the question from the point of view of British interests, it would appear that the claims of Sweden to these islands should be satisfied.'[86] This was due not only to Sweden's size

[83] FO 371/4352/f13/PC83, Howard, 'Russia', 5 Dec. 1918. This was sent to Smuts, although it had not yet been approved by Balfour. Also in CAB 29/2/P-64. A separate report dealt with Siberia.

[84] FO 371/4354/f37/PC64, R. W. A. Leeper and Zimmern, 'The Principle of Self-Determination and its Application to the Baltic Provinces', Nov. 1918, and minute by Howard, undated. See also O. Hovi, *The Baltic Area in British Policy, 1918–1921*, vol. i (Helsinki, 1980).

[85] FO 371/4355/f96/PC113, Carnegie, 'Memorandum on the Aland Islands', 12 Dec. 1918.

[86] FO 371/4354/f37/PC67. Howard, 'The Baltic Provinces and Lithuania', 28 Nov. 1918. Also in CAB 29/2/P-55.

and location, but to a fear that a reinvigorated Russia could reabsorb Finland and regain the islands. Military Intelligence, however, was ambivalent, suspecting that Sweden was just as susceptible to German influence as Finland, and therefore advocated staying out of the matter. This case shows the clear difference in analytical approach employed by the Foreign Office and the military. The former having noted the defeat of Germany, was now concerned about future adversaries, while the latter were still fixated on the now defunct German threat. In the end no definite memorandum on the question was produced. The peace conference itself was unable to resolve the issue, and left the matter to the League, where it provided the first successful test of the League machinery.[87]

A fair amount of attention was paid to Scandinavian affairs, as well as to the fate of coal-rich Spitsbergen. The Historical Section Handbook on the islands, one of the first to be completed, warned of the danger of a strong naval power obtaining Spitsbergen. Such a power would be independent of Britain for steam coal, 'and could construct a strong naval base on the Atlantic within sixty hours of the Firth of Forth'.[88] Such a fear smacks of the invasion hysteria prevalent before the war, and it undoubtedly influenced the final recommendations.[89] The general opinion arrived at in the Foreign Office and the Admiralty was that Norway should be given a demilitarized Spitsbergen, with certain reservations as to mining rights. This solution was eventually adopted at Paris.

Sir Esme Howard in the peace memorandum on Poland stated that 'the first necessity appears to be the creation of a strong compact Poland . . .'.[90] It was generally agreed that the core of the new state would be the Congress Kingdom of Poland created at the last great peace congress of 1814. Howard certainly considered Poland to be his 'most difficult problem', with the most complex questions being Polish access to the

[87] See James Barros, *The Aland Islands Question: Its Settlement by the League of Nations* (New Haven, Conn., 1968).

[88] FO 373/3/20.

[89] C. Andrew, *Secret Service: The Making of the British Intelligence Community* (London, 1985), chap. 1.

[90] FO 371/4354/f46/PC70, Howard, 'Poland', Nov. 1918. Also in CAB 29/2/P-71.

Baltic Sea and Polish claims to Eastern Galicia.[91] In the latter case Howard recommended a plebiscite, though in his opinion the best settlement from the viewpoint of the Western powers would be an independent Ruthenian state straddling the Carpathians, a view shared by the Americans. This solution would keep the strategically important Carpathian passes out of Russian hands.[92]

Namier, who had grown up in Galicia, contributed an internal memorandum on 'The Problem of East Galicia'.[93] Its tone can only be described as stridently Polonophobe. Namier lucidly argued that

The partitions of Poland were caused by the justified desire of Russia to gather in all Russian land ... which gave Poland's other neighbours a chance to grab territory to which they had no right whatsoever. If Poland once more appropriates to herself Russian land, be it White Russian or Ukrainian, and constitutes itself a new Hungary, Europe will not find peace, and in the end the new Hungary will perish, perhaps after having caused a Second World War.[94]

Namier continued with the ominous warning that, 'Should at the Peace Congress the interests of the Polish nobility prevail against those of the present nations, so much the worse for Poland and Europe'.[95] It is little wonder that this paper, which shows the force of Namier's opinions, was not circulated outside the department.[96] The differences between Howard and Namier would continue to widen, becoming one of the critical internal splits within the British delegation at Paris.

The question of Danzig was particularly involved. The Historical Section Handbook on East and West Prussia reaffirmed the German nature of Danzig, commenting that 'twenty years ago it was possible to inhabit it for some time without becoming aware that a Polish question existed'.[97] Howard recommended in the peace memorandum on Poland that Danzig should remain German, and that Poland be allowed an

[91] Howard of Penrith Diary, 18 Nov. 1918.   [92] FO 371/4354/f46/PC70.
[93] FO 371/4352/f6/PC6, Namier, 'The Problem of East Galicia', Nov. 1918.
[94] Ibid.   [95] Ibid.
[96] A good account of the development of the Polish question is Kay Lundgren-Nielsen, *The Polish Problem at the Paris Peace Conference: A Study of the Policies of the Great Powers and the Poles, 1918–1919*, trans. Alison Borch-Johansen (Odense, 1979).
[97] FO 373/2/18.

enclave nearby.[98] Sir Charles Oman, who had submitted a report on the subject for consideration, also supported Danzig remaining German, although he saw no problem with cutting off East Prussia from the rest of Germany. He observed that 'The convenience of organisation of the new German state is not a primary aim for the Entente powers.'[99] He recommended solving the problem by allowing Germany special transit rights across the Polish corridor.

Lord Robert Cecil, however, thought such a policy mistaken as it would 'only create a sore place which will never heal'.[100] He thought the best that could be done would be to allow the Poles special transit rights and for the whole matter to be reconsidered in ten years' time by the League of Nations. Howard disagreed with Cecil's view, as in his opinion, while dividing Prussia was an inconvenience, the settlement would have to be based on the principle of national self-determination. Thus Danzig would remain German, while the Poles could use the nearby port of Neufahrwasser. Namier was doubtful about Polish access to the sea, as well as its claims to Russian lands, commenting that 'For the sake of Poland's own future we must firmly oppose exaggerated Polish claims'.[101] Headlam-Morley in his summary of the European settlement recommended that Danzig, along with Stettin and Hamburg, should become international free ports. The Danzig question remained contentious, eventually dividing the British delegation at Paris.

Military Views

Under Hardinge's plan the military aspects of peace terms were handled by the Admiralty, the War Office, and the Air Ministry. Each produced a single memorandum setting out their views and suggestions on desiderata. The Admiralty's report was a product of discussions by the Board, the War Office's by the General Staff, while the Air Ministry's report was

[98] FO 371/4354/f46/PC70.
[99] FO 371/4354/f46/PC46, Oman, 'The Practicable Western Boundary for the New State of Poland', 14 Nov. 1918.
[100] Ibid., Minute by Cecil, undated.
[101] FO 371/4354/f46/PC73, Namier, 'Poland', 6 Dec. 1918.

drafted by the Chief of the Air Staff. None of these memoranda were the product of specially established research departments, although the General Staff seems to have been influenced by the work of Temperley's M.I.2(e). These military memoranda are best dealt with collectively as they are specifically concerned with military, as opposed to political, problems.

What is remarkable about these memoranda is their limited concern for European matters. The Admiralty's report on peace terms confined its primary recommendations to the destruction of Heligoland, and the placing of the Kiel Canal under an Allied Commission. Suggestions were also made on other problems of interest to the Admiralty, and included the recommendations that the Scheldt should remain Dutch, that a Dutch claim to the Ems should be favoured, that the Åland Islands should not be fortified and that Finland should have sovereignty over them, and that Spitsbergen be placed under an international commission in order to prevent another power from constructing a naval base there.[102]

The General Staff did not get around to formulating its desiderata until February 1919, and its report discussed only a limited number of European territorial questions. Belgian claims to Dutch territory were rejected, while the Scheldt question was referred to the Admiralty. In Western Europe it was warned that 'Any demands made by France and Belgium for territorial aggrandisement on their eastern frontiers will not make either of them stronger for offence, but since their demands, especially those of France, will make them stronger for defence, they should be backed'. French claims to the Saar region were also supported. The problem of uniting Luxemburg with Belgium was avoided, but it was made clear that any solution must involve some defensive alliance with France. On the other hand the General Staff believed that 'the French claim to the Rhine frontier cannot be supported' although it advocated that 'the left bank of the Rhine should be demilitarised'.[103]

[102] ADM 167/57, 'Notes on Matters Affecting Naval Interests Connected with the Peace Settlement', (3rd revise), Jan. 1919.
[103] Webster Papers 3/7/34, 'General Staff Desiderata Regarding Territorial Adjustments', 19 Feb. 1919.

In Eastern Europe the claims of the Allied states were generally supported over those of the defeated states. Unlike the Foreign Office, the General Staff suggested on strategic grounds moving Romania's frontier in the Southern Dobrudja even further southwards in order to protect the Constanza–Cernavodă railway. Romanian claims to Bessarabia up to the Dniester were also supported in order to give Romania control of the mouth of the Danube. Romanian claims to the Carpathian foothills and to Temesvar were disallowed however, as it was considered that the latter more properly belonged to Yugoslavia. On purely strategic grounds Czechoslovakia was to have the Sudeten area.

On Russian affairs the General Staff made some far-sighted observations. It was hoped that friendly relations could be achieved, as this would reduce garrison needs in the northwest provinces of India. Russian access to the sea, though, was a matter of particular concern, for as the report noted, 'it is essential for the Russian people (whatever form of government they may ultimately decide upon) to have free access to the sea, which, by the action of the Allies is at present everywhere denied them. It is inconceivable that European Russia, a nation of 130 million, can permanently acquiesce in such limitation.'[104] For these reasons it was hoped that the Baltic provinces would not become independent, but would instead be autonomous within a Russian federation.

In Poland the General Staff report suggested that East Prussia should retain a narrow land link to Germany proper, but that the Poles should have an enclave on the sea which would be reached by a special extra-territorial route across the German strip. The incorporation of Eastern Galicia into Poland was advocated, and failing this an autonomous state was recommended. The aim of the General Staff in this question was to keep the Carpathian mountain passes out of Russian hands.

The Air Staff submitted its memorandum on 22 January 1919.[105] One historian has commented on this report that 'It is remarkable that frontier questions in western Europe were not deemed of sufficient interest from the standpoint of air power

---

[104] Webster Papers 3/7/34.   [105] CAB 29/2/P-100.

and of Britain's position in the new age to warrant discussion'.[106] The Air Staff memorandum does not even mention German territorial questions. Eventually as the peace conference developed, simultaneously with the creation of the Royal Air Force as a separate service, more specific recommendations on the future implications and needs of air power were produced.

Conclusion

When the limited number of personnel involved, and the pressure of time upon the final work is considered, the breadth and vision of the recommendations is remarkable. Headlam-Morley gives some indication of the value of these preparations in a letter from the peace conference in which he discusses the problems caused by the lack of an Austrian specialist: 'As I need not point out to you, if the PID had dealt with the matter thoroughly they would have guided the Foreign Office, and of course the Peace conference would have followed the lead of the Foreign Office and all would have been well.'[107] Certainly other circumstances affected the final outcome of the European settlement; nevertheless, the result was deeply influenced by these preparatory studies. The sheer weight of the material provided, the lucidity of the peace memoranda, and the quality of the expert advisers make it difficult to underestimate the value to the delegates, or the effectiveness in negotiation, of the British preparations for peace.

[106] H. I. Nelson, *Land and Power: British and Allied Policy on Germany's Frontiers, 1916–1919* (London, 1963), p. 109.
[107] Headlam-Morley to Saunders, 20 July 1919. Headlam-Morley Papers.

5

The World Outside Europe

> It would be very satisfactory if we could find some con-
> vincing argument for not annexing all the territories in the
> world.
>
> Edwin Montagu, CAB 23/42/IWC44, 20 Dec. 1918

Preparations for the settlement of non-European territorial
questions focused on two issues: the fate of the Ottoman
Empire and the distribution of Germany's colonial possessions. Planning for the European settlement had been left to
specialized departments, which were often handicapped by a
lack of direction from the Cabinet. The preparations for the
non-European settlement followed a different pattern, with
the work of the specialized departments forming the basis for
discussion in Cabinet committees and by the Cabinet itself. As
this process developed account had to be taken of a greater
range of opinion, and the modest proposals for territorial acquisitions discussed in the early memoranda had by the
opening of the conference burgeoned into a list of desiderata
encompassing a vast array of lands. The British Empire was a
colonial empire, and to those concerned with imperial matters
success in the colonial negotiations was essential. Unquestionably the degree of ministerial involvement aided the preparation process and gave the technical experts a greater ability
to focus their efforts, making them better equipped to aid the
plenipotentiaries in the negotiations.

A major question facing the British in their preparations was
the role which national self-determination would play outside
Europe. Lloyd George had stated that Great Britain's policy
with regard to the Ottoman Empire was not to 'deprive Turkey
of its capital, or of the rich and renowned lands of Asia Minor

and Thrace, which are predominantly Turkish in race'.[1] President Wilson in his speech of the Fourteen Points proposed that 'The Turkish portions of the present Ottoman Empire should be assured a secure sovereignty'.[2] Even in the least developed regions Lloyd George considered that the native chiefs and councils 'are competent to consult and speak for their tribes and members, and thus to represent their wishes and interests in regard to their disposal'.[3] Wilson considered that colonial claims should be adjusted with 'a strict observance of the principle that in determining all such questions of sovereignty, the interests of the populations concerned must have equal weight with the equitable claims of the government whose title is to be determined'.[4] It was generally assumed that given the promise of a peace with no annexations, the successor states of the Ottoman Empire and the German colonies would be placed under the control of a mandatory power on behalf of the Allies or the proposed League of Nations. The PID naturally embarked upon its preparatory memoranda with these general principles as guidelines. The development of the delegation's peace brief shows that as it evolved from the original PID work through various committees, though a concern for native wishes was maintained, the desire not to lose any potentially important area led to a weakening of these principles.

The PID and the Ottoman Empire

At the PID the question of British policy towards the successor states of the Ottoman Empire fell to Sir Louis Mallet's Middle East Section, where Arnold Toynbee was responsible for writing most of the memoranda. Toynbee's output in this period was prodigious, yielding between early October and mid-November 1918 the essential core of reports on the Ottoman Empire. His output was so rapid that the PID was not yet prepared with a classification scheme, with the result that the Middle East reports came to be labelled the 'special series'.

[1] WM ii. 1511, text of Speech of 5 Jan. 1918.
[2] J. B. Scott, ed., *President Wilson's Foreign Policy: Messages, Addresses, Papers* (New York, 1918), pp. 361–2.
[3] WM ii. 1515.   [4] Scott, *President Wilson's Foreign Policy*, p. 360.

Toynbee's most important report, 'The Peace Settlement for Turkey and the Arabian Peninsula', was submitted on 21 November. The same day General Smuts reported to the Prime Minister and the War Cabinet on the progress of the peace brief, noting that his staff was busy with questions concerning the Middle East and Turkey.[5] Lord Curzon, concerned lest Smuts be formulating policy without him, asked the War Cabinet to instruct Smuts to consult the Eastern Committee, of which he was chairman, on any questions concerning this region.[6] Curzon's demand was met and the Eastern Committee assumed control of policy formulation on these topics for the peace conference, though the PID continued to provide factual material for the committee's discussions.

Toynbee laid the groundwork for the Eastern Committee's subsequent discussions in his memorandum of 21 November.[7] Here he listed British commitments, stated acknowledged British aims, and suggested policy to be followed. Fourteen existing British commitments were enumerated. These included such old arrangements as Britain's role in the 1861 *Règlement Organique* of the Lebanon vilayet and the secret agreements by which Great Britain pledged to support other states' claims. Potentially the most troublesome of the latter were the 1915 Treaty of London and the 1916 Sykes–Picot Agreement, which had defined what spoils the major allied states could expect in the Near and Middle East in the event of victory.

By late 1918 both these agreements were outdated, and Great Britain was eager to escape the promises it had made under the duress of war. With British forces victorious throughout the Middle East, and with British administrators in

[5] Lloyd George Papers F/45/9/23, Smuts to Lloyd George, 21 Nov. 1918. Also in Smuts Papers 101/37.

[6] CAB 23/8/WC506/5.

[7] Confidential Print 11908*, Toynbee, 'Peace Settlement for Turkey and Arabian Peninsula', 21 Nov. 1918. Originally circulated with the title 'The British Case in Regard to Settlement of Turkey and the Arabian Peninsula'. This report generated much correspondence which can be found in FO 371/3385/f747, FO 371/4368/f480, and FO 371/4352/f1/PC1. These all contain copies of Toynbee's reports in various draft forms. Hereinafter cited as Confidential Print 11908*. Some of these proposals had already been suggested by Toynbee in FO 371/4353/f25/PC25, 'The Formula of Self-Determination of Peoples and the Muslim World', 10 Jan. 1918.

control from Egypt to Persia, the British Empire was obviously reluctant to turn over vast tracts to countries which had contributed little or nothing to the defeat of the Ottomans. The Allies had pledged themselves in 1918 to a peace without annexations, and the United States was certain to take a grim view of any settlement based upon secret treaties. Great Britain, obsessed with controlling the routes to its Indian Empire, desired neither France nor Italy to become major factors in the Middle East, nor did it wish the establishment of a series of weak and potentially unstable successors to the Ottoman Empire. The problem which Great Britain would face at the Paris negotiations was how to persuade France and Italy to renounce their claims under the secret treaties, while retaining British control of the Middle East without any overt annexations.

Toynbee in his report listed fourteen aims of British policy in the area once controlled by the Ottomans:

1. *European Turkey and Anatolia*: Sovereign independence (the balance of advantage, as regards Constantinople, remaining in doubt).
2. *Black Sea Straits*: Effective international control.
3. *Dodekannese*: Friendly settlement between Italy and Greece.
4. *Cyprus*: A free hand for ourselves.
5. *Armenia*: Independence, with equal rights for all nationalities, and with assistance of an outside Power for a term of years.
6. *Arab Countries in General*: Maintenance of existing British possessions, protectorates, and treaties; widest local independence compatible with this; widest extension of British trucial system to independent Arab States; least possible interference of outside Powers in local internal administration.
7. *Arab Federation*: Desirable, but without prejudice to 6.
8. *Caliphate*: To be settled by the Muslims themselves.
9. *Arabian Peninsula, excluding Hejaz*: British trucial treaties with all independent States.
10. *Hejaz*: Independence; British trucial treaty to cover all foreign relations except those involved in the pilgrimage.

11 *Mesopotamia*: Independence, with British administrative assistance (subject to no limitations of period or function).
12 *Kurdistan*: Same desiderata as in Mesopotamia.
13 *Syria*: Independence, with outside administrative assistance if necessary; free transit for trade between Syrian ports and hinterland; independent [Arabian] Peninsula rulers whose spheres border on Syria, to have trucial treaties with Great Britain.
14 *Palestine*: Independence; administrative assistance to be either American or preferably British; free transit for trade between Palestinian ports and hinterland; British trucial treaty only in case Palestine includes country east of Jordan.

In order to achieve these goals Great Britain would have to escape from its obligations under the secret treaties, and this Toynbee proposed to do by arriving at artful interpretations of the agreements themselves.

Toynbee, like his New Europe colleagues, was a stout supporter of a Wilsonian peace and took every opportunity to remind his readers of the necessity for such a settlement. To him the principles of nationality, democracy, and self-determination were for the Allies not just one element of their aims, 'but the essential aim and expression of their cause'.[8] It was through an application of Wilsonian principles that Toynbee proposed to free Great Britain from the constraints of the secret agreements. Applied to the Middle East this meant that 'the peoples must be free to form what political groupings they chose, to establish what Governments they chose within these groupings, and to invite what outside Power they chose to assist them, without their freedom of choice being hampered by dictation or compulsion at any point'. Toynbee noted therefore that

Our Allies cannot in principle contest that the populations of Turkey, including the Turks themselves, are to constitute their own governments, as this is specifically accepted in the joint Anglo-French Declaration, from which Italy cannot dissent. . . . It seems to follow inevitably that there should not only be freedom for the Arabs, Turks,

[8] Confidential Print 11908*.

Armenians, &c., to invite what Power they like, but that the various Powers should be free towards each other to accept such invitations.[9]

Thus the spirit of the secret agreements would be met by allowing all the Allies equality of opportunity and the secret treaties would theoretically be left intact, while in fact the entire proposed settlement would be altered. Although Toynbee was most circumspect in the way he proposed this plan, it illustrates how the PID could help to generate policy, despite its terms of reference. The gap in Toynbee's argument, and it was common to most British officials, was the assumption that the local peoples themselves would choose the mandatory power which would assist them, and it seemed obvious that these peoples would naturally opt for Great Britain, or at worst the United States. Toynbee hoped that by giving each Allied power an equal opportunity to be chosen as a mandatory state the equilibrium of power could be maintained in form, while in substance France and Italy would be excluded from the region.

Hardinge and Balfour both approved the report, and while Balfour desired more discussion before endorsing it, Hardinge felt Toynbee's work was comprehensive and ordered a limited distribution since 'it contains all our cards with which we hope to negotiate a satisfactory agreement'.[10] Balfour's suggestion for further discussion was met, probably not to his satisfaction, when Lord Curzon and the Eastern Committee gained control of this subject and began discussions on negotiating policy for all matters relating to western Asia.

The Eastern Committee

The Eastern Committee met nine times in November and December 1918 to draft a set of resolutions on British policy for the benefit of the negotiators. The verbatim reports of the committee's discussions provide the most vibrant picture available of the intensity with which different views were expressed, and the difficulty of reconciling them into

[9] Ibid.   [10] FO 371/4368/f480/PID567, Minute by Hardinge.

guidelines for use at the conference.[11] Whereas the specialized preparatory departments were involved in the compilation either of background facts or of contingency negotiating plans, the Eastern Committee set about drawing up a series of short resolutions which would give a coherent direction to Great Britain's negotiations over the almost nightmarish tangle of claims and counter-claims which had followed the final collapse of the Ottoman Empire.

The Eastern Committee's membership fluctuated, but the members who attended in this period were Lord Robert Cecil, Edwin Montagu, who was often at odds with his fellow members, Arthur Balfour, who appeared occasionally, and Jan Smuts, who attended the first five discussions on peace terms until his resignation from the War Cabinet. In addition many senior experts were usually present, among whom were often to be found Hardinge, Mallet, Hirtzel, and Shuckburgh.[12]

Curzon acted as chairman, and in his handling of this committee can be seen a reflection of how the Viceroy's Council must have been dealt with during his tenure in Delhi.[13] Curzon was a consummate controller of committees, aided by his inexhaustible appetite for work and his justly famous memory for detail. He opened the first discussion of the Eastern Committee on peace terms with a lengthy and erudite lecture on the history of the region from Mosul to the Persian Gulf, a practice he continued with each new topic which came before the committee. For Curzon the eastern settlement was critical to the future of the Empire and he stated his opinion that 'Upon the fate of these territories, and the way in which our

[11] The minutes of the Eastern Committee are in CAB 27/24, and the memoranda submitted to or prepared by the committee are in CAB 27/25–39. It should be noted that Balfour often asked the secretary to suspend the taking of notes when he spoke, e.g. CAB 27/24/EC41, 5 Dec. 1918.

[12] The Eastern Committee originated in Mar. 1917 as the Mesopotamia Administration Committee, which in Aug. 1917 became the Middle East Committee. In Mar. 1918 it was amalgamated with the Foreign Office's Committee on Russia and the interdepartmental Persia Committee, the new committee being named the Eastern Committee. There is no full account of the committee's work, but a good survey is in Briton Cooper Busch, *Britain, India, and the Arabs, 1914–1921* (Berkeley, Calif., 1971), particularly pp. 208–85.

[13] For one commentary on Curzon's technique see ibid. 207–8, 272.

case is presented to the Peace Conference, and the form of administration to be set up, will depend not only the future of the territories themselves, but also the future of the British Empire in the East'.[14] Curzon's practice was to provide the committee with a set of draft resolutions he had prepared, the debate which followed therefore concerned not so much the setting of policies as the modification or acceptance of his version of policy.

The ghost at the feast in all these discussions was the Sykes–Picot Agreement, by which Great Britain, France, and Russia delimited their respective zones of influence and territorial acquisitions in Asiatic Turkey. Although the new Communist government in Moscow subsequently denounced the agreement, France insisted upon the strict application of its terms and firmly opposed surrendering any claim to territory promised under the agreement. The agreement certainly found no supporters among the members of the Eastern Committee, who turned their considerable mental powers to working out how to escape its terms. Balfour was openly perplexed by the logic behind such an arrangement, commenting, 'I never quite understood the inception of the Sykes–Picot Agreement, I never thoroughly understood it, and do not understand it to this day'.[15] Curzon referred to Sykes–Picot as 'that wretched Agreement'.[16] Smuts considered it a 'millstone' around Britain's neck.[17] The General Staff observed that 'it is difficult to see how any arrangement could be more objectionable from the military point of view than the Sykes–Picot Agreement of 1916, by which an enterprising and ambitious foreign power is placed on interior lines with reference to our position in the Middle East'.[18] Certainly this was collectively a harsh opinion of the reliability of Britain's wartime ally. Nothing could show more clearly the complex nature of the

[14] CAB 27/24/EC39, 27 Nov. 1918.   [15] CAB 27/24/EC41, , Dec. 1918.
[16] CAB 27/24/EC40, 2 Dec. 1918.
[17] Ibid.
[18] CAB 27/39/EC2824, 'The Strategic Importance of Syria to the British Empire', 9 Dec. 1918. Also in Webster Papers 3/7/28. On the Middle East settlement in general and the Sykes–Picot Agreement in particular see Elie Kedourie, *England and the Middle East: The Destruction of the Ottoman Empire, 1914–1921* (London, 1978).

Anglo-French alliance, which made them international allies, but often regional rivals.

A possible solution suggested by Smuts to the Eastern Committee was the exchange of territory elsewhere in return for a French renunciation of claims in the Middle East.[19] Cecil pointed out that the difficulty with this was that

I know that if Mr. Balfour or myself makes any proposition with regard to Africa, we shall be told that there is an aeroplane station, or a submarine base, or that it is the oldest colony, or it will bitterly offend some New Zealand politician if we do it, or something of that kind. It is always the same.[20]

The problem was that Great Britain clearly preferred to keep the French out of the Arab lands, and though Britain did not want any formal responsibility for the Caucasus itself, there was a general reluctance to allow the French anywhere into the region.

Even in such a remote area as the Caucasus there was a general suspicion that the French would cause problems for Great Britain. Smuts in particular perceived France as a potential future threat, and he considered that 'Our line of policy should be, if possible, to work with America'.[21] Curzon even indicated that a return of the Caucasian states to Russia might be preferable to allowing them to fall into the clutches of France. Curzon held a high opinion of the French, and as a result perceived them as a potential threat to British supremacy in the East. 'France is a highly organised State, has boundless intrepidity, imagination, and a certain power of dealing with Eastern peoples ....'[22] Certainly these were just the qualities envisaged as being required by an ideal mandatory power, that is if the mandate system were really to be used to prepare these states for an independent future. They were not, however, desirable qualities if the mandatory power were in a position to block British interests.

There was some hope that the United States might accept a mandate for the Caucasian states. Cecil was among those who found it unlikely that the Americans would want to become

[19] CAB 27/24/EC42, 9 Dec. 1918.   [20] Ibid.
[21] CAB 27/24/EC40, 2 Dec. 1918.
[22] Ibid.

involved in such a far distant place, though American connections with Armenia might induce it to accept an Armenian mandate.[23] Indeed the United States was a favourite choice for every mandate Britain did not desire, as at least it would keep out the French. As Cecil summed up the likelihood of an American mandate, 'They will not do the Caucasus and Armenia; they would be mad to do it, but there is an off-chance that they would take Constantinople and Palestine, one or the other, because of the great swagger of it.'[24] The committee was forced to accept that the American option was an unlikely one, and began seriously to consider the possibility of Great Britain retaining control, in some form, of Arabia, Syria, Palestine, Iraq, the Lebanon, and the Caucasian states. It was only when Balfour and Montagu objected on practical grounds that the committee returned to more moderate proposals. The difficulty was to find some way to insinuate British rule into the key Middle Eastern areas while blocking any other potential rival and simultaneously paying lip-service to President Wilson's sensibilities.

In the absence of any decision for wholesale annexation of the Middle East the most likely counterbalance to French claims was, as Toynbee had suggested, support for a policy of self-determination. Balfour claimed credit before the committee of having advocated this policy as early as January 1917, before the United States had even entered the war.[25] The committee's members were truly convinced that if given a choice, all the peoples of the Ottoman Empire and the Caucasus would prefer Britain as a mandatory power. Curzon suggested that

if we cannot get out of our difficulties in any other way we ought to play self-determination for all it is worth wherever we are involved in difficulties with the French, the Arabs, or anybody else, and leave the case to be settled by that final argument knowing in the bottom of our hearts that we are more likely to benefit from it than anybody else.[26]

---

[23] The Americans on their part were indeed considering the possibility of an Armenian mandate; see James B. Gidney, *A Mandate for Armenia* (Kent, Ohio, 1967).

[24] CAB 27/24/EC41, 5 Dec. 1918.   [25] Ibid.   [26] Ibid.

Smuts was one member of the committee who must have been painfully aware of the reality that not all peoples if given a choice would automatically opt for placing themselves under British rule. Throughout the committee's sessions Smuts maintained a rather enigmatic silence and showed a marked preference for intervening only when he might thereby tip the balance or smooth out a problem. In this instance he came out in favour of bringing in the League of Nations. Smuts believed that by giving the territories in question to the League for supervision, Britain would maintain some degree of leverage over whatever state became responsible for the day to day administration.[27] Cecil supported this idea in preference to pure self-determination on the part of the inhabitants, which he felt should be used only as an indication to the League.[28]

The future of Syria and Palestine lay at the centre of concern over the Sykes–Picot Agreement. Curzon considered Syria to be the most perplexing problem facing the Eastern Committee, as it was the most likely to bring Great Britain and France into conflict.[29] Cecil agreed that the French were mad with desire for Syria, and thought that there would be great convulsions if France were forced out. The difficulty here was that the committee was reluctant to allow the new Arab state in Syria any major seaport if it meant the French gaining control over it. Curzon thought, however, that it would be disastrous to block the new Arab state from the sea, noting archly that

It seems to me perfectly absurd to set up an Arab State under Faisal at Damascus, and to say to him: 'My dear fellow, here you are, do what you like in this region; but we are bound to block you out, by the Sykes–Picot Agreement, from the Sea, Tripoli, and Latakia.' That is an inconceivable position to put him in. The only alternative is to let him have the railway from Tripoli to Homs.[30]

Curzon favoured instead a partition of the Syrian coast, leaving the French in possession of the Lebanon and Alexandretta, and bringing the Arab state to the sea at Tripoli.

The committee decided to follow Curzon's suggestion when it adopted a set of resolutions on Syria on 18 December 1918.[31]

[27] CAB 27/24/EC40, 2 Dec. 1918.   [28] CAB 27/24/EC41, 5 Dec. 1918.
[29] Ibid.
[30] Ibid.   [31] CAB 27/24/EC44, 18 Dec. 1918.

These called for negotiations to cancel the Sykes–Picot Agreement, for Curzon's suggested division of the coast, and a predominant voice for Great Britain in the area.[32] The General Staff found no objection to Curzon's plan of allowing the establishment of French enclaves at Beirut and Alexandretta, but wanted no military organizations to be set up within them. In the Army's view Syria 'should be an Arab State under British guidance and virtual control'.[33]

As for Palestine, where Sykes–Picot called for international administration, and where the Balfour Declaration of 1917 promised a national homeland for the Jews, Curzon suggested that a mandate would be necessary as it was commonly agreed that previous experiences of international control had been a failure. Curzon had now moved away from the view he had expressed in the Imperial War Cabinet which inclined towards a United States mandate for Palestine. The committee concurred with Curzon's views on Syria without much debate.[34]

Four days after the main debate on Syria, Military Intelligence contributed a report on 'The Strategic Importance of Syria to the British Empire'.[35] The report concluded that Syria was not likely to pose a threat to the Suez Canal and Egypt. Given British command of the seas, and a favourable political situation in Egypt, 'the development of the country by her own population need not cause anxiety to the British General Staff'.[36] Events of the next year however would show the situation in Egypt was hardly favourable, while naval supremacy was under threat from the American naval building programme. They were correct in believing Syria was not a threat to the canal, and indeed there were threats closer to hand in the form of Egyptian nationalism. On a Jewish homeland in Palestine the General Staff, in one of the few references to this subject in all the preparatory memoranda and discussions, concluded that 'The creation of a buffer

[32] CAB 27/38/EC2716-A. Sir Erle Richards's restatement of these conclusions is in CAB 29/2/P-50.

[33] Webster Papers 3/7/34.   [34] CAB 27/24/EC41, 5 Dec. 1918.

[35] CAB 27/39/EC2824. Also in Webster Papers 3/7/27. Discussion in CAB 27/24/EC42, 9 Dec. 1918.

[36] Ibid.

Jewish State in Palestine, though this state will be weak itself, is strategically desirable for Great Britain so long as it be created without disturbing Mohammedan sentiment and is not controlled by a power which is potentially hostile to this country'.[37] The retention of Muslim goodwill was considered important in order to achieve a politically independent Syria under British influence.

Toynbee had already proposed that British policy should be 'to insure reasonable facilities in Palestine for Jewish colonisation, without giving Arab or general Moslem opinion an opportunity for considering that Great Britain has been instrumental in handing over free Arab or Moslem soil to aliens'.[38] Toynbee suggested that this could best be accomplished by including Palestine, at least nominally, within an Arab confederation. The military later modified its views to support for the establishment of an independent Jewish state, which should be reconciled with Arab national aspirations and be under British influence. The Jews, however, would be given enough territory to allow for an economically viable state.[39] No one suggested in practical terms how all these factions were to be reconciled to one another. The dominant thought was not of the inhabitants, but of the region's strategic value, and therefore of enhancing British control while blocking France.

The Eastern Committee's resolutions on Syria called for a cancellation of the Sykes–Picot Agreement, though French claims to a special political status in the Lebanon and Alexandretta were to be supported. Support was also given to an autonomous Arab state under Faisal with its capital at Damascus. Self-determination was to be the basis of the Syrian settlement, but British influence in the Syrian hinterland and Trans-Jordan was to be predominant. As regards Palestine the committee opposed an international administration, and recommended instead administration by a single power. France and Italy were considered undesirable, and while the United States was deemed acceptable, this role should preferably go to Great Britain. Whatever the final choice, attention

---

[37] Ibid. [38] Confidential Print 11908*. [39] Webster Papers 3/7/34.

was to be paid to both the Arabs and the Zionist communities in the country.[40]

Toynbee's memorandum on Arabia had placed its emphasis on maintaining existing British rights in the Arab regions, and ensuring that pro-British governments were installed. From Toynbee's viewpoint, 'British desiderata in the Arab countries may be summed up as a British Monroe Doctrine for Arabia'.[41] Toynbee proposed accomplishing this by concluding 'trucial pattern' treaties with the local governments, allowing Britain the leverage to maintain peace in the area. This would effectively reserve to the British Empire the right of intervening in Arabian affairs.

Arthur Hirtzel of the India Office was quick to reject the idea of extending the British trucial system with the observation that 'the prospect of His Majesty's Government having to maintain the peace throughout Arabia and the Arab countries is so alarming as to be absolutely prohibitive'.[42] Hirtzel was also less sanguine than Toynbee about the extent to which Britain could count on continued good relations with the Arabs, commenting that 'it should not be too easily assumed — as it sometimes is, when we talk of "having the Arabs behind us" and the like — that the Arabs like us and are coming to feed from our hands'.[43] Toynbee, however, found that the Arab revolt came at a fortuitous moment for long-range British policy:

the rise of the Arab movement has been a fortunate development for the British Empire at a crucial point of its history, and . . . it offers for our Moslem policy and our Middle Eastern policy a way out of serious dilemmas which were created by the situation before the war and have been accentuated by the war itself.[44]

[40] CAB 27/38/EC2717-A. Erle Richards's restatement of these conclusions is in CAB 29/2/P-49. Lloyd George told the Imperial War Cabinet on 20 Dec. 1918, when it met to discuss the reports on the Ottoman Empire and the German colonies, that Clemenceau had effectively agreed to the British retaining Palestine and Mesopotamia. CAB 23/42/IWC44.

[41] Confidential Print 11908*.

[42] FO 371/4352/f1/PC81, Hirtzel, 'Note on Settlement of Turkey and the Arabian Peninsula (in response to PID Spec. 1)', 30 Nov. 1918.

[43] Ibid.

[44] FO 371/4352/f1/PC130, Toynbee, 'French and Arab Claims in the Middle East in relation to British Interests', 19 Dec. 1918.

Toynbee saw the Arab movement as a way for Great Britain to form a link between Egypt and India without being compelled to take France into partnership. The great difficulty was the Sykes–Picot Agreement, but as Toynbee noted, 'the alternative settlement on the basis of self-determination not only safeguards our interests but it is, if anything, more favourable than the other to the interests of France'. [45] He suggested that Britain could possibly placate France with gains in Turkish and Russian Armenia.

When the Eastern Committee came to discuss the Hejaz and Arabia, Balfour suggested the radical notion that more could be achieved by Great Britain not obtaining some of the areas it was likely to gain. [46] He observed that 'All the troubles of the Foreign Office, since I have been a member of it, have been brought about by matters raised by officials looking after the twopenny-halfpenny and very often corrupt interests of France or Italy, or serving small, narrow, nationalistic objects'. [47] Balfour was willing to be satisfied with an arrangement whereby France and Italy would not conspire against Great Britain in any of these 'semi-civilized' countries. The committee agreed that Great Britain's special position in Arabia should be recognized by the other powers. No restrictions should be placed on the king of the Hejaz's foreign relations, and the Great Powers should agree not to meddle in his internal affairs. This was taken to include no diplomatic representation in the country, save perhaps an agent to deal with questions of pilgrimage or trade.

Mesopotamia was only briefly discussed by the Eastern Committee during its discussion of peace terms, undoubtedly because it had already defined British policy in previous lengthy discussions on the country. Of all the Arab countries Mesopotamia had attracted the greatest discussion throughout the war. [48] It had been during Hardinge's tenure as viceroy that British troops from India captured Mesopotamia, and it was

[45] FO 371/4352/f1/PC130.
[46] Questions relating to the Hejaz and Arabia were all resolved at the meeting of the Eastern Committee on 18 Dec. 1918. CAB 27/24/EC44.
[47] Ibid.
[48] On British policy in Mesopotamia is V. H. Rothwell, 'Mesopotamia in British War Aims, 1914–1918', *Historical Journal*, 13 (1970), 273–94.

the questionable conduct of the campaign which had clouded his last months in Delhi and led to the establishment of the Mesopotamia Committee, the predecessor of the Eastern Committee. As early as April 1918 the Eastern Committee had endorsed the recommendations of Percy Cox, the civil commissioner in Baghdad, that 'It is agreed that the administration should be under British guidance, and the more complete the British control can be, the better for the country'. [49] The idea of outright annexation, however, had to be abandoned in consideration of the publicly announced policy to conclude a non-annexationist peace.

Toynbee recommended that the backward state of the country required stronger measures than the mere extension of the trucial system to Mesopotamia. At least for a transitional period Mesopotamia would require the guidance of a foreign power, and for Toynbee the choice was obvious: 'It is a British desideratum that this should devolve, to the exclusion of other powers, upon Great Britain.' [50] To achieve this Toynbee suggested three possible solutions, all of which were based on the premiss that Great Britain would hold Mesopotamia as a mandate. It could act as a mandatory for the local population, or on behalf of an Arab federation, or one of King Husein's sons could be appointed to the throne, with Great Britain ruling on his behalf. It was this latter suggestion which was ultimately adopted by the peace conference, under the guise of a League mandate.

The India Office maintained its early interest in Mesopotamia, although an earlier idea of placing Baghdad under Delhi's control had been abandoned by the war's end. The India Office in its own report on desiderata recommended that as annexation had been ruled out, the best solution would be the establishment of an Arab state under British control. In particular it noted the fear of the strategic threat which would be posed by a Baghdad railway should Britain lose control of the district. Hardinge concurred with the India Office's concern, noting elsewhere that 'the Baghdad Railway should not be forgotten & the Germans must be made to transfer this

---

[49] FO 371/4353/f30/PC32, Percy Cox, 'The Future of Mesopotamia', 22 Apr. 1918. Also in CAB 27/25/EC173.

[50] Confidential Print 11908*.

concession & enterprise to us'. In common with several ministries the India Office had been badly frightened by the wartime
German U-boat campaign, and its implications for imperial
communications. It even had visions of 'German submarine
bases all along the Persian Gulf'. [51] While recognizing that this
was perhaps an extreme view, the India Office was desperate to
prevent a vacuum being created in the region which could only
have negative results for Britain. The India Office avoided altogether the question of what outward form British control should
take, just as long as 'the reality of British supervision and control is secured, and provided the administrative system is such
as to commend itself to the local population, and to afford them
full scope for self-development on national lines'. [52] The India
Office envisaged this new entity as comprising the vilayets of
Basra, Baghdad, and Mosul. [53]

The Eastern Committee recommended to the War Cabinet
that Great Britain should not annex any part of Mesopotamia,
and whether a single Arab state or a number of Arab states
emerged should be left to the inhabitants. The support and
protection of a European Great Power was, however, considered indispensable. It was strongly recommended that
should the inhabitants of this region express a desire for Great
Britain to fill such a role, the responsibility should be accepted. It
should be recalled that Mesopotamia was already under British
military occupation and administration. [54]

In the preparations differences began to emerge between
those favouring Greek irredentist claims, which were seen as a
way of bolstering an ally, and those opposed to Greek aims, as
likely to inflame Muslim opinion and as such pose a threat to the
security of Britain's vast Muslim domains. The question which
raised the greatest difficulty was the future of Constantinople.
Of all the cities of the Ottoman Empire, Constantinople was
undoubtedly the most important. The delegates at Paris would

[51] Confidential Print 11582*.   [52] Ibid.
[53] Mosul had been promised to France by the Sykes–Picot Agreement,
which was recognized by the India Office as creating a special difficulty.
[54] CAJB 27/38/EC2772. Erle Richards restated these conclusions in a memorandum on Mesopotamia, see CAB 29/2/P-48. The Eastern Committee held a
crucial discussion on Mesopotamia on 27 Nov. 1918. See CAB 27/24/EC39 and
Busch, *Britain, India, and the Arabs*, p. 277.

have to decide whether or not to follow Gladstone's advice and clear the Turks bag and baggage from their last remaining European toehold. Toynbee in the early phase of preparations, and the Eastern Committee at the end, found the arguments evenly balanced for and against leaving Constantinople under Turkish sovereignty. Toynbee suggested that if Great Britain should favour the transference of the office of caliph to the Arabs, then the expulsion of the Sultan would be advisable, though the ancient rivalries for the possession of Byzantium which would be triggered by removing the Turks might prove counter-productive.[55]

Harold Nicolson, who emerged as one of the leading phil-hellenes, and one of whose earliest diplomatic postings had been Constantinople, prepared in mid-November a 'Summary of the British Case in Respect of Turkey in Europe' as part of the PID's South-East European brief.[56] His report differed in no essential way from Toynbee's, who was still strongly pro-Greek, though his views would later take a dramatic turn. Turkey would nominally retain Constantinople, which would become a free port with the Straits permanently open to inter-national traffic. To guarantee these rights the entire zone of the Straits, including Constantinople, would be under a United States high commissioner, 'enjoying extensive executive powers'.[57] To assure the authority of the high commissioner, the Straits would be neutralized, and Turkish forces prohibited in the zone. This entire arrangement would be under the League of Nations, which as a corollary would guarantee to Turkey the integrity of the territory allowed to it by the peace treaty.

As for the remainder of European Turkey, Nicolson sug-gested reducing it by drawing a new frontier from Enos to Midia. Turkey's Aegean islands would be ceded to Greece, including the strategically located islands of Imbros, Tenedos, and Castellorizo. Turkey was also formally to recognize Great Britain's annexation of Cyprus. Internally Turkey was to guar-antee a parliamentary system, and the capitulation system was

[55] Confidential Print 11980*.
[56] FO 371/4354/f36/PC36, Nicolson, 'Summary of British Case in Respect of Turkey in Europe', 20 Nov. 1918.
[57] Ibid.

to be re-established. With infinite thoroughness the Legal Section of the Foreign Office prepared a draft treaty based on these points.[58]

The Eastern Committee was similarly unable to come to any definite decision as to the future of Constantinople, which they discussed at one of their last meetings concerning the peace brief, on 23 December. It was just as well perhaps that they were reaching the end of their work, as Montagu's anger at Curzon's handling of the committee, which had been simmering for some time, finally boiled over. Just before the meeting began Curzon reprimanded Montagu, within the hearing of those present, for his office's late delivery of memoranda by Arthur Hirtzel and Hamilton Grant with the words, 'Your India Office is really beyond all limits.'[59] Montagu was not a person who took such criticisms lightly, protesting that his staff were not at fault, and explaining the circumstances. Curzon subsequently sent a note of apology.[60] Montagu, however, later wrote to Curzon giving vent to his feelings on the subject of the committee's operating procedures: 'You know that I have at times been a little impatient with the method that has seemed good to you and to none of your colleagues.... documents are circulated to you so that you have the opportunity of reading them before the meeting, but your colleagues do not get them till a later date.'[61] The incident illustrates not only the personalities involved, and certainly both Curzon and Montagu could be trying, but it shows as well the tensions building within the committee as the peace conference approached. All its members were working gruelling hours by any standard, a fact Montagu realized and mentioned in his correspondence with Curzon. Although Montagu ended his letter of complaint, 'Yours in perfect peace', the differences between them were never really resolved.[62]

[58] FO 371/4354/f36/PC36 and FO 371/4354/f36/PC154.
[59] Montagu Papers AS-III-2-494, Montagu to Curzon, 23 Dec. 1918.
[60] Montagu Papers AS-III-2-494, Curzon to Montagu, 23 Dec. 1918.
[61] Montagu Papers AS-III-2-494, Montagu to Curzon, 27 Nov. 1918.
[62] Despite this amicable closing note, Montagu and Curzon continued to feud, particularly over the fate of the territories of the Ottoman Empire. This culminated in Mar. 1922 when Montagu was forced to resign from the government in a dispute with Curzon on this issue, leaving Curzon at last victorious. See Harold Nicolson, *Curzon: The Last Phase* (London, 1937), esp. pp. 267–8.

On the future of Constantinople the Eastern Committee considered reports by the India Office, the Admiralty, the General Staff, and the Foreign Office. Sir Hamilton Grant, the foreign secretary to the Government of India, focused on the importance of the city as the seat of the sultan-caliph.[63] He believed that to take the caliph from his residence of over four centuries could have a disastrous effect on the not inconsiderable Muslim population of the British Empire.[64] In this Grant was supported by Montagu, who believed that it was one thing to strip the Turks of non-Turkish territories — that was the price of defeat — but even Germany and Austria were not to be turned out of their capitals.[65] Sir Arthur Hirtzel held other views, and considered Constantinople a European question and, as such, 'if once it is admitted that India Moslems can influence the policy of His Majesty's Government in Europe a very awkward precedent will be created'.[66] This incident illustrates the different perceptions of the India Office establishment in London and the Government of India at Delhi.

The Admiralty and General Staff, showing a unique degree of co-ordination in these discussions, had consulted and concurred on strategic questions before submitting their memoranda.[67] Both wanted the Straits open to all ships, a goal generally agreed to by everybody. The General Staff emphasized the importance of the future control of the Straits with the observation that 'it is there that any future naval expansion based on a reconstituted Russia might be throttled'.[68] If a foreign power were brought in to administer the city the military considered that there were only three possible choices, Greece, the United States, and Great Britain. Greece was rejected as being too vulnerable to attack. The United

---

[63] Sir (Alfred) Hamilton Grant, 12th Baronet (1872–1937); educ. Balliol Coll., Oxford; entered India Civil Service, 1895; Foreign Secretary to the Government of India, 1914–19.

[64] CAB 27/39/EC2841, Hamilton Grant, 'The Future of Constantinople', 20 Dec. 1918.

[65] CAB 29/2/P-91, Montagu, 'The Future of Constantinople', 8 Jan. 1919.

[66] CAB 27/39/EC2841, Note to Hirtzel, 20 Dec. 1918.

[67] CAB 27/39/EC2824, General Staff, 'The Strategic Importance of Constantinople to the British Empire', 22 Dec. 1918. Also in WO 106/64. CAB 27/39/EC2823, Memorandum by Admiralty.

[68] CAB 27/39/EC2824.

States meanwhile was perceived as a not wholly altruistic ally, as 'her recently declared naval ambitions and her policy of the freedom of the seas, makes her an undesirable tenant, even in the doubtful contingency of her being willing to accept the responsibility'.[69] British control would undoubtedly create too much opposition with the other powers, and so the military concluded that the Turks should be left in control, though with the Straits declared an international waterway.

On the side of expelling the Turks stood Mallet and Curzon. Mallet observed that as Ottoman finances and sanitation were already under international control it would be an easy matter to go one step further and internationalize the city.[70] As the Eastern Committee was so divided on the issue, Curzon was asked to sum up both views as the most useful guide to the peace delegation.[71] Inclined as he was towards expulsion, Curzon's language in support of this view was the stronger.[72] He commented that 'The world is looking for great solutions. Let not this occasion . . . be missed of purging the east of one of its most pestilent roots of evil.'[73] Curzon also added the idea, recently broached, that a possible compromise might be to make Constantinople the headquarters city of the League, perhaps with the United States providing the administration.

A particularly vexing problem was how much of Anatolia to leave to the Turks, how much to award to the Greeks and Armenians, and how much to allow to the Allied Great Powers. Merely untangling Great Britain's commitments on this question proved a major task. Toynbee has left us with an excellent sketch illustrating the difficulties involved in suggesting logical frontiers.

---

[69] CAB 27/39/EC2824.

[70] CAB 27/39/EC2964, Mallet, 'Constantinople and Internationalisation', 25 Dec. 1918.

[71] CAB 27/24/EC46, 23 Dec. 1918.

[72] Indeed Montagu wrote to Curzon on 6 Jan. 1919 complaining that Curzon's summing up was not an accurate reflection of the Eastern Committee's views. Montagu Papers AS-III-3-495.

[73] CAB 27/39/EC3027, Curzon, 'The Future of Constantinople', 2 Jan. 1919. Also in CAB 29/2/P-85.

On the eve of the peace conference I was given the job (among a number of others) of suggesting — with a map — the bounds of a possible Greek enclave round Smyrna. I carried out these instructions, and learnt, in doing so, that this plan was a geographical absurdity. It was not till I visited, in 1921, the then Greek-occupied area that I realized how small the Greek minority was, even within the area that I had delimited.[74]

These difficulties in determining frontiers are reflected in the evolution of preparations on the Anatolian question.

Toynbee in particular did not care for the Italians, a view which was widely shared and which grew as the peace conference itself progressed. In discussing Italian claims he predicted that allowing the Italians south-west Anatolia would only arouse the opposition of the native inhabitants, adding that the Italians' 'record in colonial enterprises elsewhere indicates that they would be oppressive and incompetent'.[75] Concern about the rapacity of the Italians was linked to concern for the Mediterranean balance of power. Toynbee pointed out that the British aims listed in his report on the settlement with Turkey would avoid the Ottoman Empire being replaced by a great power dominion or by protectorates. Rather a series of new nation states would be erected, leaving the frontiers of the Allied states with Turkey as they stood under the status quo. Italian gains in the Mediterranean, however, would inevitably alter the overall balance of power to the detriment of Great Britain and France.[76]

On the 9 December Toynbee produced a report on the 'Future Turkish State' meant to cover subjects overlooked by his earlier report and Nicolson's memorandum.[77] Neither of these reports had dealt with the possibility of Anatolian cessions to Greece. Toynbee pointed out that such a transfer would involve great ethnographic, economic, and strategic difficulties and recommended instead that the Greeks in this region be allowed broad self-government. He suggested that the Greeks on the Black Sea littoral could be accommodated within the new Armenian state, while the Greeks on the Straits

[74] Toynbee Papers (Individuals-W), Toynbee to Arthur Walworth, 5 July 1968.
[75] Confidential Print 11908*.   [76] Ibid.
[77] FO 371/4354/f36/PC94, Toynbee, 'The Future Turkish State', 9 Dec. 1918.

and the Aegean littoral would remain Ottoman subjects, but under a special regime.

This report was followed by one which received a smaller circulation and proposed an alternative territorial settlement in Thrace and the Straits.[78] Toynbee's ideal solution was to place the entire zone of the Straits under one power, or the League. This would exclude Greece from the Straits, which could then be allowed a strip of Anatolia stretching from Smyrna to Cheshme. Toynbee also suggested various permutations of this plan involving trade-offs of Greek claims in Thrace against Anatolia in the event of the zone of the Straits not becoming a single mandate. The General Staff advised that British military security in the Middle East required that Turkey not be anti-British, and therefore Anatolia should remain independent and undivided. In particular the military advised against strangling the hinterland by denying the Turks the port of Smyrna.[79]

These different views all point to the difficulty of reaching an agreed position on the Turkish peace settlement. Having decided that the best peace in terms of durability and inherent justice would be one which took account of national-ethnic composition, the settlement for Turkey became hopelessly complicated to unravel and strategically and economically unrealistic. British policy had to date been one of support for Turkey's ethnic minorities coupled with support for a harsh line on the Turks. The dispersed locations of the ethnic minority groups and the lack of clear geographical divisions made any proposal on frontiers open to question. The military finally decided to support leaving Anatolia united under Turkish rule on purely geo-strategic grounds, a policy not in accord with the prime minister's philhellenic views. The uncertainties over this question are clearly reflected in the progress of the Turkish question at the peace conference, where a struggle emerged between the philhellenic and mishellenic factions.

Islam was a subject inextricably linked to the Turkish question, and one upon which various British officials exhibited a high degree of nervousness. John Shuckburgh of the India

---

[78] FO 371/4356/f162/PC162. Toynbee, 'Memorandum on Alternative Territorial Settlement in Thrace and the Straits', 31 Dec. 1918.

[79] Webster Papers 3/7/34.

Office noted 'the momentous fact that the sovereign of Great Britain holds sway over more Moslems than any Osmanli Sultan in the greatest days of the Ottoman Empire'.[80] The goodwill of the Muslim community was of critical importance given the vast number of Muslims already under the British crown, now being augmented by those in the Middle East. The Historical Section produced two handbooks on the subject, *The Rise of Islam and the Caliphate* and the other on *Islam in India and Islam in Africa*, to inform the delegates about the political importance of the faith.[81] Hardinge thought it undesirable to discuss arrangements for the Hagia Sophia for fear of causing 'deep offence to the Mohammedans in Egypt, Turkey & India'.[82] The Eastern Committee indeed sent a resolution to the Cabinet suggesting that Great Britain should abstain from interference in the question of the caliphate.[83]

Montagu was also concerned about Muslim opinion and was troubled when Toynbee suggested that Great Britain should avoid making any decision concerning the future of the caliphate, though he noted that Britain could influence Muslim opinion indirectly by its policy over Constantinople. Montagu was apparently so sensitive on the question and believed it 'so grave a matter that it should not be referred to at all in any written paper'.[84] Crowe was clearly angered by Montagu's reaction, and in a minute on this dispute observed that the PID existed to place Foreign Office views before the War Cabinet, for which purpose the memorandum had been written. Crowe did not want the Office muzzled, and the offending paragraph remained in Toynbee's report.[85]

[80] FO 370/f30550/183448, Shuckburgh to Historical Section, 4 Nov. 1918. Lloyd George expressed a similar opinion at the peace conference when he told the Council of Four that 'Great Britain was, perhaps the greatest Mohammedan power'. 21 May 1919. FRUS:PPC:V, p. 756.

[81] FO 373/5/6/ and FO 373/5/8. The India Office wrote to Cecil on 6 Nov. complaining that the author of the handbook on the 'Rise of Islam', Prof. Margoliouth, was too opinionated to make the book useful. Cecil Papers BL Add. MS 51094.

[82] FO 371/4354/f36/PC36, Minute by Hardinge, 20 Nov. 1918. This memorandum was revised and resubmitted on 21 Dec. 1918.

[83] CAB 27/38/EC2763-A.

[84] FO 371/4368/f480/PID573, Minute by Crowe, 25 Nov. 1918, recounting substance of a telephone call from Shuckburgh.

[85] Ibid.

The question which proved to be the most divisive and troublesome for the Eastern Committee concerned British policy for the Caucasus. Armenia, Georgia, and Azerbaijan were all enjoying a precarious independence, while Dagestan and Kurdistan seemed to be possible candidates for statehood. The difficulty facing the committee was to decide on the degree of British involvement in this remote and inaccessible area. There was general support for the national aspirations of these peoples, though it was assumed that the help of an outside power would be required for several years. The problem was to decide on the British preference for the role of assisting power. Curzon for one believed that 'We want to have an Armenia which, if not now, at some time in the future, and whether its boundaries are narrow or wide, shall be a self-governing community'.[86] He did not favour, however, Britain assuming a mandate for Armenia, recognizing that Britain's resources were already extended to the limit and that for the foreseeable future Britain would have its hands too full 'to be able to undertake any responsibility so colossal as that of being responsible for the future of the Armenian State'.[87] If there was to be a mandatory power it would have to be either the United States or France, and Curzon believed that it would be advantageous to British aims in the Arab lands to divert French attention away into the remote Caucasus.

Cecil emerged as a proponent of a greater Armenia stretching from the Black Sea to the Mediterranean, which could act as a barrier against what he considered as the scourge of Pan-Turanianism. He too favoured the idea of diverting the French into this volatile area, though he admitted that the real aim was 'to get a barrier across from the Black Sea to the Mediterranean, if it can be done reasonably'.[88] But General Wilson, Chief of the Imperial General Staff, feared allowing such a barrier to fall into the clutches of the French, and therefore proposed an unusual two-Armenia solution. Former Turkish Armenia could possibly be allowed to France if necessary, while the former Russian Armenia centred at Erivan would be left without the advantages of French tutelage. For General Wilson the chief concern was the threat posed by French control of a large

---

[86] CAB 27/24/EC40, meeting of 2 Dec. 1918.   [87] Ibid.   [88] Ibid.

block of the Levant lying between Great Britain and Britain's eastern empire. He hoped to minimize the threat by reducing France's Armenian slice.[89]

The committee followed a similar line in its discussions on Georgia and Azerbaijan, supporting independence while expressing concern over the pernicious influence another power might exert as the mandatory authority.[90] When it actually came to making a decision the committee was reluctant to allow any other Great Power to dominate this region. The future of Azerbaijan was a particularly vexing problem, for as Curzon observed, 'The really embarrassing factor of this problem is Azerbaijan . . . the difficulty about the Government of Azerbaijan at the moment is this, that it is violently pro-Turk, violently anti-Armenian, violently anti-Persian, — in fact it is everything we do not want it to be.'[91] Much of the concern expressed about the Caucasus was linked to the oil wealth of the region. To control the oil it was necessary to control the two strategically important ports of Batum on the Black Sea and Baku on the Caspian, along with the railway line between them which passed through Tiflis. The difficulty was that Baku was in Azerbaijan while Batum and Tiflis were in Georgia. The committee proposed making these port cities into free ports, thereby avoiding any state putting a stranglehold on the supply of petroleum. The Eastern Committee resolved that Great Britain should support the existence of strong independent states in the Caucasus, with the strongest claim to early recognition going to Georgia, which was considered the most advanced.[92] Strong regional states were clearly preferable to ones needing French tuition.

The most critical session of the Eastern Committee was held on 9 December 1918. In what must at times have been a heated meeting the committee at last discussed overall policy for the Middle East, and tried to come to terms with the voracious appetite with which they had envisaged the British

---

[89] CAB 27/24/EC42, meeting of 9 Dec. 1918. See also 'General Staff Desiderata Regarding Territorial Adjustments'. Webster Papers 3/7/34.

[90] CAB 27/24/EC41–43.   [91] Cab 27/24/EC40.

[92] CAB 27/24/EC43 and CAB 27/38/EC2715-A. It was recommended that Georgia should include the Muslim Georgians of Batum and Lazistan.

lion, however reluctantly, devouring the Middle East and the Caucasus. The rogue elephant at this meeting was Edwin Montagu, who clearly disapproved of Curzon's vice-regal way of guiding the committee. Montagu complained that

we treat each area, as it seems to me, according to the almost irrefutable and unanswerable arguments addressed to us by our Chairman. With the assent of the Committee we seem to be drifting into the position that right from the east to the west there is only one possible solution of all our difficulties, namely, that Great Britain should accept responsibility for all these countries. For some reason, France is objectionable *here*; for other reasons, America is objectionable *there*, and the only solution is that we should be the tutelary Power, the protecting Power, or whatever the adjective is, although we agreed that there should be no annexation.[93]

Montagu was alarmed by the situation and wanted it reviewed before final decisions were made, and in this he found an ally in Arthur Balfour.

Balfour intervened when General Wilson recommended that Great Britain should take the mandate for the Caucasus because of the need to protect India. Balfour stated the obvious reality of the situation when he said, 'If Russia is in a position to crush them, why not? We should not go there to protect them from the Russians. It would be folly, from a purely military point of view, for us to try to keep a military force there.'[94] Balfour then proceeded to demolish the argument which based British imperial expansion on the need to defend India. 'Everytime I come to a discussion — at intervals of, say, five years — I find there is a new sphere which we have got to guard, which is supposed to protect the gateways to India. Those gateways are getting further and further from India . . . .'[95] He observed that if the French were inclined to be troublesome in the Middle East they would have to get there by sea, leaving themselves open to Britain's considerable naval power. Balfour's calm observations, combined with Montagu's more excitable statements, illustrate the growing shift away from blind expansionism to considered consolidation.

[93] CAB 27/24/EC42.   [94] Ibid.   [95] Ibid.

Balfour, ever the conciliator and postponer, finally suggested ending such an acrimonious debate by leaving the decision on the Caucasus to the peace conference. At this Curzon's temper flared. He reminded Balfour that the Eastern Committee's remit was to prepare policy for the peace conference. In what must have been a memorable exchange Curzon retorted that, 'Now that we are trying to perform that task, Mr. Balfour says, "Why not postpone it to the Peace Conference?" I am trying to help you at the Peace Conference Mr. Balfour, for you will be our chief delegate there.'[96] To this onslaught Balfour blandly replied, 'I do not think it is our business to have a policy with regard to these places.'[97] Curzon concluded the exchange, in an undoubted state of frustration, with the comment that 'We shall get on very badly if we do not. I think we must have an idea of what we are working for.'[98] The committee then quietly moved on to other topics. After some discussion of the problem of the Sykes–Picot Agreement, Curzon closed the meeting noting that he had hoped in vain that the committee could have concluded its discussions. Curzon redrafted his original proposed resolutions to take into account the criticisms of the committee, and at the next two meetings most of the revised proposals were accepted with only minor modifications.

When the Eastern Committee came to discuss Persia they touched on a subject which was of one Lord Curzon's great interests. An acknowledged expert on Persia, he described it as 'one of the most puzzling, and in some respects one of the most discouraging with which we have to deal'.[99] He summed up the situation in Persia with some despondency: 'We are face to face, in the first place, with a country the government of which is weak and incompetent, the ruling classes corrupt and extortionate, the monarch worthless, and the lower classes in a deplorable condition intellectually, physically, and materially.'[100] It was a country of considerable strategic importance to the Indian Empire, and several of those present at the meeting of the Eastern Committee had previous experience of the problems involved. Among those sitting in the room were Curzon, a former viceroy; Montagu, the Secretary of State for India; and

[96] Ibid.   [97] Ibid.   [98] Ibid.   [99] CAB 27/24/EC45.   [100] Ibid.

Sir Charles Marling, the minister at Tehran. Curzon summed up Britain's traditional policy as being 'to build up, establish and fortify the independence and integrity of Persia'. [101] Now that Great Britain was extending its sphere in the East, Persia, 'instead of being a solitary figure moving about in a chronic state of disorder on the glacis of the Indian fortress, has the Indian frontier on one side of her and what is tantamount to a British frontier on the other'. [102] Curzon believed that Persia could not stand on its own and that therefore a mandatory power would be required. His aim was for Great Britain to maintain its position of general political predominance in Persia.

The India Office also wished to see some supervisory power installed in Persia, with a view to making it a tolerable neighbour. Naturally it was assumed that Great Britain was 'the nation best qualified for the task' but another power would be acceptable, since any state involved in Persia would need British support regardless. [103] The Foreign Office was concerned as to who could act as the mandatary for Persia, with the PID recommending a small state such as Switzerland, Norway, Denmark, or Belgium. Germanophobia was carried to a laughable extreme with the suggestion that if the choice fell to Switzerland, only francophone Swiss be allowed to participate. It was accepted that the Swiss might be unwilling to agree to such a restriction. While the PID thought that Great Britain would undoubtedly be the best mandatary, it was concerned as to the extent such an undertaking would strain Britain's administrative and financial commitments. Alternatively the whole matter could be avoided at the peace conference, thus leaving the solution to be dealt with by Great Britain bilaterally. [104]

Curzon was not favourably impressed with the idea of letting the Belgians loose in Persia, commenting that 'Efficiency is not the ideal with them that it is with us, and their tendency is

---

[101] CAB 27/24/EC45.   [102] Ibid.   [103] Confidential Print 11582*.
[104] FO 371/4356/f143/PC143, 'Memorandum Regarding the Policy of His Majesty's Government towards Persia at the Peace Conference.' Prepared by Forbes-Adam in consultation with Toynbee, and revised by Crowe. Also in CAB 27/38/EC2772.

to embark upon a policy of intrigue'.[105] With Norway Curzon was kinder, stating briefly, 'Her loyalty may be unquestioned, but I should have thought that her capacity was a very doubtful factor.'[106] From Curzon's point of view only one country was suited for the job — the British Empire. 'Our stake is the greatest, our knowledge of these parts of the world by far the most profound; our experience extends over a much longer period of time. We are the people naturally and inevitably to do this thing.'[107] The Eastern Committee, however, was unable to reach any definite conclusions about Persia, and Curzon contented himself with expressing agreement with a revised version of the Foreign Office memorandum.[108]

The Indian Empire

Questions concerning the Indian Empire were left to the India Office, which produced a long memorandum on desiderata, probably written by Sir Arthur Hirtzel.[109] It was divided into two parts, of which the first, on the disposal of conquered territories, dealt solely with Mesopotamia and the small Persian Gulf island of Abu Musa. The second and far longer section covered arrangements with the Allied powers. Foremost among the India Office's goals was to gain control of the remaining sub-continental pocket colonies of France and Portugal. The French possessions consisted of five settlements, with the most important one at Pondicherry being spread over ten isolated strips. Hirtzel, in summing up the problem of the French colony, explained that

So far as the four Madras Settlements (Pondicherry, Karikal, Mahe, and Yanaon) are concerned, the worst that can be said is that their continued existence constitutes an administrative inconvenience. But

---

[105] CAB 27/24/EC45. Britain had disapproved of the activities of Belgian administrators in Persia prior to the First World War. See Confidential Print 10081, particularly on the activities of M. Mornard, the acting treasurer-general.
[106] Ibid.   [107] Ibid.   [108] FO 371/4356/f143/PC143.
[109] Confidential Print 11582*, 'Indian Desiderata for Peace Settlement', 4 Dec. 1918. Also in CAB 29/2/P-42, FO 371/4355/f85/PC85, and India Office L/P&S/11/142/5441/18.

the question of really vital importance is Chandernagore. The situation there may fairly be described as intolerable.[110]

Chandernagore was a particular thorn in the Raj's side, being twenty miles from Calcutta. 'It provides an anarchist centre, within a few miles of Calcutta, where plans can be hatched, bombs manufactured, arms imported, emissaries instructed and youths depraved *with absolute impunity*.'[111] The author pointed out that in all probability the attempted assassination of Lord Hardinge in 1912 was planned there.

In addition the India Office hoped to do away with the French *Loges*, the sites of former French factories over which the French claimed to exercise certain rights of jurisdiction. A possible compromise was suggested by which the French would exchange all their territory for one enlarged and consolidated settlement at Pondicherry. Likewise it was thought that 'The elimination of Portuguese territorial rights would be an administrative convenience'.[112] A heavy price, however, was not considered justified to attain this end. The issue did not arise at the Peace Conference and Portuguese India was to survive the end of British rule by thirteen years.[113]

The India Office memorandum discussed in some detail its aims in the states bordering the Empire. In Afghanistan it was pointed out that Great Britain was pledged to the Amir not to bring up any questions concerning his country at the peace conference. On Tibet the India Office was anxious to abrogate the 1907 convention, which acted as an Anglo-Russian self-denying ordinance. Concern was also expressed over Japanese expansion, the India Office commenting that 'it is very desirable, from the Indian point of view, that Japan should not be permitted to establish herself, politically or commercially, in the two Chinese provinces of Szechuan and Yunnan, which border on Tibet and the Indian Empire'. In Persia the India Office regarded the 1907 convention as dead and considered that 'the "spheres of influence" no longer have any meaning'.[114] The future of Persia directly affected the defence

---

[110] Confidential Print 11582*.   [111] Ibid.   [112] Ibid.
[113] An end to Portuguese rights over the appointment of high Roman Catholic dignitaries in India was also thought to be desirable.
[114] Confidential Print 11582*.

of India for, unfortunately, 'Persia as a body politic, is in the last stages of decay and decomposition'. The India Office's chief concern was that Persia should have a stable pro-British government.

Russian Central Asia provided another subject for the India Office's concern, and it was agreed with the Foreign Office that as British interests in this region were almost entirely concerned with India, the case should be prepared by the India Office. It was recommended that no encouragement should be given to the establishment of an independent Muslim state in the region, and that a Russian government should be responsible for maintaining order there, preferably the government now located at Omsk.[115] Sir Esme Howard in a note summarizing the India Office's views, commented that the idea of separating Russian Central Asia from European Russia would constitute a shift in policy, and in any case it would be difficult for Great Britain to exert influence in the region.[116]

The Far East

Comparatively little work was done to prepare material on the Far East, undoubtedly because it seemed unlikely that anything of a controversial nature would arise. Macleay, who handled the PID's work on the Far East, summed up the situation concisely in a memorandum on 'The Far East and Non-African Colonies'.[117] Macleay took into consideration both the American views on the Far East and the future relations of China with the outside world, but the only potential difficulty he foresaw in achieving a smooth settlement was Japan. Macleay observed that Japan's 'aggressive policy and the exclusive and selfish spirit which the Japanese have shown towards all foreign competition in their spheres of interest are diametrically opposed to the altruistic attitude of

[115] FO 371/4352/f13/PC78, India Office, 'The Future of Russian Central Asia', 3 Dec. 1918.
[116] FO 371/4352/f13/PC78, Howard, 'Russian Central Asia', 28 Dec. 1918.
[117] FO 371/4355/f87/PC87, Macleay, 'The Far East and Non-African Colonies', 13 Dec. 1918. Discussed by the Imperial War Cabinet, 20 Dec. 1918, CAB 23/42/IWC44.

America in her relations with China'. [118] Japan, however, had been Great Britain's major Far Eastern ally since 1902 and Macleay's report supported Japan retaining the leased territory of Kiaochow, which had been captured from the Germans, although China would clearly ask for its retrocession and would look to America for support. He also recommended remodelling the administrative system of the International Settlement at Shanghai to vest control in the powers with the greatest population and whose nationals owned the bulk of the rateable property, an arrangement likely to be much in Britain's interest.

Macleay suggested as a technical measure that China should conclude short, simple agreements with the enemy countries for regulating their relationship. He favoured restoring special rights and privileges to the Austrians and Germans, since allowing the Chinese to withhold them might create a dangerous precedent. This brought a note of disapproval from the Board of Trade which recommended that the Allies conclude no agreements with the Central Powers for five years, or until they were admitted to the League of Nations. The Board of Trade was definitely opposed to a restoration of any special status to the defeated powers. [119]

Headlam-Morley in a minute on this exchange of views noted that the Board of Trade's policy would amount to 'war after war'. [120] He believed that after peace had been made and 'after satisfaction had been given to the Allies with regard to reparation and punishment, German[y] would, according to all precedent, renew her position as one of the family of European Nations, with a claim to complete equality in consideration and treatment'. The matter was resolved by referring the question to Sir John Jordan, the minister in Peking, who considered a revival of the special treaties a retrograde step. British opposition to such a move could only benefit its position in China.

Lord Eustace Percy, recently returned from the United States, shared Macleay's concern about American policies, writing that 'it is in our interest to maintain the Japanese Alliance till such time as we can really rely on consistent American

[118] FO 371/4355/f87/PC 87.
[119] Ibid., H. Fountain (Board of Trade) to Macleay, 19 Dec. 1918.
[120] Ibid., Minute by Headlam-Morley, 23 Dec. 1918.

co-operation in the Far East'. [121] As at the Washington Conference of 1922 there was the danger that the chimera of an American alliance would be allowed to replace the reality of a functional Anglo-Japanese Alliance. There was general agreement that Japan should gain something from the war, and there was little opposition to the terms of Great Britain's last wartime secret treaty, the Anglo-Japanese Understanding of February 1917. Under this agreement Japan was to receive Germany's Pacific possessions north of the equator, while the British Empire would gain those to the south, which were to go to Australia and New Zealand.

Africa and Latin America

From the first discussions in Asquith's War Committee there was a constant and unanimous agreement that Germany should lose its colonies. It was a British war aim of the first rank, and is reflected as such in the negotiating preparations. The concern lay not so much in getting the colonies from Germany, which was assumed; rather, the worry was whether the French or the Italians might become the successors of the German Empire. No matter how close the Allies had been in Europe, competition for control of the colonial world was a different matter, one in which France, Great Britain, and Italy were more often in competition than agreement.

Africa was to provide the opportunity for the greatest colonial carve-up of the peace settlement. [122] As it was assumed that none of Germany's colonies would be returned, the central question became the redistribution of Germany's overseas empire, with the three victorious European Great Powers the most likely heirs. The Mallet Committee and the Imperial War Cabinet Committee on Territorial Desiderata had already made clear that the British Empire should aim at gaining as much of the spoils as possible. South Africa was determined to

---

[121] FO 371/4353/f29/PC129, Percy, 'Anglo-Japanese Alliance and the League of Nations', 18 Dec. 1918.

[122] On British policy towards Africa see W. Roger Louis, *Great Britain and Germany's Lost Colonies, 1914–1919* (London, 1967) and by the same author, 'Great Britain and the African Peace Settlement of 1919', *American Historical Review*, 71 (1966), 875–92.

retain control of German South-West Africa, a policy aided by the presence in the British War Cabinet of General Smuts.[123] India was interested in German East Africa as a field of settlement for Indian colonists.[124] Only Togoland among Germany's African outposts excited little interest.

While the colonial negotiations at Paris would be concerned with the technicalities of disposing of Germany's colonial empire, on a broader scale what was being planned was a rearrangement of the delicate African balance of power struck at Berlin in 1886.[125] A potential new factor was the role the United States would decide to play in the African settlement.[126] Sperling, who was responsible for the PID's African Section, was concerned about America's intentions in Liberia, which seemed to amount to an unofficial protectorate. As with those involved in the Middle East discussions, Sperling believed that native peoples would naturally prefer British tutelage to that of any other state, and that this would hold true as well for Africa's only independent republic.

Sperling felt that Percy in his general memorandum on colonial policy had expressed the idea that

the United States Government should be given an opportunity of learning from actual experience that backward races must necessarily be controlled by some more highly civilised Power and, secondly, that equality of trade conditions should be instituted in all backward countries so controlled, including by implication those administered by the United States itself.[127]

Indeed there was a widely held view that American anti-colonialism could be diminished by giving it colonial

[123] Smuts resigned from the War Cabinet on 14 Dec. 1918 but continued to be active on several committees.

[124] Confidential Print 11582*.

[125] There was an exchange of notes between the CO and the FO over a memorandum on the 'Partition of Africa' prepared in May 1918. The CO was informed that it was not part of the Historical Section handbook series. The CO was therefore most surprised when this report appeared almost verbatim in this series in Dec., CO 323/776/25718 and 61912, FO 373/6/28.

[126] See W. R. Louis, 'The United States and the African Peace Settlement of 1919: The Pilgrimage of George Louis Beer', Journal of African History, 4:3 (1963), 413–33.

[127] FO 371/4355/f109/PC109, Sperling, 'Proposed United States Protectorate over Liberia', 12 Dec. 1918.

responsibilities. This had clearly been one of the Eastern Committee's motives in suggesting some form of United States
mandate over Constantinople and the Caucasus.

Sperling, however, pointed out that the United States was
not unaware or inexperienced in colonial matters, as it had
been ruling the Philippines for twenty years, and its Latin
American interventions had resulted in virtual protectorates
over Santo Domingo, Nicaragua, and Haiti. In Sperling's view
American colonial administration was usually disadvantage-
ous to the interests of British subjects, and he took every
opportunity to state his views. At the Peace Conference he
objected to giving the Americans a copy of the Historical
Section handbook on Liberia, which contained a scathing
analysis of that country, for fear that the United States would
subsequently use it against British interests with the Liberian
government.[128] In one report, concerning the possibility of
Abyssinia acquiring American advisers, Sperling commented
that 'it should be noted that United States advisers are scarcely
to be trusted after our experience in Liberia, where their violent
and high-handed suppression of disorders in the interior is in
no small degree responsible for the present troubles in that
country'.[129] Sperling recommended that the rights of British
subjects to equality of treatment should be made clear in advance of an American mandate.

The Horn of Africa with its control over the main sea route to
India was of particular strategic concern to Great Britain.
Sperling recommended support for the continued independence of Abyssinia as the most likely way to maintain stability,
and presumably to exclude other powers. Both Sperling and
the Admiralty recommended that to further this end France
should be cajoled into surrendering Djibouti, the most critical
port in the region.[130] In the event the French did not leave, and
Djibouti was to be the last colony in Africa to achieve independence.

Erle Richards's section of the peace brief on the German
colonies was not so much an outline for negotiators as a

[128] FO 370/97/f12608/94886.
[129] FO 371/4356/f128/PC128, Sperling, 'Proposals for Territorial Settlement
in North East Africa: Abyssinia and Somalialand', 17 Dec. 1918.
[130] Ibid., and ADM 167/57.

polemic against German colonial administration.[131] Richards viewed his role as Smuts's junior in preparing the peace brief as if it was intended for a judicial hearing. The result was that he produced something more akin to an indictment of Germany than to a useful set of instructions for diplomats. He supplemented his report with a vast appendix including such items as a 212-page 'Report on the Natives of South-West Africa and their Treatment by Germany', replete with photographs showing the inhuman treatment of the natives. All the documents Richards appended to his report had already been on public sale for months, and were certainly not an essential part of a negotiating brief. Richards's strongest plea was for South-West Africa to go to South Africa, a view not entirely surprising when one considers that his superior was General Smuts.

An area which received virtually no attention in the preparations was Latin America. Apart from a few handbooks prepared by the Historical Section no discussions were held nor reports prepared on questions concerning the New World. This is in striking contrast to the American Inquiry, which expended a disproportionate amount of its effort on Latin American questions.

The Military

The various military staffs were in favour of Britain keeping as much of Germany's colonial empire as possible. The Admiralty advised that it was essential from a naval viewpoint that the British Empire acquire South-West Africa, New Guinea, and Samoa from Germany. Togoland was deemed insignificant, and so could be given to the French, who would in return surrender Djibouti to Great Britain, a view shared by the General Staff. This would leave Britain in control of the Red

---

[131] CAB 29/1/P-34, Richards, 'Peace Conference: Memorandum Respecting German Colonies'. The appendices were Command Papers 9146, 8371, 8306, and 9210. Walter Long, after reading Richards's memorandum, suggested that he should consult with the Colonial Office as there were some slips. CAB 29/2/P-45.

Sea, a sea lane of increasing importance to the navy given the growing importance of Middle Eastern oil.[132]

The Air Staff put in a particular bid for German East Africa in order 'to provide an "all red" air route from Cape to Cairo'.[133] The chief concern of the Air Staff was the provision of strategically located aerodromes, with the prime sites being the Azores, Crete, Palestine, South Persia, Mesopotamia, and South Baluchistan. Given the needs of the air service, oil concessions were considered essential in Persia, Arabia, and Mesopotamia. Few of these Air Staff requests were related to questions likely to arise at the peace conference, but were more properly a subject for direct negotiations with the states concerned.[134]

The General Staff provided a long list of suggestions for the African settlement. Abyssinia was considered particularly important as 'the successful consolidation of our Middle East Empire demands either its absolute independence or the exclusion of other influence than our own'.[135] German South-West Africa and German East Africa were similarly considered essential additions to the British Empire. Curiously, the General Staff considered that an exchange of Gibraltar for the Spanish North African enclave of Ceuta might be desirable on military if not naval grounds.[136] The General Staff obviously envisaged the peace conference as taking place on a grand scale, including neutrals as well as belligerents.[137]

The Imperial War Cabinet

On the 20 December 1918 the Imperial War Cabinet met for a discussion of the various colonial memoranda and the resolutions of the Eastern Committee.[138] Lloyd George quickly dismissed any discussion of those colonies which had been

[132] ADM 167/57, 'Notes on Matters Affecting Naval Interests Connected with the Peace Settlement' (3rd revise), Jan. 1919.
[133] CAB 29/2/P-100. [134] Ibid.
[135] Webster Papers 3/7/34. 'General Staff Desiderata Regarding Territorial Adjustments', 19 Feb. 1919.
[136] A committee was appointed to consider this question in Apr. 1917, though it only met once, in Jan. 1919. See 'War Cabinet Committee on Proposed Exchange of Gibraltar for Ceuta', CAB 27/51.
[137] Webster Papers 3/7/34. [138] CAB 23/42/IWC44, 20 Dec. 1918.

occupied by Dominion forces with the assumption that there could be no question as to their fate, which had the simultaneous effect of staying the rapacious howlings of his fellow imperial premiers.[139] This left only German East Africa as the most contentious issue. Smuts, who had led the campaign to conquer the colony, put in a strong plea for Great Britain assuming a mandate for it. The old Boer leader made the interesting comment that 'The British Empire was the great African Power right along the eastern half of the continent, and securing East Africa would give us through communication along the whole length of the continent'.[140] While he wanted the United States to share mandatory obligations, Smuts did not want them in East Africa, commenting that 'There was no guarantee that the United States would understand how to govern African natives'.[141]

Curzon pointed out that the populations affected should at least be consulted before being allotted a mandatory power. The general consensus of the Cabinet, though, was that this could be only one factor, to be taken into account with geographical propinquity and security. Balfour had already expressed his view on self-determination in the Eastern Committee that

we must not allow ourselves to be driven by that broad principle into applying it pedantically where it is really inapplicable, namely, to wholly barbarous, undeveloped, and unorganised black tribes, whether they be in the Pacific or Africa. Self-determination there, I do not say has no meaning, I do not say it has not even a real meaning, but evidently you cannot transfer formulas more or less applicable to the populations of Europe to those utterly different races.[142]

Lloyd George recognized that this particular interpretation of self-determination might look like land-grabbing to President Wilson, whose goodwill was essential. It was assumed that the United States would decline any mandatory responsibility, but Lloyd George was determined to offer the United States first

[139] Hankey prepared Lloyd George for this meeting and recommended this course of action. His suggestions to Lloyd George are in Lloyd George Papers, F/23/3/30. Lloyd George's observations before the Cabinet seem to have been influenced by a memorandum by Leo Amery on 'The United States and the Occupied Enemy Territories', 20 Dec. 1918. Lloyd George Papers, F/23/3/32.
[140] CAB 23/42/IWC44.   [141] Ibid.   [142] CAB 27/24/EC41, 5 Dec. 1918.

refusal on a selection of mandates, which the British Empire could then reluctantly assume. Lloyd George added in justification of Britain's substantial list of desiderata that 'These territories could not be left to be exploited by Arabs or by European capitalists without a strong government to control them'. [143] Despite the many suggestions that the United States should be induced to participate in a mandatory system, there was the difficulty that Britain only really wanted the United States in places it could not take itself.

In the discussion on the Eastern Committee's resolutions, Lloyd George voiced the strong opinion that 'we should not let the United States into Europe, and, above all, into so dominant a position as Constantinople'. [144] Although Lloyd George had originally favoured giving the Americans Palestine, he now opposed the idea of 'placing an absolutely new and crude Power in the middle of all our complicated interests in Egypt, Arabia, and Mesopotamia'. [145] Curzon concurred and informed the Cabinet that the Eastern Committee was unanimously opposed to a United States mandate for Palestine. Indeed, he observed that if the United States took a mandate it should be for Armenia where the inhabitants clearly wanted American help. Churchill, though, opposed the idea of introducing the United States anywhere into the Mediterranean region as this might induce the Americans to become the greatest naval power. Churchill and the Admiralty both preferred to see the United States in East Africa where the British Empire already had more territory than it had the capacity to develop.

The Imperial War Cabinet drew up a set of conclusions to act as a guide for Lloyd George and Balfour in their forthcoming meeting with President Wilson, and by implication at the peace conference. It was recommended that the German colonies and the non-Turkish portions of the Ottoman Empire

[143] CAB 23/42/IWC44. This echoes his words of 5 Jan. 1918 when he said, 'the inhabitants should be placed under the control of an administration acceptable to themselves, one of whose main purposes will be to prevent their exploitation for the benefit of European capitalists or Governments'. WM ii. 1515.

[144] CAB 23/42/IWC44. Lloyd George later altered his position on an American mandate for Constantinople, himself proposing such a resolution to the Council of Four, 14 May 1919. FRUS:PPC:V, pp. 614–23.

[145] CAB 23/42/IWC44.

should not be handed back, and that instead these territories should be administered by mandatory powers on behalf of the League of Nations. The British Empire should be willing to place all the territories occupied by its forces at the disposal of the League, with the exception of German South-West Africa and the German islands south of the equator, which on geographical grounds must go to the bordering Dominions. It was proposed that Great Britain had a strong case for taking the mandates for Mesopotamia, Arabia, Palestine, and German East Africa.[146]

These discussions in the Imperial War Cabinet must have been more than Montagu could bear, and echoing his earlier comments in the Eastern Committee he acidly observed that 'it would be very satisfactory if we could find some convincing argument for not annexing all the territories in the world'.[147] Perhaps Montagu was right and the British Empire did assume too much responsibility. However, the delegation went to Paris well prepared, in part through background work of the experts on the facts, followed by discussions of the possible options in committee and the Cabinet. The meeting of the Imperial War Cabinet was the culmination of the preparations for the peace negotiations, and all this work helped to bring about the result that Great Britain left the conference gorged with almost all its colonial desiderata. Events within the next few years would show how dangerously over-extended the British Empire had become, but in the halcyon days of the immediate post-war era and within the confines of the diplomatic settlement reached at Paris, British aims had triumphed.

[146] Lloyd George Papers, F/23/3/31.   [147] CAB 23/42/IWC44.

6

Non-Territorial Questions

The most certain way of 'bolshevising' Germany would be to put an excessive burden on her.

Lord Milner, 24 Dec. 1918, CAB 23/42/IWC46/3

Preparations on questions of economics and international law were not as well organized as those on territorial problems. Whereas the PID played a co-ordinating role for much of the territorial planning it was not involved with non-territorial problems and questions relating to these areas were dealt with haphazardly. The Board of Trade and the Treasury each prepared lengthy reports on reparations. Energy needs were covered by the Petroleum Executive and the Admiralty, while communications and transit involved the Admiralty, the War Office, and the Postmaster-General. Legal questions were usually assigned to *ad hoc* committees, though the PID assisted in the planning for a League of Nations. In addition other ministries, committees, and sub-committees also submitted reports on these topics.

Political interference eventually reduced the usefulness of the reparations planning, while lack of direction seriously hampered work on a League of Nations. The experts' recommendations for moderate reparations were defeated by political support for a punitive indemnity. Very much as the Eastern Committee had taken over from the experts and inflated the definition of Britain's essential needs in the Middle East, so the Cabinet Committee on Indemnity inflated the Empire's financial requirements. At the other end of the spectrum work on developing a plan for the League of Nations virtually ground to a halt from lack of any indication of Cabinet policy, and resulted in an unprecedented letter of protest from the Foreign

Office's senior diplomats. All these topics formed part of the fabric of the Paris negotiations, and concerns about them were interwoven with the overall problems facing the British delegation.

ECONOMIC QUESTIONS

Reparations and Indemnities

Economic preparations focused on the problem of reparations and indemnities from the defeated states, together with general questions concerning the future of Britain's energy supplies, communications, and overseas transport. Demands for high reparations and an indemnity found little support among the economic experts, while the government, under the pressure of the general election campaign, took a harder line. The Treasury placed its preparations in the charge of John Maynard Keynes, who also represented the Treasury at the peace conference. It was his resignation in July 1919 in protest against the severity of the financial clauses of the German peace treaty, followed by the publication of his views in *The Economic Consequences of the Peace*, which sparked public reaction against the settlement. The harsh financial provisions of the Versailles Treaty have often been cited as the settlement's greatest flaw, and an examination of British planning on the subject reveals that the government was well aware of the dangers posed by exacting a large financial settlement, as well as the probability that Germany would be unable to pay such large sums.

The internal debate on peace aims was heavily influenced by the Paris Resolutions, adopted by the Allied Economic Conference in June 1916. Sir Albert Stanley, President of the Board of Trade, played an important role in the drafting of these resolutions, which dealt firstly with Allied wartime policy and secondly with post-war arrangements. Intended primarily to strengthen Allied co-operation on the economic front, the suggestions on post-war policy assumed that this co-operation would be continued after the war. It was recommended that Germany be denied most-favoured-nation status for a term of years, that limits be placed on its mercantile tonnage, and that devastated Allied territories should have first call upon raw materials. These resolutions did not command universal support within the British government, and, after America's entry into the war, account had to be taken of President Wilson's firm opposition to such policies.[1]

Two separate questions were involved in the discussions on the financial assessments to be levied against the Central Powers. First there was the question of reparation, which involved payment for losses of non-military property or of property lost through actions unacceptable to the laws of war. British claims here involved mostly shipping and related losses. The second question concerned the imposition of an indemnity, which was in fact a penalty imposed on the defeated powers for having waged war and lost. Wilson in the Fourteen Points had called for reparation to be made for damage done, a principle with which Germany had concurred by signing the Armistice. The difficulty therefore arose as to how best to construe these terms, and how to determine what Britain was justified in demanding payments for. At the conference it became obvious that Great Britain would have to cope with French extremist demands on one side, and America's aim of a moderate settlement on the other.

Of the early reports on the economic conditions for the peace treaty, the two most important opposed the imposition of harsh economic penalties against the defeated states.[2] The Board of Trade, responding tardily to Asquith's call for memoranda, submitted a report in January 1917 on 'Economic Desiderata in the Terms of Peace'. The Board did not desire

to impose terms of peace on the Central Powers inspired by motives of commercial revenge. The permanent crushing of the commercial and industrial power of Germany, even were it practicable, would not be to the eventual advantage of this country, while the attempt to

---

[1] A copy of the resolutions is in H. W. V. Temperley, ed., *A History of the Peace Conference of Paris* (6 vols., London, 1920–4), v. 366–9. For an analysis of the conference see Robert E. Bunselmeyer, *The Cost of the War, 1914–1919: British Economic War Aims and the Origins of Reparation* (Hamden, Conn., 1975), pp. 35–47.

[2] On this early phase of economic preparations see Bunselmeyer, *The Cost of War*, pp. 52–72.

effect it (though doomed to failure) would alienate the good opinion and outrage the moral sense of the civilised world.[3]

The Board called only for the inclusion of terms of economic defence in the treaty, but not of aggression. This moderate course found support in the Milner Committee's report to the Imperial War Cabinet, which fell short, however, of actually providing guidelines for any future negotiations.[4]

The final phase of preparations was initiated on 17 October 1918 when the War Cabinet placed General Smuts in overall charge of the peace brief, simultaneously ordering the Board of Trade to examine the economic aspects. On 26 October a report was also requested from the Treasury on indemnities.[5] The board was the first to complete its report, which was dispatched to Smuts on 15 November.[6] The Treasury was slower in organizing its case, which was placed in the charge of John Maynard Keynes, assisted by the 'A' Division of the Treasury.[7] Keynes wrote to Smuts on 19 November informing him that Sir John Bradbury, the permanent secretary at the Treasury, had placed him in charge of collecting and arranging the information for the peace conference which fell within the Treasury's sphere.[8] The Treasury's memorandum was ready by late November and was considered, together with the Board of Trade's report, by the Imperial War Cabinet on 24 December.[9]

The Board of Trade's memorandum on the 'Economic Considerations Affecting the Terms of Peace' incorporated many of the proposals of its report of January 1917. The main thrust of this memorandum was to delay German recovery long enough to give the Allies a head start. The Board now followed up its

[3] CAB 29/1/P-12. The report itself is dated 27 Oct. 1916, but Stanley only sent it to the War Cabinet on 24 Jan. 1917.

[4] CAB 29/1/P-15.

[5] CAB 23/8/WC488/1 and Bunselmeyer, The Cost of War, p. 85.

[6] Smuts Papers 101:32, Llewellyn-Smith to Smuts, 15 Nov. 1918.

[7] Keynes's authorship of the report is supported by evidence in John Maynard Keynes, The Collected Writings of John Maynard Keynes, ed. Elizabeth Johnson (London, 1971), xvi. 344.

[8] Smuts Doc. 862. Keynes wrote to his mother on 21 Nov. that 'I have been put in charge of financial matters for the Peace Conference'. Cited in R. Skidelsky, John Maynard Keynes, vol. i: Hopes Betrayed, 1883–1920 (London, 1983), p. 353.

[9] CAB 23/42/IWC 46/3.

earlier suggestions by recommending that the Allies not grant the Central Powers most-favoured-nation status for five years, or until admitted to the League. The trade of the Allied states, however, was to enjoy such status for at least twenty years. During the reconstruction period no materials were to go to the Central Powers until the needs of the devastated regions had been met. The principle of freedom of transit for persons, goods, and ships by land, sea, and air was to be included in the peace terms.[10]

The Board of Trade did not support a harsh policy on reparation, and was concerned mostly with the position of Great Britain as a maritime power. The final amount of the reparation was left open, but it was suggested that £400,000,000 should be paid in materials and the remainder in interest-bearing securities. All shipping belonging to the Central Powers in excess of 1,600 tons gross was to be allotted to the Allied states in proportion to their lossss through illegitimate action. A central inter-allied reparation fund was proposed which would accept payments, whether in cash or in kind, and redistribute them to the Allies in proportion to their requirements. Among the commonly mentioned goods to be taken in payment of the reparations were potash, gold, coal, ships, rolling stock, and materials.

It has sometimes been suggested that British preparatory efforts suffered through lack of co-ordination, a view not supported by the writing of the Board of Trade memorandum, which was prepared after informal consultation with the Treasury, Home Office, Foreign Office, Colonial Office, India Office, Ministry of Shipping, Ministry of Reconstruction, and the Department of Overseas Trade. Llewellyn-Smith in sending this memorandum to Smuts noted that it had been revised to embody the criticisms of these ministries, and while disclaiming unanimity of opinion, he believed that any remaining

---

[10] CAB 29/1/P-33, 'Memorandum by the Board of Trade on Economic Considerations Affecting the Terms of Peace', Nov. 1918, and revised Dec. 1918. Also in FO 371/4352/f14/PC14 and Keynes Papers T/12. The report is discussed in Bunselmeyer, *The Cost of War*, pp. 84–5, and in *MPC* i. 297–9. Lloyd George cites the Nov. edition of the report, but it should be noted that many of the passages he quotes were altered in the definitive Dec. edition, a fact he fails to note.

differences were minor.[11] Criticism was levelled none the less at the report. Lord Eustace Percy, in a note disapproving of the Board's recommended package of discriminatory trade measures against the Central Powers, advised that in the event of Bolshevik unrest in Germany it would be unwise for the 'capitalist' West to be seen discriminating against German trade. Conversely, if a stable and democratic government emerged in Germany such actions would not only violate Wilsonian principles, but could alienate American, Allied, and labour support.[12]

The Treasury's report on financial terms of peace was prepared primarily by John Maynard Keynes.[13] It did not differ greatly from, and took full account of, the Board of Trade's memorandum. Keynes opened with a recapitulation of Allied statements on reparations, from which he concluded that claims for the repayment of the general costs of the war were precluded. This was certainly not the opinion put forward by the French on 26 November in Paul Cambon's 'Examination of the Conditions of Peace', which proposed that Germany should pay the full cost of the war in fifty-six annual instalments.[14] Keynes observed that even assessing the damage done directly to civilians, excluding incidental damage, could well pass beyond Germany's capacity to pay. He warned that unless claims were made along the most unexceptionable lines, Germany might be able to turn excessive demands to its advantage by attempting to divide the United States from the European Allies.

In an earlier memorandum on indemnity, intended for the Armistice negotiations, Keynes had placed Germany's ability to pay at £1 billion, an amount sufficient to cover the actual damage of the war.[15] In preparing his report for the peace

---

[11] Smuts Papers 101:32, Llewellyn-Smith to Smuts, 15 Nov. 1918.

[12] FO 371/4353/f29/PC29.

[13] CAB 29/2/P-46, 'Memorandum by the Treasury on Indemnity Payable by the Enemy Powers for Reparation and other Claims'. Reprinted in Keynes, *Collected Writings*, xvi. 344–83. On Keynes's role see Bunselmeyer, *The Cost of War*, pp. 85–7; Skidelsky, *John Maynard Keynes*, vol. i: *Hopes Betrayed*, pp. 354–8; Howard Elcock, 'J. M. Keynes at the Paris Peace Conference', in M. Keynes, ed., *Essays on John Maynard Keynes* (Cambridge, 1975).

[14] FO 371/3446/f157260/198800.

[15] Keynes, *Collected Writings*, xvi. 338–43.

negotiations Keynes estimated the total amount of reparation due to the Allies for clearly accepted losses at £522,807 from Germany and £55,490 from the other defeated powers. Keynes briefly touched on the possible amount of an indemnity should this be claimed in excess of the reparations. He believed that if an indemnity were demanded it would be impossible to stop short of the entire cost of the war, which he estimated as follows:

British Empire	£6,600,000,000
France	4,150,000,000
Russia	3,500,000,000
United States	2,150,000,000
Italy	2,100,000,000
Belgium	200,000,000
Serbia	50,000,000
Romania	50,000,000
Greece	30,000,000
Portugal	10,000,000
TOTAL	£18,850,000,000

If pensions and demobilization costs were added to this sum the total indemnity could rise to £25 billion.[16]

Keynes suggested, however, that the question of an indemnity was irrelevant as he estimated Germany's capacity to pay at £3–4 billion. Keynes observed in a footnote to his report that 'If every house and factory and cultivated field, every road and canal, every mine and forest in the German Empire could be carried away and expropriated and sold at a good price to a ready buyer, it would not pay for half the cost of the war and of reparation together'. Keynes recommended that an actual payment of £2 billion 'would be a very satisfactory achievement in all the circumstances'. This was not meant to preclude Great Britain asking for more in the first instance, with the burden falling to Germany to show its incapacity to pay. But Keynes argued that should Germany's economy be devastated in the first instance, it would be unable to pay any further instalments. He observed, 'If Germany is to be "milked", she

---

[16] CAB 29/2/P-46.

must not first of all be ruined.' This remark is probably an expression of his opposition to a Carthaginian peace, and not advocacy for the policy of turning Germany into a tributary state. It must be remembered that this was meant as the Treasury's contribution to the peace brief, and as such was the work of civil servants. Keynes was unable to express openly his own views, but the tone of his words makes these clear.

Keynes closed the memorandum with a section entitled 'The Economic Consequences of an Indemnity', foreshadowing the title of his book of the following year. One concern aroused by the question of reparation payments was the effect these would have on the economies of the recipient states. Keynes and Ashley in 1916 had prepared a report showing that such large transfers of capital would not affect the receiver states provided this was spaced out over a period of years.[17] Keynes also re-iterated the danger which would be posed by a Germany forced to stimulate exports in order to meet its obligations. At best Great Britain would receive 15 per cent of the overall payment, with most of the reparations going to France. As Great Britain and Germany shared the same staple industries, any expansion of German productivity in these areas could only hurt British industry. There was, therefore, a limit to what could be demanded beyond which Germany would have to expand its exports to the detriment of British trade. Keynes believed that Britain's own best interests would be served if reparations were assessed at the relatively low figure of £2 billion.

Keynes identified two alternative policies which could be followed with Germany. The first option would be to obtain everything possible within three years, 'levying this contri-bution ruthlessly and completely, so as to ruin entirely for many years to come Germany's development and her inter-national credit'.[18] Keynes estimated this could yield £1–2 bil-lion, the amount he believed it practicable to expect. The alter-native option was to be less severe in the immediate future and to provide Germany with materials to develop its industries, 'and having thus nursed her back into a condition of high productivity to compel her to exploit this productivity under

[17] Keynes, *Collected Writings*, xvi. 313–34.   [18] CAB 29/2/P-46.

conditions of servitude for a long period of years'. Keynes's report clearly favoured the first option.

Keynes also discussed two other potential consequences, should Germany be squeezed too hard. He predicted that a German government responsible for vast annual reparations payments, together with servicing its own war debt, would face an impossible problem. Keynes warned that 'If all War Debts east of the Rhine have been repudiated, the proletariat of Western Europe may object to be shut out from the supposed advantages of such a situation. Repudiation is a contagious disease, and each breach in the opposite convention brings it nearer everywhere.' A second problem might arise if disenchanted Germans came to view the central government as an expensive luxury which turned over vast amounts annually to foreign states. This would inevitably lead to separatist movements, and occupying Germany to exact payment would not solve the problem for as Keynes observed, 'the cost of even a partial occupation may be so great as to exceed what extra it brings in a tribute': a lesson the French would learn during their occupation of the Ruhr in 1923. Keynes concluded that while Germany's capacity to pay the probable reparations bill fell short of the required amount, it could pay between 50 and 75 per cent of the bill. Under no circumstances, however, could Germany meet the full cost of the war in addition to reparations.

There was one other component in the preparation of Britain's economic policy for the peace conference, albeit of questionable value. This was the Committee on Indemnity which met briefly during November and December 1918 under the chairmanship of William Hughes, the tempestuous Australian premier.[19] The committee met ten times between

[19] CAB 27/43, 'War Cabinet, Proceedings and Memoranda of War Cabinet Committee on Indemnity'. Its final report is also in CAB 29/2/P-38. The Committee's terms of reference are in CAB 23/42/IWC38/12. The members of the committee were W. H. Hughes, chairman (Australia), W. H. Long (Colonial Secretary), G. E. Foster (Canada), W. A. S. Hewins (Treasury). In addition two businessmen were co-opted, Lord Cunliffe and Herbert Gibbs. Llewellyn-Smith, A. W. Flux, and Keynes attended all the meetings. Lloyd George gives a scathing account of the Hughes Committee in *MPC* i. 303–6. See also Bunselmeyer, *The Cost of War*, pp. 85–105. On Hughes's role see W. J. Hudson, *Billy Hughes in Paris: The Birth of Australian Diplomacy* (Melbourne, 1978), pp. 36–7.

27 November and 11 December at the Colonial Office, and considered no other reports than the Board of Trade memorandum and the Keynes and Ashley 'Memorandum on the Effect of an Indemnity'.[20] All the committee's members were supporters of a large indemnity, and the committee's final report recommended charging the entire cost of the war to Germany and her allies. After cursory examination, the committee saw no reason why Germany should be unable to pay the full amount. They believed that the British Empire's economic position would be worse off without an indemnity than with one, and suggested that the enforcement of such a penalty would operate as a deterrent to future aggression and as a guarantee of the world's peace.

The Imperial War Cabinet met on 24 December to discuss the Hughes Report, when the Australian premier explained that his committee had looked at the effects, amount, and mode of payment of an indemnity, but had not considered if the Allies were entitled to one under the Armistice terms. Hughes expressed the committee's belief that Germany could pay substantial sums, without any undesirable political affects, stating that he 'thought there was no country less likely to fall under the sway of Bolshevism'.[21] Milner strongly disagreed, and believed that a harsh indemnity would have just that result. Among the Cabinet members Milner certainly had the best understanding of Germany, having been brought up there. Churchill also disagreed with the Hughes proposals, basing his opposition on the effect such payments would have on the ordinary working-class household in Germany. He reckoned that this would mean that each household would have to produce £85 worth of goods for export a year, beyond sustaining itself. Hughes dismissed this argument by retorting that he was more concerned about the working classes in Britain and the Empire, than with the possibility of Bolshevism in Germany. Hughes was supported by Borden of Canada, who

---

[20] Keynes's report was not yet ready when the committee met. On 23 Dec. Hughes complained that the Treasury had subsequently issued a report controverting the conclusions of his committee. Bonar Law explained that it had been ordered before the Hughes Committee was appointed, and was not meant as a criticism. CAB 23/42/IWC45/3.

[21] CAB 23/42/IWC46/3, 24 Dec. 1918.

paradoxically favoured a large indemnity, while being unconvinced of Germany's capacity to pay it. The only Labour member of the government, George Barnes, advocated the same views as Keynes and supported reparations only. Despite this opposition the Cabinet concluded that the British Empire should press for the greatest indemnity possible, short of one requiring an army of occupation. This decision was undoubtedly a victory for the Hughes recommendations. Lloyd George later claimed that both he and Bonar Law 'regarded the conclusions of this Report as a wild and fantastic chimera. It was incredible that men of such position, experience and responsibility should have appended their names to it.'[22] Lloyd George did his best to ignore this inconvenient report, but the strident views of Hughes and those of like opinion helped to submerge the calmer views of the Board of Trade and the Treasury.

It was assumed that a large proportion of Germany's payments would be in kind, and attention was given in the economic preparations as to the most useful form these payments could take. The Treasury and the Board of Trade recommended that payments include important raw materials, but other ministries were quick to expand the scope of desirable assets. Francis Oppenheimer in particular contributed various memoranda on financial questions, including an exhaustive paper on Germany's amber and ambroid industry. Prussia produced most of the world's supplies of these substances, and he proposed that they should help contribute to Germany's indemnity.[23] Oppenheimer can be numbered among those who supported imposing a savage indemnity upon Germany. Though born and educated in Germany the super-British Oppenheimer held a low opinion of the Germans, as illustrated by his proposal that the peace treaty should include protection against such nefarious German practices as the imitating of British trademarks and packaging. Oppenheimer observed that, 'Given the German character and the great difficulties of export with which German manufacturers will be faced in the future, it is to be feared that this evil will assume increased

[22] MPC, i. 305.
[23] FO 371/4355/f92/PC92, 'Peace terms: Amber and Ambroid'. Oppenheimer to Crowe, 5 Dec. 1918.

proportions'.[24] Oppenheimer's recommendations were amazingly detailed, extending even to the disposal of German art treasures.

Most of Britain's actual property losses during the war were maritime, with the fishing fleet in particular being hard hit, and the Board of Agriculture and Fisheries recommended to the Foreign Office that sufficient fishing vessels be exacted from Germany to replace those destroyed.[25] The Board of Trade disagreed with this proposal as it might deprive Germany of food. The Board of Agriculture and Fisheries replied to this criticism with the comment that 'we shall be quite prepared to furnish pickled herrings to Germany — a very large importer of this article — and we may be prepared to supply her with other salt fish or even with fresh fish. It would do Germany no harm to go without fresh fish supplies.'[26] These views reflect the very deep hatred of the Germans, discernible particularly in the Hughes Committee, which was prevalent throughout important sections of the government.[27]

The debate on the financial policy Britain should follow at the peace conference was complicated by a number of external factors which eventually forced the government into a difficult position. A successful wartime campaign had been conducted to whip up public support for the war against Germany. As in all such campaigns the tide of animosity receded slowly, and cooler views did not become dominant again until around the time of the signing of the treaty. Public hostility was at its peak as a result of this policy during the period from November to January. Secondly a general election campaign was in progress, parliament having been dissolved on 25 November with polling on 14 December. Simmering public hatred of Germany was inflamed by a newspaper campaign, spearheaded by the Northcliffe press, to make Germany pay the full cost of the war. Extremist opinion can be summed up in the well-known phrase of Eric Geddes, 'The Germans, if this Government is returned, are

[24] Ibid. See also Francis Oppenheimer, *Stranger Within* (London, 1960).
[25] FO 371/4356/f168/PC168, Henry Maurice to Headlam-Morley.
[26] FO 371/4356/f168/PC168.
[27] Ibid. and MT 25/23/f62833/18, FO 368/2047/f207034/207034.

going to pay every penny, they are going to be squeezed as a lemon is squeezed — until the pips squeak.'[28]

Supporters of a Carthaginian peace ignored the implied Allied commitment of the Fourteen Points, a commitment Keynes made explicit in his report. The defeat of the moderate view, set out in the Treasury and Board of Trade memoranda, came with Lloyd George's reluctant acceptance of the Imperial War Cabinet's recommendation that Hughes and Lord Cunliffe, two of the chief authors of the Committee on Indemnity report, serve on the Reparations Committee at Paris.[29] Lloyd George claimed in his *Memoirs of the Peace Conference* that both he and Bonar Law opposed such a policy, but that given the public hysteria they could not say so explicitly.[30] Though Lloyd George's *Memoirs* must be read with caution, this statement was probably true. Lloyd George would not want to go to the negotiating table with his position already restricted by public promises. Added to this technical difficulty was the very real problem posed by the American president. Throughout the war Wilson had been a prophetic voice booming across the ocean to Europe. Now, in the midst of the Imperial War Cabinet's wrangling over negotiating policy, Wilson arrived in London. The president was adamant that no indemnity should be assessed against Germany. Lloyd George knew that he needed Wilson's support on a wide variety of issues where France and Britain disagreed. Lloyd George's ability to leave his hands unfettered by Imperial War Cabinet dictates, while simultaneously assuaging Wilson, shows the Welsh magician at his most effective. At Paris Lloyd George was undoubtedly

[28] *Cambridge Daily News*, 11 Dec. 1918, p. 3.
[29] The third member was Lord Sumner, a Lord of Appeal. Lloyd George later claimed that he hoped that Sumner would restrain his two colleagues, but Lord Sumner 'himself caught the infection and gave logical and literary form to its ravings'. MPC i. 314.
[30] Keynes indeed held preliminary talks in London with American Treasury officials who shared his views: *John Maynard Keynes*, vol. i: *Hopes Betrayed* (Skidelsky, p. 357). The Americans suffered, however, from lack of preparation, 'Questions concerning indemnities and reparations somehow remained outside the purview of the Inquiry's activities except as those matters were incidental to the consideration of other problems.' L. Gelfand, *The Inquiry: American Preparations for Peace, 1917–19* (New Haven, Conn., 1963), p. 298.

at fault in not allowing the financial experts to play a greater role, for in retrospect it can be seen that not only had they prepared accurate information, but had also developed a strategy which could have achieved a viable economic settlement with the defeated states.

Petroleum, Communications, and Transport

Economic preparations for the peace conference were not confined to reparations and the future financial relations between victors and vanquished. A number of economic questions of general interest were discussed in readiness for the conference, particularly concerning energy, communications, and transport. Of all these questions petroleum was undoubtedly the most important and increasingly critical concern of Great Britain.[31]

In 1917 the Ministry of Munitions established a Petroleum Executive under Professor John Cadman.[32] In December 1918 the Petroleum Executive drafted a memorandum for the Foreign Office on the 'Petroleum Position of the British Empire' for use at the peace conference. This report observed that 'One of the principle factors on which the commercial supremacy of the British Empire has been built up is its indigenous coal resources', but noted the development of the internal combustion engine was threatening this supremacy.[33] Great Britain

[31] On the petroleum policy of Great Britain see Marian Kent, *Oil and Empire: British Policy and Mesopotamian Oil, 1900–1920* (London, 1976), especially pp. 117–50 and App. VI. Further information on the Petroleum Executive is in Helmut Mejcher, *Imperial Quest for Oil: Iraq, 1910–1928* (London, 1976).

[32] John Cadman (1877–1941); educ. Durham University; prof. of mining and petroleum technology, University of Birmingham, 1908–20; created Baron Cadman, 1937. See also J. Rowland and B. Cadman (2nd Baron), *Ambassador for Oil: The Life of John, First Baron Cadman* (London, 1960).

[33] POWE 33/60 (old classification S.269). Also in FO 371/4356/f182/PC182. This report was printed by the PID in its PC series as PC/024. The correspondence in POWE 33/60 shows that this report was drafted by Capt. A. S. Jelf after a long discussion with Cadman. Sir Frederick Black looked it over and made some suggestions. Sir Arthur Selbourne Jelf (1876–1947); educ. Marlborough and Exeter Coll., Oxford; Malayan Civil Service, 1899–1925; seconded for Military Service (Intelligence), 1917–19; Colonial Secretary, Jamaica, 1925–35; knighted, 1932.

required an unlimited supply of oil for military purposes, and the report recalled that Britain had maintained control of world shipping by its command of bunker fuel. The Petroleum Executive considered it essential for Britain to retain its control of this commodity, whether it be oil or coal. It warned that 'It is no exaggeration to say that our existence as an Empire is very largely dependent upon our ability to maintain control of bunker fuels'. Oil was clearly the coming thing as oil fuel used in boilers was twice as economical as coal, and in an internal combustion engine four times as efficient.

The difficulty facing the British Empire was that the United States controlled 65 per cent of the world's petroleum production, and before the war supplied the United Kingdom with 62.3 per cent of its oil imports. The Petroleum Executive warned that 'it is obvious that America has it in her power to place us in a position of great difficulty if her own oil requirements or trade interests should dictate'. Given, however, that American supplies could already have peaked it was believed that the situation was 'pressing and insistent' and that at the peace conference all 'reasonable pressure' should be brought to bear to secure British control over as many new oilfields as possible. The most likely localities were Persia and Mesopotamia, where British-controlled oil companies were firmly established, particularly the Anglo-Persian Oil Co. and the Turkish Petroleum Co. The Admiralty in its own reports advocated a policy very much in accord with the views expressed by the Petroleum Executive.[34]

British energy interests were not limited to the Middle East, and the Petroleum Executive also considered the implications of British petroleum involvement in Eastern Galicia, which suggested that the region's inclusion within Poland would be the most commercially useful solution for British interests.[35] A concern very much linked to the control of petroleum was the

[34] ADM 116/1852.
[35] FO 371/4356/f185/PC185. A report communicated by the Petroleum Executive from Mr Perkins of the Premier Oil and Pipeline Co. and chairman of the International Committee appointed to protect Allied interests in Galicia. 'Memorandum on the Commercial Interests of the Allied Countries in Eastern Galicia in Relation to the Proposals Affecting its Future Political Status'. Printed by PID as PC/025.

question of coaling stations, and Percy in his memorandum on colonial matters enumerated the coaling stations considered of sufficient strategic importance for Britain to take control of.[36]

Given the geographical distribution of the British Empire, control over channels of communication was of the greatest strategic importance. During the war major realignments had occurred to the world's cable network, with the German submarine cables being seized. The Admiralty recommended that the appropriation of the German cable system carried out during the war become permanent, as might the provisional division of these cables which had been arranged with the French.[37] The Postmaster-General contributed to the preparations with a report on 'Postal and Telegraphic Communications with Germany and Austria', which considered that it was impossible that in future Great Britain should rely on a telegraphic route through Germany to India, and the Indo-European Telegraph Company was already arranging for another route.[38] The future of Germany's overseas cables was also discussed by the 'Clean Slate' Committee, which recommended not only that Germany's overseas cable and wireless stations should not be returned, but that compensation should not be paid, a policy with which the Postmaster-General concurred.[39] The Admiralty proposed that the enemy states be prohibited from constructing any high-power wireless telegraph stations for at least two years, unless they could be justified on commercial grounds.

Transport questions in particular were considered likely to pose difficulties in reaching a settlement, not only with respect to Britain's commercial interests, but in delimiting the

[36] FO 371/4353/f28/PC28. Percy listed these coaling stations as of importance: Swakopmund, Dar es Salaam, Duala, Lome, Tsingtau, Samoa, New Guinea, Solomon Islands, Pelew Islands, Marshall Islands.

[37] ADM 167/55, Board Meeting, 14 Nov. 1918.

[38] FO 371/4356/f169/PC169, Postmaster-General, 30·Dec. 1918.

[39] CAB 29/1/P-21. Percy in his memorandum on 'Colonies', FO 371/4353/f28/PC28, recommended keeping the German Pacific islands' wireless stations. Forbes-Adam in the report on Persia, FO 371/4356/f143/PC143, suggests avoiding discussion at the conference of the two telegraph lines through Persia, the Indo-European Co. line, and the line of the Indo-European Dept. of the Government of India. This agreed with the Admiralty view, ADM 116/1852.

boundaries of new states. The War Office's Director of Railways and Roads, H. O. Mance, prepared a report on the 'Transportation Aspects of Peace Negotiations: Delimitation of Frontiers', in which he warned that although a fundamental factor governing the delimitation of frontiers was frequently stated to be nationality, and that initial proposals would 'doubtless conform as closely as possible to ethnographical boundaries with due regard to physical features, it is evident that transportation considerations will play an important part in frontier delimitation and in other international arrangements which must be settled at the peace conference'.[40] With the realignment of frontiers and the creation of new states, what was once internal traffic would become international traffic, while some stats which previously had a coastline would now become landlocked.

Mance recommended that certain general principles should always be applied, otherwise 'the results will be conflicting and, in some cases, unsound, thereby laying up trouble for the future'.[41] Among the general principles Mance proposed were that railways joining different portions of the same country should not pass through an intermediate strip of foreign territory, a railway joining a land-locked state to the sea should pass through as few intervening states as possible, junctions near frontiers should be awarded to the state which was served by the majority of the lines, and where a state railway was to be divided the rolling stock should be allocated on the same basis as before the war. To assist land-locked states obtain trade outlets, Mance proposed internationalizing certain waterways, granting rights of transit over the railways of any intervening state, or the cession or lease of a river or seaport enclave to the interior state. Mance's proposals favoured no state in particular. His focus was mainly on the potential transport nightmare facing eastern Europe, and his suggestions revolved around providing equal economic opportunity and

[40] FO 371/4355/f86/PC86. H. O. Mance (1875–1966); Director of Railways, Light Railways, and Roads, War Office, 1916–20; Brevet Lt. Col.; CMG, 1917; CB, 1918; Transportation Adviser to the British Delegation, Paris, 1919–20; President, Communications Section of the Supreme Economic Council, 1919–20.

[41] FO 371/4355/f86/PC86.

minimizing friction between these new members of the international community. As such his views were very much in accord with the New Europe group, which supported Mance's efforts when the negotiations began.[42]

Special interest was shown in the future of certain railway networks, with individual memoranda covering railway problems in Switzerland, Luxemburg, and Persia. Although Great Britain had no commercial interest in the Swiss railways, it did have an interest in maintaining Swiss independence. The Swiss St Gotthard Railway and tunnel had been built with German, Italian, and Swiss finance and provided the main route between Germany and Italy. In return for these financial contributions Switzerland was bound by the 1909 St Gotthard Convention to give Germany and Italy the equivalent of most-favoured-nation status over the whole of the Swiss railway system. The Swiss considered this an infringement of their economic sovereignty and were pressing for revision of the agreement. In the interests of supporting Swiss independence from German influence it was recommended that Britain should favour Swiss claims.[43]

Concern was likewise expressed over German control of the Wilhelm–Luxemburg Railway, the most important of the four railway companies operating in the Grand Duchy. Originally a French concession, the line passed to Germany as part of the 1871 peace settlement, which controlled it through the Imperial German Railways, which also operated the network in Alsace-Lorraine. The line, which fed the Metz–Amsterdam/Antwerp main line, was only due to return to local control in 1959, when the concession expired, and Francis Oppenheimer was particularly concerned not to leave Germany in control of it.[44]

[42] Mance must have had the predictions of his report in mind when writing his comments on the 'Transportation Aspects of Frontier Questions', in Temperley, *History of the Peace Conference*, ii. 100–1. He reiterated these principles in H. O. Mance, *Frontiers, Peace Treaties, and International Organization* (London, 1946).

[43] FO 371/4353/f26/PC63, Randall, 'The Revision of the St. Gothard Railway Convention of 1909', Nov. 1918. Also in CAB 29/2/P-63.

[44] FO 371/4352/f16/PC16, 'Pre-war Rights of Germany over the Railways of Luxemburg', Nov. 1918. FO 371/4355/f74/PC74, Oppenheimer, 'Note upon the Railways of Luxemburg', 30 Nov. 1918. This memorandum is in line with the views expressed in Francis Gribble, 'The Luxemburg Railways', *New Europe*, 8:99 (5 Sept. 1918), 177–80.

A further area of concern about the control of railways was Persia, where the potential threat came not from Germany but from Russia. Railway development in Persia had been retarded by the 1890 Russo-Persian Agreement, an arrangement which was responsible for much of the chaos in Persia. Britain was naturally interested in any future rail developments, but it was thought best to avoid all Persian topics at Paris, leaving matters to bilateral talks. The General Staff in particular was concerned about this region, and realizing that Britain's current military advantage could well be temporary, they had evolved plans for a well-developed railway network as part of the defence arrangements. In Mesopotamia a system radiating from Baghdad was projected, as well as the extension of existing lines from Mesopotamia and India into Persia. The Euphrates valley line was envisaged as the backbone of the network, with priority being given to its development together with conversion to standard gauge.[45]

Internationalization of waterways was often suggested as a solution to transit problems in Europe. The successful internationalization of the Danube in the previous century had provided a powerful example in support of this policy, and in particular it was proposed that the Rhine should be placed under an international commission modelled on the Danube regime. Linked to the question of freedom of transit, by water or rail, was the necessity of creating free ports for use by landlocked states, and various suggestions were put forward as to which outlets might conveniently be declared free ports. Zimmern proposed increasing the number of European free ports from the pre-war figure of thirteen to a new total of twenty-two, together with six other Mediterranean ports. He envisaged a system which would connect the ports with the hinterland by navigable rivers, canals, and railways.[46]

[45] FO 371/4356/f143/PC143. CAB 27/38/EC2766, General Staff, 'Railway Policy in Relation to General Military Policy in the Middle East'.

[46] FO 371/4354/f42/PC42. See also FO 371/4355/f68/PC68, FO 373/151–152; FO 371/4353/f27/PC132, Headlam-Morley, 'Limburg', 18 Dec. 1918; FO 371/4355/f93/PC190, Headlam-Morley, 'The Freedom of Navigation of the Rhine and other Swiss Outlets to the Sea', 9 Jan. 1919; FO 371/4355/f93/PC93, Saunders, 'Freedom of Navigation of the Rhine', 9 Dec. 1918 (similar to Saunders's article 'Free Navigation of the Rhine', *The Nineteenth Century and After*, 85 (Jan. 1919)).

Labour

Labour matters provided one of the most likely spheres for future international regulation and organization. Against the backdrop of the increasing power of the Labour party within Britain, the planned meeting of a World Labour Conference to coincide with the peace conference, and the Bolshevik revolution in Russia, it was considered essential for the government to be seen raising labour-related questions at the conference. To prepare a policy for the government the Home Office and the Ministry of Labour produced a joint memorandum in which it was argued that the peace conference should not consider specific proposals, such as an eight-hour working day, but rather that the government should make a definite pronouncement in favour of international conventions on such topics as well as supporting an international labour organization.[47]

On the broader international level it was considered vital not to ignore labour questions in the economic negotiations at the conference as 'it would deepen the belief which has been repeatedly voiced in Labour circles since the days of the Paris Resolutions that the economic terms of peace will be framed solely in "capitalist" and commercial interests'. Although the Imperial War Cabinet scheduled a discussion on this report, it was apparently never held. The British War Cabinet, with Bonar Law filling in for Lloyd George, did discuss it on 10 January 1919 and substantially agreed with the report's conclusions.[48] British actions at Paris largely followed these guidelines, and the labour clauses of the settlement were in accord with British ideas.

INTERNATIONAL LAW

The League of Nations

Interest in some form of general international organization had been discussed by several generations of publicists. The

[47] CAB 29/2/P-41. Cave and G. H. Roberts, 'Labour Matters and the Peace Conference', 9 Dec. 1918. See also Edward J. Phelan, 'British Preparations', in James T. Shotwell, *The Origins of the International Labor Organization* (New York, 1934), i. 105–26. Phelan, who represented the Ministry of Labour at the peace conference, states that the Intelligence Division of the Ministry began planning for the conference as soon as the Bulgarian armistice was signed.

[48] CAB 23/42/IWC43/6, 18 Dec. 1918, and CAB 23/9/WC515/8, 10 Jan. 1919.

collapse of the old concert system combined with hopes of creating lasting peace and security impelled the Allied powers to convert these proposals into policy. By the time the Armistice was signed it was clear that the creation of a League of Nations would be part of any peace settlement. Woodrow Wilson's single-minded determination on this subject assured it an important place at the negotiating table, and it was quite possible that he would insist on the creation of a League as a basis for all other discussion. As early as 1917 the British government had begun to consider the desirability of such an organization, and discussions continued over the next two years as to what the framework and powers of the new league would be.[49] Part of the success of carrying a basically British view of the League in the negotiations must rest upon the fact that all those involved in the discussions at Paris were deeply involved in planning from the earliest preparatory phase.

The first discussions at a high level on the possibility of establishing some form of international organization to assist in the maintenance of peace occurred during the 1917 session of the Imperial War Cabinet. Lord Milner's sub-committee suggested that in future states which had signed the peace treaty should bind themselves not to resort to armed conflict 'without previous submission of their dispute to a Conference of the Powers'.[50] The American entry into the war later the same month added a powerful impulse to such ideas, and by early 1918 it had gathered sufficient support for Lloyd George to declare the creation of such an organization as being among

[49] On Britain and the League of Nations see Lord Robert Cecil, *A Great Experiment* (London, 1941), which unfortunately contains nothing on his work with the PID; George W. Egerton, *Great Britain and the Creation of the League of Nations: Strategy, Politics, and International Organization, 1914–1919* (London, 1979); Alfred Zimmern, *The League of Nations and the Rule of Law, 1918–1935* (London, 1936); Hugh P. Cecil, 'The Development of Lord Robert Cecil's Views on the Securing of a Lasting Peace, 1915–1919' (D.Phil. thesis, University of Oxford, 1971); C. M. Mason, 'British Policy on the Establishment of a League of Nations, 1914–1919' (Ph.D. thesis, University of Cambridge, 1970); *MPC* i. 403–29, which should be read with caution. The Noel-Baker Papers in FO 800/249 contain a useful collection of many of the most important documents.

[50] CAB 29/1/P-15.

Britain's three preconditions for establishing a permanent peace.

Lloyd George in his Caxton Hall address of 5 January 1918 advocated 'the creation of some international organization to limit the burden of armaments and diminish the probability of war'.[51] This view was reiterated three days later in Wilson's Fourteen Points speech in which the president proposed that 'a general association of nations must be formed under specific covenants for the purpose of affording mutual guarantees of political independence and territorial integrity to great and small states alike'.[52] Lord Robert Cecil, one of the strongest advocates of a League of Nations, had been pressing the government to consider how such a League could be organized, and on 3 January a committee of experts was appointed to consider the question.[53] The League of Nations Committee meeting under the chairmanship of Walter (later Lord) Phillimore was divided evenly between historians, Julian Corbett, A. F. Pollard, and J. H. Rose, and members of the Foreign Office, Crowe, Tyrrell, and Cecil Hurst. The committee met nine times between January and March 1918 and produced an interim report on 20 March and a final report on 3 July.[54]

Among the more significant recommendations of the Phillimore Committee was that force in the form of military and economic sanctions should be used if necessary to bring disputing states to international arbitration. Such states would be bound to attempt reconciliation, which naturally meant delay and which it was hoped would allow passions to cool. It was when states avoided this process that the other members of the

[51] *WM* i, 1517. Egerton notes that Lloyd George on this point was following a draft by Cecil. Egerton, *Great Britain and the Creation of the League of Nations*, pp. 60–1.

[52] J. B. Scott, ed., *President Wilson's Foreign Policy: Messages, Addresses, Papers* (New York, 1918), p. 362.

[53] Zimmern, *The League of Nations*, p. 179.

[54] Walter Phillimore, 2nd Lord Phillimore (1845–1929); educ. Westminster and Christ Church, Oxford; barrister, Middle Temple, 1868; President, International Law Assoc., 1905–8; Lord Justice of Appeal, 1913–16; author of *Three Centuries of Peace and their Teachings* (London, 1917). FO 371/3439; contains interim reports and correspondence concerning the committee. FO 371/3483, 'League of Nations Committee: Minutes and Proceedings'. Lloyd George wrongly dates the committee as having met in 1917 in *MPC* i. 405.

system would drag them into a conference to settle the matter. The report included a draft convention which proposed that the members bind themselves not to go to war with each other, to use arbitration, and in the last resort for members to go to war with a state which refused arbitration. The procedure for arbitration was an *ad hoc* affair, resembling the ambassadors' conference of the pre-war order. The Phillimore proposals did not go as far as later plans which called for an organization with a full-time staff located at a permanent headquarters. Rather the Phillimore Committee supported the creation of an agreed machinery to be activated in times of international stress.

After the Phillimore Committee had completed its main task in July 1918, Hardinge arranged for questions concerning the League to be taken by the PID, where they would be handled by Lord Eustace Percy under the supervision of Sir Eyre Crowe.[55] When the PID was reorganized in November for peace conference work, Percy was assigned to the League of Nations Section together with Alfred Zimmern, though no head was appointed, a fact which was later to cause difficulty. During the course of preparations four important plans were submitted for consideration by Percy, Zimmern, Cecil, and Smuts. The Percy and Zimmern reports were produced at the same time in November, and helped to form the basis for the later memoranda.

Lord Eustace Percy recommended that Britain should support the formation of a League of Nations which would promote regular international consultation, and which would have a permanent international secretariat. While the original members would be the Allied powers, the new states of Europe and the neutrals should be invited to join. This new league would act as guarantor of the whole peace settlement, and of the political and territorial integrity of the members. Percy envisaged this guarantee as being both collective and individual, thus allowing room for states to exercise independent judgement. Percy observed that this was not a radical proposal, but resembled the treaty guaranteeing Belgium. He proposed that Britain should put forward the Phillimore committee's report as the best scheme for pacific settlement of

[55] FO 371/4365/f253/PID253.

disputes. Percy believed it to be advisable to concentrate first on establishing a league along these lines, while leaving such volatile and potentially divisive issues as disarmament, freedom of the seas, and equality of trade conditions for future consideration. If too many issues were thrust upon the League at birth, he feared that it would be unable to cope.[56]

Zimmern's plan followed a similar line to Percy's concept of a permanent organization arranging regular conferences. He suggested, however, that while the League's guarantee of peace should be permanent, it would be wiser if all other treaties were not concluded for a duration exceeding ten years, when they could be renewed. He argued that long-term treaties were not consistent with the principles of state sovereignty. Zimmern, Percy, and the Phillimore Committee all concurred that the coercive power of the League should be limited to occasions when either arbitration had been refused or an arbitral award ignored.[57]

The greatest problem facing the preparation of a British scheme for a League of Nations was the absence of any indication of the government's views on the matter. The PID's League of Nations Section was left without a head, as it was still undecided who would lead the British negotiations on this topic at the conference. The situation was intolerable, and just three days after Zimmern and Percy had submitted their plans Crowe, Tyrrell, Howard, Mallet, and Paget sent a note protesting about this state of affairs to Hardinge, who forwarded the letter to General Smuts. In this singular communication the Foreign Office's most senior members complained in chorus that

In preparing for General Smuts and for submission to the War Cabinet the papers setting out of the aims and requirements of British foreign policy in regard to the several questions which will come before the Peace Conference, we are much embarrassed by our

---

[56] FO 371/4353/f29/PC29, Percy, 'The League of Nations', Nov. 1918. Also in CAB 29/2/P-69. Percy's memorandum also discusses the Board of Trade report on reparations (CAB 29/1/P-33), as well as freedom of the seas.

[57] FO 371/4353/f29/PC29. Also in CAB 29/2/P-68. Zimmern reprints this plan in his book on the League, and discusses at some length its place in the evolution of ideas on a league, though he does not mention that he was the plan's author.

inability, in the absence of instructions, to grapple effectively with the question of the League of Nations which encounters us at every turn. We find that it closely affects, and indeed is likely to dominate, the whole complex of arrangements, territorial, racial, economical, which the Peace Conference is to set up, and we may possibly be faced by a demand on President Wilson's part that the project of a League of Nations shall have priority, in principle, and perhaps even in time, over every other aspect of the general settlement.[58]

The letter concludes with a plea that someone should be placed in charge of the League of Nations Section without delay in order to formulate and elaborate a policy on this topic. Such a letter of protest from all the senior diplomats involved in the peace planning could not be ignored, and on 3 December Lord Robert Cecil was appointed to head the League of Nations Section, although he was unable to take up his duties until 16 December due to the general election campaign.[59]

Lord Robert Cecil had long been interested in the idea of a League of Nations, and on 17 December he submitted his own scheme for such an organization.[60] The Cecil Plan synthesized the common points of the earlier proposals, with regular conferences acting as the pivot of the League's activities. Cecil went a step further than the earlier proposals in suggesting that the League should have an independent capital, with a chancellor as chief executive officer. Cecil wanted a person of the greatest possible ability to hold this post, giving Venizelos, the Greek prime minister, as an example of the sort of individual he had in mind.[61]

Cecil, Percy, and Zimmern all perceived the new League of Nations as an institutionalization of the conference system, under which the old concert of Europe had acted for so long. As such the concept of a League was no more than an adjustment of older, traditional forms of international relations, and as Percy suggested what was proposed was no more than an

---

[58] Smuts Papers 101:46. 22 Nov. 1918.

[59] Cecil Papers, BL Add. MS 51076, fo.73. Smuts to Cecil, 3 Dec. 1918.

[60] CAB 29/2/P-79.

[61] CAB 23/42/IWC 46/1, 24 Dec. 1918. The Admiralty Board opposed Cecil's support for the binding use of military force under the League of Nations. ADM 116/1852, 'League of Nations: Admiralty Comments on Lord R. Cecil's Memorandum', undated.

extension of the old multinational guarantee of Belgian integrity to the entire peace settlement. It was this very Belgian guarantee, however, which had finally brought Britain into the war, and not everyone was convinced that a conservative organization was the correct remedy for international ills. It was Jan Smuts, undoubtedly motivated by his extra-European viewpoint, who proposed a radical scheme for the new League of Nations.

Smuts was content to keep no more than a supervisory eye over the preparations as they developed, scarcely interfering at all. He personally produced only one memorandum during this process, but this plan is memorable.[62] In his preamble Smuts notes 'that the ordinary conception of the League of Nations is not a fruitful one, nor is it the right one, and that a radical transformation of it is necessary'.[63] Smuts observed that with the destruction of the old European empires and the passing of the old European order a vacuum had been created which could only be successfully filled by a powerful league. He did not perceive such an organization as acting only to help in the prevention of wars, but rather as something which would play an integral part in the ordinary peaceful existence of people. The experience the Allies had already gained during the war in co-operating on the control and rationing of food and raw materials provided a useful precedent which could be used to extend economic co-operation through the League in peacetime.

Smuts firmly opposed a peace of annexations, rather he wanted all territories surrendered by the defeated states to go to the League, for as he warned,

The application of the spoils system at this most solemn juncture in the history of the world, a repartition of Europe at a moment when Europe is bleeding at every pore as a result of partitions less than half a century old, would indeed be incorrigible madness on the part of rulers, and enough to drive the torn and broken peoples of the world

[62] FO 371/43533/f29/PC152, 'The League of Nations: A Programme for the Peace Conference', 16 Dec. 1918. Also in CAB 29/2/P-44. Published as *The League of Nations: A Practical Suggestion* (London, 1918). Discussed in Zimmern, *The League of Nations*, pp. 209–14, and W. K. Hancock, *Smuts*, vol. i: *The Sanguine Years, 1870–1919* (Cambridge, 1962), 500–3.
[63] CAB 29/2/P-44.

to that despair of the state which is the motive power behind Russian Bolshevism.[64]

Smuts proposed that territories unable to administer themselves should become wards of the League, a plan he considered as useful for Europe as for the colonial world. The Great Powers would assist in the development of the regions formerly under Russian, Habsburg, and Ottoman rule. Smuts did not exclude Germany from participating in this work, once stability had been restored in that country. His plan would have given the Great Powers extensive control in Eastern Europe, Siberia, and Western Asia. Zimmern later observed of this plan that 'It is not surprising that no more was heard of this scheme for diverting the mandate system from a plan for the betterment of backward peoples to something not very far removed from a twentieth-century Holy Alliance'.[65]

Smuts's proposals on the organization of a League drew heavily on his experiences of the relationship between Great Britain and the Dominions. His aim was not to create a superstate, nor simply to establish an office for organizing conferences. Smuts wanted an organization of sufficient suppleness and flexibility to be able to adapt to the evolving needs of the international system. He proposed that the League have a two-tier system, comprising a council and a general conference. He agreed with the earlier proposals for a secretariat, and for the settlement of disputes along the lines suggested by the Phillimore Committee. War was not outlawed, but the system would do everything possible to prevent it by delay and arbitration.

The council was to be the permanent nucleus of the League, which would supervise the variety of tasks Smuts hoped the League would be charged with. Smuts introduced an innovation by suggesting that the council be comprised of two classes of members. The Great Powers would sit as permanent members, while the remaining states would be classified as intermediate and minor powers, each group being allowed two seats on the Council by rotation. Three adverse votes would be sufficient to defeat a resolution. The lower tier of this system was a General Conference which would meet periodically.

[64] Ibid.   [65] Zimmern, *The League of Nations*, p. 212.

Smuts concluded his proposals by focusing on what he perceived as the cause of militarism, which the League could assist in eliminating. He called for the abolition of conscription, which he considered 'the taproot of militarism', the limitation of armaments, and the nationalization of armaments production with League inspection.

Smuts's radical departure produced a variety of criticisms on the part of the Foreign Office, particularly on disarmament. Crowe was at first reluctant to criticize a paper by a member of the War Cabinet, but when Cecil gave his permission he responded readily with the observation, 'that it dangerously over-elaborates the whole scheme of a League of Nations'.[66] Crowe believed that disarmament should wait upon the establishment of a system which really guaranteed peace. Tyrrell also saw the Smuts Plan as over-ambitious, commenting tersely, 'This paper positively frightens me from this point of view.'[67] Cecil responded by observing that Britain would have to make disarmament propaganda, causing Crowe to retort that he did not see why Britain had to be the one to bring forward such proposals.[68] Headlam-Morley in particular criticized Smuts's assumptions about the link between conscription and militarism, noting that this was historically difficult to prove. If anything, Headlam-Morley contended, conscription had made war less likely by destroying the possibility of small wars.[69]

Despite these criticisms Smuts's plan was compelling. At the time Lloyd George called it 'one of the ablest state papers he had read', and years later in his *Memoirs* he described the plan as 'one of the most notable products of this extremely able man. It is pellucid in style, eloquent in diction, penetrating in thought and broad in its outlook.'[70] Much of what Smuts proposed was based on the conclusions of the Phillimore, Zimmern, and Percy plans, modified by several suggestions which have remained a part of modern international organizations.

[66] FO 371/4353/f29/PC152, Minute by Crowe, 30 Dec. 1918.

[67] Ibid., Minute by Tyrrell, 31 Dec. 1918.

[68] Ibid., Minute by Cecil, undated; Minute by Crowe, 31 Dec. 1918.

[69] FO 371/4356/f176/PC176, Headlam-Morley, 'On Conscription and Militarism', 4 Jan. 1919.

[70] CAB 23/42/IWC46/1, and Lloyd George, MPC i. 43–4.

Alfred Zimmern later concluded that Smuts had rendered a great service by adding his not inconsiderable reputation to these plans.[71] The government decided to try to achieve the creation of a League of Nations along the lines proposed by these schemes, and at Paris this early work played an important role in the shaping of this innovation in the development of the international system.

On the day before Christmas 1918 the Imperial War Cabinet met to discuss British policy on the creation of a League of Nations, a meeting held very much in the shadow of President Wilson's trip to London.[72] Smuts was unable to attend the meeting, and the discussion was relatively brief. Hughes of Australia supported the Zimmern plan, 'which he regarded as a severely practical comprehensive pronouncement'.[73] For Hughes, Zimmern's concept of a council of governments, each vested with its own sovereignty, must have reflected his own views on the form of the British Empire. The Cabinet agreed that the success of the League in preventing war would be linked to the success of disarmament. Lloyd George concluded the discussion by expressing his opinion that the best way to achieve disarmament was for conscription to be abolished in the enemy states and limits placed upon their armies. As a result their populations would not stand having to support a large army to defend themselves against a shadow. In the final settlement, in part due to British insistence on this point, anti-conscription clauses were written into the peace treaties.

Questions of International Law

The question which seemed most likely to divide the Anglo-American alliance was the doctrine of the freedom of the seas, or rather the interpretation of it. Queen Mary, when asked by Mrs Wilson what she thought about the issue, responded that 'she was not in favour of mixed bathing'.[74] In the Fourteen Points President Wilson had called for 'Absolute freedom of

[71] Zimmern, The League of Nations, p. 209.
[72] CAB 23/42/IWC46/1, 24 Dec. 1918. Lloyd George informed the Cabinet that he had given a copy of the Smuts plan to President Wilson, though he had taken the precaution of removing some examples which he thought President Wilson might not approve of.
[73] Ibid.   [74] Prothero Diary, 1 May 1919.

navigation upon the seas, outside territorial waters, alike in peace and in war, except as the seas may be closed in whole or in part by international action for the enforcement of international covenants'.[75] Britain on the other hand wanted to maintain the right to impose a blockade and to stop and search ships. Britain was a sea-borne empire and the navy was its greatest weapon, but the Americans had become embroiled in the European conflict over the issue of the freedom of the seas. To define British attitudes and to prepare for a likely dispute with the Americans, several committees and sub-committees were established during 1917–18. Although these committees' terms of reference were to consider problems of international law, their discussions came to revolve almost totally around the question of the freedom of the seas.[76]

In January 1918 an interdepartmental International Law Committee was appointed under the chairmanship of the Home Secretary, Lord Cave. Among the members were Sir Eyre Crowe, Cecil Hurst, and Sir Erle Richards.[77] It was charged with considering what additions and amendments to the established rules of international law would be advantageous to British interests. An attempt was made to learn what work the other Allies were doing in this field, and through the British embassies they were informed that France was making no preparations but would be happy to learn of British conclusions, and that American preparations were in progress under Dr James Brown Scott; the Italians failed to respond. Eventually in November the committee heard that an Italian equivalent did exist, but nothing could be learnt of their activities.[78]

The International Law Committee began its work with an

[75] Scott, *President Wilson's Foreign Policy*, p. 359.

[76] A good summary is M. G. Fry, 'The Imperial War Cabinet, the United States, and the Freedom of the Seas', *Journal of the Royal United Service Institution*, 110 (Nov. 1965), 353–62.

[77] FO 371/3467/f8362/12742, for a synopsis of the committee. ADM 116/1865 contains many of the documents relating to the committee. See also FO 372/1185–1186/f539. Committee members were Lord Cave, Home Secretary; Foreign Office, Crowe and Hurst; Admiralty, Hall and Hope; War Office, Cockerill; Supreme Court, Macdonnell; Procurator-General's Office, Mellor; Sir Erle Richards and Dr Pearce Higgins. Roxburgh and W. Stewart of the Foreign Office acted as secretaries.

[78] ADM 116/1865. Minutes of the 2nd meeting, 3 May 1918. FO 372/1186/f539/192594, Rodd (Rome) to Balfour, 14 Nov. 1918.

examination of the 1856 Declaration of Paris, which dealt with the protection of non-contraband goods on neutral ships. The committee did not meet between May and October, but when it reconvened on 11 October the committee resolved in favour of the abrogation of the Paris Declaration. A report was prepared on the freedom of the seas which recommended not only the abrogation of the Paris Declaration, but that no similar agreements should be entered into. It was agreed that while there should be full freedom in times of peace, in wartime neutrals would have to accept certain restrictions including the liability to search when attempting to break a blockade. The committee suggested that the best policy for the peace conference would be to postpone discussion of the topic until a later date. All future reports on this subject followed similar lines.

Shortly after the International Law Committee was established, which curiously included no naval member, the Admiralty Reconstruction Committee created a sub-committee to study the Naval Aspects of International Law.[79] Known as sub-committee 'A' and chaired by Admiral of the Fleet Sir William May, it did not hold its first meeting until 3 June. When the Admiralty Board began to prepare the naval case for the peace negotiations the work of this committee was taken as the basis for the naval brief on questions of international law. It agreed with the International Law Committee view that the Paris Declaration should be abrogated and that in future Britain should only be bound by general principles on international law. It also submitted practical recommendations on such questions as the marking of hospital ships. The 'A' committee supported the abolition of submarine warfare, though it recognized that this was improbable.

A special memorandum on the 'Freedom of the Seas' was also ordered by the Chief of the Naval Staff, and prepared by the Plans Division in consultation with Dr Pearce Higgins.[80] It

[79] ADM 116/1865. Contains most of the documents relating to this sub-committee.

[80] ADM 1/8545/312. Also as CAB 29/2/P-74 and ADM 1/8546/329. Pearce Higgins (1865–1935); educ. Downing Coll., Cambridge; Barrister, Lincoln's Inn, 1908; Adviser in International Law and Prize Law in Depts. of Procurator-General and Treasury Solicitor, 1914–20; Whewell Prof. of International Law, Cambridge, 1920. Higgins was also a member of the inter-departmental International Law Committee.

reiterated the views of the 'A' committee and recommended that Britain 'should endeavour to withdraw from the Declaration of Paris, denounce the Hague Conventions, and declare her intention of being guided in the future by certain recognised principles and rights, the interpretation of which will be left to the judgement of the Prize Courts'. [81] The Admiralty's aim was that in future Britain alone should act as arbiter of its rights on the world's seas.

A good example of the debate on issues at the lower levels of government and the attempt to co-ordinate views is provided by these discussions on the freedom of the seas. Initially the Admiralty sub-committee did not have an easy time. Once it wrongly addressed the interdepartmental International Law Committee as a Foreign Office committee and received back a politely worded note setting it straight. Next, sub-committee 'A' discovered that the Foreign Office Historical Section was producing a handbook on 'The Freedom of the Seas', and that although copies had been sent to Naval Intelligence they were unable to obtain one. [82] Eventually the Foreign Office agreed to supply a copy direct. The Admiralty sub-committee then busied itself with making a great fuss over the draft of this handbook, which was being written by Dr Pawley Bate. [83]

In November Dr Pearce Higgins sent a critique of Bate's handbook to the Foreign Office on behalf of the Admiralty. [84] While finding the handbook admirable, he made several suggestions to bring it into line with Admiralty policy. Higgins suggested that Bate's work could be taken to mean that Britain had made unfair use of its maritime position during the war, and Higgins was definite that 'the only possible official view is that our actions have been in accordance with the bedrock principles of International Law'. [85] The Historical Section agreed to alter the handbooks to meet Admiralty objections.

The Admiralty, despite the redrafting of the handbook, again objected to Bate's work in January, and requested that it not be published, to avoid having two different views circulating. The

---

[81] CAB 29/2/P-74.   [82] FO 370/84/f124616.

[83] Pawley Bate (1857–1921); educ. Peterhouse, Cambridge; barrister; LLD, 1898; prof. of jurisprudence, University Coll., London, 1894–1901; British Legal Representative of staff of the League of Nations, 1919–20.

[84] FO 370/84/f30550/196580 and FO 372/1186/539/119688.   [85] Ibid.

Admiralty admitted that Bate expressed a neutral viewpoint, but all the same it was not that of the government. The Foreign Office had to remind the Admiralty that the purpose of these booklets was to provide just such an unbiased background, and not to explain government policy.[86] Similar difficulties were encountered with the International Law Committee.[87]

The Imperial War Cabinet discussed the issue of freedom of the seas on 24 December, with Balfour enjoying the role of devil's advocate to put forward the Wilsonian argument. Lloyd George in response to Balfour's presentation of the American view suggested that the best policy would be to tell Wilson that Britain could not surrender rights vital to its security, but was willing to let the League examine the whole question of the rules of war at sea. A compromise might be reached by agreeing to some code on the use of submarines and mines, which had primarily been German weapons. This solution was adopted, and at Paris the issue was quietly shelved.[88]

A variety of other international law topics, beside the League of Nations and freedom of the seas, also received preparatory attention. In 1916 a Committee on Treaty Revision was appointed to consider useful post-war alternatives in treaties to which Britain was a party.[89] Some thought was given to suggestions calling for the trial and punishment of the Kaiser and other high-ranking German officials. Headlam-Morley in a note on this subject suggested that the most serious charge which could be laid against the Kaiser was that of having misled the German people, a matter for German municipal law. The only alternative would be to establish a system of international law where an international court appointed by member states could try individuals who had violated laws agreed to by all

---

[86] FO 370/96, Anderson (Admiralty) to FO, 23 Jan. 1919. Prothero to Anderson, 28 Jan. 1919. Tilley to Anderson, 19 Feb. 1919.

[87] FO 370/84/f12608/13204, letter of 24 Jan. 1919.

[88] CAB 23/42/IWC46/2. Marder observes on this question that 'The Freedom of the Seas controversy revealed to the British as in a flash the apparent American ambition to achieve naval superiority.' Arthur Marder, *From Dreadnought to Scapa Flow: The Royal Navy in the Fisher Era, 1904–1919* (5 vols., London, 1961–70), v. 242.

[89] FO 371/4356/f170/PC170.

civilized states.[90] Balfour warned in a minute that Headlam-Morley's views should not be taken as representing Foreign Office policy, although Hardinge thought the suggestions full of sound sense. Howard summed up the feeling of many officials when he wrote in his diary, 'The papers write the greatest rubbish about hanging the Kaiser. They are as mad about him as they once were over Jumbo the Elephant. We ought to have better things to think of.'[91]

A matter which was both territorial and legal was the future protection of minorities. Redrawing the map of Europe would inevitably create a number of minority problems, and the PID proposed that the new states promise by treaty to protect these groups. Hardinge, however, noted that this would depend on what enforcement powers the new League possessed.[92] The PID in its first 'P' memorandum had addressed the problem of the Jewish minority, proposing that the government should insist on the Balfour Declaration, which called for a Jewish national homeland in Palestine. The creation of such a state, however, should not prejudice Jewish rights to minority protection in countries where such rights were to be subject to treaty obligations.[93]

Conclusion

Preparations on economic problems and international law both suffered from the lack of firm government directives as to policy. Lloyd George claims in his *Memoirs* that he disagreed with the advocates of a Carthaginian settlement, but the fact remains that he allowed these men to dominate the financial negotiations with a policy which was opposed by the government's own technical advisers. As such it provides one of the

[90] FO 371/4356/f139/PC139, Headlam-Morley, 'The Trial and Punishment of Germans, including the Kaiser, for their action in connection with the war', 12 Dec. 1918. A file of interesting reports on the possibility of trying the Kaiser is in the papers of Lloyd George's private secretary, Philip Kerr, Lothian Papers GD 40/17/53.

[91] Howard of Penrith Diary, 2 Dec. 1918.   [92] FO 371/4353/f33/PC33.

[93] On the protection of minorities see A. Sharp, 'Britain and the Protection of Minorities at the Paris Peace Conference', in A. C. Hepburn, ed., *Minorities in History* (London, 1973).

earliest examples of a problem which haunted the Paris conference, the suppression of the prepared brief in favour of political opinion. The interference of the political factor in the preparations was compounded by the difficulty the experts had originally faced in determining what their own government's policy was, much less preparing for discussions by second-guessing the plans of other countries. The preparation of a scheme for a League of Nations was almost crippled by the lack of any indication of the Cabinet's policy. Despite these obstacles, definite plans, possible options, and recommendations were formulated for the use of the delegates. The most spectacular failure of the preparatory machinery at Paris was over the reparations and indemnity question, where the pre-conference work was virtually ignored, while the great triumph was the creation of a League of Nations very much along the lines envisaged by the British planners.

PART III

Implementation

7

The Paris Peace Conference

> One is always on the go & just on the brink of hope or despair.
>
> A. W. A. Leeper to R. W. A. Leeper, 5 June 1919
> (A. W. A. Leeper Papers)

An inevitable question which arises given the scope of British preparations for the peace conference is whether the British delegation arrived in Paris with an overall strategic view of the post-war world. The answer must be no. The empire's vast size, varied interests, and complex regional concerns could not allow one neat view to prevail. What did emerge was a set of basic principles which did not mutually contradict one another and which run right through British thinking on the post-war order. Three key schools can be clearly identified: the balance of power, the New Europe, and imperial expansion. All three schools recognized that 1919 was the great hinge of British foreign and imperial policy, marking the critical point of transition from the era of expansion to the era of consolidation. The recognition by these groups of this transformation in overall strategic aims had a deep impact on British actions at the peace conference, and the changing emphases can be seen in the tactical implementation of these concerns in the final settlement.

Aims for the settlement in Western Europe were guided by the traditional precepts of British foreign policy, which had for several centuries assured the security of the British isles. This policy was to prevent one power from dominating Western Europe, and in particular from controlling the Lowlands. The mechanism for achieving this end was the maintenance of a balance of power, at least in Western Europe. As a result Britain did not back, but rather blocked, many of France's more expansionist plans directed against Germany. It was accepted that Alsace-Lorraine was France's primary war aim and must therefore be allowed without reservation, but French plans to annex or control Luxemburg, the Saar, or the Rhineland were firmly opposed. As early as 1916, in their memorandum to Asquith's War Committee, Paget and Tyrrell had opposed any French gains beyond Alsace-Lorraine. Britain had no intention of replacing the German threat with a French one, and it should be recalled that France had been the historic Continental threat to well within the living memory of the negotiators.

The Eastern European settlement was dominated by the principles of the New Europe. Here it was presumed that frontiers based as closely as possible on ethnic lines would help assure a stable future, which was Britain's chief desire in this region. The adherents of this school of thought saw Czechoslovakia as the linchpin of central European stability, which would provide some redress for the power vacuum created by the dissolution of the Habsburg Empire. To the extent British policy had tactical interests in this region they were limited to the maritime fringe, and the issues which most involved Britain were the crises over the key ports of Danzig and Fiume. Britain was looking for useful maritime allies, and many officials focused on the creation of a Greater Greece as a useful regional ally. The struggle between philhellenes and mishellenes became one of the bitterest internal wrangles of the British delegation.

Ambitions for the territorial settlement outside Europe concerned a number of factions involved with Britain's imperial future. This group included old-style imperialists willing to grab any available piece of land, reformers who sought only moderate gains to tidy up the frontiers of empire, and consolidationists who saw the empire as already too large to manage and protect. They all, however, shared some common characteristics, first among which was a fear of any other Great Power, whether defeated enemy or wartime ally, intruding into any region with British interests. As British interests were global, this posed difficulties. Compromises were agreed within the delegation which led to compromises externally. Britain did take some key lands, but did not acquire more peripheral areas, such as the Caucasus. All the acquisitions were in the form of mandates, which left open the possibility of subsequent withdrawal without loss of face if the situation became strained. This mechanism was indeed used in 1929 with Mesopotamia.

Non-territorial matters, from the point of view of British diplomatic strategy, can be seen as corollaries to the territorial questions. Reparations were considered within the context of the West European balance of power. The League of Nations was shaped on the basis of British plans. It provided a useful vesting agency for the captured colonial possessions and provided a possible mechanism for international co-operation without binding Britain to specific, and potentially unwanted, commitments.

As the interests of these three groups could be roughly defined regionally, their different ideas had little opportunity to clash. Each dominated the section of the British delegation dealing with the interests of particular concern to them. So while there was not necessarily a high degree of co-ordination, there was little serious conflict, and each group with its own focused determination was able to achieve substantial success within its own sphere.

WESTERN EUROPE AND THE BALANCE OF POWER

The first region where Britain had to set about assuring a balance of power was in Western Europe, and the future of the Lowlands was closely bound up with the desired equilibrium. Germany having been routed, the potential enemy was the spread of French influence. As the Netherlands were neutral, the debate on the Lowlands centred on the future role of Belgium and the future status of Luxemburg. For Britain, Belgium and Luxemburg were merely components of a general Western European settlement, bound up with the Saar and the Rhineland questions. Several of the senior delegates intended to use concessions in one region for gains in another.

There was a clear British preference to see Belgium strengthened so as to allow it greater ability to resist German or French influence. This idea was linked to Britain's view on the future of Luxemburg. There was no general agreement that Luxemburg would even continue to exist as a sovereign state, as it, or at least its leadership, was widely viewed as having been too pro-German. France had clear annexationist intentions, and the most obvious way to block such a bid was to unite the Grand Duchy with Belgium. This would simultaneously resolve the Luxemburg question while also strengthening Belgium. This matched a consistent pattern of British diplomatic tactics in the European settlement which supported the building up of states which were seen as future key regional allies. Headlam-Morley, who served on the Belgian Committee, argued that 'Belgium *must* have Luxemburg'.[1] Failing this the aim of British policy was at least to foil any French attempts at annexation. Although Luxemburg was nominally within the American zone of occupation, there was a powerful French politico-military presence in the shape of Marshal Foch, who made the city his headquarters and who was accompanied by an unusually large personal honour guard.

Headlam-Morley was a powerful advocate of a Belgian annexation of Luxemburg, on the basis that the grand duchy was not a viable state, and that absorption into Belgium was the best solution in terms of the West European balance of power. He was advising in fact no more than putting back together the available fragments of the buffer state created in 1814, with exactly the same end in mind. Headlam-Morley's views were shared by both Balfour and Crowe, but despite this concordance of opinion, lack of communication between those involved meant that the critical moment passed in the negotiations when Luxemburg might have been gained for Belgium. Headlam-Morley in despair at this commented, 'in regard to this matter our diplomacy failed'.[2] He had become very involved in this question, and its failure stung him badly. Nevertheless the basic aim of keeping Luxemburg out of France's grasp succeeded. Luxemburg was allowed a plebiscite, which decided in favour of continued independence. The ideal aim of creating a greater Belgium failed, but the optimum

[1] FO 608/18/2/4/5147, Minute by Headlam-Morley, 7 Apr. 1919.
[2] FO 371/6970/W5008, Headlam-Morley, 'History of the Luxemburg Question', 9 May 1921.

aim of preventing any increment in French control in the Low-lands succeeded.[3]

In the Saar the French hoped to see a broad interpretation of Anglo-American support for the return of Alsace-Lorraine, which would include the entire historic principality of Lor-raine. Such an understanding had already been reached in the February 1917 Franco-Russian Secret Agreement. Britain, how-ever, consistently offered support only for a restoration of the 1871 frontier, which would return the Franco-German border to that established at Vienna in 1814, which Britain had been instrumental in formulating. Britain was willing to consider some special economic arrangements in the Saar for France as reparation for the damage caused to France's own coalfields. The American experts had reached a similar conclusion, and the French themselves by January 1919 had accepted that the Saar problem would have to be approached from the point of view of reparations.

The Saar question arose in February with Headlam-Morley proposing the idea that France should obtain the Saar coalfields as compensation, but should not receive sovereignty over the district. A meeting of the Anglo-American experts followed, during which the basic outline of the solution finally adopted was evolved. Headlam-Morley observed that 'members of the American and British delegations, working without any instructions from their political chiefs, had, in the middle of February, agreed on proposals which were in general very similar to the final solution, though the details were to be much modified and improved'.[4]

On 28 March 1919 the Supreme Council met and a wide divergence of views soon became apparent between the leaders.[5] Clemenceau wanted French annexation of the Saar,

---

[3] See also S. Marks, *Innocent Abroad: Belgium at the Paris Peace Conference of 1919* (Chapel Hill, NC, 1981), pp. 200–54. An indication of French intentions is shown by the report of the *Comité d'études*, which considered Luxemburg in vol. i with Alsace-Lorraine, rather than in vol. ii with other claims.

[4] Confidential Print 12150, Headlam-Morley, 'The Saar Valley', 28 May 1923. Confidential Print 12150. Also in FO 371/8762/C9743/493/18.

[5] Paul Mantoux, *Les Délibérations du Conseil des Quatre, 24 mars–28 juin 1919*, vol. i (Paris, 1955). This is the only account of the meeting, which does not appear in FRUS: PPC.

while Wilson would only agree to coal deliveries from the district. Lloyd George in attempting to hold the middle ground between his two stiff-necked protagonists proposed French ownership of the mines without any territorial annexation, the administration being placed under a special local regime. This plan is noticeably similar to that drawn up by the experts. Headlam-Morley later observed of this development that 'The English, therefore, in close touch with the Prime Minister, were working towards conciliation, and in this they were helped by members of the American delegation, who were more sympathetic to the French claims than was their President'.[6] The following day Lloyd George and Balfour summoned Headlam-Morley, who outlined the Anglo-American experts' solution, of which they were apparently unaware, but with which they immediately concurred. Wilson held similar consultations with his own experts. The Anglo-American experts then held a further meeting and agreed a joint proposal for Lloyd George and Wilson based on their original conclusions. The French were also busily at work on a possible solution and proposed that the Saar be given to France as a League of Nations mandate with a consultation of the inhabitants after fifteen years. While the French proposal would still give France an iron grip on the district it did provide one element used in the final solution, with the proposed consultation becoming a plebiscite.

On 30 March the Council of Four met and accepted the general concept of the Anglo-American experts' proposal. A committee was established to work out the details, consisting of Headlam-Morley, Tardieu, and Charles Haskins of the American delegation. The key problem facing them was the future administrative arrangement for the Saar, and on this point Headlam-Morley succeeded in convincing both Crowe and Balfour of the need for a special arrangement which would limit Franco-German friction, especially if the mines were under French control. On 8–9 April the Council of Four discussed the problem and reached what was probably their most original and effective solution of the conference. Basing their conclusions on the experts' proposals they evolved the final

[6] Confidential Print 12150.

compromise, which placed the Saar under a League commission, with a plebiscite after fifteen years, the French in the mean time receiving control of the mines.

Britain had succeeded in maintaining its favoured Congress of Vienna frontier, restricting excessive French territorial expansion, while still in Headlam-Morley's view meeting the reasonable demands of the French. The key actor in the solution reached was Headlam-Morley, who noted in his diary, 'For the general conception of this scheme, I am, I believe, originally responsible.... Eventually I had an opportunity of drawing the Prime Minister's attention, together with that of Mr. Balfour, to this solution, and he took it up.'[7] This was indeed true. The solution he proposed combined the traditional British concern for the balance of power with the ideas of the New Europe, which opposed detaching large coherent pieces of territory against the obvious wishes of its inhabitants. France would receive its desired economic compensation, the old territorial balance in Western Europe was restored, and the principles of the New Europe had been followed.

The third component of the Western European settlement was the future of the left bank of the Rhine. Control of the Rhineland had long been an aspiration of French foreign policy, in order to complete France's natural frontiers. France had at times controlled the area but the 1814 Vienna settlement put it firmly within the German sphere. For the rest of Europe the Rhineland was seen as a barrier to French predominance. France's desire for the region was now all the stronger because of its perception of a continuing German threat. For France, therefore, control of the Rhineland was more than a historic, irredentist claim, but a specific strategic aim with an immediate purpose — to serve as a buffer against Germany. For Britain, on the other hand, the aim was to maintain the regional equilibrium. The problem facing British diplomacy was how to meet the French demands for greater security while not detaching the Rhineland from Germany against the wishes of its inhabitants.[8]

[7] J. Headlam-Morley, *A Memoir of the Paris Peace Conference, 1919*, ed. A. Headlam-Morley, R. Bryant, and A. Cienciala (London, 1972), pp. 166–7, diary entry for 25 June 1919.

[8] On French aims see Walter A. McDougall, *France's Rhineland Diplomacy, 1914–1924: The Last Bid for a Balance of Power in Europe* (Princeton, NJ, 1978).

Headlam-Morley in his retrospective assessment of the Rhineland negotiations concluded that Britain acted at a disadvantage. The Rhineland was such a central French goal that all the French officials involved at all levels worked in close harmony, while the British 'had no definite instructions, nor were they provided with clear ideas as to the general object to be obtained'.[9] It is all the more notable therefore that Britain achieved its alternative solution while the bulk of French aims in the Rhineland were thwarted.

In mid-March Tardieu submitted the French plan in a meeting with Kerr and Mezes. He proposed a 50-kilometre demilitarized zone to the east of the Rhine, the Rhine bridgeheads to be garrisoned by an inter-allied force, while the left bank would become either a single independent state or a group of independent states under the League. Kerr went so far as to accept the demilitarized zone, but the other points were considered unacceptable. He proposed a British guarantee of French security, which appears to be the origin of the Anglo-American Guarantee Treaty meant to protect France from future German aggression.

There followed the pivotal month of the conference, between 25 March and 22 April, when the great Allied powers threatened to break up over the question of reparations and the Rhineland. For France these questions were key aims, for Wilson they involved essential principles of the New Diplomacy, while for Britain the diplomatic necessity was to keep the conference together without allowing one side or the other to distort the balance. This critical month was inaugurated by Lloyd George's Fontainebleau Memorandum, in which he for the first time considered the Carthaginian treaty being designed for Germany as the sum of its parts. This first clear analytical view of the overall treaty showed that the demands which it was envisaged to force upon Germany were unworkable, possibly in the short term, certainly in the long term. Lloyd George in particular opposed separating the Rhineland from Germany. The eventual solution was worked out at the highest political levels of the conference and left the Rhineland

---

[9] Confidential Print 12347, Headlam-Morley, 'The Left Bank of the Rhine', 13 Feb. 1924. Also in FO 371/9825/C2924/2924/18.

to Germany, but demilitarized the entire district. The French in return received an Anglo-American guarantee, which in fact collapsed with the failure of the Versailles Treaty in the United States Senate. French ambitions in the Rhineland continued to be a destabilizing factor in European relations until 1924, but British foreign policy remained consistent in withholding support for French ambitions in the region. At the Paris conference Britain succeeded in restraining the French drive to the Rhine. All the frontiers of Western Europe agreed in 1919 are still in place, based in great measure on the Vienna frontiers of 1814. The British aim of maintaining the status quo had persevered.

The most fundamentally flawed part of the settlement concerned German reparations payments, for which all of the parties concerned must bear the blame. Headlam-Morley later observed, 'It seems impossible to avoid the conclusion that whatever may have been the case with other parts of the treaty, in this, at any rate, there were demonstrable errors, both in policy and procedure, which it would have been possible to avoid.'[10] Unquestionably the failure to grasp the importance of economics for diplomacy seriously weakened, and it has been argued terminally weakened, the Paris settlement. From the viewpoint of British negotiating strategy, though, the issue must be seen as forming part of the concerns over the future Franco-German balance in Western Europe. The perception of reparations as a serious problem only grew slowly within the British delegation as its impact on the Continental balance became more evident. Assessing punitive reparations upon Germany might prove a popular political measure at home, and could raise hopes of less budgetary strain, but there was the danger that they would so weaken Germany that it would cease to be an effective counterweight against France. This might well suit French ambitions, but not British conceptions. Reparations were seen by some as forming part of France's bid for predominance in Western Europe. Keynes observed at an Anglo-American meeting in December 1918 that the 'French

---

[10] Confidential Print 11984. For an analysis of the financial details considered at Paris see J. A. Hemery, 'The Emergence of Treasury Influence in British Foreign Policy, 1914–1921' (Ph.D. thesis, University of Cambridge, 1988).

demand for a huge indemnity was to be the basis for continued occupation and ultimate acquisition of the Rhine provinces'. [11] Keynes opposed heavy reparations on several grounds, as his preparatory memoranda make clear, but he was also among the first to perceive the impact of financial instability on the balance of power. As concerns grew about French aims in Western Europe, in the midst of the Rhineland question, so British thinking on reparations began to shift.

The linkage of economic consequences to future diplomatic development was only just coming to be seen as an integral part of statecraft. Lloyd George almost crippled Britain's ability to deal with this issue at the outset by appointing Cunliffe, Hughes, and Sumner as the British members of the Reparations Commission. Hughes and Cunliffe had already made their views clear in the Cabinet Indemnities Committee, and they were firmly 'pledged to the two propositions that Germany ought to pay the complete cost of the war, and that she was capable of doing so'. [12] They were inflexible in their desire for a Carthaginian peace against Germany, but inflexibility is a dangerous stance in the diplomatist's art where suppleness of response is everything. As Lloyd George became aware of the significance of the reparations question he had to spend much of his time and energy in neutralizing the views of his own representatives.

The questions of reparations and of the left bank of the Rhine proved the greatest crises of the conference, threatening to shatter the fragile British–French–American co-operation. When Woodrow Wilson returned to the conference on 14 March, after a brief visit to Washington, he found these linked crises rapidly heading for an explosion. It was in response to this state of affairs that conference procedure was streamlined with the creation of the Council of Four, and indeed within a month solutions were found. Lloyd George was now convinced that the intransigent views of Hughes and Sumner had

[11] Quoted in H. Elcock, *Portrait of a Decision: The Council of Four and the Treaty of Versailles* (London, 1972), p. 49. A strong argument that reparation demands were not a function of France's Rhenish policy is made by Marc Trachtenberg, *Reparation in World Politics: France and European Economic Diplomacy, 1916–1923* (New York, 1980).

[12] Confidential Print 11984.

to be jettisoned. Increasingly the concerns of Keynes and his Treasury colleagues over the future financial stability of Germany meshed with worries over French aims to create a shift of attitude.

The cause of moderation was aided by Woodrow Wilson, who in exasperation with French demands ordered the *George Washington* to Brest in readiness to depart. Though the theatrics of the Italians, who later tried to mimic Wilson's threatened walkout, were generally ignored, it was obvious that Wilson did not dabble in idle gestures. The same afternoon the French capitulated and agreed to a moderation of the reparations assessment. In the choice between winning on reparations and losing the American alliance there was no contest. But for Lloyd George the great battle was not in the Council of Four but within his own delegation. Meeting with them on 11 April he bludgeoned the hardliners, with the help of Bonar Law, into submission.[13]

A way still had to be found out of the wretched problem of setting the actual amount Germany should pay. In the end it was Keynes who found the mechanism of leaving the sum blank in the treaty, to be determined in the future by an inter-allied commission. This removed the irritant of setting a specific amount at the conference, which could be held over for discussion in a calmer atmosphere. As Nicolson later observed, 'By leaving it to the Reparation Commission to fix the sum which Germany should eventually have to pay, he was able both to satisfy immediate opinion at home, and to secure that the Reparation question could subsequently be dealt with by technicians and in a saner atmosphere without thereby violating the treaty as signed. For this wise achievement he is seldom given credit.'[14]

It had been amply pointed out during the preparatory phase that what was involved was more than a financial transaction between victor and vanquished; it was a question which critically affected the future power of Germany by its effects on its financial stability, political equilibrium, and industrial infrastructure. The ramifications were many, and the recognition of

[13] Lloyd George Papers F/28/3/24.
[14] H. Nicolson, *Peacemaking 1919* (London, 1933), pp. 90–1.

this limited. The failure of the British handling of this matter was to see it initially as a financial affair and not a diplomatic one. As a result nobody concerned with foreign affairs was involved on Britain's behalf in the reparations negotiations at Paris. This meant that the financial side was not integrated into diplomatic thinking. It was the greatest failure of co-operation of the negotiations, and it was due to oversight. It was only when matters became critical, and Lloyd George became cognizant of the looming crisis and its implications, that attempts were made to redress the situation. Lloyd George managed to regain some of the lost ground when he succeeded in having the determination of the final amount to be paid put off to a later date, but this was only a successful rearguard action rather than a diplomatic forward movement.

British interests, while global in scope, had to be considered regionally in terms of application to France, as the surviving Continental Great Power presented unusual complexities in the formulation of a coherent foreign policy. France might be a potential rival in the Middle East, an irritant in Colonial Africa, and a nuisance in India, but in Europe it was a key element in the restructuring of the European order, provided that its more extravagant desires could be kept in check. France was after all still an ally which had fought loyally together with Britain in the bloodiest war in history. Emotionally a bond was inevitable, if only in the public imagination, but it was therefore a bond which could not be casually severed. Diplomatically France continued to be an ally, leading Headlam-Morley to observe that France 'gave unswerving support to nearly all British claims'. [15] France could have objected to many important British desiderata, particularly in the colonial sphere or on naval matters. It did not. France expected a traditional, straightforward political transaction. There were relatively few seriously conflicting aims and France hoped for a trade-off. Britain could not afford to push the western frontier questions so far as to obtain a new solution constructed to meet Britain's wildest expectations. Instead Britain had to content itself with a return to the traditional status quo, which it had helped to shape and maintain. On the most important question for

[15] Confidential Print 12150.

France, the Rhineland, Britain did refuse support and this almost shattered the Entente Cordiale. This was probably the Entente's most crucial test. Anglo-French rivalry was the historic norm, a united front against Germany a radical departure. Was the diplomatic revolution wrought in 1904 a substantive one, or was it so thin that the veneer would be pierced once the immediate German threat was crushed? The crisis passed. A compromise was achieved which met the substantive demands of both. Britain could not afford to be inflexible on all three components of the western settlement if a compromise was to be reached. Being comparatively inflexible over the Rhineland, it had to be more accommodating in the Saar. A French failure in both areas would have forced France to concentrate on Luxemburg to obtain a substantive gain, and this would have brought about a real Anglo-French confrontation in the Lowlands. If a crisis in relations were to occur it was best that it was in the district furthest from Britain. British diplomatic craftsmanship in the western settlement can in retrospect be seen as adroit and successful. On paper Britain gained nothing. Its victory was that neither did any other state.

EASTERN EUROPE AND THE NEW EUROPE

In Eastern Europe Britain faced an entirely different situation. There was no status quo, but only a fluid and increasingly volatile situation created by the collapse of the old multi-ethnic empires and the rise of nationally oriented states with vague frontiers. Here the task facing British diplomacy was to take this still shapeless mass and, if not to determine the final form, at least to assure that the final product was not displeasing. This was the sphere where the New Europe played its greatest role. The adherents of this school of thought had a general plan in mind, which resembled Wilson's ideas in advocating states based upon national self-determination. There was a difference, however, in that these officials were British diplomats, and as a result were concerned with the promotion of British interests. Their principles were in general accord with Wilsonism, but their application of them was British.

In the negotiations over Eastern Europe one difficulty was

that each party to these negotiations had differing motivations. The Americans were entranced by the 'scientific' principles of President Wilson. The French as a Continental power were already concerned with laying the foundations for an alliance system in Eastern Europe, which would eventually become the Little Entente, as the basis for future security. Italy had no grand strategy, but rather calculated its moves according to the particular tactical needs of achieving its various irredentist claims. For Britain, while adapting to the changing circumstances in Eastern Europe, there was some continuity with the concepts of the Congress of Vienna. Too many small, and therefore weak, states would cause instability, and Britain as a result consistently pushed for the creation of larger states, which would of necessity encompass smaller ethnic groups, whose rights were to be protected by a series of minority treaties. In Central Europe Czechoslovakia would have Ruthenia tacked on to it, not because of irredentist demands, but as the best cartographic solution. Poland was to be resurrected as a state and given generous frontiers. The Balkans would be dominated by a Greater Greece, a Greater Serbia in the form of Yugoslavia, and a Greater Romania. It was assumed that Albania would disappear, and that the enemy kingdom of Bulgaria would be left as the only unenlarged state. The cornerstone of British strategy in the region was the development of Greece as its regional proxy. Greece was the pivotal state, simultaneously Balkan, Mediterranean, and Near Eastern. An Anglo-Greek alliance stood to profit both partners. All Britain's reactions on the Balkan and Turkish territorial settlements must be seen as emanating from the Greek epicentre. Decisions on the future of all the Balkan states were related to the effect territorial and power changes would have on the new Greater Greece.

Greece

The First World War saw the collapse of the old multi-ethnic empires, among them the Ottoman Empire. Having lingered on, terminally ill, as the sick man of Europe for several decades, its final demise created a potentially volatile power vacuum in the Eastern Mediterranean. British concerns as a maritime power in this region were focused on the Straits and the Suez Canal. The latter was clearly primary and Britain planned to keep this strategic asset firmly under its own control in any Middle Eastern settlement. Attempting to secure control of the Straits, in addition to the other regions now coming under British rule, threatened a serious over-extension of its strategic capabilities. British policy preferred to see a friendly power dominating this critical waterway, and one obvious candidate was Greece, seen as a potential ally ever since Eleftherios Venizelos took power in 1917, with British assistance.

British officials were sharply divided between philhellenes and pro-Turks. It is worth noting that this division often reflected the individual's educational background, those with a classical education favouring Greece, those without, in particular military officers, preferring the Turks. Lloyd George emerged as one of the most strident philhellenes, but his circumstances were unusual. As a Welshman he empathized with the Greeks as a fellow nationality which had suffered long oppression by an imperial state. The experts of the PID were among the philhellenes, the most important being Allen Leeper, Nicolson, and to a lesser extent Toynbee. At Paris they were joined by Crowe, and together they formed a powerful group which promoted the idea of a Greater Greece which would serve as Britain's regional counterweight.

Greece benefited from the Turcophobia of many of these officials, an emotion which may have been a more potent factor than any philhellenism. Sir Eyre Crowe observed that 'The policy of allowing the Turk to remain in Europe is so contrary to our most important interests and so certain to involve the continuance of all the abomination associated with the rule of the Turks, that we cannot afford to treat this as a matter of just humouring Moslem feeling.'[16] Crowe consistently placed the reduction of Turkish power and the consequent increase in Greek power above any concerns as to the potential reaction from the British Empire's substantial Muslim population. His views were shared not only by his PID colleagues but also by such figures as Lord Curzon.[17]

---

[16] FO 608/37/92/1/1/4392, minute by Crowe, 22 Jan. 1919.
[17] On Curzon's views see CAB 27/24/EC46, 23 Dec. 1918.

Greece also stood to benefit from the superb diplomatic craftsmanship of its prime minister, Eleftherios Venizelos. The Greek leader fascinated many of the British delegates. Allen Leeper remarked, on hearing Venizelos present the Greek case before the Great Powers, 'We all thought it was the most brilliant thing we've ever heard, such amazing strength and tactfulness combined.'[18] Venizelos was a polished diplomatist, frequently dining for his country, often with the British delegates involved with the Greek settlement. He was seen as a reliable ally, as Leeper and Nicolson noted in their survey memorandum on South-Eastern Europe: 'M. Venizelos has merited our complete support. ... So long, therefore, as M. Venizelos remains in power little anxiety need be entertained as to the internal conditions of Greece, or her relations to this country.'[19] The British military representative in Bulgaria later recalled Philip Kerr telling him 'that Mr. Venizelos had done more than any single person to further the Entente action in the Near East during the war, and intimated that whatever he asked for must be granted'.[20] A constant fear among the philhellenes was that if Venizelos obtained insufficient gains to satisfy Greek opinion he would be toppled and Britain would thereby lose a useful ally. As Nicolson argued, 'It is a direct British interest that M. Venizelos' personal influence should be maintained and strengthened.'[21] In general the philhellenes wanted British support for Greece, but the key to it was a phil-Venizelist policy.

Support for Greece was located within the Foreign Office, while the mishellenes were dominant in the military. Only minimal support was forthcoming for Greek aims, mostly out of fear of angering the Turks. The General Staff considered 'the peaceful settlement of Turkey a legitimate interest'.[22] Both Foreign Office and War Office were concerned with the same

[18] A. W. A. Leeper to R. W. A. Leeper, 3 Feb. 1919. AWAL.

[19] FO 371/4355/f68/PC68.

[20] H. D. Napier, *The Experiences of a Military Attaché in the Balkans* (London, 1924), p. 243.

[21] FO 608/37/92/1/1/775, Nicolson, 'Summary of Memorial Presented to Peace Conference by M. Venizelos', 28 Jan. 1919.

[22] FO 608/37/92/1/1/1575, Maj.-Gen. Thwaites, 'Memorandum on Greek Claims by General Staff', 7 Feb. 1919.

issue, the stability of the Eastern Mediterranean, but their approaches differed widely. The Foreign Office hoped to assure this aim with the assistance of a dynamic regional power closely linked to Britain, the War Office sought the same end through a passive Turkish state which would simply not cause problems, but which need not be a British ally. Certainly the Foreign Office approach was the more imaginative and potentially a significant addition to the exercise of British diplomacy.

The whole Greek question was referred by the Supreme Council to the Greek Committee at the beginning of February, with Britain being represented by Sir Eyre Crowe and Sir Robert Borden, the Canadian premier, assisted by Harold Nicolson. During these discussions there was often Anglo-French agreement with frequent American concurrence, but the discussions were punctuated by continual Italian dissent. Italian aspirations conflicted with Greek aims, with Italy hoping to gain control of Albania and receive a section of Anatolia, while retaining control of the Dodecanese.

Greek aspirations lay in three areas, Northern Epirus, Thrace, and western Asia Minor. In the Greek Committee, Greek claims received strong British support. Greek control of Northern Epirus meant reducing any Italian gains in Albania. Crowe, when taxed with evidence that the frontier proposed by Britain would give some clearly Albanian districts to Greece, brushed aside the problem by noting 'the great power of assimilation possessed by the Greeks'. [23] The philhellenes found support within the military from Harold Temperley, who though temporarily in uniform had more in common with the PID types than with his career brethren. He argued that whatever the area's ethnic composition, 'None the less the importance of strategic security to Greece must be insisted upon'. [24] The point was to gain control of the area for Greece, and Crowe and Nicolson proposed a number of solutions to achieve this end. Suggested variants ranged from the outright annexation of the district to Greece, to making Greece the League mandatary for the area. By the end of May Nicolson

[23] FO 608/37/92/1/4/4117, Minutes of 10th Meeting of Greek Territorial Committee, 4 Mar. 1919.
[24] FO 608/29/76/2/3/8333, Minute by Temperley, 28 Apr. 1919.

was reaching the end of his patience and proposed one final compromise which must rank as one of the most bizarre schemes of a conference riddled with curious proposals. He proposed dividing Albania into four sections. The Kossovo region would go to Yugoslavia as an autonomous province, central Albania would become an autonomous Muslim state under an Italian mandate, while Northern Epirus would be ceded outright to Greece with the intention that Greece would then trade the Muslim areas to Italy in return for the Dodecanese. The remainder of Albania, consisting of the strategically important Koritza district, was to be 'rendered the seat of a Central Albanian University under United States protection, in which the idea of eventual Albanian unity would be preserved and stimulated'. [25] It is difficult to tell if Nicolson was wholly serious, or if having seen more sensible solutions fail he opted for a silly one. Balfour authorized him to discuss it with the Americans who, despite being mostly university professors, remained uninterested.

The question of Thrace was linked closely to control of Constantinople. The fate of this city was as yet undecided, so it was impossible to set a definite eastern frontier, but a notional line was agreed running from Enos to Midia which would have given Greece an outlet on the Black Sea. Agreement was reached here with surprising ease, but as so often at Paris the clearest agreements could come unstuck. In July when the territorial settlement was being reviewed the Americans unexpectedly changed their view and called for a return to the 1915 frontiers of Thrace. Crowe and Nicolson were enraged, as of course the final agreement on frontiers had involved give and take in a number of regions in order to achieve a balanced solution. The British were particularly put out as the United States had never declared war on either Bulgaria or Turkey. Crowe decided the American move was due to their delegate, W. H. Buckler, who he believed was 'a notorious out-and-out pro-Turk and hates everything Greek'. [26]

---

[25] FO 608/29/76/2/3/11124, Nicolson, 'Albania', 28 May 1919.
[26] FO 608/55/120/6/1/15321, Minute by Crowe, 11 July 1919.
William Hepburn Buckler (1867–1952); educ. Trinity Coll., Cambridge, and University of Maryland; Secretary US Legation, Madrid, 1907–9; US Embassy London, 1914–19; US Commission to Negotiate Peace, 1919.

The philhellenes were anxious that Greece should make the greatest possible gains and saw no reason why Bulgaria or Turkey should profit from the settlement. In addition Venizelos implored Crowe to push for the original agreement, as he was soon due to return to Greece, and as no final decision had yet been reached on any of Greece's frontiers. He feared that this might cause his political support to erode, which was the last thing Britain desired as British interests centred on the continuation of a Venizelist Greece. There was always the danger that King Constantine might be restored, and given Britain's role in deposing him in 1916 there could be little doubt that he would be less well inclined to Britain than Venizelos.

Greek claims in Asia Minor were the most debatable, and even the philhellenes realized the potential difficulties. Here there was an absence of clear geographic frontiers to correspond with a roughly national demarcation. There was also the additional danger that Greece might overstretch its resources, thereby weakening it and creating a much less useful ally. The British representatives on the Greek Committee, however, started from the position that Greece should have its Anatolian irredenta, and this by direct annexation without the palliative of a League mandate. This would not only help to achieve the *Megali Idea* but would also place a British ally firmly astride the Aegean Sea. As with other elements of the settlement, when the British view was not agreed to alternatives were proposed which would provide the substance if not the visible form of British aims. Nicolson again devised a series of possible compromises, such as allowing Greek annexation of Smyrna, but with a Greek mandate over the remainder of the region, though for this proposal Nicolson increased the area to pass under Greek control.[27]

There was of course opposition from the mishellene faction, which included Mallet, one of the few senior diplomats at Paris with direct experience of the area. Mallet's views were mirrored by General Milne, the commanding officer at Constantinople, and by General Thwaites, the Director of Military Intelligence.

[27] FO 608/37/92/1/4/4212 and FO 608/37/92/1/1/4392. On the negotiations on the future of Turkey see Paul C. Helmreich, *From Paris to Sèvres: The Partition of the Ottoman Empire at the Paris Peace Conference of 1919–1920* (Columbus, Ohio, 1974).

Crowe dismissed one admonitory dispatch from Milne with the observation that 'I should attach more importance to this paper if it did not betray in every line of it the traditional prejudice against everything Greek which is the stock-in-trade of our pro-Turks in the East'.[28] Crowe was concerned about the long-term development of British interests and saw Greece as the most likely guarantor of regional stability. He considered that the military's assessments were influenced by political views, which should be the concern of the diplomatists. General Thwaites, however, took the opportunity to retort that 'Policy, unless leavened with understanding is apt to make an early call on strategy. Do we desire such a call at present and could we respond to it?'[29] It was a view that could profitably have been recalled during the subsequent Chanak crisis. The split between mishellene and philhellene extended to the War Office as well, for the day after Thwaites made his comment Military Intelligence produced a memorandum which supported Greek control of Smyrna, a view entirely consistent with its reports as far back as December 1918.[30]

The various attempts to find a solution to the Anatolian problem in committee were overtaken by events at a higher level in late April. Irritation with Italian intransigence on a whole range of questions had been growing among Lloyd George, Wilson, and Clemenceau. If they agreed on anything it was probably their exasperation with the methods of Italian diplomacy. On 24 April the Italian delegation walked out of the conference, a serious error as it turned out, as it simply allowed the remaining three to move forward rapidly on a number of outstanding problems. Among these issues were reports of a possible Italian landing in Anatolia to pre-empt the conference. None of the Great Powers was particularly interested in providing forces to block their erstwhile ally. It was Lloyd George who proposed on 6 May that Venizelos be allowed to send two or three divisions to Smyrna, ostensibly to protect his fellow countrymen. Wilson and Clemenceau immediately

[28] Milne could not have been too mishellenic as he chose for one of his armorial supporters 'an officer of the Greek Evzone Guard'.

[29] FO 608/103/383/1/1/3968, Note by Thwaites, 20 Mar. 1919.

[30] FO 608 103/383/1/1/4795, 'The Economic Importance of Smyrna to Anatolia'. FO 371/4356/f192/PC192, 'Notes on Greek War Aims', 27 Dec. 1918.

agreed, and on 13 May the Greek force sailed for Smyrna under the protection of four British warships.[31] While American delegates on the Greek committee had opposed Greek aspirations in Asia Minor, President Wilson was more philhellenic. With his personal involvement American opposition ceased. British aims were now significantly advanced. With a Greek army on the ground Venizelos would be able to negotiate from strength. The tragedy which overtook the philhellenes, as well as Venizelos's dreams, were the reports of Greek atrocities in the occupied area. As these reports filtered through to Paris opinion began to change. Those who had not supported either faction within the British delegation now turned firmly against Greece. By July Eric Forbes-Adams was commenting, 'We do not want to increase the already prevalent, though erroneous, opinion that *we* alone are responsible for the Greek occupation of the Smyrna zone.'[32] The conference dealt with the problem by one of its favourite mechanisms, postponement.

British policy towards Constantinople was also very much tied up with the aims of the philhellenes and the opposition of the pro-Turks. Venizelos had been careful not to claim the city, well aware of the fact that it was likely to be at the vortex of Great Power rivalry. Two questions arose on the future of this historic capital of the East, first as to its future administration and second as to whether or not the Turks should be expelled. As with other problem cities, such as Danzig and Fiume, a solution which grew in favour was the creation of a city-state under League control, perhaps in this instance even becoming the seat of the League. Britain's aim here was to prevent any other power from gaining control of the city.

Initially some consideration was given to making Constantinople an American mandate, a solution which found favour with Crowe, Nicolson, and Toynbee. The Americans were less happy with the idea, the navy in particular aware that its link to the mandate would be along an extended sea route where the Royal Navy controlled all the critical chokepoints. Curiously these fears of naval projection of power were mirrored on the British side. When the question of

[31] FRUS:PPC:V, Minutes of Council of Four, 6 May 1919.
[32] FO 608/104/383/1/6/14003, Minute by Forbes-Adam, 1 July 1919.

Constantinople was discussed within the delegation, the Admiralty warned that 'a mandate given to the U.S.A. by the League of Nations would afford opportunity and pretext for basing a strong American fleet in the Mediterranean — a danger which, from a strategical point of view, must at all cost be avoided'. [33] At least in naval terms, with the defeat of Germany, the United States had become the greatest potential rival. However, as the possibility of an American mandate receded and the debate over Anatolia continued, the possibility emerged of allowing Greece to take Constantinople in return for surrendering its Anatolian claims.

The future of Constantinople also concerned the India Office, which was disturbed by the possible civil unrest in India by Muslims if the sultan-caliph was deprived of his historic capital. Britain's overwhelming concern about the security of its Indian empire acted as a particular constraint to its policies on Turkey, and the India Office was particularly torn about Constantinople, an issue on which even the Eastern Committee had been unable to decide. Montagu advocated the status quo, while Hirtzel warned that 'if once it is admitted that Indian Moslems can influence the policy of His Majesty's Government in Europe a very serious precedent will be created'. [34] Curzon, however, was a staunch Turcophobe and was all for ousting the Turks from Europe.

By July no decision had yet been reached on any part of the Greek settlement, mostly due to the problems of Italian intransigence, combined with some erratic American inflexibility. At the end of the month, however, the Italians and Greeks had a dramatic *rapprochement* and a solution emerged on lines favourable to the philhellenes' plans. The Northern Epirus frontier was left to an international commission, and virtually all of Thrace was awarded to Greece, as was the Smyrna region. The philhellenes had succeeded in piloting through the bulk of their aims, despite opposition within the delegation, together with the opposition of some of the other Great Powers. The Greeks had benefited not only from their own statesmanship, but from the vision of a team of philhellenic British diplomats at

[33] 'The Future of Constantinople', Minutes of meeting of 30 Jan. 1919. Montagu Papers (Trinity) AS-IV-4/743.
[34] CAB 27/39/EC2841, Note by Hirtzel, 20 Dec. 1918.

Paris. However, their plans in the final instance came to nought. In November 1920 Venizelos, unexpectedly defeated in a general election, was replaced by the dreaded King Constantine. Even then some of the philhellenes still pushed for the Greek option, but with little success. Aid to Greece was cancelled, which helped to weaken the Greek military, so involuntarily assisting in their defeat at the hands of the Turks. The philhellenes were proved right, as Britain now found itself without an eastern Mediterranean ally.

Yugoslavia

After Greece the next most favoured Balkan state was Yugoslavia. This union of the South Slavs, centred on the old Serbian kingdom, evoked British sympathy because of the events at Sarajevo in 1914 which had sparked the European conflict. A more important geopolitical reason for British goodwill was that Yugoslavia and Greece were on good terms and the new state was considered safely Anglophil. Brigadier General Plunkett, the military attaché at Belgrade, reported to Military Intelligence that the new state was worthy of support as it would provide 'A solid block of 10 to 12 millions, splendid fighters, very pro-English and pro-American, intensely anti-German and Austrian and Italian, [who] would block the way effectively from central Europe to Salonika and Constantinople'.[35] Yugoslavia would act therefore as a Balkan buffer for the new Greece. But the crisis in determining the frontiers of the new state became inextricably linked to the Italian problem and what role Britain envisaged Italy playing in the post-war order.

Italian intransigence spawned a number of diplomatic imitators, in particular the Romanians. Since Yugoslavia's southern frontier with Greece was relatively uncontroversial, it could have been hoped that the frontiers with Romania could also be easily settled. Romania's aim, though, was to achieve the

[35] FO 608/51/117/1/2/1231, Plunkett to DMI, 1 Jan. 1919. A similar message from Plunkett somewhat garbled in transmission is in FO 608/42/98/1/3/2034. Edward Abadie Plunkett (1870–1926); Head, British Military Mission to Royal Serbian Army, 1918; Military Attaché, Belgrade, 1918–20; Inter-Allied Commissioner of Control, Bulgaria, 1920–2.

creation of a Greater Romania. The difficulty was that the ir-redenta of the nascent South Slav state and the prospective Greater Romania overlapped. The result was that the Italians backed the Romanians on the principle of troubling the Yugo-slavs, while the French backed the Yugoslavs probably in order to irritate the Italians. American policy remained idealistic and incoherent, while British policy tilted to Yugoslavia out of the dual necessity of securing the new Greece while simultan-eously restricting any growth in Italian maritime power.

The union of the South Slavs in the new Yugoslav kingdom, while still awaiting formal diplomatic recognition, was now a reality, but a reality without definite frontiers. The complex forces which swirled about in the maelstrom of domestic Yugoslav politics prevented the development of a co-ordinated national case for presentation to the peace conference, in con-trast to Venizelos's masterful presentation of Greek aims. The Yugoslav premier and chief delegate, Nikola Pašić, envisaged a new regional order where Balkan stability would turn on a Yugoslav–Greek axis, a concept which naturally found favour with the British philhellenes.[36]

The work of the Yugoslav Committee went relatively smoothly, in no small measure because it was debarred from discussing the sensitive Italo-Yugoslav border, which was reserved for Great Power negotiation. Leeper during the com-mittee's discussions pushed vigorously for a large Yugoslavia, in particular continually pointing out that the proposed fron-tiers would leave up to 400,000 of the 1,500,000 Slovenes under foreign rule. As Plunkett pointed out, the bigger the Yugoslav state the better. The creation of a great South Slav state had been a prime aim of the New Europe group, and of British policy. Such a union would, it was hoped, create not only greater regional stability, but would also help to fill the vacuum left by the collapse of the old regional empires.

Romania

Romania, unlike Greece, was not central to British concerns. The Great Power chiefly interested in the country was France,

[36] On Yugoslav aims see I. J. Lederer, *Yugoslavia at the Paris Peace Conference: A Study in Frontiermaking* (New Haven, Conn., 1963).

which projected the creation of a French-dominated East European alliance system, a grouping which eventually emerged as the Little Entente. The French had particular links with Romania through the image of a common Latin heritage, and many senior Romanians had been educated in France. Popular British interest in Romania was limited to the fascinating Queen Marie, whose household was viewed by the local British representatives as the centre of pro-English ideas.[37] From the British viewpoint Romania suffered from two important disadvantages, its erratic behaviour during the war, and the personality of its premier, Ioan Bratianu, an abrasive personality who went down badly with almost every British official with whom he came into contact. From Bucharest in early January the British Minister, Sir George Barclay, warned that Bratianu had 'tendencies towards megalomania'.[38] Allen Leeper wrote on meeting him for the first time that he 'was not very favourably impressed. He's quite a fish out of water here ....'[39] Harold Nicolson in reviewing the problems of Romania's future relations with Yugoslavia observed that 'we do not feel that M. Bratiano is sufficiently honest or advanced to cope with a situation requiring moderation, honesty and disinterestedness'.[40] The tactics necessary for political victory in Bucharest were not the same as those required at the peace conference. Despite these shortcomings Bratianu achieved a remarkable amount at Paris, proving himself one of the most effective small-state leaders.[41]

Bratianu could not be counted upon to act in as friendly a way as Venizelos would. Certainly he made no attempt, unlike his Greek counterpart, to establish cordial relations with the British delegation. Given Romania's marginal strategic position from Britain's viewpoint, combined with the unpleasant image of its leader, the British delegates saw no significant role for the country in Britain's future diplomatic-strategic arrangements.

[37] FO 608/51/114/1/17/5156, 'Secret No. 2. Report on Roumanian Mission', 10 Jan. 1919.
[38] FO 608/49/114/1/9/1617, Telegram from Sir George Barclay, 11 Jan. 1919.
[39] A. W. A. Leeper to R. W. A. Leeper, 2 Feb. 1919. AWAL.
[40] FO 371/3141/f629/198694, Minute by Nicolson, 2 Dec. 1918.
[41] On Bratianu's diplomacy see S. D. Spector, *Rumania at the Paris Peace Conference: A Study of the Diplomacy of Ioan C. Bratianu* (New York, 1962).

It was clear, however, that Britain consistently wished it was dealing with a different Romanian leader, the favoured candidate being Take Ionescu. Allen Leeper even went so far as to suggest in July, after months of dealing with the slippery Mr. Bratianu, that if a government containing Ionescu 'came into power, it would be not only politic but just to give them a chance of securing more generous treatment than M. Bratianu has deserved'. [42]

At the beginning of February the Romanian Committee was appointed. Britain was represented by Eyre Crowe and Allen Leeper, but as Crowe was now deeply engaged in many facets of the conference's activities much of the technical work was left to Leeper. The Romanians could hardly have hoped for a better choice than a British diplomat who knew Romanian, was secretary of the Anglo-Romanian Society, and was the expert primarily responsible for Romania during the preparatory phase. Now Leeper would have the opportunity of putting his training to direct use and his negotiating skills were to leave a permanent mark upon the frontiers of the country.

The Romanian Committee met for the first time on 8 February, and prior to this first session the British and American delegates met to discuss their views, with the result that a common position was rapidly agreed. [43] In the preparatory phase both the British and Americans had independently arrived at virtually the same conclusions on Romania. [44] Their joint discussions now revealed just how close their views really were. Unusually for the territorial negotiations it emerged in the early sessions that there were few points of disagreement with the French, at least initially. It was therefore commonly agreed that Romania should receive Bessarabia and Transylvania, as well as the bulk of Bukovina. The Americans, however, felt that the Ruthenian areas should be

[42] FO 608/49/114/1/9/14571, Minute by Leeper, 8 July 1919.

[43] FO 608/30/79/1/1/1646, 'Future Frontiers of Rumania: Recommendations submitted by British Delegates on the Inter-Allied Commission', 8 Feb. 1919. A. W. A. Leeper to R. W. A. Leeper, 8 Feb. 1919, AWAL. These views were finally expressed in the British Recommendations to the Roumanian Committee, FO 608/49/114/1/8/1788.

[44] L. Gelfand, The Inquiry: American Preparations for Peace, 1917–1919 (New Haven, Conn., 1963), p. 220.

detached to form part of an independent Ruthene state which the British saw as impractical, preferring that Bukovina be kept intact. The Banat, though forming a neat geographic and historic unit, would have to be partitioned between Yugoslavia and Romania on ethnic grounds. The only area of potential Great Power disagreement was over the Southern Dobrudja, an ethnically Bulgarian area acquired by Romania in 1913. Here Britain and the United States desired its return to Bulgaria on ethnic grounds, while France opposed taking any territory from an Allied state. Given this rough concordance on Romania's future it should have been comparatively easy to reach a quick settlement, but as Allen Leeper was eventually to exclaim,'such problems in tracing a frontier'. [45]

Throughout the Romanian discussions the Italians proved troublesome, supporting the maximalist Romanian claims for two reasons, first that they were based on one of the wartime secret treaties similar to those which Italy was also using as a justification for claims, and secondly to isolate Yugoslavia. The Italians were concerned by the potential threat posed by the new Yugoslav state, and on the basis of chequerboard diplomacy were looking for an ally to Yugoslavia's rear. The United States as usual rejected the validity of any of these secret treaties, much to Britain's delight. Crowe argued that American entry into the war and 'the proclaiming of the principle of self-determination, and other factors, have necessitated its [the secret treaties] complete revision, if not extinction'. [46] What Crowe was arguing was that American entry into the war had caused a fundamental change of circumstances and if the international law concept of *rebus sic stantibus* was applied this could provide a legal basis for declaring the wartime secret treaties invalid. The British delegation never formally made this argument, perhaps because it was potentially too volatile in the unstable atmosphere of the conference, but it was undoubtedly there in reserve in the minds of the diplomats. It was hoped that if America could carry its views on this point it would help to liberate Britain from a whole series of unfortunate promises made under the duress

[45] A. W. A. Leeper to R. W. A.Leeper, 12 Feb. 1919. AWAL.
[46] FO 608/48/114/1/4/551, Minute by Crowe, 25 Jan. 1919.

of war. Romanian links with Italy irritated the British negotiators, who considered them an unwholesome influence. Allen Leeper commented that 'if Mr. Bratianu's Govt. insists on quarrelling with the Serbs & putting their trust in Italy, no one can save them from ruin'. [47]

The Romanian Committee reported to the Central Territorial Committee at the beginning of April and with only minor modifications these frontiers were sent to the Council of Foreign Ministers. Since most of the senior officials at the conference were concentrating their efforts on completing the German treaty, the Romanian report was not considered until the beginning of May, after the German treaty was completed. It was not until the 21 June that the Council of Four finally approved the report, virtually unchanged from the original version. In general Leeper was successful in implementing Britain's views, though as he realistically summed up the negotiations, 'I carried some & lost others of my proposals.' [48] Romania did well out of the proposed settlement, in particular receiving much of what had been promised of Transylvania by the 1916 secret treaty. Romania was not central to British concerns, and while no doubt finding the current leadership distasteful, Britain was willing to acquiesce in most Romanian demands. When these demands posed a threat to Yugoslavia, which did fit into the British strategic scheme, opposition was evident.

The increasingly pragmatic New Europe supporters, such as Leeper, were clearly erring in the application of their ideas in favour of wider British aims where such disputes arose. Bratianu, however, continued to take a maximalist position. Whereas the Italians had the power to take such a stand, Romania's imitation was a dangerous ploy. No doubt Lloyd George and Wilson would have been sorely tempted to expel Romania from the conference, an action they contemplated in June, if it had not been for the events in Hungary. With the establishment of a Communist republic in Hungary, Romania suddenly took on an enhanced strategic position. Poised between this new Communist state and Soviet Russia, it

[47] FO 608/49/114/1/11/5676, Minute by Leeper, 31 Mar. 1919.
[48] A. W. A. Leeper to R. W. A. Leeper, 2 Mar. 1919. AWAL.

became a potentially important military base for any anti-Bolshevik operations. As a result Romania emerged, in the short term at least, as a state to be kept reasonably strong given the regional political situation. It was this set of circumstances which allowed Bratianu to reap such great rewards from the reluctant powers.

Czechoslovakia

The creation of a Czechoslovak state was a secondary issue for British policy, just as in 1938–9 the destruction of this landlocked European country would be acquiesced in as it was not of critical strategic importance to Britain. What the Czechoslovak leaders, such as Masaryk, relied upon in 1919 were the close relations they had established with the New Europe group. Masaryk was particularly close to Seton-Watson, who in turn was in close consultation with Leeper and Nicolson. As Nicolson later recalled, they 'never moved a yard without previous consultation with experts of the authority of Dr Seton-Watson who was in Paris at the time'.[49] As Leeper noted during the negotiations, 'I find that from whatever corner of Europe we start, we always run into the Czechs. They are especially valuable to us at present when we are trying to get together the peoples of South-Eastern Europe to form a *bloc* as an example and instalment of the League of Nations in Eastern Europe.'[50] Czechoslovakia was pivotal to the New Europe group, if not to the more traditional diplomatists. When the Czechoslovakia Committee was appointed, Masaryk's policy of courting this group seemed justified, as the British delegate was Harold Nicolson, along with the New South Wales premier, Sir Joseph Cook, who remained a cipher in the negotiations.

Nicolson intended to apply the principles of the New Europe to the Czechoslovak settlement, and while this led him to reject some of the more extreme proposals of the Prague government, it did mean that the new state obtained most of its goals. The most difficult problem, as Namier had

[49] Nicolson, *Peacemaking 1919*, p. 126
[50] A. W. A. Leeper to R. W. A. Leeper, 21 Feb. 1919. AWAL.

identified in the preparatory phase, was what to do about Bohemia's German population. It is interesting to note that in the British delegation's summary of the Czechoslovak case, probably prepared by Nicolson, the argument is made that 'German Bohemia cannot form a separate political unit owing to its geographical position, nor be allowed what it asks, i.e. union with German Austria'.[51] The author is attempting to explain approval of an obvious violation of the principle of national self-determination, but as Namier had already pointed out, to strip Czechoslovakia of the Sudeten region would be to deprive it of one of the best defensible frontiers in Europe.

Czechoslovakia was also to be favoured over Poland, which was perhaps seen to be too much under French influence, while the Czechoslovaks were seen as pro-British. Namier observed when comparing them, 'They [the Czechs] have been our most faithful and most devoted allies in Central and Eastern Europe throughout the War and have raised entire armies of volunteers'.[52] On the troublesome question of who should get Teschen, the military section, which was not always in accord with the diplomats, agreed that it should go to Czechoslovakia on the grounds that its strategic railway junction and the Jablunka Pass would help 'to weld Czecho-Slovakia into a State which combines economic independence with military and political stability'.[53] Clearly the Czechs were considered more reliable than the Poles.

This concurrence over Teschen should not be taken to mean that the military supported the New Europe group's positive view of Czechoslovakia. The General Staff expressed strong reservations about Czechoslovakia obtaining the Grosse Schutt, which would give it a Danubian frontier. The military objections were 'based mainly on the unsettling effect which this transfer is likely to have on the balance of military power in Central Europe, as it may tempt the Czechs to further territorial aggrandisement in the Danubian region'.[54] This smacks of a military fear of the unknown, perhaps fuelled by

[51] FO 608/6/35/1/1/1486, 'The Cheko-Slovak Case', 3 Feb. 1919.
[52] FO 608/7/35/1/5/2823, Memorandum by Namier, 15 Feb. 1919.
[53] FO 608/7/35/1/5/1782, 'The Problem of Teschen', 7 Feb. 1919.
[54] FO 608/7/35/1/5/3815.

the reputation of the Czech Legion. It was a lone argument, however, as the Czechoslovak Committee had already reached a unanimous decision in favour of the Czechs on this issue. The result was the creation of a new state which more than fulfilled the expectations of its early supporters, becoming the Central European bastion of the ideals envisaged by the New Europe group.

Poland

It was over the Polish question that the greatest struggle between members of the British delegation occurred, with two factions emerging. One group favoured a Greater Poland encompassing significant minority populations, while the other pushed for frontiers drawn along New Europe lines. The later view was ardently championed by Headlam-Morley, who eventually overturned many of the early victories of his opponents and succeeded in rewriting the Polish settlement. The thinking behind the pro-Polish group coincided with that of the French, 'who looked on the problem from the point of view of the balance of power, [and believed] that it was necessary to create a State intervening between Russia and Germany . . . a State depending for the defence of its territory on a great army'. [55] Indeed a Greater Poland could potentially command an army of four million men and could possibly become one of the European great powers. This obviously held attractions for France, which could replace its old Eastern European counterweight, Russia, with a new powerful Poland. France certainly viewed Poland as a potential regional ally. General Carton de Wiart, who was dispatched as the British member of the Inter-Allied Mission to Poland, noted that during his briefing, 'I learnt that Poland had been earmarked as the French sphere, and the French did not allow us to forget the fact for a single instant'. [56] There was some concern, particularly among the New Europe group, of the implications of a pro-French Greater Poland. Allen Leeper observed of French actions, 'they are obsessed by the dream of a great Poland

[55] Confidential Print 13917.
[56] Adrian Carton de Wiart, *Happy Odyssey* (London, 1950), p. 93.

which could and should never exist'.[57] Given the historic Franco-Polish connection and French sympathy for Polish aspirations, combined with strong French support for Polish claims at the conference, France could expect amicable relations with the new state. It fell to Headlam-Morley to push forward a solution which adhered to the basic principles of the new Europe, while not adversely affecting British interests. A pragmatic idealism became increasingly evident in the actions of the New Europe adherents at Paris.

Headlam-Morley later observed that 'The other attitude was that taken by the British delegation, who urged the danger of including large numbers of Germans in a Polish State, and felt that if a strong Poland were to be established the principle of self-determination must be taken into account.'[58] Headlam-Morley wanted 'to reduce the causes for dispute to a minimum', as 'It seemed possible that an extensive Poland might really prove in practice to be weaker than a smaller Poland'.[59] A large German minority could be a volatile force, and to give Poland its pre-partition frontier on the west would place it within striking distance of Berlin, inevitably forcing Germany on security grounds to have revisionist aims.

The initial negotiations over Poland were left to Sir Esme Howard. During the preparatory phase in London he had advocated only a medium-sized Poland. Released, however, from his PID staff his views began to change, and Headlam-Morley reported to Namier that 'What we both anticipated has in fact, I think, undoubtedly happened, and Howard has been more and more falling under the influences of Paris and drifting away'.[60] His view seems justified for on 6 February Howard reached an agreement on Poland's frontiers with the American delegate, Robert Lord, heavily in Poland's favour.[61] Headlam-Morley on seeing the Howard–Lord agreement commented, 'This raises serious problems of policy.'[62] Headlam-Morley was

[57] A. W. A. Leeper to R. W. A. Leeper, 17 Mar. 1919. AWAL.   [58] Ibid.
[59] Ibid.
[60] Headlam-Morley to Namier, 10 Feb. 1919. Headlam-Morley, *Memoir*, p. 25.
[61] FO 608/66/130/6/1/20216, 'Papers and Correspondence dealing with the Establishment of Danzig as a Free City'.
[62] Headlam-Morley, *Memoir*, p. 21.

already concerned at this stage that the settlement of Germany's frontiers was not being dealt with as a whole, and that a compartmentalized approach could only lead to disaster.

A Polish Committee had been appointed quite early on in the conference in order to liaise with the Allied Mission in Poland. On 26 February the Supreme Council assigned the task of defining Poland's frontiers to this committee, which in turn delegated it to a sub-committee of experts. This sub-committee was in effect the equivalent of the other territorial committees established by the conference. The British delegate was Lt.-Col. F. H. Kisch, as Howard was away on a special mission to Poland.[63] The committee moved quickly. The chief Polish delegate, Dmowski, presented his country's case on 6 March, and on 19 March the committee reported, the first territorial committee to do so. Alone among the leaders Lloyd George voiced concern about including two million Germans within the new Poland, precisely the same point which worried Headlam-Morley. There is no definite evidence that Headlam-Morley influenced the prime minister, but it seems likely, as he was already in regular contact with Philip Kerr, who did have direct access to Lloyd George. As a result of Lloyd George's objections the report was returned to the committee for reconsideration. Led by Kisch, it unanimously stood by its report. Headlam-Morley then provided ammunition for the prime minister with some 'Notes on the Report of the Polish Commission'.[64]

The question of Poland's frontiers receded as other more immediate crises claimed the conference's attention. Smuts again raised the problem of Poland on 1 June in the British delegation's discussion on the German treaty. He was not sanguine about the future of the nascent Polish state, observing that 'Poland was an historic failure, and always would be a failure, and in the Treaty we were trying to reverse the verdict

[63] Frederick Hermann Kisch (1888–1943); educ. RMA Woolwich; entered Royal Engineers, 1909; served France, 1914–15; Mesopotamia, 1916–17; retired 1922; chairman Palestine Zionist Executive, 1922–31. See also Norman Bentwich and Michael Kisch, *Brigadier Frederick Kisch: Soldier and Zionist* (London, 1966). Howard left for Warsaw on 9 Feb. 1919, and did not return until 6 Apr. Howard of Penrith Diary.

[64] Headlam-Morley, *Memoir*, pp. 60–3.

of history'.[65] Smuts in these internal discussions was a leading spirit for the modification of the harsh terms being envisaged for Germany. These views must have influenced the prime minister, for the next day Lloyd George, who had continued to block an overly pro-Polish settlement, announced that it was the unanimous British view that 'the British Army should not be allowed to march or that the fleet should take part in the blockade', in order to impose a treaty as it currently stood upon Germany. Among the necessary changes were modifications of the very pro-Polish frontier.[66] Such a blunt statement from the leader of the world's greatest empire had to be taken into account. Woodrow Wilson has often been criticized for compromising the principles he enunciated in the Fourteen Points when he might have backed them up with America's new economic and military might. Lloyd George on the other hand was willing, if necessary, to play such a hard diplomatic game.

As a result of Lloyd George's objections, which threatened to block any German settlement, a new committee was hastily created to reconsider the problem. The membership was exactly the same as that of the previous committee, except that Headlam-Morley replaced Kisch. Headlam-Morley had now won the battle within the British delegation, and held the vital support of the prime minister. He proceeded to bend the committee to Britain's newly defined will. He observed that 'The position of the British representative was therefore not an easy one, and he repeatedly found himself in a minority of one, and had much difficulty in getting the substantial changes agreed upon.'[67] Headlam-Morley achieved just this, later commenting that 'I found myself from the beginning thrown into complete opposition to all the other members. However, ultimately I succeeded in getting the report in a general way based on the lines which seem to me the only ones legitimate. . . .'[68] As a result Poland's frontiers with Germany were revised, much reducing the size of the German minority in Poland.

[65] FO 608/156/511/1/3/11558, 33rd Meeting of British Empire Delegation, 1 June 1919.
[66] FRUS:PPC:VI, p. 139.   [67] Confidential Print 13917.
[68] Headlam-Morley, *Memoir*, p. 152.

Danzig

The most critical question within the complex Polish problem was the future of Danzig, which 'was the cause of acute differences of opinion within the British delegation itself'.[69] Here too Headlam-Morley won the battle within the British delegation by achieving access to the prime minister.[70] Indeed Headlam-Morley claimed that 'The one section of the treaty for which I am really responsible, and for which I am prepared to accept responsibility, is that concerning Danzig'.[71] The evolution of the Danzig solution was, however, particularly twisted.

The original proposal in the preparatory phase, suggested by Professor Oman, was to leave the city to Germany. Howard agreed with this, even suggesting a German corridor linking East and West Prussia. Two months later, however, in the Howard–Lord Agreement, Howard reversed his opinion and supported allocating the city to Poland, leaving the Germans control of a railway line to East Prussia. Both Hardinge and Crowe strongly disagreed with this change. The Danzig problem led to the brief re-emergence of George Prothero as an important actor. The head of the Historical Section had been in Paris for some weeks, officially as Historical Adviser to the British Delegation, but nobody seemed to want historical advice, to Prothero's growing frustration. He was at last asked to prepare a report on Danzig, and in a masterly memorandum succeeded in convincing Hardinge, and possibly others, of the danger of giving Danzig to Poland.[72] Within days Headlam-Morley had put forward, as an alternative, the creation of a city-state, which would allow the inhabitants to rule themselves, but would meet Poland's desire not to allow the city to Germany.[73] H. J. Paton, who had replaced Howard as adviser on Polish affairs,

---

[69] Confidential Print 12760.   [70] Ibid.

[71] Headlam-Morley, *Memoir*, p. 169.

[72] FO 608/141/477/1/6/2523, Prothero, 'Future of Danzig and West Prussia', 20 Feb. 1919. Prothero was asked to prepare the memo on 16 Feb., and completed it on 19 Feb. Prothero Diary.

[73] FO 608/141/477/1/6/2864, 25 Feb. 1919.

immediately produced a memorandum in rebuttal to Headlam-Morley.[74]

Headlam-Morley in explaining his views observed that 'I cannot reconcile myself to the policy of handing over a city such as Danzig to an alien Power, completely disregarding the wishes of the inhabitants. . . . I still believe the right solution is to be found in the conception of the autonomous and, perhaps, semi-independent city-state.'[75] The future of Danzig was as such very much tied up with the entire solution being proposed for Poland. Headlam-Morley in commenting on Lloyd George's objections to the Polish Committee report noted that the prime minister could hardly be expected to have expert knowledge of these problems. As a result, 'The great point was who should be chosen to advise him? It was in accordance with his general method of procedure that he did not turn to the higher members of the Foreign Office staff and diplomatic service. They appear not to have been consulted at all.'[76] The operative word here seems to be 'higher', as it seems clear that the solutions were coming from the comparatively 'lowly' Headlam-Morley. Indeed, as Headlam-Morley noted at one stage, 'The practical suggestion put forward to him [Lloyd George] was that Danzig should be handed over by the Germans, not to Poland, but to the Allies.'[77] The proposal in fact originated with Headlam-Morley.

On 1 April Lloyd George, adopting Headlam-Morley's ideas, brought the issue before the Council of Four, which in turn referred the question to a special committee of two, Headlam-Morley and the American, Charles Haskins. It is not clear why no Frenchman was appointed, though Headlam-Morley later presumed this was perhaps a French protest at any revision of the Polish Committee's markedly pro-Polish report. In drafting their suggestions Headlam-Morley and Haskins took direct advice from Lloyd George on the question

[74] FO 608/141/477/1/6/3075, 'The Polish Claims to Danzig and West Prussia', 27 Feb. 1919. Henry James Paton (1887–1960); educ. Glasgow University and Balliol Coll., Oxford; fellow and praelector in classics and philosophy, Queen's Coll., Oxford, 1911–27; Naval Intelligence, 1914–19; prof. of logic and rhetoric, Glasgow, 1927–37; White's Prof. of Moral Philosophy, Oxford, 1937–52; Foreign Office Research Dept., 1939–44.

[75] Headlam-Morley, Memoir, p. 40.   [76] Confidential Print 12760.

[77] Ibid.

of sovereignty, and a week later they submitted a proposal for a city-state.[78]

In the debate over the Polish question it is worth noting the emergence of Headlam-Morley's influence, and the consequent displacement of opposing views. Headlam-Morley, like his PID colleagues, had a clear vision of the Europe he wanted to emerge from the wreckage of the war and was willing to fight tenaciously for these aims. This group could not have succeeded as far as it did without the tacit support of Lloyd George. It was not that they were ever in league, but rather that the prime minister's instincts were much in accord with the group's views. The PID and the ideas of the New Europe group gave an intellectual and strategic form to Lloyd George's general inclinations. The combination of the Welsh Wizard's forensic talent and native guile when married to the intellectual strength of the New Europe proved a potent force in the final European settlement.

Fiume

One of the great crises of the conference developed over the future of the Adriatic port of Fiume. It was the keystone to the debate over the frontiers of Italy, and it should be recalled that in 1919 these frontiers stretched as far as the Aegean Sea, with ramifications for the Asia Minor settlement. The whole mass of Italian claims proved so interlocking that as Headlam-Morley later recalled, 'Of all the problems discussed at the Peace Conference of Paris none proved so intractable as the settlement of the new frontiers of Italy.'[79] The problem at one time threatened to break up the conference, culminating in the Italians' theatrical walkout on 24 April, and their sheepish return by 5 May. The conference never did resolve the Fiume question, which in September 1919 was pre-empted by the comic opera occupation of the city by the eccentric poet Gabriele d'Annunzio. During the period of negotiations the British delegation opposed the Italian claim to Fiume on principle, but denial of it to Italy was an important strategic aim as well.

[78] Ibid.
[79] Confidential Print 12200, Headlam-Morley, 'Fiume and the Adriatic', 13 Apr. 1923.

Orlando laid claim to Fiume on the grounds of ethnicity, as he could not invoke the justification being used for Italy's other claims which were based on the secret treaties. This provided Britain with its only legitimate opportunity to object to Italy's extravagant irredentist claims. As a result of Italian insistence this question was not sent to the Yugoslav Committee, but remained a topic for the Council of Four. President Wilson, with backing from Lloyd George and Clemenceau, refused to give in to Italian demands, with the result that Orlando left the conference on 24 April.

Wilson's view, supported by Lloyd George, was also the view of the New Europe group. Leeper, very much concerned about the viability of the new states, commented that 'Fiume is vital to Jugoslavia'. [80] Crowe held similar views, though probably more out of concern to limit Italian power, observing that 'The Italians have no case as regards Fiume, *on the merits*'. [81] A reasonably strong Yugoslavia would prevent Italy from turning the Adriatic into an Italian lake, thereby allowing British maritime power greater leverage. The Army, or at least General Wilson, had other concerns. In November 1918, at the end of the hostilities, one British battalion was dispatched to Fiume as a token contribution to an inter-allied occupation force. In March 1919 General Wilson requested permission to withdraw these troops as they were needed as reserves for Turkey or Egypt. [82] Crowe, while not judging the military necessity, was concerned about the diplomatic impact, noting that 'It seems to me however unfortunate to proceed with this before we have come to a clear understanding with Italy'. [83] General Wilson was clearly irritated at having to pay attention to what he considered a peripheral issue from the viewpoint of immediate military needs. When Temperley reported on the eve of the Italian walkout that in his opinion the Serbs would fight for Fiume, if not now, certainly within two or three years, General Wilson commented with some asperity, 'I thought one of the decisions of the Paris Conference was that these young nations were not to have armies

[80] FO 608/51/117/1/6/5307.
[81] FO 608/35/89/1/2/4334, Minute by Crowe, 17 Mar. 1919.
[82] FO 608/8/39/1/1/7262, Minute by General Wilson, 7 Apr. 1919.
[83] Ibid., Minute by Crowe, 8 Apr. 1919.

that could fight'.[84] This certainly would have made the British army's immediate task easier. There was under the circumstances no hope of affecting these negotiations with military assistance and therefore the experts focused their efforts on diplomatic means.

There was no great surprise among the experts at Orlando's abrupt withdrawal, with Allen Leeper blandly commenting that 'Well, one always knew the break wd. come some time', and the following day Leeper was already busy constructing an Adriatic compromise.[85] The Americans were consulted and willing to accept Leeper's scheme, but this agreement came unstuck when President Wilson decided to take a firm stand against Italy's behaviour. As a result it was decided to apply diplomatic pressure on Italy by recognizing the new Yugoslav kingdom. This had been a long-term objective of the New Europe group, which now saw formal acceptance of the transformation of Serbia into a great South Slav state.

Leeper's plan was formally proposed by him, together with Nicolson and their junior PID colleague, Major J. S. Barnes, on behalf of the delegation's South European section on 1 May. It consisted of a minimum scheme and provided for three progressive lines of concession. By this plan all the components of Italy's various demands were considered together, ranging from the Tyrol to Asia Minor. Their view on Fiume was clear, stating that 'No peaceful settlement can be secured if Fiume is placed under the Italian flag'. They therefore recommended that Fiume be placed under Yugoslav sovereignty, with suitable international guarantees. The only possible concession envisaged was that Fiume might be placed directly under the League but with full economic union with Yugoslavia. Fiume, it was clear, must be denied to Italy.

On 7 May the Italians returned to Paris, concerned no doubt about what was being connived at in their absence. As a result the British delegation became immersed in the Adriatic negotiations between 13 and 16 May. One of the difficulties continually encountered by the British diplomats was lack of information as to the twists and turns of Lloyd George's

---

[84] FO 608/35/89/1/4/7939, Minute by Gen. Wilson, 1 May 1919.
[85] A. W. A. Leeper to R. W. A. Leeper, 24 & 26 Apr. 1919. AWAL.

negotiations. Leeper complained on the day that Italy returned to the conference, and in the midst of trying to work out a compromise, that 'one is quite vague as to what terms Ll.G. proposes to make with the Italians'. [86] In retrospect this should not be considered particularly surprising. Having put his staff on to a problem, and given the myriad of problems he was dealing with, the prime minister could not succeed in keeping his staff informed. The answer to Leeper's question was probably that Lloyd George had no terms in mind and was awaiting further suggestions.

Work continued simultaneously on the linked question of the Austrian frontiers. The situation in the Klagenfurt basin was becoming critical, and the inter-allied delegates on the spot asked for troops to be dispatched by the Great Powers. The only British forces in the region were the battalion at Fiume. In this instance the prime minister, Crowe, and Thwaites showed a rare degree of unanimity, refusing to weaken the force at Fiume. In a choice between inland and maritime questions Britain instinctively ranked the latter as the most important.

These negotiations help illustrate one aspect of the experts' role, which can be compared with solicitors briefing barristers, the role of the barristers being played by the political leaders. Leeper prepared a draft resolution on this problem in consultation with Temperley and Mance, which was accepted by the Yugoslav Committee, with only Italy dissenting. After this Crowe and Leeper called on Balfour and as Leeper noted they 'coached him up on the subject. At 4 Council of Five which for once was a great success. Balfour using our arguments with considerable skill so that finally Sonnino gave way & they all adopted the draft I'd prepared for the committee prolonging the Austrian frontier to the W. to N. of Tarvis. It was a great triumph for us & I hope may prove the starting point for a real settlement of the whole Italo-Yugoslav question on proper lines.' [87] A solution did indeed begin to emerge.

Tardieu proposed a compromise based on the Leeper–Nicolson–Barnes plan which gave Yugoslavia most of

[86] A. W. A. Leeper to R. W. A. Leeper, 7 May 1919. AWAL.

[87] A. W. A. Leeper to R. W. A. Leeper, 10 May 1919, AWAL. FRUS:PPC:IV, pp. 696–703, contains a copy of the Yugoslav Committee report based on Leeper's draft.

Dalmatia, though Italy received a mandate for Albania, while Fiume would become a free city under the League with an eventual plebiscite as to its future. The free city would have a large, mostly Slavic hinterland, effectively predetermining any future plebiscite. It should have been sufficient to meet Italy's overall aims and avoid any loss of face. The Italians, however, were unwilling to compromise, and expected to receive anything they demanded. Their diplomacy had in fact become paralysed by lack of flexibility. This scheme was presented to Orlando on 7 June, who rejected it the following day, and on 21 June his government fell with his resignation. In August an informal committee including Nicolson and Tardieu met to try to work out a solution, but their deliberations were disrupted by the fresh crisis of d'Annunzio's occupation of Fiume.

Britain therefore in the final outcome failed to deny Fiume to Italy, which formally annexed it in January 1921 after bilateral negotiations with Yugoslavia. The acceptance of d'Annunzio's hoped-for *fait accompli* was a military failure rather than a diplomatic one. If the Great Powers, led by Britain, had forced a withdrawal it seems likely that the Tardieu proposal, based on the British plan, would have been implemented. The British military already had extensive short-term concerns elsewhere, particularly in the Middle East, and were less concerned by the Foreign Office's long-term perspective. Italy succeeded by abandoning diplomacy and resorting to force, an indication of the growing collapse of the conference's authority in the late summer of 1919.

THE NON-EUROPEAN WORLD AND THE IMPERATIVES OF EMPIRE

Negotiations on the future of the Arab lands of the Ottoman Empire fell more clearly within the sphere of interest of those concerned with Britain's imperial future. This group itself falls into two factions, one pushing to make certain that Britain acquired any territory currently available in the immediate post-war power vacuum, while the other wished to focus on certain key strategic gains out of fear that any imperial gluttony might seriously overstretch an already mammoth empire.

Early 1919, however, was a period of supreme exultation and confidence for the imperialists. The war was won and the British Empire once again stood victorious. What was more British armies were in occupation of most of the Middle East. It was not so much a question of what Britain could get, but rather what it would choose to keep. Undoubtedly some dregs would have to be provided for France, preferably in darkest Africa, while some gristle would be found for the Italians' seemingly curious colonial appetite, and a particularly vile mandate might be graciously offered to the Americans to teach them the arduous nature of an imperial burden. The euphoria evaporated, however, as the negotiations, and 1919, wore on. By the year's end Ireland had erupted, Egypt was in revolt, there was war with Afghanistan, and most seriously the Indian Empire had been ignited by the spark of the Amritsar massacre. In the wake of these catastrophes, and the need to think about the security of an empire based on the usual parsimonious peacetime budget, the imperial reformers began to gain an edge in the negotiations.

The future of Syria rapidly developed as the most contentious issue in Middle East affairs. Britain had already promised it to the Emir Faisal in 1915, and then agreed that it should fall within the French sphere in the 1916 Sykes–Picot Agreement. The Eastern Committee when confronted by these potentially conflicting promises resolved that Sykes–Picot should, if possible, be cancelled, presumably because it recognized a role for France. Faisal, it was agreed, could have his state centred on Damascus, but Britain was to be predominant in the region. France would receive, as a sort of *pourboire*, enclaves for the Alexandretta and Lebanon districts; its regional presence would thereby be neatly contained.

The traditional Anglo-French rivalry continued in the Middle East long after the Entente Cordiale had eased relations in other areas. Many officials continued to see France as Britain's prime adversary in the Middle East. Mallet warned that if France 'goes to Syria and holds Alexandretta and Cilicia, she will be astride the land communications between Great Britain and the British Empire in the East'. [88] He recommended

---

[88] FO 608/116/385/2/2/4605, Minute by Mallet, 17 Jan. 1919.

instead that France be given Constantinople, from which it would undoubtedly merrily intrigue in the Balkans, away from any important British interests.

The Syrian question rapidly became one of the greatest strains on Anglo-French relations. When Pichon approached the British in early February with a suggestion that Syria could quickly be dealt with along the lines of the Lloyd George–Clemenceau understanding of December 1918 he was staggered by the British response. Clemenceau by this agreement had acquiesced in Britain taking Palestine, which under Sykes–Picot was to be internationalized, and gave up French claims to Mosul, though retaining a half-share in any petroleum exploitation. No doubt the French were under the impression that they had already made significant concessions to Britain, but the latter's response proved otherwise. They were anxious to keep France's sphere as small as possible, as the thinking in the Eastern Committee indicates, and therefore in return suggested frontiers which removed all of south-east Syria, giving the Palestine mandate a border virtually outside Damascus.

The supporters of an Arab client kingdom in the Middle East received a boost when the Emir Faisal made a skilful presentation before the Supreme Council on 6 February. The French, seeing him as a British creature, attempted to make things difficult, but Faisal managed with exquisite politeness to be rude in return. Bratianu of Romania could have learned much from Faisal's style. The man to convince was President Wilson, who held the balance in such circumstances, and here Britain had managed the situation well, appearing as the supporters of an authentic Arab leader who only asked for national self-determination for his people. The French eventually presented a tame Syrian of their own, who in fact lived in Paris and who presented his case with such excruciating loquacity that even the usually patient Wilson became fidgety after two hours. Faisal's standing can only have benefited in comparison.[89]

There were some officials, though, who saw such proposals

---

[89] FRUS:PPC, vol. iii, pp. 889–94. Nicolson, *Peacemaking 1919*, p. 142. Hardinge to Chirol, 8 Feb 1919, Hardinge Papers 40. C. Andrew and A. S. Kanya-Forstner, *France Overseas: The Great War and the Climax of French Imperial Expansion* (London, 1981), p. 186.

as either impossible, or if forced through at all costs as wrecking the Anglo-French entente. They considered that some regional advantage might have to be sacrificed for the greater good of the empire. Hirtzel in particular was becoming increasingly concerned at the growing tension in Anglo-French relations. On 14 February he submitted a memorandum giving his personal assessment, which differed somewhat from received India Office wisdom. Hirtzel was no Francophil, as the India Office suggestions on eliminating the French enclaves in India reveal, but he was sensible of the difference between a map-tidying exercise and the loss of a Great Power ally. Hirtzel plead for an understanding with France, noting 'I have all along urged that we should not carry our support of Arab claims to a point that would involve us in a conflict with France. But we are now within measurable distance of doing so'. He pointed out the unfortunate but obvious fact that, 'After the war, as before it, we shall have to live next door to the French all over the world. They may not be pleasant neighbours in detail, but there it is . . .', and he presciently warned that 'it is quite conceivable that the U.S.A. may withdraw into their shell again, leaving us to bear the odium of disappointed hope'.[90] This view was shared by General Thwaites, who wanted the issue resolved by a committee of experts whose interest was in preserving Anglo-French harmony.

The general situation also began to deteriorate due to factors beyond anybody's control. On 14 February Sir Mark Sykes, one of the few British officials who worked well with the French, died in the influenza epidemic then raging in Paris, while on 19 February Clemenceau was severely wounded by a would-be assassin. During this period Lloyd George had delegated the task of negotiating with Clemenceau over Syria to Lord Milner. Out of concern for the premier's health after the assassination attempt Milner refrained from continuing discussions. This so infuriated Clemenceau that he refused to have anything more to do with

---

[90] FO 608/107/384/1/7/2256, Hirtzel, 'The French Claims in Syria', 14 Feb. 1919. Also in Montagu AS-IV-4-751. Busch discusses this memo in *Britain, India, and the Arabs, 1914–1921* (Berkeley, Calif., 1971), p. 289, together with a foonote on the historical debate about it.

Milner. As a result discussion of Middle East questions lapsed for some days.[91]

By mid-March Clemenceau had become incensed by Lloyd George's continual changes of tack, particularly over France's future role in Turkey. On 14 March he angrily exclaimed his view that 'Lloyd George is a cheat'.[92] In fact this exasperation may have been due to the growing realization of Britain's diplomatic success, and not in Middle Eastern affairs alone. It has been observed that Clemenceau's focus was on France's security in Western Europe, and that he was willing to make significant concessions to Britain in return for support for French aims against Germany.[93] By mid-March Clemenceau was undoubtedly feeling the better part of French ambitions in the Rhineland, the Saar, and Luxemburg beginning to slip from his grasp.[94] He was beginning to sense the tightening diplomatic hug of the many-tentacled British empire.

When the Council of Four held its first meeting on 20 March, Syria emerged as the first problem, possibly because Clemenceau wished to indicate his displeasure with British policy over an expendable issue. Wilson in an attempt to resolve the problem proposed a commission of inquiry to examine local opinion. Clemenceau readily accepted, provided areas potentially falling to Britain were included. Clemenceau probably intended by this to please Wilson and irritate Lloyd George, knowing that the commission would take months to report and wanting Wilson's goodwill now on German questions.[95]

There matters rested as the conference turned to other concerns, only to resurface violently on 21 May. Relations among

[91] Milner was apparently irritated at being left in charge by Lloyd George as he wrote on 10 Feb., 'The last thing I expected or wished was that L.G. should hop off & leave me to take his place in the British Delegation....Meanwhile evrything is at sixes & sevenses ....' Milner to Lady Edward Cecil, quoted in Sotheby's Sale Catalogue of English Literature and History, 22–3 July 1985. Attempts to find the original have been unsuccesful.

[92] Raymond Poincaré, *Au Service de la France*, vol. xi, *À la récherche de la paix, 1919* (Paris, 1974), p. 245, entry for 14 Mar. 1919.

[93] Andrew and Kanya-Forstner, *France Overseas*, p. 181.

[94] Louis Loucher, *Carnets Secrets, 1908–1932*, ed. J. de Launay (Brussels, 1962), p. 71, entry for 12 Mar. 1919.

[95] FRUS:PPC, vol. v.

the Allies had been going well for some time, particularly in the absence of the Italians, who had become the target of available animosity. Now, however, Clemenceau felt he was being made a fool of by the British. He had agreed to give way over French claims in Palestine, Mosul, and Cilicia, but was receiving nothing in return. Matters reached a head when Clemenceau became convinced that Lloyd George also intended to go back on a promise, only two days old, on France's future role in Turkey. In what must unquestionably have been the nadir of Anglo-French relations Clemenceau apparently challenged Lloyd George to a duel.[96] Lloyd George remained adamant, and the following day reminded Clemenceau of Britain's powerful position by refusing to remove the British army from Syria until he was satisfied as to the demarcation of frontiers. The British prime minister knew Clemenceau was caught in the toils of his own policy objectives. French security after the negotiations on the Rhineland now depended on an Anglo-American guarantee treaty, an assurance which would be worthless if Britain were badly antagonized. The Welsh magician had trapped the tiger. Clemenceau, outraged and helpless in his plight, gave vent to his views on British aims: 'England frightens me with the cynicism of her claims and her unbridled avarice, not merely in what she demands but also in what she takes.'[97] The question of Syria was therefore left in abeyance for future consideration.

In mid-summer, after the German treaty had been dealt with and attention could focus on the other treaties, an agreement was quickly reached on Syria. It had by then lost its value as a diplomatic lever. Vansittart noted the need to give France a paper concession and after all Syria was hardly critical. He observed that in any case British 'desiderata go much further than anything yet mentioned, or suspected, by the French'. The French of course were not unaware of this, as Clemenceau's pained outburst makes clear. In September Lloyd George finally ordered the evacuation of Syria. President Wilson was in increasing political difficulty at home, and was soon to be incapacitated by a stroke, and the Versailles treaty was in

---

[96] Andrew and Kanya-Forstner, *France Overseas*, p. 197.
[97] Quoted ibid., p. 198.

danger of failure in the Senate. Any plans for using the United States as a counterweight against France were becoming increasingly moot. Even more disturbing was the possibility that with the rejection of the treaty, and the American security guarantee for France upon which the British pledge was contingent, France might reactivate its plans for control of Western Europe. This would wreck Britain's carefully constructed regional equilibrium. A gesture of amity towards France was in order, and selling out Faisal but a small price to pay.

Faisal was told he would have to negotiate with the French, who were to have a mandate over Syria and Lebanon, and he had but little choice with the removal of British support. The French moved carefully but with purpose and by July 1920 had defeated Faisal and forced him to flee. Syria had never really been a key British desideratum, but rather a useful plum to pluck if possible and otherwise an even more useful piece of territory to be used to advantage in the hard bargaining of the peace conference.

The question of Syria was closely linked to what Britain's policy should be towards the Arabs in general. This was further complicated by divisions among the Arabs themselves. Britain had so far aligned itself with the Hashemites, whose power base at Mecca was under threat from the forces of Ibn Saud. Faisal's father, Husain, who was ruling in Mecca, was in difficulty, in part, as Vansittart noted, 'because we made him. But as we made him we've got to stick by him. Strength is the only thing appreciated in the East; and if we were weak enough to let our man go under we shd. lose more than by seeing him through in spite of his unpopularity. The whole of our prestige is at stake.' Vansittart advised that 'the only "realpolitik" for us is to take a line in the Near East that will keep in with the French (much as I dislike it) and the Jews, and not be too nervous of Arab susceptibilities. We cannot sacrifice the reality of France for an Arab unity that will never materialise.'[98] It was precisely the importance of this reality which was emerging by the end of June, and even Mallet was now taking a softer view of the French than he had at the opening of the conference. Crowe agreed, pointing out that Britain had never

[98] FO 608/80/342/2/8/13141, Minute by Vansittart, 19 June 1919.

wanted a united Arab kingdom and wished to deal with different Arab states, though he agreed that Husain should be saved if possible. Crowe pointed to the weakness in British policy in the Middle East as due to never having come to a satisfactory understanding with France.[99] Britain had of course come to many agreements with France, but so far had been unable to stick to one.

African questions did not cause significant difficulties for Britain, and all the key aims defined in the preparatory phase were achieved. No difficulty arose with the French once the technicalities of the mandates system were worked out. Britain acquired a mandate for German East Africa while South Africa was to administer German South-West Africa. The Cameroons and Togoland were amicably split with France on the basis of their wartime division. Fears on the part of some officials about what would happen if the United States was allowed a mandatory role proved unfounded when the Americans themselves rejected any such arrangement. The only heated problems arose over Italian claims, which must be seen in the context of the wider Italian question. Italy seemed to be more interested in generating problems for the conference than in finding solutions. The result was a pervasive anti-Italian attitude within the British delegation. As all the other Great Powers were also thoroughly disgusted with Italian demands and tactics there was a rare unanimity in denying Italy its claims. All Italy finally received were small slices from French Algeria and the Juba Valley from Britain on the Somalia–Kenya frontier, both amounting to no more than token border rectifications.

Africa was in fact no more than a subset of a far greater British problem, the security of the routes to India. Colonel Meinertzhagen observed in late January that 'the consolidation of our Middle East Empire should form the focus of all our African negotiations, as they protect our communications with India and the East'.[100] Britain's key territorial aspirations involved reaffirmation of its paramountcy over Egypt, control of Tanganyika, and bolstering South Africa with German

[99] FO 608/80/342/8/13141, Minute by Crowe, 24 June 1919.

[100] Meinertzhagen Diary, 30 Jan. 1919. He was present as a member of the Military Section, and advised on Middle Eastern and colonial affairs.

South-West Africa. All three were considered important in safeguarding the two maritime routes to India. The German U-boat campaign, however, had shown the vulnerability of relying solely on maritime communications. While in the first instance this lesson demanded stripping Germany of its colonies so that in future submarine bases could not be developed, it also led to a longer term concern to create alternative means of communication. Acquisition of Tanganyika would allow at long last the possibility of a Cape to Cairo route, a possibility already noted by the Air Staff in the preparatory phase. It is perhaps significant that the man in ultimate charge of the colonial negotiations was Lord Milner, whose two great colonial experiences had been in Egypt and South Africa. Nor was the potential of new technology overlooked, as shown by an early concern to acquire locations, appropriate to contemporary aerial technology, to create an all-red air route to India. France, the only other significant power seeking colonial gains, was well satisfied with West African spoils. British aims in Africa when seen in an Indian context emerge as clearly defined, and they were achieved.

On 28 June 1919 the victorious allies assembled at Versailles to sign their peace treaty with Germany. Over the following fourteen months they were to assemble again at various chateaux around Paris, St Germain, Neuilly, Triannon, and Sèvres, to formalize similar agreements with the other defeated states. The signing of the German treaty was the psychological and emotional apex of the peace process, and with its conclusion public interest began to wane. The diplomats themselves were nearing physical exhaustion, while the politicians needed to return home to attend to neglected affairs of state. Accounts of the peace conference usually overlook the exhaustion felt by the delegates after six months of negotiations.[101] Their aim was to rebuild the international system, but by this point they were themselves on the verge of collapse. During the summer of 1919 many of them dispersed on holiday to recoup their strength. Those who returned to Paris in the early autumn found no more than a

---

[101] Nicolson, *Peacemaking 1919*, p. 67.

shadow conference. The peace process slowly petered out, with no great triumphant flourish to mark the completion of its labours.

Britain's diplomatic achievement at Paris was substantial. Inevitably it compromised on various claims and aims, but the essential core of its desires was accomplished. Some British aims, while seemingly successful at the conference, did not develop as hoped. The collapse of the Venizelist regime in Greece deprived Britain of its hoped-for regional ally. The occupation of Fiume by d'Annunzio so complicated and prolonged that question that eventually Italy was able to take the city. Both these failures, however, were due to a failure to back up the diplomatic result with military force when necessary. The empire was overstretched, and military assets were desperately required elsewhere. The result was that those primarily concerned with Continental problems had to witness the negation of some of their efforts. But the negotiators had done their job with skill, and a diplomatic strategy was evolved for a new era of international relations.

In comparison to the other Great Powers, Britain was notably successful, and of all the Great Powers to come to Paris in 1919 the British Empire unquestionably left the negotiating table as the most satisfied, if not satiated, state. President Wilson, after having been forced to give in on a wide range of issues in order to achieve his primary objective, the creation of a League of Nations, then had to watch his country reject the entire settlement. The tragedy for American foreign policy in this instance was that the enemy was the enemy within. Clemenceau's quest to arrange for a substantive guarantee of French security collapsed with America's withdrawal. France sacrificed much for this end, and gained nothing but the most basic irredenta. Italy left with most of its irredentist desires unfulfilled, becoming that rare creature, a victorious state which emerges as a revisionist power. British preparations, the training of an expert staff, and the deployment of these resources at Paris allowed Britain to reap what rewards there were from the bitter harvest of the Great War.

8

Conclusion

> It will be too awful, if after winning the war we are to lose
> the peace.
>
> > Harold Nicolson, 24 Mar. 1919,
> > *Peacemaking 1919* (1933), 289

Diplomacy is the art of the possible, not of the ideal. At Paris
the British Empire Delegation attained the maximum possible
in the circumstances, and Britain left with more of its aims
attained than any of its allies. But many of the British delegates
were men of high ideals, and despite their successes they felt
dissatisfied with the final result. This air of dissatisfaction has
clung to the British achievement at Paris, clouding much of the
diplomatic reality. Robert Cecil advised Harold Nicolson that
'the test of our value was the extent of our dissatisfaction'.[1]
Settlements as complex as the one evolved at Paris in 1919 are
not just the product of what the leaders say to each other across
the green baize-covered table, but are very much the product
of the detailed and integrated work of the delegation's staff.
The experts proved invaluable in assisting Britain in the negotiations, for they were the source of much of the intellectual
vision which provided the underlying coherence in British diplomatic strategy.

Europe had been at war for two years when Britain began to
consider its position for the eventual peace negotiations. The
memoranda prepared for Asquith's War Committee in 1916
were more a debate on war aims than policy planning for a
peace conference. Organized preparations were the result of
the simultaneous concern of two individuals, Leo Amery and
Lord Hardinge. Amery, spurred on by Toynbee and Zimmern's

---

[1] H. Nicolson, *Peacemaking 1919* (London, 1933), p. 210.

proposal for a Peace Terms Intelligence Section, was able to initiate the collection of material under the auspices of Admiralty Intelligence. Hardinge, newly returned from India, was appalled by the decline in Foreign Office influence and began to organize the Office so that it could reassert itself once the military phase of the war was concluded. Both Amery and Hardinge believed that research was essential if the delegates at the peace conference were to be adequately prepared, and by the spring of 1918 all the machinery needed was in place.

Hardinge was particularly incensed by the role of Lloyd George's 'Garden Suburb', and in the PID he created a Foreign Office alternative. The PID, because of its unique role as a co-ordinator, together with its outstanding staff, played a central part in the story of British preparations for the conference. By bringing the Historical Section, the War Trade Intelligence Department, and the War Trade Statistical Department under Foreign Office control, Hardinge drew together the various wartime creations spawned by Amery's original suggestions. Hardinge was carefully gaining control of most of the preparatory machinery, while establishing links with such specialized departments as the military, the Treasury, and the Board of Trade to ensure co-operation.

The Political Intelligence Department, the Historical Section, and at an earlier stage the Geographical Section were the chief instruments of Britain's preparations for the peace conference, though there were other important components of the rambling machinery engaged in preparing for the negotiations. The War Trade Intelligence Department became increasingly responsible for providing the other departments with data, for assisting with the peace handbooks, and finally for supervising the administrative arrangements for the conference. The Director of Military Intelligence created a special section to report on political, historic, and ethnic questions. These reports formed the basis for the General Staff's contribution to the preparations. The other government departments did not create special sections for such work, but did provide memoranda on their particular areas of concern. Use was also made of such non-governmental organizations as the Royal Geographical Society. The aim of all this work came within view in October 1918 as the collapse of the Central

Powers became inevitable. It was in this period that Hardinge and Hankey were forced to define and divide responsibilities for the coming congress, while Hardinge and Smuts were involved in the final articulation of the peace memoranda.

The appointment of Smuts to prepare the peace brief may well have proved initially disappointing to Hardinge, who had no doubt hoped to play such a part himself. In fact Smuts proved to be the ideal solution to what might otherwise have been the fatal flaw in Foreign Office plans. Having carefully gathered together the various threads of the preparatory process, there was still no channel by which to get to the prime minister. That Lloyd George disliked Hardinge, and that this feeling was reciprocated, is evident in the writings of both men. Hardinge, by putting his preparatory apparatus at the disposal of General Smuts, found a way to present his material to the Cabinet and eventually to the delegates under the cover of Smuts's imprimatur. The struggle for predominance between Hardinge and Hankey mirrored the larger struggle between the Foreign Office and the Cabinet Office for predominance. This conflict was very much in line with developments in the capitals of all the major states, where power was shifting to the central political figures away from its traditional locus in the foreign ministries.

It would be impossible to sustain any argument that the British delegation was unprepared. They were amply provided for by 174 Historical Section handbooks, 71 PID memoranda, and 35 Military Intelligence reports. In addition these writings were supplemented by an array of memoranda from the specialized committees. For good measure a number of the authors of these works were taken to Paris as technical advisers, where they served on the various committees established by the conference. Britain could hardly have found better-trained representatives. The preparatory organization had recruited an unusually competent staff, and these men after having spent months studying the facts and preparing the British case were then brought to Paris to assist in the negotiations. The extent of the British success at Paris is due in great measure to the thoroughness of its delegation's preparations, especially when seen alongside those of the other powers.

The offices created to consider the post-war settlement were staffed for the most part by temporary civil servants recruited chiefly from the academic world. This development was mirrored in France, and particularly in the United States. The reliance on the universities was something of a departure for Whitehall, which no doubt tolerated it as one of those unfortunate impositions required by the exigencies of war. Certainly these temporary departments, often staffed by seemingly eccentric individuals, did at first experience difficulty in obtaining the co-operation of the permanent officials, but their eventual acceptance can be noted by the large number who were offered regular appointments when the war ended.

One of the most notable aspects of the British preparations for the peace conference is the personnel who were employed in the work, and their future careers provide ample evidence of the talent deployed within these departments. The most familiar names are Keynes, Namier, Nicolson, and Toynbee, but many of the others went on to positions of great influence and high rank. Several of them would be numbered in succeeding decades among Britain's leading historians. Lewis Namier, Arnold Toynbee, H. W. V. Temperley. J. R. M. Butler, E. H. Carr, C. K. Webster, E. L. Woodward, and Lillian Penson all served an early apprenticeship in these departments. Alfred Zimmern, who before the war had lectured on ancient Greek history, went on to become professor of international relations and a founder of the School of International Studies at Geneva, together with André Tardieu, who had himself been a central figure in the French preparations. Arnold Toynbee made a similar transition from a pre-war interest in the ancient world to become director of studies at the Royal Institute of International Affairs, an organization that many of these experts were instrumental in establishing. The preparations for the conference not only assisted Britain in the negotiations and provided it with a reservoir of talent for use at the conference, but also helped to train a generation of historians in the realities of international relations and assisted in the development of the study of modern history in Britain.

Diplomatic strategy towards the post-war settlement evolved slowly, responding to the various changes caused by the war. At no point was it clear what the military situation would be at the end of hostilities. Preparations therefore had to consider other possibilities than outright victory. As a result the planning had a certain fluidity to it, responding to the pressure of contemporary events. Out of the mass of detail provided by the preparatory reports and proposals a few key concepts began to emerge, themes which developed more fully during the course of the negotiations. Some of these ideas can be traced to the earliest discussions, before being elaborated during the preparations, and culminating in their attempted implementation at Paris. Both the PID, as the co-ordinator of the Foreign Office effort, and Military Intelligence, which played a similar role for the War Office, made important contributions, together with various other departments. There was, however, a critical difference in approach. The Foreign Office focused on the long-term implications of the settlement, being more concerned with possible new adversaries. By its very defeat Germany had ceased to be the enemy. Diplomatic strategy needed to consider who had now emerged as the British Empire's prime adversary. Particular concern was expressed as to possible friction with France, Britain's traditional sparring partner, while reservations were expressed about the United States. The military, conversely, concentrated on the shorter-term implications, and with four years of fighting as comrades in arms they found it hard to view the French as potential enemies.

Already the future balance of power in Western Europe was emerging as a concern. In Eastern Europe the situation was still so amorphous as almost to defy description. The basic contours of the new political map only began to emerge as the conference opened. It was clear that Britain would benefit from befriending some of the new states for purposes of regional leverage, though as yet it was unclear which states would benefit from British patronage, while simultaneously benefiting their patron.

The ideas on the settlement of the New Europe supporters in the Foreign Office, despite internationalist undertones, need to be seen as those of patriotic Britons. Their recommendations were not just born out of concern for the future peace and stability of the Continent, but were the product of genuine concern as to what would be best for Britain. Crowe and the New Europe group helped to develop a diplomatic strategy at

Paris for the British Empire in a new diplomatic age, a strategy which was concerned not with the myth of empire, but rather the reality of survival in a radically altered world. The era of expansion was over, the era of consolidation about to begin. The ending of great wars usually sees the international system in a state of flux, malleable and ready to be shaped for succeeding years. Those are the critical moments for diplomats to attempt to shape the settlement to their own national interests, before the heat of war subsides and the international system once again hardens. Crowe and the New Europe group combined to provide the clearest vision of British strategy in the new age, with the recognition that the focus of activity had now returned to Europe. Their actions complemented those of the imperial reformers who recognized the need for consolidation and an end to ceaseless expansion.

At the apex of these competing groups stood the prime minister, Lloyd George, whose role in the negotiations has come in for much criticism, often ill-founded. He was of course a controversial figure; having been a voluble opponent of the Tories up to the outbreak of war, he acquired the enmity of many Liberals by his role in Asquith's political demise. George Prothero on seeing Lloyd George at the opening of the Peace Conference noted, 'It is humiliating to be represented by such a little cad.'[2] Yet within a month, after having read the back papers of the conference, he was forced to recognize Lloyd George's ability to bring off compromises in Britain's interest.[3] Lloyd George did not want to deal with the myriad matters arising at the conference, and by agreeing that much of the conference's work would be done in committees, and by accepting the appointment of Foreign Office officials as the British representatives on those committees, he was accepting the re-establishment of the Foreign Office as a key component in representing Britain's interests. This led Nicolson to tell his father that far from trying to subordinate the Foreign Office Lloyd George 'has been extremely good to the Foreign Office, and . . . the whole direction of all but essentially non-political and economic questions is entirely in our hands'.[4] As the

[2] Prothero Diary, 18 Jan. 1919.   [3] Ibid. 22 Feb. 1919.
[4] Nicolson, *Peacemaking 1919*, p. 271, Nicolson to Lord Carnock, 25 Feb. 1919.

experts came into closer contact with him their opinion of Lloyd George rose. In the aftermath of the decision to send the Greeks to Smyrna, Nicolson wrote, 'Poor Ll.G.! It is so easy for us irresponsible people to criticise him ....'[5]

Lloyd George's role was a difficult one at Paris. Gordon Craig, in his analysis of the British Foreign Office, suggests that 'Lloyd George became wearied of the advice of experts from whatever department they might be drawn and closeting himself with Wilson, Clemenceau, and Orlando, undertook to solve the problems of the conference by his own intuition'.[6] He was indeed continually involved in negotiations, but in these he did rely on briefings, provided either personally by the experts, or through the medium of Philip Kerr. His diplomatic craftsmanship was more than a match for his fellow Allied leaders. It was in such discussions that he was able to deploy his considerable charm, forensic talent, and native guile to achieve British ends. What disturbed many of the British observers was his unconventional behaviour, but as Harold Nicolson later observed, 'Mr. Lloyd George taught me that apparent opportunism was not always irreconcilable with vision, that volatility of method is not always indicative of volatility of intention.'[7] Lloyd George was a politician, not a diplomatist. The tactical approach of a politician to a problem often differs from that of a professional diplomat, but it should be remembered that in the Council of Four Lloyd George was dealing not with diplomats, but with fellow politicians.

Lawrence Gelfand concludes his analysis of the Inquiry with observation that 'At least the American plenipotentiaries were able to compete successfully with the weapons of facts, figures, and previously assembled recommendations of other national delegations when the peace conference began in earnest'.[8] The same holds true of Britain, which was even better prepared. Victor Rothwell ends his book on British war

---

[5] Ibid., diary entry for 16 May 1919.

[6] Gordon A. Craig, 'The British Foreign Office from Grey to Austen Chamberlain', in Gordon A. Craig and Felix Gilbert, eds., *The Diplomats, 1919–1939* (New York, 1972), i. 20.

[7] Nicolson, *Peacemaking 1919*, p. 209.

[8] L. Gelfand, *The Inquiry: American Preparations for Peace, 1917–1919* (New Haven, Cann., 1963), p. 333.

aims with this conclusion: 'Always one comes back to the point that British foreign policy in the era of the First World War was truly concerned with the interests of the British Empire.'[9] There is no reason to suggest why British policy should have been otherwise. It was, however, the detailed preparation of the British case which allowed the delegation to put policy into practice as well as it did among the myriad complexities and crises which bedevilled the Paris Peace Conference.

No neat strategic view can be identified from a definite Cabinet decision. The British system did not function that way when it came to foreign policy formulation. Instead, a number of ideas and individuals willing to push for their concepts helped to produce a viable diplomatic strategy. It was not a case of muddling through, nor was it a product of central decision-making; rather, it evolved organically from those with knowledge of their particular spheres, which were synthesized at Paris into a supple and responsive approach to the post-war world, and which in turn allowed effective negotiations against the ambitions of the other participants. Many factors made Paris a far from perfect conference, and the result in many ways was grossly inadequate to the challenge faced. Nevertheless the British achievement at Paris should not be devalued. Within the context of a settlement flawed by many factors beyond British control, and contrasted against other participants, the British Empire was outstandingly successful. Unlike any other major participant it achieved its key aims. Britain had not only achieved victory in war, but it won the peace as well.

[9] V. H. Rothwell, *British War Arms and Peace Diplomacy, 1914–1918* (Oxford, 1971), p. 287.

Bibliography

I. PRIMARY SOURCES: GOVERNMENT ARCHIVES

A. Public Record Office, London (Kew)

Admiralty Papers
    ADM 1/   Admiralty and Secretariat Papers.
    ADM 116/   Admiralty: Secretary's Department.
              ADM 116/1852, Board Discussions on Peace Settlement, Nov. 1918–Jan. 1919.
              ADM 116/1861, Peace Terms, 1918–20.
              ADM 116/1865, International Law Committee, 1918–19.
    ADM 137/   Historical Section: War Histories.
    ADM 167/   Board Minutes, Memoranda, etc.

Air Council Papers
    AIR 1/   Air Historical Branch Records: Series 1.

Board of Trade Papers
    BT 61/   Estimate and Account Papers.

Cabinet Papers
    CAB 15/   Committee of Imperial Defence: Committee on Co-Ordination of Departmental Action.
    CAB 16/   Committee of Imperial Defence Ad-Hoc Sub-Committees of Inquiry: Proceedings and Memoranda.
    CAB 21/   Registered Cabinet Office Files: Miscellaneous Papers.
    CAB 23/   Cabinet Minutes.
              CAB 23/1–12, Minutes of Meetings. Series W. C. Dec. 1916–Oct. 1919.
              CAB 23/40–44A, Imperial War Cabinet.
    CAB 24/   Cabinet Memoranda.
    CAB 27/   Cabinet Committees: General Series.
              CAB 27/24–39, Eastern Committee.

CAB 27/43, War Cabinet Committee on Indemnity.
CAB 29/ Peace Conference and Other International Conferences.

Colonial Office Papers
CO 323/ Colonies (General).
CO 378/ Colonies, General: Register of Correspondence.

Command Papers 8306, 8371, 9146, 9210.

Confidential Prints 10081, 10968, 11004, 11022, 11582*, 11908*, 13680.

Foreign Office Papers
FO 366/ Chief Clerk's Dept.: Archives.
FO 368/ General Correspondence: Commercial.
FO 370/ General Correspondence: Library.
FO 371/ General Correspondence: Political.
        FO 371/3452–3483, Miscellaneous: General.
        FO 371/4352/4346, PID (Peace Conference Series).
        FO 371/4357–4387, PID, 1918–20.
FO 372/ General Correspondence: Treaty.
FO 373/ Peace Conference of 1919–20, Handbooks.
FO 383/ General Correspondence: Contraband.
FO 395/ General Correspondence: News.
FO 608/ Paris Peace Conference of 1919–20: Correspondence.
FO 794/ Private Office: Individual Files.
FO 800/ Private Collections.
        FO 800/147–58, Curzon of Kedleston Papers.
        FO 800/199–217, Earl of Balfour Papers.
        FO 800/243, Sir Eyre Crowe Papers.
        FO 800/249, P. Noel-Baker Papers.

Ministry of Power Papers
POWE 33/ Petroleum Division: Correspondence and Papers.

Ministry of Shipping Papers
MT 25/ Correspondence and Papers, 1917–21.

Treasury Papers
T 12/ Out Letters: Foreign Office.
T 172/ Chancellor of the Exchequer's Office: Miscellaneous Papers.

War Office Papers
WO 32/ Registered Papers: General Series.
WO 106/ Directorate of Military Operations and Intelligence Papers.

B. *Public Record Office, London (Chancery Lane)*

Treasury Solicitor Papers
TS 14/ War Trade Intelligence Department.

C. *India Office Library, London*

L/P&S/10 Departmental Papers: Political and Secret Separate
Files, 1902–31.
L/P&S/11 Departmental Papers: Political and Secret Separate
Files, 1912–30.

D. *National Archives, Washington, DC*

Record Group 256, Records of the Inquiry.

II. PRIMARY SOURCES: BIBLIOGRAPHIES AND REFERENCE GUIDES

GUNZENHAUSER, M., *Die Pariser Friedenskonferenz 1919 und die Friedensvertrage 1919–1920: Literaturbericht und Bibliographie.* (Frankfurt-on-Main, 1970).

HANCOCK, N. J., *Handlist of Hardinge Papers at the University Library Cambridge* (Cambridge, 1970).

MOIR, M. I., 'A Study of the History and Organization of the Political and Secret Departments of the East India Company, the Board of Control and the India Office, with a summary list of records' (Unpublished Diploma in Archive Administration thesis, University of London, 1966).

PUBLIC RECORD OFFICE, *The Records of the Cabinet Office to 1922* (London, 1966).

——*The Records of the Colonial and Dominions Offices* (London, 1964).

——*The Records of the Foreign Office, 1782–1939* (London, 1969).

UNITED STATES, NATIONAL ARCHIVES AND RECORDS SERVICE, *Records of the American Commission to Negotiate Peace: An Inventory of Record Group 256* (Washington, 1974).

WHEELER, K. V., *A Guide to the Political Papers, 1874–1970, Deposited by the First Beaverbrook Foundation* (London, 1975).

III. PRIMARY SOURCES: PRIVATE COLLECTIONS AND PERSONAL PAPERS

British Museum, Central Archives, London.
J. R. M. Butler Papers, Trinity College, Cambridge.

Cecil of Chelwood Papers, British Library (Add. MSS 51071–51204).
Cozens-Hardy Papers.
H. W. C. Davis Papers, Bodleian Library, Oxford.
W. H. Dawson Papers, University of Birmingham.
Admiral Sir Reginald Hall Papers, Churchill College Archive Centre, Cambridge.
Hankey Papers, Churchill College Archive Centre, Cambridge.
Hardinge Papers, University Library, Cambridge.
Headlam-Morley Papers, Prof. Agnes Headlam-Morley, London. (Original documents at University of Ulster, Coleraine).
Howard of Penrith Papers, Cumbria Record·Office, Carlisle.
J. M. Keynes Papers, Marshall Library, Cambridge.
A. W. A. Leeper Papers.
Lloyd George Papers, House of Lords Record Office.
Lothian Papers (Philip Kerr), Scottish Record Office, Edinburgh.
R. Meinertzhagen Papers, Rhodes House Library, Oxford.
Milner Papers, Bodleian Library, Oxford.
Montagu Papers, India Office Library, London.
Montagu Papers, Trinity College, Cambridge.
G. W. Prothero Papers, Royal Historical Society, London.
G. W. Prothero Papers, Mr C. W. Crawley, Trinity Hall, Cambridge.
Reading Papers, India Office Library, London.
Royal Geographical Society Archives, London.
George Saunders Papers, Churchill College Archive Centre, Cambridge.
Smuts Papers, University Library, Cambridge (Microfilm MSS).
A. J. Toynbee Papers, Bodleian Library, Oxford.
C. K. Webster Papers, British Library of Political and Economic Science, London.
Barrett Wendell Papers, The Houghton Library, Harvard University.
A. F. H. Wiggin Papers.
Zimmern Papers, Bodleian Library, Oxford.

IV. PRIMARY SOURCES: PUBLISHED DOCUMENTS.

BARNES, J. and NICHOLSON, D., eds., *The Leo Amery Diaries*, vol. i: *1896–1929* (2 vols., London, 1980–8).
COMITÉ D'ÉTUDES, *Travaux du Comité d'études* (Paris, 1918–19).
The Foreign Office List and Diplomatic and Consular Year Book for 1919, (London, 1919).

GREAT BRITAIN. Admiralty, Naval Intelligence Division. Geographic Handbook Series.

——Foreign Office, *Documents on British Foreign Policy, 1919–1939*, First Series (London, 1947–67).

——Foreign Office, Historical Section, *Peace Handbooks* (25 vols., London, 1920).

——*Parliamentary Debates*, House of Commons, 5th series.

HANCOCK, W. K., and VAN DER POEL, J., eds., *Selections from the Smuts Papers*, vol. iii: *June 1910–November 1918*, vol. iv: *November 1918–August 1919* (7 vols., Cambridge, 1966).

India Office List for 1918 (London, 1918).

JONES, T., *Whitehall Diary*, vol. i: *1916–1925*, ed. K. Middlemas (London, 1969).

KEYNES, J. M., *The Collected Writings of John Maynard Keynes*, ed. Elizabeth Johnson, vol. xvi: *Activities 1914–1919: The Treasury and Versailles* (30 vols., London, 1971–89).

MANTOUX, P., *Les Délibérations du Conseil des Quatres, 24 mars–28 juin 1919*, vol. i (2 vols., Paris, 1955).

PROTHERO, Sir G. W., *A Select Analytical List of Books Concerning the Great War* (London, 1923), with a Prefatory note by Stephen Gaslee.

SCOTT, J. B., ed., *President Wilson's Foreign Policy: Messages, Addresses, Papers* (New York, 1918).

R. W. Seton-Watson and the Yugoslavs: Correspondence, 1906–1941 (2 vols., London and Zagreb, 1976).

SEYMOUR, C., *Letters from the Paris Peace Conference* (New Haven, Conn., 1965).

SMUTS, J., *The League of Nations: A Practical Suggestion* (London, 1918).

THORPE, A. W., ed., *Burke's Handbook to the Most Excellent Order of the British Empire* (London, 1921).

UNITED STATES, Department of State, *Papers Relating to the Foreign Relations of the United States: The Paris Peace Conference, 1919* (13 vols., Washington, DC, 1942–7).

WADE, J. R., ed., *The War Office List, 1918* (London, 1918).

V. SECONDARY SOURCE: MEMOIRS

AMERY, L. S., *My Political Life*, vol. ii: *War and Peace, 1914–1929* (3 vols., London, 1953–5).

CARTON DE WIART, A., *Happy Odyssey: The Memoirs of Lieutenant-General Carton de Wiart* (London, 1950).

CECIL, Lord R. (Viscount Cecil), *A Great Experiment: An Autobiography* (London, 1941).

GREGORY, J. D., *On the Edge of Diplomacy: Rambles and Reflections, 1902–1928* (London, 1928).

HARDINGE OF PENSHURST, Lord, *Old Diplomacy: The Reminiscences of Lord Hardinge of Penshurst* (London, 1947).

HEADLAM-MORLEY, J., *A Memoir of the Paris Peace Conference, 1919*, ed. A. Headlam-Morley, R. Bryant, and A. Cienciala (London, 1972).

HOWARD OF PENRITH, Lord, *Theatre of Life*, vol. ii: *Life Seen from the Stalls* (2 vols., London, 1935–6).

LEEPER, Sir R., *When Greek Meets Greek* (London, 1950).

LLOYD GEORGE, D., *Memoirs of the Peace Conference* (2 vols., New Haven, Conn., 1938).

——*War Memoirs of David Lloyd George* (2 vols., London, 1938).

McFADYEAN, A., *Recollected in Tranquillity* (London, 1964).

NAPIER, H. D., *The Experience of a Military Attaché in the Balkans* (London, 1924).

O'MALLEY, O., *The Phantom Caravan* (London, 1954).

OPPENHEIMER, F., *Stranger Within* (London, 1960).

PERCY, E., *Some Memories* (London, 1958).

POINCARÉ, R., *Au Service de la France*, vol. xi: *À la recherche de la paix, 1919* (11 vols.; i–x, Paris, 1926–30; vol. xi, Paris, 1974).

SEYMOUR, C., *Letters from the Paris Peace Conference* (New Haven, Conn., 1965).

SHOTWELL, J.T., *At the Paris Peace Conference* (New York, 1937).

TARDIEU, A., *The Truth About the Treaty* (Indianapolis, 1921).

TOYNBEE, A.J., *Acquaintances* (London, 1967).

VANSITTART, Lord, *The Mist Procession* (London, 1956).

WOODWARD, E. L., *Short Journey* (London, 1942).

VI.   SECONDARY SOURCES: BIOGRAPHICAL ACCOUNTS

BENTWICH, N. and KISCH, M., *Brigadier Frederick Kisch: Soldier and Zionist* (London, 1966).

BINDOFF, S. T., 'Charles Kingsley Webster', *Proceedings of the British Academy*, 48 (1961), 427–47.

BUSCH, B.C., *Hardinge of Penshurst: A Study in the Old Diplomacy* (New York, 1980).

BUTLER, R., 'Sir Eyre Crowe', *World Review*, NS 50 (1953), 8–13.

CARR, E. H., *From Napoleon to Stalin and Other Essays* (London, 1980).

CECIL, A., 'Sir George Prothero, KBE Litt.D.', *Quarterly Review*, 473 (Oct. 1922), 213–18.

CECIL, H. P., 'The Development of Lord Robert Cecil's Views on the Securing of a Lasting Peace, 1915–1919' (D.Phil. thesis, University of Oxford, 1971).

CRAWLEY, C. W., 'Sir George Prothero and His Circle of Friends', *Transactions of the Royal Historical Society*, 5th Series, 20 (1970), 101–27.

ELCOCK, H., 'J. M. Keynes at the Paris Peace Conference', in M. KEYNES, ed., *Essays on John Maynard Keynes* (Cambridge, 1975).

EYCK, F., *G. P. Gooch: A Study in History and Politics* (London, 1982).

GOOLD, J. D., 'Old Diplomacy: The Diplomatic Career of Lord Hardinge, 1910–1922' (Ph.D. thesis, University of Cambridge, 1976).

HANCOCK, W. K., *Smuts* (2 vols., Cambridge, 1962–8).

HARROD, R. F., *The Life of John Maynard Keynes* (London, 1963).

HUDSON, W. J., *Billy Hughes in Paris: The Birth of Australian Diplomacy* (Melbourne, 1978).

JAMES, Sir W., *The Eyes of the Navy: A Biographical Study of Admiral Sir Reginald Hall* (London, 1955).

LEES-MILNE, J., *Harold Nicolson: A Biography, 1886–1929*, vol. i (2 vols., London, 1980–1).

NAMIER, Julia., *Lewis Namier: A Biography* (London, 1971).

NICOLSON, H., 'Allen Leeper', *The Nineteenth Century and After*, 118 (Oct. 1935), 473–83.

——*Lord Curzon: The Last Phase* (London, 1937).

PENSON, H., 'Lord Cozens-Hardy', *The Times*, 29 May 1924.

POWICKE, F. M., 'Henry William Careless Davis', *English Historical Journal*, 43 (1928), 578–84.

ROSKILL, S., *Hankey: Man of Secrets* (London, 1970–4).

ROWLAND, J., and BASIL, Second Baron CADMAN, *Ambassador for Oil: The Life of John, First Baron Cadman* (London, 1960).

SETON-WATSON, H. and SETON-WATSON, C., *The Making of a New Europe: R. W. Seton-Watson and the Last Years of Austria-Hungary* (London, 1981).

SKIDELSKY, R., *John Maynard Keynes*, vol. i: *Hopes Betrayed, 1883–1920* (London, 1983).

SUAREZ, G., *Briand: sa vie — son œuvre*, vol. iv: *Lu Pilote dans la tourmente, 1916–1918* (6 vols., Paris, 1938–52).

TAYLOR, A. J. P., *Beaverbrook* (London, 1972).

WEAVER, J. R. H., *Henry William Careless Davies, 1874–1928: A Memoir* (London, 1933).

VII. SECONDARY SOURCES: MONOGRAPHS AND ARTICLES

ANDREW, C., *Secret Service: The Making of the British Intelligence Community* (London, 1985).

——and KANYA-FORSTNER, A. S., *France Overseas: The Great War and the Climax of French Imperial Expansion* (London, 1981).

BARROS, J., *The Aland Islands Question: Its Settlement by the League of Nations* (New Haven, Conn., 1968).

BAUMONT, M., *La Faillite de la paix, 1918–1939* (2nd edn., Paris, 1946).

BINKLEY, R. C., 'New Light on the Paris Peace Conference', *Political Science Quarterly*, 46 (1931), 335–61, 509–47.

BROWN, R.C., 'Sir Robert Borden and Canada's War Aims', in B. Hunt and A. Preston, eds., *War Aims and Strategic Policy in the Great War, 1914–1918* (London, 1977).

BUNSELMEYER, R. E., *The Cost of the War, 1914–1919: British Economic War Aims and the Origins of Reparation* (Hamden, Conn., 1975).

BUSCH, B. C., *Britain, India, and the Arabs, 1914–1921* (Berkeley, Calif., 1971).

——*Mudros to Lausanne: Britain's Frontier in West Asia, 1918–1923,* (Albany, NY, 1976).

CALDER, K. J., *Britain and the Origins of the New Europe, 1914–1918* (Cambridge, 1976).

CHILD, C., 'Introduction'. In Great Britain, Foreign Office, *Weekly Political Intelligence Summaries*, vol. i (16 vols., Millwood, NY, 1983), pp. v–xxii.

COX, F. J., 'French Peace Plans, 1918–1919', in Cox *et al.*, *Studies in Modern European History in Honor of Franklin Charles Palm* (New York, 1956).

CRAIG, G. A. and GILBERT, F., eds., *The Diplomats, 1919–1939* (New York, 1972).

CURATO, F., *A conferenza della pace, 1919–1920,* vol. i (2 vols., Milan, 1942).

DOCKRILL, M. L., 'The F.O. and Chatham House, 1919', *International Affairs*, 56 (1980), 665–72.

——and GOOLD, J. D., *Peace without Promise: Britain and the Peace Conferences, 1919–23* (London, 1981).

——and STEINER, Z., 'The Foreign Office at the Paris Peace Conference in 1919', *International History Review*, 2 (1980), 56–86.

EGERTON, G. W., *Great Britain and the Creation of the League of Nations: Strategy, Politics, and International Organization, 1914–1919* (London, 1979).

ELCOCK, H., *Portrait of a Decision: The Council of Four and the Treaty of Versailles* (London, 1972).

FEST, W., *Peace or Partition: The Hapsburg Monarchy and British Policy* (London, 1978).

FLOTO, I., *Colonel House in Paris: A Study of American Policy at the Paris Peace Conference, 1919* (Princeton, NJ, 1980).

FOWLER, W. B., *British–American Relations, 1917–1918: The Role of Sir William Wiseman* (Princeton, NJ, 1969).

FRY, M. G., 'The Imperial War Cabinet, the United States, and the Freedom of the Seas', *Journal of the Royal United Services Institution*, 110 (Nov. 1965), 353–62.

GELFAND, L., *The Inquiry: American Preparations for Peace, 1917–1919* (New Haven, Conn., 1963).

GIDNEY, J. B., *A Mandate for Armenia* (Kent, OH, 1967).

GLUCK, G., 'Die britische Mitteleuropapolitik nach dem Ersten Weltkrieg. Von der Unterzeichnung des Waffenstillstandes bis zum Ende des Jahres 1920' (Erlangen-Nuremberg, Phil. Diss., 1964).

GOLDSTEIN, E., 'British Peace Aims and the Eastern Question: The Political Intelligence Department and the Eastern Committee, 1918', *Middle Eastern Studies* 23:4 (1987), 419–36.

——'The Foreign Office and Political Intelligence, 1917–20', *Review of International Studies*, 14:4 (1988), 275–88.

——'Hertford House: The Naval Intelligence Geographical Section and Peace Conference Planning, 1917–1919', *The Mariner's Mirror* 72:1 (1986), 85–8.

——'New Diplomacy and the New Europe at the Paris Peace Conference of 1919: The A. W. A. Leeper Papers', *East European Quarterly*, 21:4 (1988), 393–400.

——'Great Britain and Greater Greece, 1917–20', *Historical Journal*, 32:3 (1989), 339–56.

GRIBBLE, F., 'The Luxemburg Railways', *New Europe*, 8:99 (5 Sept. 1918), 177–88.

HANKEY, Lord, *The Supreme Command, 1914–1918* (London, 1961).

——*The Supreme Command at the Paris Peace Conference, 1919. A Commentary* (London, 1963).

HEADLAM-MORLEY, J., 'Mittel-Europe Again', *New Europe*, 6:74 (14 Mar. 1918), 257–63.

HELMREICH, P. C., *From Paris to Sèvres: The Partition of the Ottoman Empire at the Paris Peace Conference of 1919–1920* (Columbus, Ohio, 1974).

HEMERY, J. A., 'The Emergence of Treasury Influence in British Foreign Policy, 1914–1921' (Ph.D. thesis, University of Cambridge, 1988).

Hovi, O., *The Baltic Area in British Policy, 1918–1921*, vol. i (Helsinki, 1980).

Hunczak, T., 'Sir Lewis Namier and the Struggle for Eastern Galicia, 1918–1920', *Harvard Ukrainian Studies*, 1:2 (1977), 198–210.

Kedourie, E., *England and the Middle East: the Destruction of the Ottoman Empire, 1914–1921* (London, 1978).

Kendle, J. B., *The Round Table Movement and Imperial Union* (Toronto, 1975).

Kent, M., *Oil and Empire: British Policy and Mesopotamian Oil, 1900–1920* (London, 1976).

Kernek, S. J., *Distractions of Peace During War: The Lloyd George Government's Reactions to Woodrow Wilson, December 1916–November 1918*. (Philadelphia, 1975).

——'Woodrow Wilson and National Self-Determination Along Italy's Frontier: A Study of the Manipulation of Principles in the Pursuit of Political Interests', *Proceedings of the American Philosophical Society*, 126:4 (1982), 243–300.

Keynes, J. M., *The Economic Consequences of the Peace* (London, 1919).

Kitsikis, D., *Le Rôle des experts à la Conference de la Paix de 1919: Gestation d'une technocratie en politique internationale* (Ottawa, 1972).

Laffan, R. G. D., 'Rumania and the Redemption of the Rumanians', in H. W. V. Temperley, ed., *A History of the Paris Peace Conference*, q.v.

Lederer, I. J., *Yugoslavia at the Paris Peace Conference: A Study in Frontiermaking* (New Haven, Conn., 1963).

Loucher, L., *Carnets Secrets, 1908–1932*, ed. J. de Launay, (Brussels, 1962).

Louis, W. R., 'Great Britain and the African Peace Settlement of 1919', *American Historical Review*, 71 (1966), 875–92.

——*Great Britain and Germany's Lost Colonies, 1914–1919* (Oxford, 1967).

——'The United States and the African Peace Settlement of 1919: The Pilgrimage of George Louis Beer', *Journal of African History*, 4:3 (1963), 413–33.

Lundgren-Nielsen, K., *The Polish Problem at the Paris Peace Conference: A Study of the Policies of the Great Powers and the Poles, 1918–1919*, trans. A. Borch-Johansen (Odense, 1979).

McDougall, W. A., *France's Rhineland Diplomacy, 1914–1924: The Last Bid for a Balance of Power in Europe* (Princeton, NJ, 1978).

Macfie, A. L., 'The British Decision Regarding the Future of Constantinople, November 1918–January 1920', *Historical Journal*, 18 (1975), 391–400.

McKercher,, B. J. C., *Esme Howard: A Diplomatic Biography* (Cambridge, 1989).

Mance, O., *Frontiers, Peace Treaties, and International Organization* (London, 1946).

Marder, A., *From Dreadnought to Scapa Flow: The Royal Navy in the Fisher Era* (5 vols., London, 1961–70).

Marks, S., 'Behind the Scenes at the Paris Peace Conference of 1919', *The Journal of British Studies*, 9:2 (1970), 154–80.

——*Innocent Abroad: Belgium at the Paris Peace Conference of 1919* (Chapel Hill, NC, 1981).

Marston, F. S., *The Peace Conference of 1919: Organization and Procedure* (London, 1944).

Mason, C. M., 'British Policy on the Establishment of a League of Nations, 1914–1919' (Ph.D. thesis, University of Cambridge, 1970).

Mejcher, H., 'British Middle East Policy, 1917–21: The Interdepartmental Level', *Journal of Contemporary History*, 8 (1973), 81–101.

——*Imperial Quest for Oil: Iraq, 1910–1928* (London, 1976).

Namier, L. B., *Avenues of History* (London, 1952).

Nelson, H. I., *Land and Power: British and Allied Policy on Germany's Frontiers, 1916–1919* (London, 1963).

Nicolson, H., *Peacemaking 1919* (London, 1933).

Percy, E., 'Foreign Office Reform', *New Europe*, 11:134 (8 May 1919), 77–82; 11:137 (29 May 1919), 197–250.

Phelan, E. F., 'British Preparations', in J. T. Shotwell, *The Origins of the International Labor Organization* (New York, 1934).

Roskill, S., *Naval Policy between the Wars*, vol. i: *The Period of Anglo-American Antagonism, 1919–1929* (3 vols., London, 1970–4).

Rothwell, V. H., *British War Aims and Peace Diplomacy, 1914–1918* (Oxford, 1971).

——'Mesopotamia in British War Aims, 1914–1918', *Historical Journal*, 13 (1970), 273–94.

Saunders, G., 'Free Navigation of the Rhine', *The Nineteenth Century and After*, 85 (Jan. 1919), 179–87.

Seton-Watson, R. W., *Treaty Revision and the Hungarian Frontiers* (London, 1934).

Sharp, A., 'Britain and the Protection of Minorities at the Paris Peace Conference', in A.C. Hepburn, ed., *Minorities in History* (London, 1978), pp. 170–80.

Spector, S. D., *Rumania at the Paris Peace Conference: A Study of the Diplomacy of Ioan I. C. Bratianu* (New York, 1962).

Steiner, Z., *The Foreign Office and Foreign Policy, 1898–1914* (London, 1969).

STEVENSON, D., *French War Aims Against Germany, 1914–1919* (Oxford, 1982).

TAYLOR, P. M., 'The Foreign Office and British Propaganda during the First World War', *Historical Journal*, 23 (1980), 875–98.

TEMPERLEY, H. W. V., ed., *A History of the Peace Conference of Paris* (6 vols., London, 1920–4).

TILLMAN, S. P., *Anglo-American Relations at the Paris Peace Conference of 1919* (Princeton, NJ, 1961).

TORRE, A., *Versailles: Storia della conferenza della pace* (Milan, 1940).

TRACHTENBERG, M., *Reparation in World Politics: France and European Economic Diplomacy, 1916–1923* (New York, 1980).

TURNER, J., *Lloyd George's Secretariat* (Cambridge, 1980).

WALWORTH, A., *America's Moment: 1918* (New York, 1977).

WARMAN, R. M., 'The Erosion of Foreign Office Influence in the Making of Foreign Policy, 1916–1918', *Historical Journal* 15:1 (1972), 133–59.

ZIMMERN, A., *The League of Nations and the Rule of Law, 1918–1935* (London, 1936).

Index

'A' Division, Treasury 54–5, 112, 194
Abu Musa 179
Abyssinia 82, 185, 187
Admiralty 53–4, 57, 62, 128, 144,
    146–7, 169, 185, 189, 191, 205,
    206, 215n, 221, 250
    Admiralty Reconstruction
    Committee, 221
    Admiralty Sub-Committee A,
    221–2
Afghanistan 180
Africa 43, 158, 173, 183–90, 270,
    276–7
Agriculure and Fisheries, Board
    of 202
Air Board, Ministry, & Staff 54, 146,
    149, 187, 277
Akers-Douglas, A., 80n, 112
Åland Islands 143–7
Alaska 16, 42
Albania 82, 135–6, 242, 245–6, 269
Alexandretta 160–2, 270
Allied Economic Conference (1916),
    192
Alsace-Lorraine 11, 13, 16, 53, 69,
    106, 126, 233, 230
Amber and Ambroid 201
American Geographical Society 100
Amery, Leo 14–15, 20–3, 26, 27, 30,
    49, 96, 188n, 279–80
Anatolia (Asia Minor), 82, 150–1,
    153, 170–2, 245, 247–50, 267
Anglo-American French Guarantee
    Treaty (1919), 236–7, 274–5
Anglo-Japanese Understanding
    (1917), 183
Anglo-Persian Oil Co., 205
Anglo-Rumanian Society 71, 254
d'Annunzio, Gabriele 265, 269, 278
Arabia 17, 44, 82, 102, 103, 152–5,
    159, 163–4, 187, 189–90, 275
Argentina 63
Arland, J.A. 52, 137
Armenia 53, 141, 153, 159, 164, 170,
    171, 174–5, 189
Arms Limitation, see Disarmament
Ashley, P.W.L. 14n, 198, 200
Asia Minor, see Anatolia

Asquith, H.H. 9
Asquith Government 10
Australia 16, 183
    (See also Dominions)
Austria-Hungary 12, 13, 16, 43, 72,
    81, 85, 131–2
Austria 63, 127, 132, 140, 182, 268
    See also Austria-Hungary
Azores 187

Baden, Prince Max 90
Baghdad Railway 165
Bailey, J., 59, 69–70, 77, 80
Balance of power 10, 12, 119, 124–6,
    171, 184, 229, 231–2, 235, 238,
    259
Balfour, Arthur 10, 13, 23, 40, 44, 58,
    60, 61, 79, 90–2, 101, 115, 155,
    156–9, 164, 176–7, 188–9, 223–4,
    232, 234–5, 246, 268
Balfour Declaration (1917), 161, 224
Balkans 21, 43, 59, 81, 85, 113,
    133–40, 242
Baltic 81, 84, 143, 148
Baluchistan 187
Banat 136, 137, 255
Barclay, George 253
Barnes, George 201
Barnes, J.S. 267–8
Bate, Pawley 222–3
Baghdad 166
Baku 175
Basra 166
Batum 175
Beaverbrook, Lord 60–2, 64
Beirut 161
Belgium 11, 16, 43, 53, 63, 69, 80, 84,
    127, 147, 178, 179n, 197, 213,
    216, 231–2
Belgium and Denmark Affairs
    Committee 117, 232
Benoist, Charles 105
Berlin 11
Bessarabia 40, 137, 141, 254
Bevan, E.R. 59, 72, 77, 82, 117
Bikanir, Maharaja of 15n
Binkley, Robert 1
Black, Frederick 204n

Blockade, Ministry of 24, 26, 56
Bonar Law, A., 200 n, 201, 210, 239
Borden, Robert 15 n, 200, 245
Bourgeois, General Leon 105
Bowman, Isaiah 100
Bradbury, John 194
Bratianu, Ioan 253–4, 256–7, 260–1
Brenner Pass 139, 140
Briand Government 104
British Academy 31
British Guiana 16
British Honduras 42
Buchan, John 60
Buckler, W. H. 246
Bukovina 137, 254–5
Bulgaria 63, 134–5, 137, 242, 246–7, 255
de Bunsen, Maurice 20
Bureau d'études economiques 104
Burgenland 129 n
Butler, J. R. M. 52, 52 n, 282
British Empire Delegation 110–19, 145

Cables 53, 206
Cadman, John 204
Caliphate 153, 167, 169, 173, 250
Cambon, Paul 106, 107, 196
Cameroons 17, 276
Campbell, C. W. 40
Carnegie, E. H. W. Fullerton-, see Fullerton-Carnegie
Carpenter, Rhys 115
Carr, E. H. 65, 68, 72, 74, 80, 128, 139, 141, 282
Carton de Wiart, General Adrian 259
Castellorizo 167
Caucasus 53, 82, 158–9; 174–7, 185, 231
Cave, Lord 220
Cave Committee of International Law 55
Cecil, Algernon 31, 35, 37–8
Cecil, Robert 15 n, 44, 48, 58, 83, 94, 102, 112, 138, 146, 156, 158–60, 174, 213, 215, 218, 279
Central Asia 181
Central Territorial Committee 256
Central Organization for a Durable Peace 33–4
Ceuta 187
Chamberlain, Austen 15 n, 17
Chandernagore 180
Cheshme 172
China 40, 43, 63, 180, 181–2
Chirol, Valentine 14, 58

Churchill, Winston 189, 200
Clean Slate Committee 206
Clemenceau, Georges 106, 107–8, 109, 111, 163 n, 233, 248, 266, 271–4, 278, 285
Clerk, G. R. 14 n
Coaling Stations 206
Cockerill, George 220 n
Colonial Office 34, 195
Comite d'études 103–7
Committee of Imperial Defence (CID), 47
Committee on Indemnity, see Hughes Committee
Committee for National Patriotic Orgnisation 31
Committee on Staffs 37
Committee on Treaty Revision 223
Congress of Berlin (1878) 40
Congress of Vienna 2, 11, 40, 110, 127, 233, 235, 242
Constantine, King (of the Hellenes) 247, 251
Constantinople 153, 159, 166–9, 173, 185, 189, 246–7, 249–50, 251, 271
Constanza-Cernavoda Railway 148
Cook, Joseph 257
Coolidge, Archibald Cary 100, 103
Coordinating Committee 117
Corbett, Julian 212
Cox, Percy 165
Cozens-Hardy, W. H. 22, 32, 34–5, 38, 39, 47, 49
Craig, Gordon 285
Crete 187
Crewe House, see Propaganda Services
Crowe, Eyre 15 n, 36, 45, 79–80, 82, 85, 88, 96, 112, 117, 118–19, 124, 127, 128, 173, 178 n, 212, 213, 214, 218, 220, 232, 234, 243, 245–9, 254–5, 263, 266, 268, 275–6, 283–4
Crutwell, C. R. M. F., 52
Cunliffe, Lord 199 n, 203, 238
Curzon, Lord 3, 16, 23, 152, 155–61, 168, 170, 174–9, 188–9, 243, 250
Curzon Committee 15–18, 183
Cyprus 137, 153, 167,
Czechoslovakia 13, 53, 132, 138, 148, 230, 242, 257–9
Czechoslovakia Affairs Committee 257, 259
Czernowitz-Kiev Railway 137

Dagestan 174

Daily Chronicle, 60, 72, 74
Danube River 148
Danzig 69, 145–6, 230, 249
Davies, J.T. 92
Davis, H.W.C. 29, 48–9
Dawson, W.H. 40
Declaration of Paris (1856), 221–2
Dedcagach 134
Demobilization Committee 95
Denmark 16, 43, 63, 69, 127, 128–9, 178
Dennis, Alfred 103
Department of Information Intelligence Bureau (DIIB) 59–61, 62
Djibouti 185, 186
Dickson, H.N. 27–30, 42, 49, 96
Disaramament 214, 218–19
Dmoski, Roman 66, 261
Dniester River 148
Dodecanese Islands 82, 137, 153, 245–6
Dominions, British 16, 17, 62, 85, 95, 188, 190, 217
Donald, Robert 60
Drummond, Eric 92, 94

East Prussia 145–6, 148, 263
Eastern Committee 152, 155–79, 185, 187–90, 191, 250, 270–1
Egypt 82, 161, 164, 173, 266
Emmott, Lord 48
Enos 167, 246
Epirus, *see* Northern Epirus
Ernle, Lord, *see* Prothero, Rowland
Estonia 141

Faisal, Emir 162, 270–1, 275
Falk, Oswald 112
Falkland Islands 44
Finland 53, 63, 81, 84, 141–4, 147
Fisher, H.A.L. 15n
Fishing fleet 202
Fitzmaurice, Gerald 19n, 31
Fiume 12, 52, 139, 230, 249, 265–9, 278
Flanders 127
Flux, A.W. 199n
Foch, Ferdinand 106
Forbes-Adam, Eric 86, 178n, 206, 249
Foreign Office Library 24, 28, 36–7, 78–9
Foreign Office Registry 25
Foster, G.E. 199n
Fountain, H., 14n

France 11, 13, 14, 16, 17, 43, 45, 59, 63, 70, 80, 83, 84, 124, 126, 147, 153–5, 157–62, 164, 174–6, 183, 185, 193, 196–9, 203, 206, 220, 229–42, 245, 252–5, 258–60, 270–8, 282–3
    preparations 98–9, 103–9
Franco-Russian Secret Agreement (1917) 233
Frankfurter, Felix 199
Free Ports 83, 134, 146, 167, 175, 209
Freedom of the Seas 41, 55, 170, 214, 219–23
French India 14, 32–3, 179–80
French Somaliland 14, 17
Fry, Geoffrey 54
Fullerton-Carnegie, E.H.W. 76, 77–8, 81, 128, 141, 143

Galapagos Islands 44
Galicia 145, 148, 205
Gambia 17
'Garden Suburb', 58, 280
Gathorne-Hardy, Geoffrey 38
Geddes, Eric 202
Gelfand, Lawrence 2, 285
General Staff, *see* War Office
Georgia 174–5
German East Africa 17, 184, 187–90, 276–7
German South-West Africa 184, 186–7, 276–7
Germany 3, 11, 12, 13, 43, 59, 63, 69, 72, 73–4, 84, 104, 124, 125, 126–9, 138, 140, 142, 145–6, 148–9, 182, 217, 231, 235–9, 241, 250, 259–64, 273, 277
    colonies 3, 14, 16–17, 40, 43, 68, 101, 150–1, 182–4, 186–90, 277
    disarmament 106; navy, 18, 53, 166, 277
    reparations and indemnities 192, 194–203, 208
Gibbs, Herbert 199n
Gibraltar 187
Gleichen, Edward 45, 59, 60
Gooch, G.P. 49
Grant, Hamilton 168–9
Greece 16, 63, 137–8, 153, 166–7, 169–72, 197, 230, 242–51, 252, 278, 285
Greek and Albanian Affairs Committee 117, 245, 247
Greenland 16, 44
Gregg, W.W. 38
Gregory, J.D. 73

Grey, Edward 23, 82
Grosse Schutt 258
Gubbins, J. H. 40

Hagia Sophia 173
Hague Conventions 222
Hall, Admiral Reginald 22, 24, 26–7,
    28, 30, 35, 47, 49, 53–4, 55–6,
    128, 220n
Hamburg 146
Hankey, Maurice 15, 20, 21–3, 25,
    93, 113–14, 188n, 281
Hardinge, Lord 13, 23–6, 35–6, 39,
    50, 57–62, 64, 66, 67, 78, 79, 80,
    82, 85, 86, 87–9, 90–8, 107,
    110–14, 117, 127, 128, 129, 139,
    155, 156, 164, 165, 213, 214, 224,
    263, 279–81
Harwood, R. E. 51
Hashemites 275
Haskins, Charles 234, 264
Hazen, J. D. 15n, 16.,
Headlam-Morley, J. W. 2, 45, 79,
    103, 218
    P. I. D. 56, 59, 60, 68–9, 75, 76, 77,
        80, 82, 84, 86, 87, 96
    Intelligence Clearing House 112–13
    Peace Conference 117, 118, 232–7,
        259–65
    views on European
        Settlement 123–31, 139, 140, 142,
        146, 149, 182
    trial of Kaiser 223–4
Headlam-Morley, Mrs. J. W. (Else
    Sontag), 68
Hejaz 153, 164
Heligoland 40, 53, 147
Henderson, Arthur 15n
Henderson, Bernard 38
Hertford House, see Naval
    Intelligence Geographical Section
Hewins, W. A. S. 199n
Hirtzel, Arthur 32–3, 156, 163, 168–9,
    179–80, 250, 272
Higgins, Pearce 220n, 221
Historical Section 22, 24, 26, 27,
    30–47, 49, 56, 58, 78, 83, 87, 186,
    280
    handbooks 32, 38, 39–47, 49, 50,
        56, 101–2, 137, 144, 146, 173,
        184, 185, 186, 222
Holderness, William 14n
Holding, Thomas 19n
Home Office 195, 210
Hope, G. P. W. 220n
Horn of Africa 17, 185

House, Edward 43–4, 99–102
Howard, Esme 64, 81, 112, 127, 139,
    141–6, 181, 214, 224 260–1, 263
Howard-Lord Agreement 260, 263
Hudson, Manley 100
Hughes, William 15n, 199–203, 219,
    238
Hughes Committee (on Indemnity),
    191, 199–203, 238
Hungary 132–3, 256
    See also Austria-Hungary
Hurst, Cecil 55, 79, 83, 106, 112, 212,
    220
Husain 275–6

Ibn Saud 275
Iceland 63
ID 27, see Historical Section
ID 32, see Naval Intelligence
    Geographical Section
Imbros 167
Imperial War Cabinet 9, 15, 18, 42,
    161, 187–90
Indemnity and Reparation 10, 13, 45,
    84, 97, 104, 108, 182, 191–204,
    224, 231, 233, 237–40
India 17, 148, 153, 164, 173, 176,
    177–81, 185, 206, 209, 250, 276
    See also French India, Portuguese
    India
India Office 32–3, 82, 94, 165–6,
    168–9, 178–83, 195, 250, 272
Indo-European Telegraph Co., 206
Information, Department (later
    Ministry) of 26, 59, 60–1
Inquiry 24, 28, 42–4, 85, 98–103, 106,
    109, 186, 203, 285
Intelligence Clearing House 50,
    112–14
Inter-Allied Mission to Poland 259
International Law Committee 220–3
Ionescu, Take 254
Iraq, see Mesopotamia
Islam, see Muslims
Islington, Lord 14n
Istria 11, 139
Italy 11, 43, 45, 59, 63, 70, 81, 82, 85,
    132, 137, 139–40, 153–5, 162, 164,
    171, 183, 197, 208, 220, 239, 242,
    245, 246, 248, 250, 252, 255–6,
    265–9, 270, 274, 276, 278

Jablunka Pass 258
James, Admiral William 50
Japan 16, 43, 63, 180, 181–3
Jelf, A. S. 204n

Jews 139, 161–3, 224, 275
Johnson, Douglas 28–9, 44, 102, 103, 106
Johnstone, Henry 19n
Jones, Thomas 20, 21
Jordan, John 182
Juba Valley 276
Jumbo 224

Kaiser, trial of 223–4
Karikal 179
Kavalla 134
Keltie, John 50n
Kerr, Philip 58, 69, 73, 114, 236, 244, 261
Keynes, John Maynard 54–5, 97, 112, 192, 194, 196–201, 203, 237–9, 282
Kiaochow 182
Kiel Canal 40, 147
Kisch, F.H. 261–2
Klagenfurt Basin 268
Klotz, Lucien 106
Koppel, Percy 76, 77–8, 80, 84, 86, 88
Koritza 246
Kossovo 246
Kurdistan 154, 175

Labour 210
Labour, Ministry of 210
Laffan, R.G.D. 52, 134–5
Lambert, H.C.M. 14n
Landsdowne, Lord 10
Lansing, Robert 99
Latin America 453, 100, 186
Latvia 141
Lavisse, Ernest 104
Lazistan 175n
League of Nations 101, 142, 146, 170, 182, 195, 257, 278
    British proposals 41, 55, 56, 63, 73, 83, 85, 191, 210–19, 225, 231
    mandates and supervised areas 151, 160, 165, 167, 172, 190, 234–6, 247, 249–50, 257, 267, 269
League of Nations Committee, see Phillimore Committee
Lebanon 152, 159, 160–2, 270
Leeper, A.W.A. 40, 59, 64n, 70–1, 72, 77, 81, 88, 103, 110, 112, 113, 114, 115, 117–19, 130, 133–8, 243–4, 253–7, 259, 266–8
    memorandum on South-Eastern Europe and the Balkans, 133–8, 244, 252

memorandum on Question of Italian Claims, 139–40
Leeper, R.W.A. 59, 70–1, 74, 77, 81, 88, 118, 141, 142, 143
Le Rond, General 107
Lenin, V.I. 143
Liberia 184
Lippman, Walter 100
Lithuania 127, 141
Little Entente 242, 253
Litvinov, Maksim 71
Llewellyn-Smith, Hubert 14n, 195, 199n
Lloyd George, David 10, 12–13, 15, 18, 23, 25, 28, 34, 84, 90, 92–3, 94–5, 96, 97, 109, 111–16, 132n, 152, 163n, 172, 173n, 187–90, 195n, 199n, 201, 203, 210, 211–12, 218–19, 223–4, 234, 236, 238–40, 248, 256, 261–8, 271–4, 281, 284–5
Lloyd George Government 9, 23, 58
Long, Walter 15n, 16, 186n, 199n
Lord, Robert 100, 260
Lorin, Henri 104–5
Lowlands 13, 229, 231, 233, 241
Luxemburg 43, 53, 80, 84, 147, 208, 230–2, 241, 273

Macdonnell, John 220n
Macdonough, General 14n
McFadyean, Andrew 54
Macleay, Ronald 83, 112, 181–2
Mahe 179
Mallet, Louis 10, 81–2, 112, 151, 156, 170, 214, 247, 270
Mallet Committee 14–15, 18, 20, 21, 24, 54, 183, 275
Malmédy 127
Mance, H.O. 207–8, 268
Manchester Guardian, 75
Marie, Queen (of Romania), 253
Marling, Charles 178
de Martonne, Emmanuel 105, 107
Masaryk, Tomas 4, 257
Massey, William 15n
Matthews, W.T. 51
Maurice, General 14n
May, Admiral William 221
Media 167, 246
Meinertzhagen, Richard 276
Mellor, John 220n
Memelland 127
Mesopotamia 17, 23, 24, 44, 70, 102, 154, 159, 164–6, 179, 187, 189–90, 205, 209, 231

Mesopotamia Committee 156n, 165
Meston, J., 15n
Mezes, Sidney 100, 236
Middle East 59, 85, 153, 157, 158, 159
    see also individual countries
Military Intelligence, *see* War Office
Military Intelligence Geographical Section, *see* War Office
M.I.2(e), *see* War Office
Milne, General 247–8
Milner, Lord 3, 15, 18, 110, 200, 272–3, 277
Milner Committee 15, 18, 21, 22, 194, 211
Minorities 69, 133, 138–9, 224, 242
Montagu, Edwin 3, 10, 13, 94, 156, 159, 168–9, 170n, 173, 190, 250
Montenegro 136
Morel, Jean 104
Moresnet 127n
Mornard, Monsieur 179n
Morning Post, 73
Morocco 82,
Morris, Edward 15n
Morrison, Samuel Elliot 100
Mosul 156, 166, 271, 274
Munitions, Ministry of 204
Munro, Dana 102
Murray, Lt.-Col. A.C. 87
Murray, Oswyn 53–4
Muscat 14
Muslims 63, 153, 162, 163, 166, 169, 172–3, 243, 246, 250

Namier, Lewis 59, 66, 72–3, 74, 77, 81, 118, 133, 138, 145–6, 257, 282
Namier, Mrs Lewis (Clara Edeleff-Poniatowski), 72
The Nation, 72
Naval Intelligence 20, 24, 27, 30, 44, 47, 56, 280
Naval Intelligence Geographical Section (Hertford House), 21, 22, 26, 42, 49, 56, 280
Naval Intelligence Historical Section, see Historical Section
Netherlands 43, 80, 127, 147, 231
Neufahrwasser 146
New Europe Group 4, 62, 70, 117–19, 124–5, 130, 133, 138, 154, 208, 229–30, 235, 241, 252, 256–60, 265–7, 283–4
New Europe, 66, 72, 74, 87, 114, 118, 124–5, 130, 136
New Guinea 186

New Hebrides 14
New Statesman, 70, 75
New Zealand 16, 182
Nicholson, W.F. 14n
Nicolson, Harold 45, 58, 62, 65–6, 76, 81, 92, 112, 113, 114, 117–19, 133–8, 167, 171, 239, 243–7, 253, 257–8, 267–9, 279, 282, 284–5
    memorandum on South-Eastern Europe and Balkans 133–8
    memorandum on Question of Italian Claims 139–40
Nixon, Frank 54
Northcliffe Press 202
Northern Epirus 137, 245–6, 250
Norway 63, 144, 178–9
    see also Spitsbergen

Oil, *see* Petroleum
Oliphant, Lancelot 33, 45
O'Malley, Owen 67
Oman, Charles 140, 146, 263
Oppenheim, Francis 39, 41, 208
Oppenheimer, Francis 201–2
Orlando, Vittorio 111, 266, 269, 285
Ottoman Empire 20, 40, 43, 63, 82, 103, 106, 150–73, 189–90, 242–51, 266, 269–76
Overseas Trade, Department of 48, 50, 195
Oxford Union 38

Paget, Ralph 10, 81, 130, 139, 214; Paget-Tyrrell memorandum 10–12, 230
Palairet, Michael 141
Palestine 17, 154, 159, 160–2, 187, 189–90, 224, 271, 274
Paris Resolutions (1916), 192, 210
Parker, Alwyn 29, 36–8, 78–9, 91, 92–3, 102, 112, 117
Pašić, Nikola 252
Paton, H.J. 263, 264n
Peace Books, *see* Historical Section Handbooks
Penson, Henry 38, 47–50, 79, 112
Penson, Lillian 38, 49, 282
Perry, Eustace 73, 82, 83, 86, 87, 112, 118, 138, 182, 184, 213–15, 218
Persia 43, 82, 177–9, 180–1, 187, 205, 206n, 208, 209
Persian Gulf 17, 156, 206
Petroleum 175, 186, 204–5
Petroleum Executive 191, 204–5
Phelan, E.J. 210n

Philhellenes 137–8, 167, 172, 230, 243–5, 247–51, 252
Phillimore, Lord 39, 41, 212
Phillimore Committee 55, 56, 212–14, 217–18
Pichon, Stephen 106, 271
Pickthorn, K. W. M. 52
Piggot, Francis 41
Plunkett, General E. A. 251–2
Poincaré, Raymond 104, 106
Poland 11–12, 13, 16, 21, 43, 63, 72–3, 81, 85, 127, 132, 141, 142, 144–6, 148, 242, 258, 259–65
Polish Committee 117, 261, 264
Political Intelligence Department (PID), 2, 4, 24, 26, 28, 37, 40, 44, 50, 53, 56, 57–89, 90, 96–8, 102, 110, 113, 114–15, 118, 123–4, 127, 130–1, 139, 142, 151, 152, 155, 167, 173, 178, 191, 204n, 213–14, 224, 243, 245, 265, 280, 283
  Sections, 79–83, 130–46, 151, 184, 212–15
Pollard, A. F. 212
Pondicherry 179–80
Portugal 17, 43, 80, 197
Portuguese India 180
Postmaster-General 191, 206
Powell, J. C. 59, 76, 77, 80, 81
Powicke, Maurice 49
Premier Oil and Pipeline Co., 205n
Propaganda Services 60
  Crewe House 62
  Wellington House 68, 70, 72, 74, 76
Prothero, George 30–2, 34–43, 45–7, 50, 61, 69, 79, 96, 102, 112, 263, 284
Prothero, Rowland 30–1

Quarterly Review, 30, 31, 41, 69, 72

Radolin, Prince 66
Railways 207–9
  see also individual railways
Randall, A. W. G. 76, 77, 80, 88
Rapa 14
Read, H. J. 14n
Reading, Lord 34, 94
Reconstruction, Ministry of 195
Reparation, see Indemnity
Reparations Commision, Paris Peace Conference 203, 238–9
Rhineland 104, 105, 106, 147, 230–1, 235–8, 241, 273, 274

Richards, Erle 95, 161n, 166n, 185–6, 220
Robertson, General 10, 12–13
Romania 13, 53, 63, 132, 133, 134, 136–37, 141, 148, 197, 251–7
Romania and Yugoslavia Affairs Committee 117, 252, 254, 256, 266, 268
Rose, J. H. 212
Round Table, 3, 74, 75
Royal Geographical Society 21, 27, 56, 100, 280
Royal Historical Society 31
Royal Institute of International Affairs 282
Rothwell, Victor 285
Roxburghe, R. F. 50n, 76, 77–8, 84, 88, 220n
Ruhr, French Occupation (1923) 199
Russell, Harold 31, 35
Russia 11–12, 43, 53, 59, 63, 74, 81, 82, 85, 126, 137, 140–5, 148, 157–58, 169, 176, 197, 210, 256, 259
Russo-Persian Agreement (1890) 209
Ruthenia 145, 242, 254–5

Saar 69, 147, 230–1, 234, 241, 273
Safrastian, Mr., 59n
St. Gothard Convention (1909) 208
St. Gothard Railway 208
St. Pierre and Miquelon 14, 16, 44
Salisbury, Lord 40
Samoa 186
Satow, Ernest 39, 40
Saunders, George 59, 74–5, 77, 80, 88
Scandinavia 81, 84
Scheldt 80, 127–8, 147
Schleswig-Holstein 11, 28, 53, 127, 128–9
Scott, James Brown 220
Secret Intelligence Service 57
Self-Determination 133, 134, 146, 150, 154, 160, 164, 188, 241, 255, 271
Serbia 13, 51, 136, 197, 242, 267
  see also Yugoslavia
Seret River 137
Service Geographique de l'Armée 105
Seymour, Charles 115, 116
Shanghai 182
Seton-Watson, R. W. 4, 59, 62, 71, 72, 114–15, 117–18, 130–3, 136, 257

Seton-Watson, R. W. (*cont.*)
  memorandum on Austria-
    Hungary 132
  memorandum on Future Frontiers
    of Hungary 132–3
Shipping, Ministry of 195
Shotwell, James 106
Shuckburgh, John 32–3, 37, 156, 172
Siam 43
Simpson, J. Y. 59, 74, 77, 141, 142
Sinha, Satyendra 15 n, 17
Slovakia 51
Smith, Vincent 32–3
Smuts, Jan Christian 15 n, 22–3,
    60–1, 84, 85, 88, 93, 94–8, 110,
    123, 152, 156–8, 160, 186, 188,
    194, 195, 213–14, 216–19, 261–2,
    281,
Smyrna 137, 171, 172, 247–50, 285
Society Islands 14
Sonnino, Sidney 268
South Africa 95, 183, 186, 276
Southern Dobrudja 134, 137, 148,
    255
Spain 43, 59, 63, 70, 80
Sperling, R. A. C. 44, 184–5
Spicer, Gerald 82
Spitsbergen 43, 44, 144, 147
Stanley, Albert 192
Stanmore, Lord 31, 35
Steed, Wickham 19 n
Strachey, C., 14 n
Stettin 148
Stewart, W. 220 n
Straits, The 134, 153, 167, 169–72,
    243
Sudetenland 258
Suez Canal 161, 243
Sumner, B. H. 52, 137
Sumner, Lord 45, 203 n, 238
Sweden 63, 143–4
Switzerland 63, 76, 80, 84, 178, 208
Sykes, Mark 21, 272
Sykes-Picot Agreement (1916) 17,
    152, 157, 160–2, 164, 177, 270–1
Syria 53, 154, 159, 160–2, 270–5
Szechuan 180

Tanganyika, *see* German east Africa
Tardieu, André 104, 107, 234, 236,
    268–9, 282
Temesvar 148
Temperley, H. W. V. 20–1, 22, 49,
    51–2, 56, 134, 135, 245, 266, 268,
    282
Tenedos 167

Teschen 258
Thrace 172, 245–6, 250
Thwaites, General William 247–8,
    268, 272
Tibet 180
Tiflis 175
Tilley, John 78, 79, 85
Times, 72, 74, 75
Timor 14
Togoland 17, 184, 186, 276
Toynbee, Arnold 9, 26, 40, 59, 65,
    72, 74–5, 77, 82, 86, 103, 112,
    113, 118, 137, 142, 159, 163–5,
    167, 170–3, 178 n, 243, 249, 282
  proposed Peace Terms Intelligence
    Section 18, 20, 27, 49, 279–80
  memorandum on Turkey and
    Arabian Peninsula, 151–5
Trade, Board of 50, 83, 97, 182,
    191–6, 199–203, 280
Trade Clearing House 47–8, 51
Trans-Jordan 162
Transylvania 254, 256
Treasury 37, 54–5, 64, 76–8, 86–7, 97,
    191–2, 194–9, 201, 203, 239, 280
Treaty of London (1915) 12, 51, 136,
    139
Trentino 139
Trieste 139
Tripoli 160
Trotsky, Leon 143
Trouton, Rupert 54
Turkey, *see* Ottoman Empire
Turkish Petroleum Co. 205
Tyrol 139–40, 267
Tyrrell, William 10, 14 n, 29, 56, 58,
    65–8, 79, 96, 62, 82, 84, 85, 86,
    88, 93, 128, 212, 214, 218
  Paget-Tyrrell memorandum, 10–12,
    230

Ukraine 132, 137, 141, 142
United States 16, 42, 44–5, 46, 63,
    124, 130, 153–5, 158–9, 161, 162,
    167, 169–70, 174, 176, 181–3,
    184–5, 188–9, 196, 197, 205, 211,
    220, 232–4, 237–40, 242, 245–6,
    249–50, 252, 254–5, 267, 270, 272,
    275–6, 278, 282–3

Vansitart, Robert 45, 76, 82, 88, 112,
    274–5
Vatican 76
Venizelos, Eleftherios 215, 243–4,
    247–9, 251, 252, 253, 278
Vidal de la Blache, Paul 105

Vienna 11

War Cabinet 22, 60, 85, 92, 94, 98,
    150, 152, 156, 194, 210, 214, 281
War Committee 9–13, 18, 20, 230,
    279
War Office 57, 62, 144, 191
    General Staff reports 53, 128, 144,
        147–8, 161, 169, 172, 186–7, 209,
        244, 248, 258, 280
    Military Intelligence 44, 47, 51, 56,
        66, 248, 280
    M.I.2(e), 22, 51–3, 144, 147
    Military Intelligence Geographical
        Section 42
War Trade Department 47–8, 51
War Trade Intelligence
    Department 22, 24, 26, 27, 34,
        38, 41–2, 47–51, 56, 280
War Trade Statistical Department 22,
    42, 50–1, 56, 280
Ward, Dudley 54, 112
Ward, Joseph 15n
Waterways, internationalization 209
Weaver, J. R. H. 49
Webster, C. K. 40, 52, 282
Westminster Gazette, 70, 72
Weygand, General 106
White, Henry 99
Wied, Wilhelm zu 135n
Wiggin, A. F. H. 31, 35, 38

Wilhelm–Luxemburg Railway 208
Wilson, Admiral Arthur 14n
Wislon, General Henry 174, 176, 266
Wilson, Woodrow 90, 99, 108, 109,
    110, 111, 116, 117–18, 159, 188–9,
    193, 203, 211, 214, 219, 234, 236,
    238–9, 242, 248–9, 256, 262,
    266–7, 271, 273–4, 278, 285
    Fourteen Points 101, 126, 131, 133,
        151, 193, 203, 212, 219, 262
Wilsonism 71, 117–18, 124, 130, 154,
    196, 223, 241
Wireless Stations 206
Wiseman, William 43–4, 101–2
Woodward, E. L. 38, 40, 282

Yanaon 179
Younghusband, Francis 19n
Yugoslavia 53, 132, 134, 136, 140,
    148, 242, 246–7, 255–6, 266–9
    see also Serbia
Yunan 180

Zambesi River 17
Zanzibar 14
Zimmern, Alfred 9, 26, 74, 75, 77–8,
    83, 143, 209, 213–15, 217–19, 282
    proposed Peace Terms Intelligence
        Section 18–20, 27, 49, 279–80
Zinoviev, G. E. 143
Zionism 44, 53, 72, 163